The Dissemination of Economic Ideas

The Dissemination of Economic Ideas

Edited by

Heinz D. Kurz

Professor of Economics, University of Graz, Austria

Tamotsu Nishizawa

Professor, Institute of Economic Research, Hitotsubashi University, Japan

Keith Tribe

Department of History, University of Sussex, UK

Edward Elgar

Cheltenham, UK • Northampton, MA, USA

Published by
Edward Elgar Publishing Limited
The Lypiatts
15 Lansdown Road
Cheltenham
Glos GL50 2JA
UK

Edward Elgar Publishing, Inc.
William Pratt House
9 Dewey Court
Northampton
Massachusetts 01060
USA

A catalogue record for this book
is available from the British Library

Library of Congress Control Number: 2011925799

MIX
Paper from responsible sources
FSC® C018575
FSC
www.fsc.org

ISBN 978 0 85793 557 1

Typeset by Servis Filmsetting Ltd, Stockport, Cheshire
Printed and bound by MPG Books Group, UK

Contents

List of contributors vii

The dissemination of economic ideas: introduction 1
Heinz D. Kurz, Tamotsu Nishizawa, Keith Tribe

PART I SYSTEMS OF POLITICAL ECONOMY

1 Cameralism as an intermediary between Mediterranean Scholastic economic thought and classical economics 13
Bertram Schefold
2 The ideal statesman: the influence of Richelieu on Davenant's political thought 41
Seiichiro Ito
3 *Polizei* and the system of public finance: tracing the impact of Cameralism in eighteenth-century Portugal 65
Alexandre Mendes Cunha

PART II EUROPEAN AND AMERICAN INTERACTIONS

4 The development of economic theories in Germany: from Karl Heinrich Rau to Wilhelm Roscher 87
Yukihiro Ikeda
5 German influences in the making of American economics, 1885–1935 108
Bradley W. Bateman
6 Marshall's ideas on progress: roots and diffusion 125
Katia Caldari and Tamotsu Nishizawa

PART III THE DIFFUSION OF ECONOMIC IDEAS IN SOUTH-EASTERN EUROPE AND BEYOND

7 The dissemination of economic thought in South-Eastern Europe in the nineteenth century 161
Michalis M. Psalidopoulos and Nicholas J. Theocarakis

8 Adventures of an Austrian trio abroad: the influence of Schumpeter, Polanyi and Hayek in Turkey and the dissemination of their work 192
Eyüp Özveren

PART IV THE EXCHANGE OF IDEAS BETWEEN JAPAN AND THE REST OF THE WORLD

9 The diffusion of economic ideas: Lionel Robbins in Italy and Japan 223
Atsushi Komine and Fabio Masini
10 The *Kyoto University Economic Review* (1926–44) as importer and exporter of economic ideas: bringing Lausanne, Cambridge, Vienna and Marx to Japan 260
Robert W. Dimand and Masazumi Wakatabe
11 The background of K. Akamatsu's *Gankou Keitai Ron* and its development: early empirical analysis at Nagoya 292
Tadashi Ohtsuki
12 Was *Sozialforschung* an Aesopian term? Marxism as a link between Japan and the West 315
Kiichiro Yagi
13 The contributions of two eminent Japanese scholars to the development of economic theory: Michio Morishima and Takashi Negishi 337
Heinz D. Kurz

Index 365

Contributors

Bradley W. Bateman, Provost, Denison University, Ohio, USA.

Katia Caldari, Assistant Professor of Economics, Università di Padova, Italy.

Alexandre Mendes Cunha, Associate Professor, Department of Economics, Universidade Federal de Minas Gerais, Brazil.

Robert W. Dimand, Professor of Economics, Brock University, Canada.

Yukihiro Ikeda, Professor of Economics, Keio University, Japan.

Seiichiro Ito, Professor of Economics, Ohtsuki City College, Japan.

Atsushi Komine, Professor of Economics, Ryukoku University, Japan.

Heinz D. Kurz, Professor of Economics, Universität Graz, Austria.

Fabio Masini, Associate Professor of History of Economic Thought, Università di Roma Tre, Italy.

Tamotsu Nishizawa, Director, Institute of Economic Research, Hitotsubashi University, Japan.

Tadashi Ohtsuki, Postgraduate student, Tokyo University of Foreign Studies, Japan.

Eyüp Özveren, Professor of Economics, Middle East Technical University, Ankara, Turkey.

Michalis M. Psalidopoulos, Professor of Economics, National University of Athens, Greece.

Bertram Schefold, Professor of Economics, Johann Wolfgang Goethe-Universität, Frankfurt am Main, Germany.

Nicholas J. Theocarakis, Assistant Professor of Economics, National University of Athens, Greece.

Keith Tribe, Department of History, University of Sussex, UK.

Masazumi Wakatabe, Professor of Economics, Waseda University, Japan.

Kiichiro Yagi, Professor of Economics, Setsunan University, Japan.

The dissemination of economic ideas: introduction

Heinz D. Kurz, Tamotsu Nishizawa and Keith Tribe[1]

In March 2009 a joint meeting of the Japanese and European Societies for the History of Economic Thought was held in Tokyo and Kyoto, dedicated to the theme of 'The Dissemination of Economic Ideas'.[2] This volume presents selected papers from that conference, marking a significant stage in our growing understanding of the manner in which the ebb and flow in the development of national traditions of economic thought has been affected by the interaction of internal and external factors. We should also note that the possibility of discussing the dissemination process in such a context was itself made possible by the existence of a European society which has over the past decade and a half provided a framework for regular meetings of scholars who are themselves also members of national bodies.[3] While the subject matter of this collection reaches back to the seventeenth century, regular interchanges of the kind represented by the Tokyo and Kyoto meetings go back no more than 20 or 30 years. And so this book places an explicit agenda – study of the dissemination of economic ideas over a period of four centuries – within an implicit framework which is, relatively speaking, quite new. This introduction is directed to both of these issues, but begins necessarily from the intentions framing the March 2009 meetings.[4]

Consideration of the propagation and dissemination of economic ideas comes naturally to Japanese scholars, for the Meiji Restoration of 1867 inaugurated a period of rapid change for Japanese society, characterized by the extensive importation of ideas and institutions from the West. This opening of Japan to the West coincided with the ending of the American Civil War and the creation of an independent Germany; during the later nineteenth century these became the most dynamic world economies and consequently important influences upon Japanese development. Social and cultural reform in Japan was heavily influenced by German models; for example, the Imperial University Act of 1886 followed the Prussian model and Tokyo Imperial University was inaugurated, then in 1896 an association modelled on the Verein für Socialpolitik was founded, while the forerunners of Hitosubashi University itself drew heavily on the curriculum of the new German *Handelshochschulen.*[5] This period, in which modernization implied the importation of Western models, came to an end in the later 1920s. From the early 1930s onwards Japan sought to exploit its new-found industrial and military power to establish itself as the dominant Asian power, a course which brought the invasion of China in 1937 and ultimately led Japan into the Second World War, in which the United States became its enemy and Germany its ally. The ensuing defeat of Japan by United Nations[6] forces in August 1945 led to occupation by the United States and a continuation of the economic modernization initiated in the later nineteenth century. This succeeded in transforming Japan into a global economic power which, while international in orientation, remains culturally distinctive, despite the social, political and economic turmoil of its development during the century following the Meiji Restoration.

Against such a background it was for many years accepted by both Japanese and non-Japanese scholars that the development of modern economics in Japan has been dominated by the assimilation firstly of European ideas and institutions, and subsequently by those of the United States (Sugihara and Tanaka, 1998). However, as our understanding of the diffusion of economics has developed during the past two or three decades, this simple story of the transmission and reception of modern economics has been progressively modified. Simple citation of one economist by another, or lack of such citation, is clearly inadequate. Access or lack of such access to literature through translation provides many insights,[7] as does knowledge of library holdings.[8] But while the catalogue of Adam Smith's library (Mizuta, 2000), together with that of the Edinburgh Advocates' Library, gives us a clear idea of what he actually read above and beyond what is cited in his writings, we still have to recognize that his works passed into the hands of readers of variable consistency, ability and understanding. And so while, for example, scholars still debate the nature of Smith's allusion to an 'invisible hand', generations of readers have confidently assumed that this is little more than a central metaphor for the market mechanism built upon an allusion to Mandeville's distinction of private vices and public benefits. Historians are aware that such a view is faulty, but that does not prevent repetition of the idea.

Even if we restrict our attention to the dissemination of Adam Smith's ideas, it quickly becomes apparent that in the process of transmission his economic ideas can easily become transformed into platitudes which in turn shape 'common knowledge' of his work. This is not merely a matter of 'expert' versus 'lay' readings of a text. The history of economics is a trail littered with examples of successive and self-reinforcing misreadings on the part of economists who might otherwise have been thought to ‘know better’, as the sorry history of the ‘Keynesian Revolution’ also testifies.[9] And so although it might appear that the primary object in studying the dissemination of ideas is to track the flow of ideas from one period to the next, and from one part of the world to another, much as we might monitor the migratory patterns of barnacle geese,[10] there is in fact an inherent instability in the object of our attention. For concepts are not invariant objects that are moved around like so many pieces of Lego, always the same shape and colour, no matter to what use they are put. And the history of economics should not be conceived as a means of rectifying this natural tendency for ideas to transmute through repetition, but instead adopt this process of transformation as an object of study in itself.

Consequently, the history of the dissemination of economic ideas becomes a history of the flux of economic ideas, rendering any easy generalization difficult, even impossible. For example, given the American occupation of post-war Japan and the fact that this period was characterized by the development of an international economics dominated by American textbooks and teaching, we might conclude that the combination of these circumstances would necessarily have served to reshape the thinking of Japanese economists along American lines. But this did not in general happen; in fact, during the post-war period Marxist economics flourished in Japan as nowhere else outside the Soviet Union and its satellite states (Akama, 2000), alongside some cross-fertilization and international dissemination of Japanese non-Marxist economics (Yagi, 2000). There are good institutional reasons for both of these trends, but this only underlines the fact that one cannot ignore the context into which ideas are introduced and domestically recycled. The Japanese experience of ‘reception’ also highlights the fact that choices can be made: while some scholars turned to German models in the later nineteenth century, others opted for a more liberal tradition and turned to Mill, Fawcett, Marshall and Pigou. And the history of translation also complicates assumptions we might make about ‘transmission’ and ‘reception’: the writings of Walras and Gossen were translated into Japanese respectively 50 and 80 years before their first translation into English. Partly at least as a consequence of this last development, general equilibrium theory took a firm hold among Japanese economists during the 1930s, so much so that it has been argued that Japan here was in advance of developments among Anglophone economists (Nishizawa and Ikeo, 2008).[11]

We could turn the argument with which we started on its head, and suggest that far from Japan being a clear case of dissemination and influence, what we see in Japan is only a more obvious case of a universal phenomenon in the history of economic thought. It is the scale of the initial cultural divide between Japan and the West, and the ‘late start’ of Japan’s ‘modernization’, that has lent the Japanese case unusual clarity, not least to the Japanese themselves. But the same mixed process of dissemination and lack of response has characterized the flow of ideas around Europe over the last 200 years. Coming back to Adam Smith again, it is today too easily forgotten that English only became a world language in the twentieth century, before which French and German were the prevailing world languages. In nineteenth-century Europe, Adam Smith's *Wealth of Nations* was indeed widely read – but in French translation, which as Karl Marx's notebooks show is how he read Smith. During the nineteenth century Smith was widely read not primarily as part of 'English' classical economics, but rather in the context of contemporary French liberal economists such as Joseph Garnier and, indeed, Frédéric Bastiat.

While Japanese scholars might therefore have a special interest in the process of the dissemination of economic ideas, this is no less an issue for European historians. The early foundation of the Japanese Society for the History of Economic Thought (JSHET) reflects the long-standing interest among Japanese economists in the historical development of their discipline and its discourse.[12] The American equivalent was not founded until 1974,[13] since when several national societies have been created. The European Society for the History of Economic Thought was a departure from this national model since it aimed to bring together scholars many of whom were already members of their national bodies, but who had a common interest in a more international perspective for their work. In this respect, it is worth noting that the international project on the institutionalization of political economy developed during the 1980s[14] was the first large-scale international collaborative project among historians of economic thought, and that it relied initially for its administration on the resources of the King's College Cambridge Research Centre and not on any existing national association. While the European Society is conceived as a body to promote the scholarship of its members, rather than to undertake projects on its own account, its inherent international composition makes it a natural vehicle for consideration of the international dissemination of economic ideas. Linked to Japanese scholars in the sister Japanese Society who are more conscious than most of the impact of this process, this makes the topic chosen for the joint meeting in 2009 a more than appropriate choice.

The papers selected for publication here are chronologically ordered, although this apparently simple editorial approach itself reveals important aspects of the phasing of the dissemination process. The first chapter relates to the early seventeenth century: Bertram Schefold's account of the work of Kaspar Klock and its connection with the Salamanca School. This is however not a simple account of dissemination and reception, not least because this process is usually conceived as a form of exchange between nation-states and their national languages. Klock was writing at the time of the Thirty Years' War, when the European political space was being recast, and he wrote in Latin, which was still a transnational language. Consequently Schefold's study demonstrates the manner in which Klock drew on the wide array of sources available to him in the European space, without regard to national languages or political boundaries. Reading Klock in this way makes it possible to establish the nature of his sources; Schefold appends a translation of Klock's account of Japan, for which Klock drew on reports by Jesuit fathers.

Seiichiro Ito's chapter takes us to the late seventeenth century and the rivalry between European powers. Davenant, being an Englishman, sought to promote the strength of Britain; Spain was no longer the power that it had been, and the hostilities with the Netherlands having been resolved through the recruitment of a Dutch monarch, the prime rival was France, which threatened to overturn the balance of emerging powers. But this did not prevent Davenant drawing upon French sources in creating arguments regarding the restoration of British power, which he treated as primarily a fiscal issue. Ito demonstrates that Davenant drew heavily upon Richelieu's *Testament politique*, so that much of his argument depends not, as previously assumed, upon a Florentine political tradition embodied by Machiavelli's treatise, but instead on the more immediate and relevant practical issues of governance and power in seventeenth-century France.

Cunha tracks the reception of Cameralistic principles and *Polizei* in eighteenth-century Portugal together with its empire. Here there is no direct link through translation besides the publication of a Portuguese version of Bielfeld's *Institutions politique*, a work which reflects French rather than German conceptions of 'police'. However, there is a connection through translations into Spanish, a language accessible to the Portuguese, whose rulers would in any case have had command of the French language. Cunha shows how the process of fiscal and administrative reform in the wake of the Lisbon earthquake drew on the models advocated in the German states, rather than in France, and suggests that here an indirect process of diffusion was at work.

With Yukihiro Ikeda's chapter we move into the nineteenth century and the influence on the textbooks of Karl Heinrich Rau and Wilhelm Roscher of English classical economics. It has long been recognized that both writers synthesized their writings from many sources without great regard to the finer points of theoretical controversy involved. Ikeda examines the manner in which the two German writers drew upon the writings of James and John Stuart Mill in constructing their conceptions of 'value' and 'good', demonstrating that Rau and Roscher's writings are more systematic in their approach than hitherto assumed.

The most well-known nineteenth-century instance of German influence on other traditions is that on American economics, which Bradley Bateman examines in his chapter. As is well known, substantial numbers of young American students sought their doctorates in Germany in the last third of the century, but as Bateman points out, this flow was already diminishing in the 1880s as new American universities such as Johns Hopkins offered attractive alternatives. It is therefore important to emphasize that American students of economics came under the influence of the 'Older School' of German Historical Economics, which was primarily interested in the reconstruction of economic theory via a historical appreciation of that theory. Returning students thus brought with them a familiarity with emergent Continental marginalism as well as a historicist inclination, and did not regard the two as being in any way opposed. Bateman goes on to demonstrate that this insight alters our perspective on the development of American economics in the early twentieth century, and shifts the clear emergence of Neoclassicism close to the mid-twentieth century, and not before.

Katia Caldari and Tamotsu Nishizawa consider another aspect of the dissemination of economic ideas – from teacher to student. They consider Alfred Marshall's views on social and economic progress as evidenced by *Industry and Trade* and his manuscript notes for a planned book: *Progress: Its Economic Conditions*. They demonstrate that the arguments that he advanced during the last years of his life are continuous with his involvement with progressive associations – related to housing, working conditions and industrial democracy – from the 1880s. However, it was only in his later writings that his ideas were fully articulated and expressed. Marshall's students broadly shared these views, but Sydney Chapman, A.C. Pigou and D.H. MacGregor were of course taught by Marshall during the 1880s and 1890s, when Marshall's ideas in this area had not yet been fully formulated. The Marshallian tradition to whose formation they contributed consequently did not therefore fully reflect what the older Marshall himself thought to be of greatest importance, but instead tended to lay emphasis upon a number of theoretical, rather than ethical, principles.

Michalis Psalidopoulos and Nicholas Theocarakis examine the influence of economic teaching and policy during the formation in the course of the nineteenth century of new countries in South-Eastern Europe with the dissolution of the Ottoman Empire. The path they trace broadly mirrors the political history of Europe in this period: initially French and English liberal ideas had some purchase, although these quickly gave way to protectionist sentiment. The emergence of Germany as a European power in the last third of the century lent German economics, especially the writings of List and Schmoller, a greater profile, and made Germany a natural destination for students of economics. However, in the Balkans Russia remained a major influence, and it was from this source that revolutionary ideas regarding agrarian and industrial development were imported, rather than from Germany.

Eyüp Özveren considers the changing reception of three Austrian economists – Schumpeter, Hayek and Polanyi – all of whom lived through the Keynesian Revolution, emigrated to North America, and whose work was more influential and well known in the later twentieth century than it was in the 1950s and 1960s, when a Keynesian synthesis was the dominant international orthodoxy. The Turkish reception of the three Austrians was in two distinct waves, whose ranking changed from one phase to the other. The comparison of Turkey with Japan is motivated by their parallel paths in terms of economic modernization and receptiveness to foreign influences. Hence the way in which the differences between Hayek, Schumpeter and Polanyi have been received in Japan is suggestive of the modernization process in Japan, and hence in Turkey too.

Komine and Masini compare the reception of the writings of Lionel Robbins in Italy and Japan chiefly during the 1930s and 1940s, which implies two separate issues. Firstly, Robbins published during this period his infamous essay on the contemporary depression, his *Essay on the Nature and Significance of Economic Science*, and a number of texts on the international order and federalism. Secondly, Italy was during the 1930s increasingly corporatist in orientation, while Japan was increasingly ruled by a military clique. It might be thought that the latter would rule out any reception of the former, but they demonstrate that this was far from the case. Partly this was because the local academic culture was not entirely homogenous and closed to outside influence, but also because even those who proved most hostile to Robbins's views – chiefly Marxists – nonetheless had a use for his works as the butt of their criticism.

The contribution of Dimand and Wakatabe focuses on the *Kyoto University Economic Review* as a medium for communication between Japan and the rest of the world. Founded in 1926 as a semi-annual English-language journal, suspended in 1944 then resuming publication in 1950, the *Review* provided ready insight into the work of Japanese economists. The *Review* published translations from a monthly Japanese publication issued by the Kyoto Imperial University Economics Department which reflected the prevailing strong interest in European and American developments, rendering the work of the Japanese economists even more accessible to those outside Japan. While contributions by Japanese economists to international discussion of business cycles, economic growth and of course Keynes's *General Theory* (1973) were thus made available, in fact little attention was paid to them at the time, and even recent commentators on the development of Japanese economics have overlooked this important source.

Ohtsuki devotes his chapter to the way in which empirical methods were introduced at Nagoya University following Akamatsu's return in 1926 from Harvard Business School, where he had encountered both the case study method and early economic research into local industry. This led to study of the local woollen industry and a series of reports, and also to his formulation of a 'flying geese pattern' of economic development moving from the import of finished goods, through the local production of such goods, and then to the eventual development of exports. This was also linked to a theory of long-wave economic development which in the 1930s drew on the work of Kondratiev.

Yagi traces a linkage between three Marxist-oriented institutes in Germany, Japan and Moscow. Starting out from a lecture he attended in 1973 in which Felix Weil talked of the foundation of the Institut für Sozialforschung in Frankfurt, he points out that '*Sozialforschung*' was at the time a German neologism, related possibly to the existence of an Institute for Social Research in Japan. The link between the two was provided by Kazuo Fukumoto, a leading Japanese Communist, who possibly suggested the name to Weil when he was casting about for a name that would not arouse the suspicions of the authorities in the University of Frankfurt. From this detective puzzle Yagi develops a fascinating account of the development of Japanese social research, the role of Marxism and the Communist Party, and the common link of both institutes to Rjazanov's Moscow Institute involved in publishing the *Collected Works of Marx and Engels*.

Finally, Heinz D. Kurz reviews the work of two world-famous Japanese economists, Michio Morishima and Takashi Negishi, demonstrating how their own thinking has developed in dialogue with the 'Western canon', from Adam Smith to Piero Sraffa, competing this volume with a clear example of the impact of Japanese economists on an increasingly international environment.

NOTES

1. The preparation of this volume was generously supported by a grant from the Japanese Society for the History of Economic Thought, for which the editors are very grateful.
2. The conference was in two parts, meeting on 21–22 March at Hitotsubashi University, Tokyo, and on 24 March at Kyoto University. This was the second such joint conference, the first having been held in Nice in 2006.
3. The European Society for the History of Economic Thought (ESHET) was founded at a meeting in Nice in December 1995, while the Japanese Society for the History of Economic Thought (JSHET) was founded as early as 1950.

4. The conference topic had been agreed in discussions between Heinz D. Kurz, Tamotsu Nishizawa, Cristina Marcuzzo, then President of the European Society and Tetsuo Taka, then President of the Japanese Society. Five main themes were identified in the call for papers addressed to the international dissemination of economic ideas: (a) the development of economic ideas and their transmission across national borders; (b) the impact of imported ideas upon the framing of responses to perceived domestic economic and social problems; (c) more detailed consideration of policies developed upon this basis; (d) the influence of imported ideas in forming new institutions; (e) identifying three critical episodes in the dissemination period: the Enlightenment, Historicism and the interwar period.
5. Hitotsubashi developed originally from the Commercial Training School founded in 1875 and with an American as its director (Ikema, et al., 2000; 7ff, 32ff)
6. While the United Nations formally came into existence in October 1945, official use of the term to designate the Allied forces dates from the signing of the Atlantic Charter on 1 January 1942.
7. See Carpenter (2002).
8. For example, if you search the Oxford University catalogues for the writings of Karl Marx, the earliest records date from the 1880s and not from the 1840s or 1850s. This is because in such cases libraries reflect the reception and influence of a writer, not his personal publishing history.
9. Akerlof and Shiller's *Animal Spirits* (2009) misreads Keynes in much the same way that, for example, George Stigler misunderstood Smith's conception of 'self-interest', inverting the original sense. Keynes introduced the idea of 'animal spirits' in the *General Theory* (1973; 161–2) to suggest that humans were prone to act more on impulse than on deliberate reflection. However, the overall argument of the *General Theory* is directed not to this human propensity to instability, but to the different fact that economies as a whole can become too stable, prone to settle into suboptimal equilibria. Akerlof and Shiller's suggestion that we should instead conceive the inherent instability of economies as rooted in human psychology owes nothing to Keynes, yet by using Keynes's striking phrase claims his reputation.
10. In 2009 four barnacle geese were fitted with satellite transmitters that enabled their wintering flight from Svalbard in the Arctic to the Solway Firth, Scotland to be tracked in real time.
11. Similarly, Schumpeter's *Das Wesen und der Hauptinhalt der theoretischen Nationalökonomie* was translated into Japanese and published in 1936, but no English version has ever been published.
12. In fact when the Japanese Economic Association was founded in 1934 several historians of economics and of economic thought were founding members; and four from six of those who proposed the foundation of JSHET in 1950 were themselves members of the pre-war Japanese Economic Association.
13. The journal *History of Political Economy* with an international (Anglo-North American) editorial advisory board was first published in 1969.
14. For an account of the origins of this project, see Claeys et al. (1993).

REFERENCES

Akama, M. (2000), 'Marxian economics', in A. Ikeo (ed.), *Japanese Economics and Economists since 1945*, London: Routledge, pp. 123–39.

Akerlof, G. and R. Shiller (2009), *Animal Spirits*, Princeton, NJ: Princeton University Press.

Carpenter, K.E. (2002), *The Dissemination of the Wealth of Nations in French and in France 1776–1843*, New York: Bibliographical Society of America.

Claeys, G., I. Hont, A. Kadish and K. Tribe (1993), 'Editorial Preface: The institutionalization of political economy', in A. Kadish and K. Tribe (eds), *The Market for Political Economy: The Advent of Economics in British University Culture, 1850–1905*, London: Routledge, pp. viii–ix.

Ikema, M. Y. Inoue, T. Nishizawa and S. Yamauchi (2000), *Hitotsubashi University, 1875–2000*, Basingstoke: Palgrave.

Keynes, J.M. (1973), *The General Theory of Employment, Interest and Money*, Collected Writings of John Maynard Keynes Vol. VII, London: Macmillan.

Mizuta, H. (2000), *Adam Smith's Library: A Catalogue*, Oxford: Oxford University Press.

Nishizawa, T. and A. Ikeo (2008), 'Japan, economics in', in S. Durlauf and L. Blume (eds), *The New Palgrave Dictionary of Economics*, 2nd edn, Vol. 4, Basingstoke: Palgrave, pp. 603–12.

Sugihara, S. and T. Tanaka (eds) (1998), *Economic Thought and Modernization in Japan*, Cheltenham, UK and Lyme, NH, USA: Edward Elgar.

Yagi, K. (2000), 'Economics in the academic institutions after 1945', in A. Ikeo (ed.), *Japanese Economics and Economists since 1945*, London: Routledge, pp. 50–92.

PART I

Systems of political economy

1. Cameralism as an intermediary between Mediterranean Scholastic economic thought and classical economics

Bertram Schefold[1]

1.1 INTRODUCTION: TRANSFER OF ECONOMIC THOUGHT

This chapter traces how ideas on money and taxation made their way from the School of Salamanca in Catholic Spain to the world of the Cameralists in Germany, many of whom were Protestants. I here follow persons and ideas, rather than discussing the wider context (a different task). Cultural differences prompt many questions regarding the transference of economic insights in space and time, and consequent shifts of meaning. As a modest preparation for a larger study, I shall summarize the views on money and usury and on indirect taxation of three of the most famous representatives of the School of Salamanca: Azpilcueta, Molina and Lessius. These represent three successive generations; I shall consider their reception by Kaspar Klock (see Schefold, 2009), one of the most eminent representatives of early German Protestant Cameralism at the time of the Thirty Years War. Klock's work contains a vast, ordered collection of economic facts and ideas from all over the world, and for over a century his many readers were like the visitors to a museum who come in great numbers to admire an exquisite selection of rare artefacts, until his style was thought outmoded. I may extend the study of his contribution to the transfer of ideas to other authors at a later stage, and also plan to investigate the extent to which central European economic thought in the mercantilist and Cameralist period was influential for the development of classical political economy in Great Britain.

Links between the School of Salamanca and Adam Smith have already been studied by de Roover (1955). De Roover describes Scholastic economic thought as a coherent body of doctrines, held together not only by the Church as such, but by the teaching of Thomas of Aquinas and a focus on ethical problems of price formation, competition and monopoly, money, exchange and usury. Scholastic thought ultimately foundered because of mistaken assumptions about usury, and because of the inherent limitations of its method; hence the new departures made by mercantilists were necessary. 'Economics, in the modern sense, occupied a very subordinate position and was still viewed as an ethical and legal matter involving the application of natural law to civil contracts' (de Roover, 1955, 162). However, in the attempt to overcome the obstacles to trade arising from the prohibition of usury, Scholastic ideas and Aristotelian philosophy would continue to contribute to the emerging discipline of economics, long after Scholasticism in its strict sense had been rejected; de Roover mentions Hugo Grotius (1583–1645) and Samuel Pufendorf (1622–94). De Roover describes the mercantilists as extremely heterogeneous authors, each often seeking personal gain such as employment in office or royal protection, and many finding truly new departures. There is a recurring concern with a favourable balance of trade. De Roover mainly discusses English mercantilists, but he also mentions the Neapolitan Antonio Serra. Scholastic influence he finds hard to detect, except in a few cases (Gerard de Malynes), and even then his adscription remains hypothetical (de Roover, 1955, 183): the 'differences between mercantilism and Scholastic economics are striking and profound'.

I choose one example for de Roover's question of how the scholastics influenced the mercantilists; more detailed studies will be necessary to determine how much an author like William Petty owed to his education by the Jesuits.[2] Petty's writings stand out among those of his contemporaries as daring and original, but he must have had his teachers, and several scholars have tried to identify them (editorial introduction to Petty, 1963; Roncaglia, 1985). There was the Hartlib circle, Petty's French connection and, it seems to me, also the influence of his Jesuit teachers at school: sharp analytical distinctions characteristic of the Jesuit 'modern' Scholasticism, were coupled with the scepticism – almost cynism – resulting from Petty's refusal of the Catholic faith, and hence of the orientation which the Jesuits gave to their scientific work. Lessius, as we shall see, recognized the autonomy of the market (Lessius, 1999). He was the leading thinker among the Jesuits in Belgium, when Petty's teachers were young. But how can such a connection be proved? Petty, like most mercantilist authors, typically made very few explicit references. A new study by Cosimo Perrotta (2004) argues that the humanists made a significant contribution to the revival of the sciences of antiquity but that, in so doing, they also adhered to the economic valuations of ancient philosophy, with its disdain for commercial activities. The mercantilists, it seems, had no option but simply to leave behind this intellectual heritage of the past, as far as economic matters were concerned. This was Petty's attitude.

One great mercantilist, Serra, in 1613, adored the ancients, stating that the moderns were superior only insofar as navigation was concerned. But even he pointed out that what we call 'the economy' formed a set of connections to be marvelled at, as the Greeks would marvel at new scientific insights; but that these connections were neither to be understood in the traditional terms of politics (following Aristotle) nor in terms of law (following Roman law and Justinian). They were something new, for which he had no name (Schefold, 1994). The mercantilists seemed to make a fresh start and they were truly innovative in some ways, as Serra was when he spoke of a new science, but – though they would scarcely admit it – they were also dependent on earlier ideas. The difficulty is to demonstrate this dependence in the absence of explicit quotations; de Roover was not really able to overcome this problem, and it has not I think been solved satisfactorily since.

However, bridges between the tradition of Scholastic thought and mercantilist ideas can be shown to exist: in Cameralism (mentioned only briefly by de Roover). The Cameralists were learned like the humanists, lovingly displaying their erudition by quoting from ancient poets, historians and philosophers. They did not feel that the ancients were to be discarded. They were predominantly lawyers, studying texts and citing from them with explicit references. Their system of abbreviations is not easy to decipher, but they quoted often not only from antiquity, but also from Scholastic authors, and they were confronted with mercantilist ideas. Hence we here have a body of continental European knowledge where the lines of intellectual dependency are easier to trace; it is the purpose of this chapter, in relation to the general theme of this book, to show this interdependency by means of the example of Kaspar Klock. A subsidiary aim is to introduce Klock as an author who is little known today.

I first have to remind the reader of Klock's intellectual environment: the older Cameralists of the seventeenth century, as opposed to the younger ones of the eighteenth. The broad background of the older Cameralists made it difficult for them to come forward with single important theoretical ideas. Individual insights disappear among a mass of legal arguments, empirical examples, learned quotes and flowery rhetoric. One can enjoy the baroque richness of the texts (Zielenziger, 1914) or shrink in horror from massive books in sometimes rather mediocre Latin (Monroe, 2001 [1923]); to isolate a coherent body of doctrines seems impossible in either case (Nielsen, 1911). But the Cameralists created the language for the new sciences of the state (Krauth, 1984; Tribe, 1988).

Mercantilism and Cameralism meant state-building, according to Schmoller (1884 [1967]). It was certainly not the ambition of the older

Cameralists to produce theory – the conception did not exist for them; rather they strove to provide just and equitable rules for the good governance of principalities, which presupposed a decent organization of economic matters. To this end, they were prepared to learn wherever models of good administration could be found, be it in antiquity, in distant countries or in their own neighbourhood, with a pragmatism coloured sometimes by passion, religious ideals and social preconceptions. They opened up a very large area for modern research on the transfer of ideas, because they shared the humanist ideal of being part of the intellectual culture created by the poets, philosophers and historians of antiquity. To refer to the stream of ideas handed down from the ancients, and which was being renewed in successive waves of rebirths – including late Scholasticism – was to participate in a collective endeavour to continue a cultural creation, looking both backward and forward. Cosimo Perrotta (2004) has criticized the sterile conservatism of the humanists who looked backwards, but there were also innovators among them. Klock endeavoured to represent a balance between both.

1.2 KASPAR KLOCK: AN OVERVIEW[3]

Kaspar Klock is little known (but see Vecchiato, 1977), even among historians of economic thought in Germany, but dictionaries and some interpreters name him as the main founder of the economics of public finance in the German realm in the first half of the sixteenth century (Stein, 1884; Mann, 1937). We also know that his books circulated widely, were reprinted and remained important up to the first half of the eighteenth century, when the early Cameralists like Klock himself, Bornitz and Obrecht had been replaced by a younger generation (Becher, Hörnigk, Justi, Sonnenfels and many others). The younger Cameralists shared their main concerns with the older, but their teaching was more systematic, they had created subdisciplines, they were established in universities (as the first professors of economics) and in special schools of agriculture, mining and so on. A comprehensive treatment is to be found in Tribe (1988); see also Schefold (1997) on Hörnigk, concerning the link between economics and state-building and on a comprehensive conception of economic policy by Justi (Schefold, 1993).

The historical importance of Klock for economists rests on his enunciation of principles of taxation, drawn from the tradition of Roman law, discussed in the context of a multitude of historical and contemporary examples, and influential indirectly through Adam Smith. The medieval discourse on the moral problems in the emerging economic sphere had been enriched by new practical concerns in Italian and French debates, in the School of Salamanca and following the German tradition. I intend here to reconsider Klock's arguments on taxation after a fresh reading of his voluminous main text, but I regard it as equally important to reread Klock as a Cameralist forerunner of the German Historical School. I propose (apparently for the first time) to read the first of the two books which constitute his main work, *De aerario* (2009 [1651]), as a survey of the economic styles of the world, as it could be known to a learned scholar working in Germany under the difficult conditions of the Thirty Years War. 'Economic style' here refers to the conception proposed by Arthur Spiethoff (1932) in the Festschrift for Werner Sombart. It denotes an economic system, characterized by an 'economic spirit', that is, by a common mentality for which conceptual expressions are sought in early economic texts.

Klock was born in 1583 as a son of the well-to-do Patrician family Klocke in Soest. They were Protestants, and Kaspar Klock studied for some years in the Protestant university of Marburg. He soon worked with his cousins as a lawyer, accredited with the Reichskammergericht at Speyer, and he wrote his doctoral dissertation on fiscal problems, which was accepted 1608 in Basel. He became Chancellor of three principalities in succession and was influential as a legal advisor all over Germany. He nonetheless found time to develop his dissertation, a short text of extreme density and erudition where the roots of the theory of taxation are sought in Roman law and applied to the conditions of the Holy Roman Empire, into a vast treatise, entitled *Tractatus nomico-politicus de contributionibus in Romano-Germanico imperio et aliis regnis ut plurimum usitatis*; this work was printed first in 1634 and then in 1656, 1676, 1699 and 1740. Klock started from the legal definitions of the different kinds of state revenues in his dissertation. He later saw that these distinctions could never be either practically useful or exhaustive – he eventually concluded that to pursue this line of investigation would be as vain as the work of Sisyphus (book one, II, 20). He sought an economic analysis of taxation, as I shall show below, but did not entirely succeed in his attempt to overcome the constraints of legal terminology.[4] His reports on legal matters (many largely written by his colleagues) were collected into three (later four) massive volumes published in 1649, 1650 and 1676, with the earlier ones reprinted in 1673, and then all of them again in 1703. This collection of essays contains an introduction with important biographical material; in particular, there is an especially moving and eloquent evocation of the suffering brought about by war. Klock always published in Latin. He was a humanist with a true and spontaneous love for the texts of the ancients. He adorned his book with Latin poems – some quite good, some rather trite – and many Latin poems were composed in his honour and printed in appendices to his books. He died in 1655.

None of his works seems to have been translated, neither into German nor into any other language, and this is one of the reasons why his voluminous main work, the *De aerario* (a folio with more than 1100 pages, each with two columns in the 1671 edition) is rarely read, apart from a few passages (invariably the same) which are quoted to illustrate his basic views on taxation. *De aerario* was written during the Thirty Years' War after the publication of *De contributionibus* in 1634, partly in response to the rival and much inferior work by Maximilian Faust (published in 1641 and clearly indebted to *De contributionibus*). *De aerario* was finally printed in 1651. A new edition with additional material in the form of notes was published in 1671 by Christoph Peller, and this was reprinted in 1699. This version is available on the Internet (Klock, 1671).

We teach not only by expounding theories, but also by means of examples drawn from our own actions, by stories, and by historical analogies; and certain truths are better expressed in such indirect ways, rather than as abstract statements, to be supported by formal proofs. Edgar Salin, a late descendant of the Historical School, characterized certain nonformal approaches as 'intuitive' or 'visual' (*anschauliche*) theory (Salin, 1967). This would represent the different dimensions of the economy as essentially interrelated, as a whole, ideally as a gestalt. Salin thought that intuitive theory could unite the rational approach with the descriptive and the visual, and that it should therefore be of greater generality than formalistic model-building (Schefold, 2004). He thought that both approaches were artfully combined in Smith, Marx and Keynes, and, in the German tradition, in von Thünen and certain members of the Historical School. Certainly, the Historical School places more emphasis on the 'visual' aspect of theorizing than on the 'rational', at least compared to the Austrian, let alone the Walrasian school, and there are several early forerunners. As we shall see, Klock's theorizing is overwhelmingly visual; reading him makes one feel that the loss of a visual theory would render economics poorer.

Klock begins with methodological chapters which set the problem of taxation in a historical perspective. He distinguishes between *ars civilis* and *prudentia civilis* (book one, I, 100): between, one could say, (visual) theory and policy (practice). The former is based on general principles, the latter concerns their application to infinitely varying circumstances, and he cautions against confusing the two; for he who attempts to subsume all methods of taxation to a single principle will end up as someone who proposes to exercise the art of riding in Venice and that of sailing in Nuremberg. In order to demonstrate the variety of circumstances in which

Table 1.1 Economic styles and Klock's descriptive programme

Economic styles	Klock's concepts
1. *Wirtschaftsgeist* (economic spirit)	*ratio Reipublicae* (governance)
2. *Natürliche und technische Grundlagen* (natural and technical conditions)	*regionis et populi natura* (nature of the region and the people)
3. *Wirtschaftsverfassung* (economic constitution)	*Regnorum jura* (legal systems of the kingdoms)
4. *Gesellschaftsverfassung* (social constitution)	*populi conditio* (condition of the people)
5. *Wirtschaftsdynamik* (dynamism of the economy)	*reditus regnorum* (revenues of the kingdoms)

the problems of taxation arise, Klock dedicates the first part or 'book' of his work to a description of the countries of the world:

> not all the modes in which a financial system can be established are applicable in any given republic, for in the same way as change the legal frameworks of the kingdoms (*ut variant Regnorum jura*) change their revenues as well. And so those modes are to be used, if the constitution of the state and the nature and condition of the region and of the people admit it. (book one, I, 100)

This is reminiscent of Arthur Spiethoff's conception of an economic style (*Wirtschaftsstil*) as an economic system, located in time and space, characterized in five dimensions combining rational and intuitive elements; in this context Spiethoff went on to adopt explicitly Salin's concept of visual theory (Spiethoff, 1932; Schefold 1994–95, here: 1994). Table 1.1 shows the five dimensions or characteristics (*Merkmale*) of Spiethoff's 'economic style' (*Wirtschaftsstil*), and the five main concepts used by Klock in one coherent passage which explains the methodological principles deployed in his country descriptions.

There is, of course, no strict correspondence. In particular, there is greater stress in Klock on the forms of rule – the political constitution, if one prefers. The expression *ratio Reipublicae* stands for what Machiavelli and Botero called *ragione di Stato* and the French *raison d'état*. Spiethoff, mainly known for his theory of the business cycle (Spiethoff, 1955), was interested in the economic initiative of entrepreneurs, hence in his fifth characteristic, and Klock in the finances of the state. We do not claim that Klock anticipated debates over economic systems and about the appropriate methodologies for comparisons of systems which took place in the twentieth century, but it has often been said that Cameralism paved the way for the later Historical School (Campagnolo, 2004), and for this we here have a splendid, so far neglected example. One could mention Gustav von Gülich (1830), a year earlier than Richard Jones (1831 [1964]) in England, as an intermediary in an intertemporal comparison. Von Gülich preceded Roscher (the self-appointed founder of the German Historical School) with a vast comparative historical work on the trade and the forms of production in different European countries (Marx referred to him: Marx, 1969, 19); Gülich thus connected the Cameralist tradition and the programme of the Historical School, of which Spiethoff represents a 'young' outgrowth. Intratemporal comparisons are more difficult in this case. I know of no contemporary of Klock who would also have attempted to compare the economic and political forms in a similar panorama, going beyond comparative history or geography.

Klock begins his country descriptions with ancient Rome, Emperor Augustus having created the model for a reliable system of state expenditure and taxation. The Holy Roman Empire is in a sad condition (book one, III, 33), due in large measure to mistakes of political and fiscal administration; for example, Emperor Charles IV sold the Italian possessions of the empire with their revenues (book one, IV, 61), making it difficult to maintain an imperial army. Klock then turns to dangerous rivals, in the first place the Ottoman Empire where religion and form of government differ, also economic institutions, other forms of revenue (book one, V, 15 ff.), and also differences in the pattern and scope of state expenditure, especially with regard to the military. Klock studies France intensely, which is politically more modern and economically more efficient than Germany; Spain, overextended with its vast colonies; and the Netherlands, with the most modern economy – Klock describes its globally trading shareholding companies (book one, XIV, 106 ff.) and colonization. Each country then serves to illustrate particular points. Britain is protectionist (book one, VIII, 106 ff.); Sweden a monarchy, but also relatively democratic in its economic institutions; there are the republics like the Swiss and, quite different, Venice; and there is the prime example of centralized rule and economic exploitation in the form of the system maintained by the Grand Duke of Russia. Political, social and economic institutions vary even more as non-European countries are considered, such as China, Japan, Moghul India, Abyssinia, Morocco and the Kingdom of Congo. Especially in the case of Africa, the contrast between natural riches and the simplicity, indeed poverty of economic life becomes his prime concern: they have linen, but they do not know how to weave; they have sugar cane, but do not know how to produce sugar (book one, XXV, 25–6).

Klock's works are available in an international language, in Latin, and my German introduction (Schefold, 2009) contains extensive summaries of the main chapters of *De aerario*. The Appendix to this chapter contains my translation into English of a relatively short chapter of Klock's book on Japan.[5] I have chosen Japan not only for reasons of brevity and because this paper was first given at Kyushu. The chapter also illustrates Klock's endeavour to give facts and explanations (in terms of 'visual' theory), even where information was difficult to come by (Japan's closure), and he provides a minimum of information regarding his source by alluding to the Jesuits. Klock points out essential differences between Japanese and European feudalism, he mentions rice production under 'royal' control – it contrasts with the 'bourgeois' city of Osaka – and the yearly forced visits of the *daimiyos* at Edo.

Klock's long second book of *De aerario* describes institutions, starting with agriculture, moving on to mining, craftsmanship, trade and banking, and so on. It culminates in chapters on taxation; I shall concentrate on these. Klock wants to be just and balanced, not to establish one-sided theories. He is a metallist and wishes big coins to circulate at full value, but he is a nominalist regarding small coins. He is for competition, but also for big companies. He is against cartels but admits guilds, as long as they do not fix prices. He is for free trade, but with restrictions on luxury imports and gold exports, and so on in many other matters. He insists repeatedly that taxes should be introduced to fulfil specific tasks: in his dissertation he describes arrangements similar to Lindahl taxation (Klock, 1610 [1608]). He proposes a general principle, in a marginalist formulation, to limit taxation: taxes should rise at most up to the point where they cause an inconvenience which is as great as it would be if the state expenditure, for which the taxes are to be used, were not undertaken.

Klock is critical of excise taxes where they are impractical and to the extent that they fall primarily on the poor. Klock here anticipates arguments of the later famous *Akzisenstreit*, the German debate mainly during the years 1717–18 over excise taxes (Mann, 1937; Blesgen and Welter, 2006). Indirect taxes, such as the famous French tax on salt (*gabelle*) had existed since the high Middle Ages and longer, but had always been controversial: as a burden on the poor, because of the high cost of collection and the possibilities of corruption. On the other hand, excise taxes were a tax on (in modern terms) expenditure, and this was felt to be just. Klock seems to believe that excise taxes raise the necessary wage of workers, so that it will be easier for the Dutch, who are richer and stronger in their export trade, to levy indirect taxes, because they can afford to pay higher wages, whereas Germany is regarded as backward. I shall return to this point and try to isolate what was taken over from the Spanish and what was new.

He relies explicitly on the Aristotelian theory of justice in order to analyse direct taxation. Regular direct taxation did not yet exist; he discusses historical forms of extraordinary taxation levied in times of war, especially against the Turks. But he clearly moves towards the idea of more regular direct taxation, more frequent, but also lower than in past emergencies. Such a tax must be based on justice in distribution, according to the law of proportions. If A and B are persons and C and D rewards, the formula $A{:}B = C{:}D$ symbolizes justice in distribution, for the proportion between the persons and the rewards will also hold, after these have been enriched by the benefits they receive: $A{:}B = (A + C){:}(B + D) = C{:}D$ (Schefold, 1994–95). The weight (*onus*) of taxation must correspond to what someone can carry (*ferre*), and this is first illustrated by means of a differential treatment of lands of different fertility and location (Klock thus comes close to the discovery of differential rent) and it is then extended to the taxation of revenues and possessions of persons (to the extent that possessions 'bear fruit'), some arguments indicating that he has progressive, rather than proportional taxation in mind, consistent with his idea that excise taxes primarily fall on the poor (book two, LII, LXXVIII, LXXX).

But he does not explicitly reach the idea that it is the total income of a person which should be taxed in this way. Both the concept of total income and the institutions necessary to measure it are absent. Hence he envisages a 'mixed' form of taxation of property and persons, where property should be taxed because it is capable of yielding revenue, and persons because they can produce (book two, LXXX, 35). His references to Leonardus Lessius and to Johannes de Lugo (book two, LXXX, 28) concern these two as authorities on the moral justification of such taxation. They are not quoted in order to underline the analytical advance in argument, but in order to justify the appeal to distributive justice (Lessius) and the consideration of the needs of the people, as opposed to those of the prince (de Lugo).

Klock thus emerges as the propagator of sensible compromises in this domain as well. He similarly tried to maintain his Protestant convictions while respecting the Catholic institutions of the realm; he combined paternalism with freedom, natural right with tradition, religious tolerance with the obligation of civil obedience; and even if one disliked the usury of Jews, one had allow them to take up the crafts. Banks nevertheless were indispensable. Here we shall find interesting continuities and departures with respect to the Spanish School.

Klock is most significant in his combination of 'law and economics' which some still regard as a modern achievement, but which has been traditional ever since the School of Salamanca, and the field was cultivated later primarily by the Historical School. Klock was richer in his approach than most modern representatives of institutionalism and the economics of development, in that he took cultural and religious motives into account (Vecchiato, 1977); he was, after all, a contemporary of one of the most bloody religious wars in history. Authors and descendants of the School of Salamanca like Azpilcueta and Lessius had sharper analytical minds – at any rate they presented more sophisticated arguments (Schefold, 1998a, 1999) – but they had much less vision regarding the potentials for development in different parts of the world, and they lacked the unifying idea which we find in Klock, for which he has no name, but which I have tried to explain by means of the comparison with the conception of economic style. His broad historical perspective, allowing him to contrast the globalizing tendencies of the early seventeenth century with the still vigorous worlds of tradition in Europe and the other continents, perhaps came to him through his reading of the ancients – did not Roscher found his idea of the Historical School on his reading of Thucydides? His humanism was the basis for tolerance, coupled with patriotic pride, a deep sense of justice and his Protestant faith. This combination of gifts enabled him to become a mediator of economic ideas across cultures. I now consider specific views of representatives of the School of Salamanca and shall then return to Klock in order to see what he made of them.

1.3 MARTIN DE AZPILCUETA ('EL NAVARRO'): CLEAR LIMITS ON INTEREST-TAKING

Martin de Azpilcueta (1492–1586) studied philosophy, theology and law and taught successively in Toulouse, Salamanca and Coimbra. He was called to Rome in 1567 and became Councillor to Popes Pius V, Gregor XII and Sixtus V. He was famous for his successful public lectures, one in the presence of Emperor Charles V. He cautiously insisted on the sovereignty of the people, based on natural law.[6] Azpilcueta's fame in the history of economic thought rests on his *Manual de Confesores* for priests as confessors (see Schefold, 1998a). The stormy development of the Spanish economy in consequence of the colonization of the Americas and the influx of American silver had transformed trading relationships, and was accompanied by inflation. Priests, always confronted with the problem of assessing the legitimacy of the actions of merchants in the confessional, now had to be informed about new trade practices so as to be able to encourage Christian behaviour, and also demand restitution if the actions of a merchant seemed incompatible with standards of the Church. In this function, Azpilcueta's book remained influential for a long time: 'El *Manual de Confesores* era uno de los libros predilectos de las bibliotecas públicas y particulares de todas las provincias de las Indias' has been said of its use in Latin America down to the eighteenth century (Popescu, 1986, 168).

Azpilcueta's central concern is with problems of usury. He begins with a subtle reinterpretation of a characterization of an important form of interest-taking by Pope Gregory IX: 'He who lends to a sea-merchant or to one travelling to a fair and receives something more than the capital because he has assumed the risk is to be regarded as a usurer.'[7] Azpilcueta now says that the scholars of Salamanca had interpreted this passage to mean: 'He who lends, because he insures and because he receives interest, is a usurer.' But Azpilcueta, who once had accepted this interpretation himself, now regards it as absurd, since all Christians know that insurance is legitimate and costly. His reinterpretation, partly based on a grammatical analysis of the Latin phrase (for details see Schefold, 1998a, 23), consists of a proposal to consider that the formulation 'is to be regarded' as the central message, for only God can know whether the creditor demands interest because a real risk has to be covered, or whether the taking of risk (*periculum*) is only a pretext in order to obtain interest in a transaction which is in fact certain. And Azpilcueta now believes that Gregory had commanded the Church to start from the position that usury might be involved even in cases where risk normally occurs (as in maritime trade) so as to ensure an investigation in each particular case. The Church uses the confession to find out the truth, while civil law will treat a normal charge for an insurance premium as licit.

A modern interpretation of Azpilcueta's argument could be based on the observation that contracts were incomplete, so that it was not really clear who took the risk – the creditor or the merchant – provided the latter left some security. Azpilcueta instructs the priests that risk premiums should not be criticized; the confessing lender is however to be encouraged to return interest payments in excess of the risk premium. It is to be understood that restitution is to be paid to the merchant concerned, but if the confession takes place long after the event, restitution should be made for a beneficial purpose or be paid to the Church. Azpilcueta regards the formulation by Pope Gregory IX as exorbitant, since it presupposes guilt where innocence is likely. The prescription is therefore to be used cautiously. On the other hand, usury is to be fought not only where lending for the poor is concerned, but also as regards lending among the rich.

Azpilcueta's *Manual* contains very advanced passages on monetary theory, in particular on the quantity theory of money (long prior to Bodin), on international trade and international exchanges. He uses quantity theory and purchasing power parity to explain exchange rates and hence the trade in bills of exchange (charges for payments due to differences in location are licit; charges for payments due to differences in time are not). He thus is concerned with the business of changing moneys, and here he introduces an interesting distinction concerning usury.

Interest to cover risk is licit, as we have seen, and so is interest to cover damages incurred because of a delayed repayment. But what about opportunity cost (*lucrum cessans*)? A money-changer must be paid for his work of money-changing. If a money-changer lends money to somebody else, he can charge for his lending to the extent that, because the money lent is not in his hands, he cannot use it for trade, therefore it is licit for him to take interest if he is forced to interrupt or at least to restrict his money-changing. Azpilcueta thus explains the gain of the money-changer as a reward of work performed, not as a profit on capital advanced. The money-changer, having less money-capital at his disposal, is compelled to reduce his activity and cannot change his method of operation in such a way that the amount of work performed remains the same despite the reduction of capital. Fixed coefficients, we might say. Azpilcueta seems to think that less work performed implies less money earned. Foregone profit here consists of a foregone compensation for work, not a forgone alternative use of a capital which would be productive as such. Azpilcueta pursues his approach with a consistency which one may find admirable or quixotic: he insists that banks should charge for deposits held, instead of paying interest on them. Both the bank and the depositor sin if, instead of charging for the deposit, a bank pays the depositor because it can use the money in usurious manner; the depositor then becomes a usurer indirectly. If this kind of indirect usury is to be avoided, the owner of the money must pay the bank for the service of custody.

1.4 LUIS DE MOLINA: REAL OPPORTUNITY COST, BUT NOT ANY KIND OF OPPORTUNITY COST, JUSTIFIES INTEREST

Molina, a Jesuit, was some 40 years younger than Azpilcueta and had been one of his students. Azpilcueta's influence is present in Molina's *De Justitia et Jure* (1659). Molina was born 1535. He studied law at the University of Salamanca, philosophy at the University of Alcalá and became a Jesuit in 1553. After further studies of philosophy in Coimbra at the College of Jesuits, he taught for most of his life at the University at Evora. His main work, *De iustitia et iure*, about a third of which was published only posthumously (first edition published 1595–1609), became influential and was reprinted several times.[8] His commentaries on Thomas of Aquinas, by contrast, created a stir during his lifetime because of Molina's position regarding freedom of will. He also taught and wrote in Lisbon, at Cuenca near Madrid, and in Madrid itself.

For the economist, possibly the most interesting aspect of his vast work concerns the theory of just price. It will have to be dealt with on another occasion, since I do not find a trace of this aspect of his theory in Klock. He is also interesting on monopoly, but I here concentrate on usury. Following the Aristotelian tradition of Thomas Aquinas, money is to be used in exchange and cannot be lent like a durable good for a rent payment. Aquinas accepted *damnum emergens* as an ultimate reason for interest-taking and also *lucrum cessans*, but only within narrow limits, as justified by the division of a commercial gain in a company. Molina develops the argument especially with regard to exchange. He remains cautious with regard to *lucrum cessans*, for if someone sees a profit opportunity, he could realize it. Why should it then serve as a pretext for demanding usury? Hence, Molina distinguished between two kinds of *lucrum cessans*: *in potentia propinqua* and *in potentia remota* (Molina, 1659, vol. II, quaestio 315, 13). The first case means a profit forgone in cases where money had been reserved for a specific activity which was not however realised only for the reason that the money had already been given as a loan. Profit *in potentia remota* by contrast occurs if the money could have been used for a specific form of acquisition, but the reservation of the money for the purpose has not yet taken place ('pecunia aut aliud quod mutuo datur, non erat destinatum negotiationi, poterat tamen destinari', Molina, ibid.). In the first case, there is *lucrum vero cessans*, a profit which is really foregone. In this case, interest is licit, but not in the other. The distinction is compared with one made by Thomas Aquinas. It is not the same as that made by Azpilcueta, but reminiscent of it. Both authors wish to avoid the inclusion of possibilities among opportunity costs which are not in some sense concrete.[9] At the same time, profit cannot arise without the assistance of labour: capital is not productive as such.

It follows that there must be a similarity between the Scholastic and the Marxian position. Capital, in Marx, is not in itself productive. He treats interest not as an intertemporal price but as a phenomenon occurring in monetary and especially in capitalist economies, where capital acquires the power to generate profit: workers can be exploited to obtain surplus value, part of which is turned into profit. Interest then is the price of capital – a *verrückte* ('displaced' / 'crazy') form of price. The Marxian critique of the concept of money-capital thus is a denunciation of a contradictory reality (Schefold, 1998b). The price of a commodity is for Marx the monetary expression of its value in exchange, hence a quantity of money; but in the case of money-capital, money – in the form of money-capital – itself is being priced in terms of money. There is thus an analogy between the Scholastic and Aristotelian view of interest as something unnatural, and the Marxian view of its being illogical.

1.5 LEONARDUS LESSIUS: EVEN THE STOCK EXCHANGE TO BE TOLERATED

Leonardus Lessius's *De iustitia et iure* represents the highest and most majestic tree in the vast forest of late Scholastic works on economic justice. He was born in 1554 in Brecht, a small city not far from Antwerp on the border of modern Belgium and the Netherlands, into a family of poor artisans. The child, eager from an early age to read and to pray, was to learn a trade, but he insisted that he be allowed to attend a school. A priest taught him Latin, his gifts were noted and he won a competition at 13 for a grant to study at the University of Leuven. He came out top in the final examination but, to the regret of his professors, he rejected an offer for an academic career and entered the order of the Jesuits. This was announced to the General of the Jesuits: 'Admisimus primum universitatis istius, adolescentem Brechtanum 17 annorum, optimis corporis at animi dotibus praeditum'.[10]

At the time, the northern and southern Netherlands were the most prosperous region of the world, belonging to the Habsburgs as part of the heritage of Burgundy; they yielded seven times as much as the silver of the Americas to Emperor Charles V. The stock exchange of Antwerp was the centre of European monetary trade. The religious wars and wars of liberation of the Netherlands began when Lessius was a child; they would last until 1648. Shortly after having become a Jesuit, Lessius had to flee because of an attack of the northern Protestants in 1572. He began to teach at the college of the Jesuits in Douai at 20. Having become a priest in 1580, he went to Rome in order to study at the Collegium Romanum in 1583, and he taught philology in Leuven from 1585 to 1601. His main work, *De iustitia et iure*, originated from his lectures, which were attended not only by young Jesuits but also by students of the university. Like Molina, Lessius defended the theory of the freedom of the will against the teaching of predestination. Lessius continued to write and to give advice to people of both high and low rank after his retirement in 1601; he died in 1623, much revered by the population.

De iustitia et iure is concerned with the cardinal virtues, in particular with justice. After a very sophisticated overview of the different kinds of justice, of rights of possession and hence also of the obligation to return goods in unrightful possession, Lessius turns to economic applications, distinguishing always between obligations due to civil law, to natural law and to the law of the Church. I concentrate again on usury (Schefold, 1999).

This is dealt with in the long twentieth chapter. A loan (*mutuum*) is a transfer of a determinate amount of a thing which the recipient has to return in similar kind and quality. He speaks of an exchange (*permutatio*), if something else is to be given back in exchange. Usury now is defined as a gain which springs immediately from the contract (*immediate, ex vi pacti mutuationis*), by the force of the loan (*mutuum*) contract. The gain (*lucrum*) is a monetary surplus, estimated in money above and beyond the capital, whose existence has no other reason than that a loan has been made.

Such a gain is contrary to the Old and to the New Testaments, and also to canonical law. It is also unjust according to natural law, for the money received by the borrower would be paid twice, by means of the return of the money and by paying interest on top. This is the traditional argument, and Lessius also takes up the other traditional argument that it is not the use of capital that can be sold and hence paid; the use of money consists in the spending of the sum, hence it is not the use of capital that must be paid for, rather it is necessary to replace what has been given away. The fact that civil law does not forbid all interest payments is not a proof that usury is not against nature. And the law does not permit usury in general.

A *mutuum* without interest and hence usury is not necessarily an act of altruism, since one possibly expects advantages out of friendship, and Lessius approaches licit exceptions with caution. 'Notandum est, damnum emergens et lucrum cessans communiter vocari interesse' (Lessius, 1605, 2.20.68). This states that damages and opportunity costs are called *interesse*. A tort can simply consist of returning the sum later than originally agreed. *Lucruum cessans* is now interpreted so widely, since money 'est enim veluti semen foecundem lucri per industriam' (Lessius, 1605, 2.20.80): money is like seed fruitful of gain by industry. By giving away one's money, one loses its potential yield. One can hope for such a yield, and this 'hope' can be estimated. If merchants are forced by princes to give loans to the state, they are entitled to receive compensation payments by virtue of the hopes they entertained concerning potential uses of their money. Lessius here criticizes Thomas Aquinas, stating that the compensation for a reasonable hope of a gain foregone can be part of a licit contract, for the lending of money is similar to the lending of instruments for work.

But even Lessius regards it necessary to consider more closely what the alternative gains might be. Such possibilities are the buying of rent-bearing land, or houses. On the other hand, Lessius criticizes older authors who had said, as we saw with Azpilcueta, that idle money could not be lent at interest. For if money is idle, this shows – according to the traditional view – that gains are made only by means of other capital. Lessius's critique involves the observation that the possession of idle money may be a necessary part of business, since what we nowadays call reserves for transactions and as a precaution are needed.

After dealing with risk in an interesting manner, Lessius even admits a lack of money (*carentia pecuniae*) on the stock exchange as a licit cause of interest (Gordon, 1975). If traders lack present money, nobody will provide a loan without interest. What is licit then depends on the habits of the traders. The example is that of the stock exchange at Antwerp ('usus Bursae seu Peristylii Antverpiensis', Lessius, 1605, 2.20.124–126). He thus recognizes the autonomous laws of the market and asks that they be respected.[11]

It becomes difficult after this to identify cases of real usury. Lessius mentions the village poor who have to turn to local money-lenders and pay usurious interest rates. Like others before him, he recommends pawn shops, instituted and supervised by the state in order to render the local money-lenders superfluous. This beneficial solution, widely applied in pre-modern Europe, can be recognized as a good thing by all concerned, but the definition of usury has been emptied of content. Whether Lessius's stance was influenced by the Reformation or by other causes is a matter of debate. Instead of following this argument, which I have pursued elsewhere (Schefold, 1999), I return to Klock.

1.6 KASPAR KLOCK: ON USURY AND INDIRECT TAXATION

Klock was a Protestant: not a Calvinist, but a Lutheran. The prosperity of the Netherlands impressed him and is often mentioned in his work. He lived under more primitive conditions in Germany, devastated by the war and almost ruined. Usury is dealt with in his chapter 19 of the second book. It is an evil (*malum*) to be contained and prohibited, but the usurers always find new techniques (*artes novas,* book two, XIX, 1) to circumvent prohibitions. Interest-taking is clearly against the law of nature, for nothing originates from nothing ('foenerandi ratio . . . planè contra naturae regulam, cùm ex nihilo nihil gignatur' book two, XIX, 5). Main new techniques are the purchases of rents (*venditiones redituum*), anticipated purchase (*locationes fructuum*: the merchant buys the fruits of agriculture prior to the harvest) and contracts to buy and resell (*venditiones cum pacto de retrovendendo*: the creditor provides money to the debtor by buying something from him and agreeing on the spot to resell the good to him after some time at a higher price, the higher price reflecting interest). Klock mentions yet other methods. For every law prohibiting such techniques there is a new fraud. But usury is to be demanded from one's enemy, not from one's neighbour. The belief that giving credit to the helpless will help them is like giving wine to the sick: the sick will get some immediate relief but will soon feel worse. Klock distinguishes four kinds of collecting money: there is the natural exchange of things; a change of moneys from place to place; buying cheap and selling at an elevated price; and usury where money is taken for a loan provided for a given amount of time. Exchange in kind is natural; usurious exchange is to be blamed; the other forms are in between.

Klock conducts his critique of usury at three levels. First is the level of tradition. As elsewhere in his book, he takes up the heritage of antiquity and the Middle Ages. There is no need to follow him in this and to repeat his quotations from Cato and other Roman authors. The second level is sociological. The usurer is described as one sitting at home (book two, XIX, 19), waiting for the calamities which must befall others so that they have need of his money. The usurer is anxious to lend out his entire fortune. If he succeeds, he lives, like the Apostles, without money in his hands, but not for altruistic reasons. At the third level, Klock returns to the sources and restates that the Bible decrees the provision of loans without demanding interest (the well-known *mutuum date nihil inde sperantes*, book two, XIX, 49–51). The distinctions made by the Scholastic authors, like *damnum emergens* and *lucrum cessans* (book two, XIX, 66), are mentioned – Klock seems to know them well – but they are invalid. There are legally accepted rates of interest of 5 per cent or 4 per cent which have been defended by different authors, among them the School of Salamanca. To this extent, interest-taking must be tolerated.

In order to demonstrate that his approach is manageable, Klock lays out criteria for when a contract involving selling and reselling or pawning is to be regarded as usurious. It is likely to be usurious if the difference in price is large. A suspicion arises if the creditor has customarily acted as usurer. There has to be a just price for the pawned object. The rate of interest implied by it should not exceed the legal rate. It is also an indication of usury if the creditor can resell at a given date or at his pleasure, but Klock's final conclusion is that such contracts are not really licit, even if they are legal.

In substance, therefore, Klock insists on the simplicity of the Christian command not to take interest. He tolerates moderate interest and he deplores forms of usury which seem to him predatory. Eventually, he seeks practical solutions in the context of a book on taxation. He therefore warns against the introduction of draconic laws against usurers, as has often been done, and recommends that usurers be fined to the benefit of the Treasury. Practical proposals in later chapters then also include the introduction of state pawn shops (*montes pietates*), as in Lessius, and a discussion of state borrowing – to introduce new borrowing is simpler than to impose new taxes.

It would thus seem that the ideas of the School of Salamanca were transferred to Klock but that the reception was negative, in that he made little use of their distinctions between licit and illicit forms of interest-taking. But this is not generally true. In other cases, for instance in the case of indirect taxes, Klock explicitly approves of the ideas of Molina, Lessius and others. He learns from them to regard the taxation of necessaries as a form of taxation which is directly proportional to consumption and insofar it is just, as well as being practical. But it does not reflect individual earning potential; in more traditional terms, the poor should pay less. Hence Klock approves of Lessius, who says that luxury goods should be taxed at a higher rate. Klock sees a possible injustice even in this case: if a specific luxury good which is in reality needed by few people, such as a medicine from India, is taxed heavily, the total burden of taxation has to be borne only by those in need. Klock therefore recommends the taxation of a variety of rare goods in order to reach 'geometric equality', that is, distributive justice. He also follows the School of Salamanca when it is a question of whether foreigners should pay such taxes. 'No', says Cajetan, according to Klock, but 'Yes' thinks Molina, and Klock follows him, for if an exemption were granted to foreigners, some who are not actually foreigners would pretend to be so, and generally foreigners enjoy the advantages of the location where they have chosen to live (book two, LXXVIII, 19–21).

Klock also considers (book two, LXXVIII) whether indirect taxation is feasible in Germany. He knows that indirect taxation is much used in 'Belgium', but it would be wrong to imitate the Dutch: 'In Belgio enim . . . ob infinitam populi et commerciorum multitudinem . . . alia collectarum ratio . . ., quae heîc in exemplum trahi nequit' (book two, LXXVIII, 4). Why does Klock feel that the time for the general introduction of indirect taxation has not yet arrived in Germany? Why is the difference in the standard of life between the advanced Netherlands and backward Central Europe relevant in this context? Klock seems to think that the poor in Belgium are less poor than the poor in Germany, and that the rich are taxed heavily in the Netherlands by means other than indirect taxation. The imposition of indirect taxation is unpopular. Does this make any difference? Sanchez and others regard it as unjust, since indirect taxes fall more heavily on the poor. It is regarded as more just by Molina, Suarez and Lessius. These recognize that the poor are forced to pay indirect taxes, but the rich buy more because they have bigger households with more dependents (family members and servants). And now Klock recognizes that indirect taxes are transferred to the rich, as employers in big families or in small enterprises, for the rich have to pay out higher wages because of taxation: 'Sentiunt tamen mediatè idem onus: quia cum artifices, operarii,

& alii majori pretio comparent sibi victum proper tributa, quae in illis rebus solvunt: carius suas operas divitibus locant' (book two, LXXVIII, 19). Hence, in the middle of his treatment of justice, which ends partly in rhetorical and partly in casuistic arguments, we find this brilliant economic idea: the tax is imposed on the poor, but the tax is transmitted to the rich since the poor – in this case artisans and workers – receive a necessary wage. It is a minimum wage, but this minimum wage can be higher in the richer country; the prices of necessary goods also include the tax on those necessaries.

Adam Smith would later say that indirect taxes were an imposition on income and a substitute for an income tax which was, for technical reasons, not yet feasible. We also find in Smith the idea that the consumption of the lower classes is much larger than that of the middle and the upper classes, so that indirect taxation leads to higher wages: 'A direct tax upon wages of labour . . . though the labourer might, perhaps, pay it out of his hand . . . would in reality be advanced by the person who immediately employed him' (Smith, 1961 [1776, 1904], 393). A few pages later, Smith adds: 'It is thus that a tax upon the necessaries of life operates exactly in the same manner as a direct tax upon the wages of labour. The labourer . . . cannot . . . be . . . said even to advance it. It must always in the long run be advanced to him by his employer in the advanced rate of his wages' (Smith, 1961 [1776, 1904], 400). Only the more advanced country can afford these higher wages. It seems that Klock felt this connection, and that he was therefore sceptical regarding the possibilities of indirect taxation in Germany, while high taxes were feasible in the Netherlands and also necessary, because of infrastructural expenses (the system of dikes and drainage) and the war against Spain. To the extent that wages were still paid in kind in Germany (the more backward country, dominated by agriculture), it was obvious that indirect taxes would fall on the employer.

These more progressive ideas were developed by Klock in his intellectual interchange with international authors, especially those of the School of Salamanca, and in this sense Cameralism is not an isolated phenomenon but reflects a wider European discussion. Klock's book is full of references to the observations and legal opinions of others; we can therefore in his case relatively easily identify the way in which economic ideas were transferred. It is different with Adam Smith: he provides not one single reference to the sources for his ideas in the section 'Taxes upon the wages of labour' from which I have quoted. So I come back to de Roover's question of how the Scholastics influenced the mercantilists. Having confirmed that an important proposition advanced by Smith had been discussed by the school of Salamanca and by Cameralists, I leave to future research the identification of the subsequent path to Smith. Schumpeter asserted: 'The

Wealth of Nations does not contain a single analytical idea, principle or method that was entirely new in 1776' (Schumpeter, 1954, 184; see also Streissler, 1981). Mann (1937) insists that the Cameralists, and Klock in particular, anticipated the principal arguments concerning taxation right into the nineteenth century.

While we can find continuity regarding the discussion of taxation, a relatively technical matter, there is clearly a discontinuity regarding the discussion of interest. In normal times one tends here to identify with Klock: he is right that the New Testament unambiguously forbids interest-taking, while the modernization of the economy imposes the need to introduce instruments of credit; and so practical solutions, such as those based on legal rates of interest, have to be found. The critique of usury is continued textually, even radicalized, but in effect it is abandoned. On the other hand, one also feels that the continuing convoluted discussions of Scholastic authors must have reflected a serious concern, and these are perhaps more easily understood at a time of monetary crisis such as that of early 2009. When we read of 'structured products' are we not reminded of Scholastic authors and their sayings, such as *venditur it quod non est*',[12] that nothing can come from nothing?

APPENDIX: ENGLISH TRANSLATION OF THE CHAPTER 'JAPAN' IN KASPAR KLOCK'S: *DE AERARIO* (1651, HERE TEXT OF PELLER EDITION, 1671)

Liber I, Caput XXIV, 1–19, pp. 358–9

> *IAPONIAE Rex milliones bis duo*
> *Auri lucratur ex oryzae semine.*
> *Hic unionum & aureorum plurimum est;*
> *Et offerunt tributa Regi reguli.*
> [The King of Japan gains twice 2 million in gold from the seed of rice. Here are plenty of pearls and goldpieces, and the princes offer tributes to the King.]

(1) Iaponia or Iapania is a body of many and various islands. To the East, these islands are opposite New Spain. To the North they have the Tatars[13] and other peoples which are of unknown ferocity.

(2) To the West they look to China. To the South they are opposite unexplored lands with a wide sea in between.

(3) In the same way as they are different from the other lands of the world with regard to their position, they are populated by a people very different from the others in their mores and manners.

(4) There are 66 principalities in these islands, divided into three main parts. Of these, the first comprises nine, the second four, the third 53 principalities. Of these, the five principalities of Coquinai are more noble and famous, of these Meacum[14] is the principal city of the entire island.[15] It happens most often that whoever obtained the rule of the five principalities was called Emperor or King of Japan and sometimes Lord of Tenza, where those five principalities are situated, close to Meacum.

(8) Such were in recent years Nabunanga[16] and Fassaha[17] who, as lords, were superior in extent and power to all their predecessors:

(9) for Nabunanga had brought together 36 principalities or districts, and so Faxiba or Fassaha got at least 50 under the yoke.

(10) There is a triumvirate at Meacum which holds supreme control over what is to be achieved. The first, who is called Zazo, equivalent to the highest priest, oversees the holy affairs. The second, Voo, the ranks and honours, the third, Cucabama,[18] peace and war, and, by the way, by means of the power of the Prince.

(11) But the way of governing this realm is very different from what is known to us in Europe.

(12) For the power and magnificence of this Prince neither consists in his annual incomes and ordinary revenues, nor in the benevolence of the people and the friendship of neighbours, but in mere authority and command.

(13) For whatever he obtains from an enemy, he divides between his friends and clients, whose perceptible fidelity he can obtain by the following law: that they should dedicate themselves to him, the King, at their own expense, whether there be peace or war, having procured a certain number of soldiers. Those in turn share their lands and properties with their dependents and clients in order to oblige them. Hence it comes to pass that all the riches of Japan, both private and public, are shifting and depend on a few lords, and those few to the Lord of Tenza, who gives and takes at his pleasure, what and to whom he likes; he lifts up and casts down, he renders the princes rich and poor.

(14) Therefore whenever he takes away or changes a principality, he changes also all the nobles and soldiers of that district, leaving only the artificers and peasants.

(15) This form of government entails perpetual transformations and changes of rule. Hence it comes to pass that the princes of Tenza, and other princes, appear to be tyrants and usurpers of the goods of others, as destroyers of the monarchy and as enemies of the greatness of Japan. And so they are, being so disposed, forced by the people, and otherwise by their companions, to live perpetually in arms.

(16) It happens that the princes, since they are repeatedly changed, are not loved as much by the people as natural lords are. And these princes, fearful of sudden change, do not reciprocate the enduring love of their people, being sure that, with the same facility with which they obtained one principality, they may obtain another, perhaps a better one, in the future. Hence they either alone or jointly with other princes always aspire to something new, and involve the island in eternal wars. They never lack reasons for discord and war, since the borders of the districts are narrow.

(17) Hence Faxiba, in order to establish absolute power, was in the habit of transferring princes from one region to another, so that they might not find it easy to rebel against him when they were made to rule a new populace. And so, in order to break their power, he divided the principalities into several smaller prefectures, so that they might not only be unable to undertake anything against him in such confined provinces, but so that they would quarrel among themselves about their borders. Moreover, he wished that, regardless of all changes, both he who obtained a better condition and he who was reduced had to come every year to his royal palace, and that they pay homage and swear fidelity and, at the same time, offer gifts and presents to the King. And in this manner he attracted the chief riches of all the island to himself.

(18) Apart from those gifts and tributes which the lesser princes have to give to him out of duty, 2 million in gold are believed to flow to him every year. Of the rice which is collected in royal estates, the inhabitants sell a

great amount to foreign merchants, together with pearls. And there are also large amounts of gems [to be found], and not a little gold. Since it can easily be collected, this realm must be judged [to be] very rich because of the abundance of these things.

(19) Ossacaeia[19] is a powerful and free city and, as some think, the richest of all in the Orient. There is a great and widespread traffic of competing merchants, and those of mediocre means are thought to possess 30 000 in gold.

It can easily been seen how considerable are the forces of this realm by considering that Faxiba, when he had subjugated all the islands with their 50 principalities, then determined upon sailing to China, having collected an enormous army, and to invade that realm. To this end, he ordered that many trees be felled for the making of 2000 ships, so that his troops be transported. Xaverius and Turrianus, the Jesuits, dedicated much work and study to this and converted many to the Christian belief.

NOTES

1. I should like to thank Keith Tribe for helpful suggestions.
2. See the forthcoming dissertation on Petty by Holger Wendt, to be submitted at Goethe-University Frankfurt.
3. This section of the chapter is a slightly modified version of the paper presented to the Japanese Society for the History of Economic Thought (JSHET) conference in Kyushu, May 2007. This was in turn based on a draft of my introduction to a reprint of the *De aerario* by Kaspar Klock, now published (Schefold, 2009). Complete references to Klock can be found there; they are given here only in summary as (book, chapter, section).
4. Hence his originality could not be understood by a historian of law like Schulz (1982), who fails to see the essential difference between Klock's early thesis and *De aerario* (Schulz, 1982, 51–2).
5. The section on Japan is about one page long in book one, which contains Klock's description of countries. Book one has a length of 173 pages in the edition of 1651. For comparison: chapters on the Holy Roman Empire, on the Ottoman Empire, on the Dutch Republic are 22, 9 and 14 pages long, respectively.
6. His thesis was: 'El reino no es del rey, sino de la comunidad, y la misma potestad, por derecho natural, es de la comunidad y no del rey; por esta causa no puede la comunidad abdicar totalmente de su poder', in Azpilcueta (1965, xvi).
7. 'Naviganti, vel eunti ad nundinas certam mutuans pecuniae quantitatem, eo quod suscepit in se periculum, recepturus aliquid ultra sortem, usurarius est censendus', as quoted in Schefold (1998a) on Azpilcueta from Gregor IX, *De usuris*.
8. The editions of 1659 and 1759 are available on the Internet, Goldsmith-Kress Library of Economic Literature.
9. I owe these observations on Molina to the Diploma thesis on Molina by Stefan Schweighöfer (2009).
10. Sull (1930, 26): 'We have admitted the best of this university, a boy from Brecht of 17 years, with excellent gifts of body and spirit' (my translation – BS).
11. Decock (2009, 58) writes of the 'disruptive character of Lessius' thought' (meaning that traditional Scholastic teaching on usury was being undermined). Lessius is found

'rewarding the prudent businessman playing on the impersonal mechanisms at work in the market'.

12. Literally: 'It is sold what is not', which means: They sell something which does not exist.
13. 'Tartars'.
14. Latin name of Kyoto.
15. Klock here refers to the main island, Honshu.
16. Klock here seems to refer to Oda Nobunaga.
17. The first edition of 1651 has 'Fahissa', the Peller edition of 1671 has 'Fassaha' and 'Faxiba', as in our translation below. (Other small differences between the editions are unimportant.) Klock probably means Hashiba Hideyoshi, one of the names adopted by Hiyoshi (or Hiyoshimaru), who had earlier adopted the name Kinoshita Tokichiro and later was called Toyotomi Hideyoshi, and who invaded Korea in 1592–93.
18. Tokugawa?
19. Osaka.

REFERENCES

Azpilcueta, Martin de (1965), *Comentario resolutorio de cambios*, Introduccion y texto critico por A. Ullastres, J.M. Perez Prendes y L. Pereña, Madrid: Consejo Superior, Introduction, p. xvi.

Blesgen, Detlef J. and Ralf P. Welter (2006), *Der Akzisen-Streit. Schriften zur finanz-theoretischen Kontroverse deutscher Frühkameralisten*, Zusammengestellt und mit einer Einleitung herausgegeben von Detlef J. Blesgen und Ralf P. Welter, (Historia Scientiarum (Wirtschaftswissenschaften), Ein Editionsprogramm der Fritz Thyssen Stiftung zur Geschichte der Wissenschaften in Deutschland), Hildesheim: Olms.

Campagnolo, Gilles (2004), *Critique de l'économie politique classique: Marx, Menger et l'école historique*, Paris: Presses Universitaires de France.

Decock, Wim (2009), 'Lessius and the breakdown of the Scholastic paradigm', *Journal of the History of Economic Thought*, **31**(1), 57–78.

Faust, Maximilian (1641), *Consilia pro aerario civili ecclesiastico et militari, publico atque priuato sive iurium, artium ac remediorum omnium, universi orbis terrarum* . . ., Frankfurt: Schleich für den Verfasser.

Gordon, Barry (1975), *Economic Analysis before Adam Smith: Hesiod to Lessius*, London: Macmillan.

Gülich, Gustav von (1830), *Geschichtliche Darstellung des Handels, des Gewerbes und des Ackerbaus der bedeutendsten handeltreibenden Staaten unserer Zeit*, 2 vols, Jena: Frommann.

Jones, Richard (1831), *An Essay the Distribution of Wealth and on the Sources of Taxation*, reprinted (1964), New York: Kelley.

Klock, Kaspar (1610), Dissertatio theoretico-practica [as in 1608], in: *Disputationes duae* . . ., von Thomas Michael and Caspar Klocke (*sic*), Speyer: J. Taschner; reprint of (1608), *Dissertatio theoretico-practica de contributionibus hodie, ut plurimum in Germania usitatis* . . ., Basel: Genathius.

Klock, Kaspar (1649), *Consiliorum Casparis Klocki JC. Eminentissimi comitis Caesar Palatini studia & opera collectorum.* Frankfurt: Endter 1649–50, 3 vols, 4th vol. (supplementum), 1676 et al.

Klock, Kaspar (1651), *Tractatus juridico-politico-polemico-historicus de aerario,*

sive censu, per honesta media, absque divexatione populi, Licite conficiendo, libri duo . . ., Nürnberg: Endter.
Klock, Kaspar (1671), *Tractatus juridico-politico-polemico-historicus de aerario, sive censu, per honesta media, absque divexatione populi*, Licite conficiendo, libri duo . . ., Nürnberg: Andreas & Endter 1671 u.a. (with comments by Christoph Peller), available at http://galenet.galegroup.com/servlet/MOME?af=RN&locID=suf&d1=19010013100200&srchtp=a&c=1&an=19010013100200&ste=12&stp=Author&docNum=U100217297&cid=ocm20885785&ae=U100217297&tiPG=1.
Klock, Kaspar (2009 [1651]), *De aerario*, edited with introduction by Bertram Schefold, (Historia Scientiarum, Fritz Thyssen Stiftung), Hildesheim: Olms.
Krauth, Wolf-Hagen (1984), *Wirtschaftsstruktur und Semantik. Wissenssoziologische Studien zum wirtschaftlichen Denken in Deutschland zwischen dem 13. und 17. Jahrhundert*, Berlin: Duncker & Humblot.
Lessius, Leonardus (1605), *De iustitia et iure caeterisque virtutibus cardinalibus libri IV*, Lovanii: Johannes Masius.
Lessius, Leonardus (1999), *De iustitia et iure caeterisque virtutibus cardinalibus Libri IV*, (Klassiker der Nationalökonomie). Düsseldorf: Verlag Wirtschaft und Finanzen. Together with: *Vademecum zu einem Klassiker der spätscholastischen Wirtschaftsanalyse*. Kommentarband zum Faksimile-Nachdruck der 1605 in Leuven erschienenen Erstausgabe von Lessius, Leonardus: *De iustitia et iure caeterisque virtutibus cardinalibus Libri IV*. (Klassiker der Nationalökonomie). Düsseldorf: Verlag Wirtschaft und Finanzen.
Mann, Fritz Karl (1937), *Steuerpolitische Ideale. Vergleichende Studien zur Geschichte der ökonomischen und politischen Ideen und ihres Wirkens auf die öffentliche Meinung 1600–1935*, Jena: G. Fischer.
Marx, Karl (1969), Nachwort zur zweiten Auflage [1873], in: *Das Kapital*. Marx–Engels–Werke, Vol. 23, Berlin: Dietz, pp. 18–28.
Molina, Luis de (1659), *De Justitia et Jure. Tomus Secundus. De Contractibus*, Moguntiae: Schönwetter.
Monroe, Arthur Eli (2001 [1923]), *Monetary Theory before Adam Smith*, Kitchener, Ontario: Batoche.
Nielsen, Axel (1911), *Die Entstehung der deutschen Kameralwissenschaften im 17. Jahrhundert*, Jena: G. Fischer.
Perrotta, Cosimo (2004), *Consumption as an Investment, Vol. 1: The Fear of Goods from Hesiod to Adam Smith*, Routledge Studies in the History of Economics 71, London: Routledge.
Petty, William (1963), *The Economic Writings of Sir William Petty*, Charles Henry Hull (ed.), reprint, New York: Kelley.
Popescu, Oreste (1986), *Estudios en la historia del pensamiento economico Latinoamericano*. Antología del pensamiento económico y social de América Latina, Vol. 10, Bogota: Plaza y Janes.
Roncaglia, Alessandro (1985), *Petty: The Origins of Political Economy*, Cardiff: University College Press.
Roover, Raymond de (1955), 'Scholastic economics: survival and lasting influence from the sixteenth century to Adam Smith', *Quarterly Journal of Economics*, **69**, 161–90.
Salin, Edgar (1967), *Politische Ökonomie. Geschichte d. wirtschaftspolitischen Ideen von Platon bis zur Gegenwart*. 5. erw. Aufl. der Geschichte der Volkswirtschaftslehre. (Hand- u. Lehrbücher aus dem Gebiet der Sozialwissenschaften). Tübingen: Mohr and Zürich: Polygraphischer Verlag.

Schefold, Bertram (1993), 'Glückseligkeit und Wirtschaftspolitik: Zu Justis "Grundsätze der Policey-Wissenschaft"', in: *Vademecum zu einem Klassiker des Kameralismus*. Kommentarband zur Faksimile-Ausgabe der 1756 erschienenen Erstausgabe von Justi, Johann Heinrich Gottlob von: *Grundsätze der Policey-Wissenschaft*. Klassiker der Nationalökonomie. Düsseldorf: Verlag Wirtschaft und Finanzen, 5-27.

Schefold, Bertram (1994), 'Antonia Serra: der Stifter der Wirtschaftslehre?', in *Vademecum zu einem unbekannten Klassiker*. Kommentar zur Faksimile-Ausgabe der 1613 erschienenen Erstausgabe von Serra, Antonio: *Breve Trattato delle cause, che possono far abbondare li regni d'oro, & argento*. Klassiker der Nationalökonomie. Düsseldorf: Verlag Wirtschaft und Finanzen, 5-27.

Schefold, Bertram (1994–95), *Wirtschaftsstile Bd. 1: Studien zum Verhältnis von Ökonomie und Kultur*, (Fischer Wissenschaft Bd. 12243), *Wirtschaftsstile Bd. 2: Studien zur ökonomischen Theorie und zur Zukunft der Technik*, (Fischer Wissenschaft Bd. 12505), Frankfurt am Main: Fischer Taschenbuch Verlag.

Schefold, Bertram (1997), 'Ph. W. v. Hörnigk: Oesterreich ueber alles / wann es nur will. Zum Geleit', in *Vademecum zu einem Klassiker absolutistischer Wirtschaftspolitik*. Kommentarband zum Faksimile-Nachdruck der 1684 erschienenen Erstausgabe von Hörnigk, Philipp Wilhem von: *Oesterreich über alles, wann es nur will*. Klassiker der Nationalökonomie. Düsseldorf: Verlag Wirtschaft und Finanzen, 5-45.

Schefold, Bertram (1998a), 'Spanisches Wirtschaftsdenken zu Beginn der Neuzeit', in *Vademecum zu zwei Klassikern des spanischen Wirtschaftsdenkens*. Kommentarband zum Faksimile-Nachdruck der 1556 in Salamanca erschienenen Erstausgabe Azpilcueta, Martin de: *Comentario Resolutorio de Cambios* sowie der Abschrift der 1558 entstandenen Handschrift Ortiz, Luis: *Memorial del Contador Luis Ortiz a Felipe II*. (Bibl. Nac. Ms. 6487). Klassiker der Nationalökonomie. Düsseldorf: Verlag Wirtschaft und Finanzen, pp. 5–38.

Schefold, Bertram (1998b), 'The relation between the rate of profit and the rate of interest: a reassessment after the publication of Marx' manuscript of the third volume of *Das Kapital*', in Riccardo Bellofiore (ed.), *Marxian Economics: A Reappraisal. Essays on Volume III of Capital, Vol. 1: Method, Value and Money*, Basingstoke: Macmillan, pp. 127–44.

Schefold, Bertram (1999), 'Leonhard Lessius: Von der praktischen Tugend der Gerechtigkeit zur Wirtschaftstheorie', in *Vademecum zu einem Klassiker der spätscholastischen Wirtschaftsanalyse*. Kommentarband zum Faksimile-Nachdruck der 1605 in Leuven erschienenen Erstausgabe von Lessius, Leonardus: *De iustitia et iure caeterisque virtutibus cardinalibus Libri IV*. Klassiker der Nationalökonomie. Düsseldorf: Verlag Wirtschaft und Finanzen, pp. 5–32.

Schefold, Bertram (2004), 'Edgar Salin and his concept of "Anschauliche Theorie" ("Intuitive Theory") during the interwar period', *Annals of the Society for the History of Economic Thought*, **46**, 1–16.

Schefold, Bertram (ed.) (2009), 'Das *De aerario* von Kaspar Klock. Eine Einführung in Leben und Werk', in Klock (2009 [1651]), *De aerarie*, Hildesheim: Olms, pp. vi–cxiii.

Schmoller, Gustav von (1884), *The Mercantile System and its Historical Significance*, transl. of *Das Merkantilsystem in seiner historischen Bedeutung*, Reprinted (1967), New York: Kelley.

Schulz, Hermann (1982), *Das System und die Prinzipien der Einkünfte im werdenden Staat der Neuzeit, dargestellt anhand der kameralwissenschaftlichen Literatur (1600–1835)*, Berlin: Duncker & Humblot.
Schumpeter, Joseph Alois (1954), *History of Economic Analysis*, London: Allen & Unwin.
Schweighöfer, Stefan (2009), *Naturale pretium unde iustum – Weshalb der natürliche Preis gerecht ist*, thesis written for the requirement of the Diploma, Frankfurt am Main: Johann Wolfgang Goethe-Universität, unpublished.
Smith, Adam (1961 [1776, 1904]), *An Inquiry into the Nature and Causes of the Wealth of Nations*, Vol. 2, Edwin Cannan (ed.), London: Methuen.
Spiethoff, Arthur (1932), 'Die allgemeine Volkswirtschaftslehre als geschichtliche Theorie. Die Wirtschaftsstile', *Schmollers Jahrbuch*, **56**, 51–84.
Sprethoff, Arthur (1955), *Die wirtschaftlichen Wechsellagen: Aufschwung, Krise, Stockung*, Tübingen: Mohr.
Stein, Lorenz von (1884), 'Zur Geschichte der deutschen Finanzwissenschaft im 17. Jahrhundert', *Finanz-Archiv*, **1**, 1–44.
Streissler, Erich (1981), 'Adam Smith oder nur Wachstum? Paradoxa einer wissenschaftlichen Revolution', *Studien zur Entwicklung der ökonomischen Theorie*, Vol. 1, Fritz Neumark (ed.), Berlin: Duncker & Humblot, pp. 9–52.
Sull, Charles van (1930), *Léonard Lessius de la Compagnie de Jésus (1554–1623)*, Museum Lessianum Publications, Section Théologique No. 21, Louvain: Museum Lessianum.
Tribe, Keith (1988), *Governing Economy: The Reformation of German Economic Discourse, 1750–1840*, Cambridge: Cambridge University Press.
Vecchiato, Francesco (1977), *Note sul Cameralismo tedesco. La dottrina economico-finanziaria di Caspar Klock*, Verona: Palazzo Giuliani.
Zielenzieger, Kurt (1914), *Die alten deutschen Kameralisten. Ein Beitrag zur Geschichte der Nationalökonomie und zum Problem des Merkantilismus*, Beiträge zur Geschichte der Nationalökonomie 2, Jena: Fischer.

2. The ideal statesman: the influence of Richelieu on Davenant's political thought

Seiichiro Ito

2.1 INTRODUCTION

Although Charles Davenant was long described as a 'country Tory' or a 'new Tory' in the fields of political history and the history of political thought, he has mainly been discussed as a 'neo-Machiavellian' or a 'civic humanist' since the publication of J.G.A. Pocock's *Machiavellian Moment* in 1975.[1] Davenant did indeed quote and refer to Machiavelli on a wide range of topics, and in this literal sense he certainly may be considered a 'Machiavellian'. What Davenant learned from Machiavelli, however, was not 'civic virtue' but rather 'public virtue'; in other words, not the virtue of citizens, but rather that of rulers. The title of Davenant's lengthy unpublished manuscript of 1696 (much of which was later published in pamphlets), *Essay on Publick Virtue*, clearly reflects this.[2] For Davenant, virtue was wisdom, and wisdom was knowledge, and hence by 'public virtue' Davenant meant the knowledge required for statesmen to restore a disaster-stricken country such as his contemporary England. The central message of Davenant's work is that a wise and able statesman (or a 'legislator', a term synonymous for Davenant with 'statesman'), armed with 'public virtue', would be essential to England's recovery. The particular challenge facing the leader whom Davenant describes is that of restoring English trade from the miserable state to which the long and profligate war with France had reduced it. The goal towards which the able statesman should lead is economic prosperity, and the means to this end is a sound fiscal policy – specifically a reduction of public debt – which would restore credit conditions to normal, enabling trade to recover. For Davenant, the key to economic recovery for the nation was thus sound fiscal policy, and this depended in his understanding on the wisdom of the statesman.[3]

The war against France was the starting point not only of Davenant's political economy but also of his career as a pamphleteer. Since his first pamphlet in 1695, *An Essay upon Ways and Means of Supplying the War* (Davenant, 1771, Vol. I), France never left his mind as his country's most formidable rival, the role Holland had played for England during most of the seventeenth century. The 'universal monarchy' no longer implied the menace of Spain; it seemed inevitable that France would seize the balance of power in Europe.[4] At the same time, just as Holland had offered a model for England to imitate, France came to represent an enviable ideal in many respects, drawing the attention of Davenant as well as his contemporary English pamphleteers.

Davenant therefore turned to Cardinal Richelieu, particularly his posthumous *Testament Politique* (published in 1688) as a guide to good management in financing the war against France (Richelieu, 1995 [1688]). Throughout his writings, Davenant refers to Richelieu as the epitome of the able statesman. In discussing public credit – as far as Davenant is concerned the central issue for the statesman – he unfailingly relied on the wisdom of Richelieu, employing *Testament Politique,* with its emphasis on frugality, as his textbook. Davenant's notion of political arithmetic, that a statesman needs 'a true knowledge of the manufactures, trade, wealth, and strength of his country' (Davenant, 1771, vol. i, 86.), also has its origins in Richelieu. Although Davenant credited William Petty as the founder of political arithmetic[5] in his *Discourses on the Publick Revenues, and on the Trade of England* (1698), his conception of political arithmetic as an instrument of the able statesman comes from Richelieu. Hence Davenant's trust in the wise and able statesman was not exclusively based upon the traditional account of the classical republican legislator, nor did it simply adopt Petty's Baconian-flavoured political arithmetic.[6]

This chapter offers a re-examination of the Anglo-French relationship in the early modern English history of ideas, focusing on what Davenant learned from Richelieu. Notwithstanding decades of research on the economic thought of early modern England (and Britain) from the viewpoint of civic humanism in Pocock's sense, as well as into natural law and natural jurisprudence traditions,[7] the reality of the international situation of England in this period as demonstrated by recent research in political and economic history[8] necessitates the re-examination of this situation in the context of existing discussion of *raison d'état.*[9] While encompassing the Machiavellian point of view as traditionally understood before Pocock (summed up in the phrase *salus populi suprema lex*), I here suggest a source for a political economy different to that of Adam Smith's 'system of natural liberty', in which the roles of states and statesmen were minimized as much as possible. Although this argument, by locating the foundations of Davenant's thought in Richelieu, is not literally Machiavellian, it nonetheless exposes a certain type of Machiavellian political economy at the heart of Davenant's political thought.

2.2 THE WAR AGAINST FRANCE AND POLITICAL ARITHMETIC

A triad of concerns – the war against France, good administration, and political arithmetic – appear repeatedly throughout Davenant's pamphlets of the 1690s. His debut pamphlet, *An Essay upon Ways and Means*, begins with pessimistic remarks about the war: 'In the course of this war we are engaged in with France, nothing seems more to have hurt our affairs than an opinion . . . that the war could not last'. According to Davenant, this mistaken prospect of war was due to 'overrating our own strength, and undervaluing that of our enemies' (Davenant, 1771, vol. i, 3), an analysis demonstrating that, from the outset of his career as a pamphleteer, Davenant recognized the close relationship between war, governance and knowledge.

Central to Davenant's thought in regard to his triad of concerns is the balance of power in Europe, accurate knowledge of which he regarded as crucial to effective governance. He viewed the prospect of universal monarchy as a dangerous threat to the liberty of the English people. In view of the manifold power of France under Louis XIV, Davenant admits: 'we cannot pretend to have secured our liberties, or defeated his designs of universal monarchy' (vol. i, 10). However, Davenant does not simply describe the nature of these threats in his *Essay*, he also constructively proposes a new art of knowledge, which he would later term 'political arithmetic'. In Davenant's conception, France is not just an opponent to defeat, but also a model to imitate. His analysis of 'what a powerful enemy we have to deal with' consequently traces the history of French governance. He concludes that the source of France's strength is her 'great princes on the throne' and 'able men in the ministry' (vol. i, 7). The excellence of France's 'art of war' is undeniable in Davenant's view, but her strength springs above all from well-managed fiscal policy: 'Harry the Fourth . . . set himself to bring the treasury of his kingdom into some order; in which he was assisted by the duke of Sully, a frugal man, who, by natural wisdom and mere honesty, brought the revenue out of infinite debts into such a flourishing condition, that . . . they had ready four or five years provision for a war' (vol. i, 6); 'What the duke of Sully but began, Colbert brought to perfection in the publick revenue' (vol. i, 7); Louis XIV's revenue was 'skilfully brought in, and frugally laid out' (vol. i, 8).

Davenant did not intend his analysis of the English economy as what we today might consider scientific. He rather attempted to set forth a method for correctly assessing the relative 'strength[s]' of his own country and its rivals, and for finding the best strategy for beating them. In the strategy at which he arrived, England would have to show 'more than ordinary virtue and resolution'; what England 'chiefly' had to do was to avoid 'giv[ing] our enemies any room to believe . . . that we shrink and give back' (Davenant, 1771, vol. i, 8). However, at the heart of Davenant's political arithmetic was his idea that accurate knowledge of his country and its rival mattered, a notion that he would elaborate a few years later in his magnum opus, *Discourses on the Publick Revenues*. For Davenant, war and peace with France depended on the state of public revenues: 'the most proper season to conclude a peace with the French, in all appearance, will be when they are impoverished, and exhausted of that money by which they have so much prevailed, and when that sinew of war begins to slacken' (vol. i, 12).

Luxury and expense have nothing to do with loss of virtue or ethical corruption for Davenant. Rather, they are products of the lack of 'balance' between 'buying commodities in one nation' and 'selling them in another'. The 'prince's revenue' has to comprise 'a due proportion and share out of this balance' (vol. i, 13), and thus, the financial situation of England and France for Davenant is merely a criterion for determining the most advantageous timing for making peace. According to his calculation, the 'ordinary revenue' of France is 'much impaired by the effects of the war' and therefore it is implausible that the French would maintain their 'government, fleet, and armies' (vol. i, 14).

In developing his political arithmetic, Davenant compares France, Holland and England with regard to fiscal policy. France has 'thriven by trade' for 40 years and Holland for 100 years, and both countries are under 'the burthen of heavy taxes'. Nonetheless, Davenant observes their respective successes, though he offers contrasting reasons: French governance is 'exact and right' to the extent that it enables the French to 'enlarge their traffic'; whereas the Dutch are simply 'so long inured to . . . parsimony, that the more they are to pay the state, the more they save at home'. In contrast, people in England, a country 'where the administration of affairs is loose', incline to the 'expensive and luxurious', and in concert with this, face high taxes, duties and impositions, 'inevitably occasion[ing] a decay of trade' (Davenant, 1771, vol. ii, 284).

Yet in Davenant's discussion of France, he invariably describes the country in the context and language of the century-long discourse on the balance of power in Europe, and the understanding that this balance depends on the ambition for universal monarchy.[10] Davenant regards

France and its governance from the perspective of the shifting balance of power in Europe, and in particular its shift from Spain to France.

Two of Davenant's pamphlets in particular, *An Essay upon the Balance of Power* and *An Essay upon Universal Monarchy*,[11] examine England's involvement in the Spanish and French struggles for universal monarchy. *An Essay upon the Balance of Power* accuses English country gentlemen of political corruption and a resulting indifference to the 'common welfare', and specifically, of giving little thought to 'what becomes of the balance of Europe', 'the growth and power of France' and 'the dangers that threaten England' (Davenant, 1771, vol. iii, 300). Davenant argues that corrupt ministries have led the country into alliances that work against the national interest. Davenant warns that: 'every step which increases the strength of [the] French, leads towards our ruin' (vol. iii, 302). Whereas Elizabeth, despite Spain's clear progress towards universal monarchy, shrewdly managed the balance of power, the court of James I was in Davenant's view charmed by 'Spanish gold'. This prince, Davenant argues, chose to follow 'the pernicious advice of his favourites and ministers, than the faithful and disinterested counsel of his parliament, who addressed to him to arm, and enter into such leagues as might oppose the growth of the Spanish monarchy' (vol. iii, 304). As Davenant argues, however, the power balance in Europe during the civil war in England moved from Spain to France: 'the Spanish monarchy, heretofore so dreadful to us, was declined in strength, wealth, fleets, armies and discipline'. The pamphlet offers the conclusion that it was 'the succession of two able ministers, Richlieu [*sic*] and Mazarin' who accomplished this shift in power (vol. iii, 305).

In *An Essay upon Universal Monarchy*, Davenant surveys the history of 'the restless ambition of mankind for universal monarchy' (Davenant, 1771, vol. iv, 6). In considering the cases of Spain and the Ottoman Empire, noteworthy examples of states that pursued this 'game' of seeking universal monarchy, as had preceding empires 'for near 4000 years', including 'the Assyrian or Babylonian, the Persian, Macedonian, and Roman Empires' (vol. iv, 5–6), Davenant concludes that these empires each ultimately failed because they grew too fast to 'cement strongly together' (vol. iv, 22), and their depopulation proved fatal to trade and the ability to wage war. In contrast, France seemed to Davenant to have 'the fairest prospect' of achieving universal monarchy (vol. iv, 23), for during the reigns of Louis XIII and the 'present' king, that is, Louis XIV – here Davenant returns to a central theme – France has been 'all the while under a strong government' due to two able ministers: 'though factions did now and then prevail a little, in the main the reins were held by the unerring and severe hands of Richelieu and Mazarin' (vol. iv, 25).

2.3 RICHELIEU'S TESTAMENT POLITIQUE

Church (1972) seeks to demonstrate that in Richelieu, Christian morality and *raison d'état* are wholly consonant. In keeping with the conventional notion of Richelieu as the personification of *raison d'état*,[12] Davenant often refers to him, sometimes together with Mazarin, as the epitome of the able statesman, betraying no recognition that Richelieu was also a cardinal. Since as far as I have been able to determine Davenant in his writings refers exclusively among Richelieu's works to *Testament Politique*, a work which appeared just as Davenant was launching his career as an anti-court writer, one might reasonably conjecture that Davenant read none of Richelieu's other works, including the religious ones. Let us therefore reconsider this lengthy 'testament', beginning with Richelieu's discussion of what a statesman should be like.

Richelieu clearly intended *Testament Politique* as a literal final testament, to be read posthumously.[13] Accordingly, the work was first published in 1688 in Amsterdam, 46 years after his death. It should be noted that no consensus has been established concerning either Richelieu's actual authorship of the text, or on the date of composition of the manuscript. However, Church's argument that 'certain portions of the *Testament* . . . could only have been written or dictated by the Cardinal himself' (Church, 1972, 481), as well as the broad consensus among historians that *Testament Politique* represents Richelieu's thought at first hand,[14] amply support an exploration of the relationship between Richelieu and Davenant, especially since Davenant always bases his discussion of the details of Richelieu's arguments in *Testament Politique*. Although Richelieu's approach in *Testament Politique* differed in some respects from English mercantilist literature of the same period, such as the large amount of space devoted to Richelieu's discussion of reform of the ecclesiastical order and of the nobility, *Testament Politique* shares an essential message with Charles Davenant: that to govern well, the prince of a country should seek the advice of counsellors who tell the truth, and keep away from flatterers. In Davenant, this idea is evidently an application of Machiavelli's thought on the same topic in *The Prince*, inflected by the country-court schema of his age,[15] but although it is difficult to place Davenant's political thought in linear succession, Davenant clearly owed much not only to Machiavelli but also to Richelieu, particularly concerning the role of statesmen and financial policy. Moreover Richelieu, like Machiavelli, was an essential source for Davenant's political arithmetic.

Testament Politique consists of two parts. In the first, Richelieu proposes reforms in the social order of France, and specifically, to the clergy, the nobility and the third estate. It furthermore offers advice concerning the principal actors in governance, such as the state, the person of the king, the household economy of the royal family, and the king's counsellors. Chapter 8, 'Of the council of the prince' (*Du conseil du prince*), which is the last, crucial chapter of the first part, is an indispensable source of Davenant's political thought, as well as, significantly, the basis for Richelieu's argument on governing in the second part.

Richelieu's contention in the first of the seven sections of Chapter 8 is that 'the best princes need a good council' (1995, 211).[16] This is just what Davenant learned from Machiavelli's *The Prince* (1988), but it bears noting that the influence of Machiavelli on Richelieu is a subject requiring discussion beyond the scope of my argument here.[17] Richelieu observed that an able prince was a 'great treasure' (*grand trésor*) for a state, but he added that a 'skilful council' (*conseil habile*) was no less valuable. Since states are happiest where the princes and the counsellors are 'wisest' (*les plus sages*), and since few princes can govern their states themselves, he concludes that good counsellors are indispensable.[18] To be a perfect counsellor, in Richelieu's view, quite a few qualities are required, including ability (*capacité*), fidelity (*fidélité*), courage (*courage*) and application (*application*),[19] each of which he analyses in an ensuing section. A 'perfect accordance between the understanding and the will',[20] Richelieu argues, comes from ability and probity (*probité*), and 'an honest boldness to say to kings what is useful for them, even if it is not always comfortable for them, comes from probity and courage' (p. 226).[21]

In addition to these elements of character, Richelieu's trust in and reliance on reason (*raison*) is evident throughout *Testament*.[22] His argument for the necessity of reason comprises a typical Enlightenment argument: 'the light of nature makes it clear to all that a human being, having been made to reason, should not do anything but with reason, for otherwise he would act against his nature, and consequently, even against the one who is its author' (p. 245).[23] Characteristically, Richelieu's trust in reason is often accompanied by condemnation of passion in women:

> It is true that usually their [women's] weakness renders them incapable of the masculine virtue necessary for governance, and that it is almost impossible that their government would be exempt from baseness or depression caused by the weakness of their sex, or from injustice or cruelty, the true source of which is the deviation of their passions displacing reason. (p. 248)[24]

Although many discounted the abilities of women in this period – including Davenant, though he made an exception for Queen Elizabeth, whom he recognized as the best monarch in English history[25] – Richelieu's negative views of women were clearly affected by a personal matter, namely, his complicated relationship with the king's mother.[26]

Such an image of women as inclined to passion contributed to Richelieu's political analysis of favour and flattery. The prince's favour (*faveur*) was often the source of trouble in governments, even those originally constructed in accordance with reason.[27] In discussing the propriety of employing officers in government, Richelieu asserts that naming officers to government posts in consideration of 'particular interests' (*intérêts particuliers*) is harmful, and that kings are responsible for the consequences if they employ officers 'by pure favour' (*par pure faveur*) (p. 275). Richelieu's assumption that favour (*faveur*) and merit (*mérite*) are opposed, and his condemnation of favour, are reminiscent of the tension between *fortuna* and *virtù* in Pocock's *Machiavellian Moment*: 'it is a sinister augury for a prince if he whose merit is most considerable is not most considered for favour . . . In that case, neither the estimation of the sovereign, nor the love which people have for him, nor the expectation of recompense excites anyone to virtue any longer' (p. 275).[28] In Richelieu's thought, however, it is reason, rather than virtue, that is supposed to secure a country from the harm of favour 'raised by fortune' (*eslevés par la fortune*). The 'false goddess' (*fausse déesse*), or favour, placed above reason, 'innocently' comes to hold sway everywhere, in Richelieu's argument. As those who are raised by fortune make little use of reason, the prince's favourites, who are such people, are desperately dangerous.[29] Richelieu equates the danger of favour to that of women, who are under the control of passion: nothing is more ruinous for Richelieu than 'the appetite of such people [of favour] or the changeableness of woman' (p. 277).[30] On the other hand, a prince's own excessive passion – for women – may be his downfall.[31] In any case, reason does not appear for Richelieu sufficient to keep favour and passion under control: 'there is not reason enough to open the eyes of a prince who has covered them with favour and passion' (p. 277).[32] Thus, Richelieu concludes that reason alone should be the guide (*guide*) to governing.

In the ensuing chapter, Richelieu describes the harmfulness of flatterers: 'There is no plague with greater power to ruin a state than the flatterers, slanderers, and schemers who have no designs beyond forming cabals and plots at court' (p. 279).[33] Thus, those who would produce factions and confusion should be excluded from the court. Here too Richelieu mentions women as a noxious source of such trouble; more than 'the malice of flatterers', Richelieu maintains, 'the industry of women' (*l'industrie des femmes*) has more power to 'trouble and overthrow' (*troubler et renverser*) cabinets, courts and states than the other subtle, malicious intrigues (p. 283). Richelieu here names names: Catherine and Marie de Médici, whom he accuses of taking advantage of their positions to achieve the aims of their passions (*passions*) (p. 284).[34]

After considering the people around a prince, Richelieu turns to military affairs and commerce: 'It is a common but verified view that, just as states often extend themselves by war, so do they generally enrich themselves during peace through commerce' (p. 333).[35] For Richelieu, the benefits of commerce have been proven by the successful examples of Holland, England and Genoa. Given that France is rich in resources and product, Richelieu sees no other option than increasing her commerce. Richelieu adopts a typically mercantilist framework, which Hildesheimer characterizes as 'la théorie du mercantilisme'. Richelieu's argument virtually defines the notion of balance of trade: 'we will draw money from those who will want to have our merchandise, which is most necessary for them, and we will take little of their products, which are seldom useful for us' (p. 335).[36] Richelieu's views on commerce, moreover, may be understood as typically mercantilist in the sense that he sees the prosperity of commerce as dependent upon sea power (*la puissance de mer*) (p. 333).

While Richelieu's notion of balance of trade does not seem to have influenced Davenant, his ideas on other economic matters, and in particular his analysis of public finance, however simple, were essential for Davenant, providing a foundation for his political and economic thought. Richelieu's France and Davenant's England shared similar situations in regard to public finance. France was involved in a long-drawn-out struggle with Spain, as England was with France. Although the most serious finance problems for France in the sixteenth and early seventeenth centuries were corruption and excessive debt (Bonney, 1999, 152), the necessity of 'a clear limit to the fiscal burden to be borne by the taxpayer' was also acknowledged even by 'the distinguished advocate of *raison d'état* Richelieu' (Gelabert, 1995, 540–41).[37]

Richelieu's political economy was in the tradition of European realism, which has often been described by Cicero's well-known phrase: 'money is the sinew of war'. As Richelieu expressed the idea: 'finance is the nerve of the state' (1995, 343).[38] In his theory of finance, there is a proper proportion between 'what the prince extracts from his subjects' (*ce que le prince tire de ses sujets*) and 'what they can give him' (*ce qu'ils luy peuvent donner*) (p. 343). A prince should levy only what is necessary. Richelieu's realism led him to insist that balance was the essential point. Only 'true enemies of the state' (*vrays ennemis de l'Estat*) would say that a prince should not extract anything from his subjects. Yet it is 'the flatterers and the true pests of the state and of the court who breathe to the ears of the princes that they can demand what seems good to them' (p. 344).[39] To find the right balance, passion and its products, such as flatterers, must be excluded from the process of deciding what is 'reasonable' (*raisonable*) (p. 344). For Richelieu, the expenses of the state must be restricted to what is 'absolutely necessary for the subsistence of the state' (p. 344).[40]

2.4 DAVENANT'S DISCOURSES ON PUBLIC REVENUE AND RICHELIEU

Davenant argued consistently that sound management of public revenue by an able statesman was required for a nation to thrive on trade. In Davenant's political arithmetic the key to the recovery of English trade, badly damaged by William's war with France, was that of credit in trade, and this depended on the soundness of public credit. In making this argument Davenant turned again to Richelieu for his approach to balancing public revenue and expenditures as a means for establishing the conditions for England's recovery.

Davenant's essay 'Of our payments to the public, and in what manner the balance of trade may be thereby affected'[41] begins with the central premise of his financial theory: 'Whether it be under a commonwealth, an absolute monarchy, or in a mixed government, the affairs of a country can never go on prosperously, unless the Public Revenues are well and wisely ordered.' Davenant presents this idea as an application of the famous maxim of Archimedes, as paraphrased by Richelieu: 'Cest le point d'Archimede qui estant fermement establi, donne moyen de mouvoir tout le monde' (Davenant, 1771, vol. ii, 260). In Richelieu, this is the opening sentence of a section of *Testament Politique* on the management of state finances. In this sentence, Richelieu conveys his central idea, discussed above, that 'finance is the nerve of the state'.

As a country pamphleteer, however, Davenant needs to introduce into this financial argument a constitutional framework that Richelieu does not employ in *Testament*. According to Davenant, a commonwealth is 'seldom to blame in this part of polity [finance]', but in an absolute monarchy, a prince is 'compelled by his want to flea [*sic*] and rack his subjects' (vol. ii, 260). Davenant argues that, 'where the regal authority is limited by laws', that is, under a mixed constitution, '[p]rofusion has the same ill effects' as in an absolute monarchy. In support of this argument, he quotes Richelieu: 'A necessitous Prince can never undertake a glorious action; and necessity ingendering [*sic*] contempt, he can never be reduced to that condition without being exposed to the attempts of his enemies' (vol. ii, 260; Davenant's translation).

Although in his analysis of public finance Davenant, like Richelieu, was most concerned with the 'ill effect' of 'profusion', he adheres in his discussion of the subject to its constitutional aspects. Financial balance in a mixed government, he argues, is brought about by striking a 'balance of power' between 'the people' and the prince, that is, between the legislative and executive powers authorized by the constitution (vol. ii, 260–61). In Davenant's view, the people are inclined to 'hold the purse to entrench upon such prerogatives as are necessary for the Prince's safety, and to keep the kingdom's peace', but the prince tends to take 'the wicked counsel . . . of making himself easy, by subverting his people's rights' (vol. ii, 261). In explaining how a balance is to be maintained, Davenant again turns to Richelieu, with whom he is in perfect accord in the view that the critical factor is the statesman's ability. Davenant quotes from *Testament Politique*: a 'good order in the revenue depends more on those who have the administration than on laws and regulations' (vol. ii, 261; Davenant's translation). Davenant then applies his constitutional vocabulary to this view: 'The legislative part of the constitution gives the money, but it principally belongs to the ministerial part to take care that what is granted be not wasted, diverted, or misapplied'. Thus, Davenant frames his discussion of finance by locating that of Richelieu in a constitutional framework. Although Davenant acknowledges that the public finances belong to the 'ministerial part', he nevertheless notes, as a country Tory, that when the ministerial authorities do not manage the public finances well, it is 'incumbent on the Legislature to interpose, and call them to a strict account' (vol. ii, 261).

Within Davenant's properly English constitutional framework of discussion, however, he enriches his analysis of finance with examples from Richelieu's France. For instance, Davenant observes that after Henri III in a short time 'consumed an immense sum', his debts were settled not by his successor, Henri IV, but through 'the infinite application, prudence, and honesty of the Duke of Sully, his treasurer' (vol. ii, 261). These essential qualities of the able statesman – that is, 'application, prudence, and honesty' – undoubtedly derive in Davenant from Richelieu's *Testament*, which, as discussed above, identifies ability (*capacité*), fidelity (*fidélité*), courage (*courage*), and application (*application*) as the qualities of the perfect counsellor (Richelieu, 1995, 212). Arguing that the Spanish did not become rich solely because of 'the silver mines of Potosi', Davenant concludes: 'the wealth or poverty of the Public does, in a manner, wholly depend upon the good or bad administration of its affairs' (Davenant, 1771, vol. ii, 262). The source of this idea is also to be found in Richelieu, indeed, in a similar conclusion drawn from a Spanish example; specifically, Richelieu argues that public interest should be 'the unique aim' (*l'unique fin*) of the government, on the basis of the experience of Spain:

> I cannot but remark appropriately that the prosperity which Spain has enjoyed for several centuries has no other cause than the care that its council has taken to prefer the interests of the state over all others, and that most of the misfortunes that have befallen France were caused by too great an attachment on the part of many employed in the administration to their own interests at the expense of the public. (Richelieu, 1995, 249)[42]

Recalling that Davenant was primarily a Machiavellian, it is interesting that he coupled Richelieu with Machiavelli repeatedly when he referred to Richelieu in connection with fiscal policy. After referring to Richelieu's politics in insisting on the importance of good governance, Davenant quotes several sentences from chapter 16 of Machiavelli's *The Prince*, which is entitled 'Generosity and meanness': 'a frugal Prince shall be accounted noble to all from whom he takes nothing away, which are an infinite number'; and, 'he shall be esteemed near and parsimonious only by those few to whom he gives but little' (Davenant, 1771, vol. ii, 262).[43] According to Davenant, Machiavelli did not consider 'liberality' to be 'a necessary virtue' in a prince.

In considering what Davenant learned from Richelieu, and what he took from Machiavelli, it is suggestive that Davenant's reference to Machiavelli is here limited to matters relating to the *liberalità*[44] of a prince, a virtue harmful to state finances in Machiavelli's view. Machiavelli himself, in chapter 22 of *The Prince*, 'The secretaries of rulers', and in the subsequent chapter, 'How flatterers should be shunned',[45] also deals with the ministers and flatterers surrounding a prince, but neither chapter touches on financial topics; for Richelieu (and Davenant), counsellors and flatterers are primary concerns in the consideration of state finances.

Thus Davenant may be understood to have extended his own theory of finance on the basis of Machiavelli's understanding of frugality, in view of Richelieu's political theory of counsellors and favourites. Machiavelli maintains that the finances of kingdoms are 'ill managed' due to the prince's liberality or lack of frugality, but Davenant argues further that people fall into two groups in responding to this ill management. One group, comprising those 'who heretofore have had the Prince's ear and favour . . . were swayed by another sort of interest; they like profusion'. Such people are 'more than balanced by a great place, or a large pension' (vol. ii, 262). In contrast, members of the second group, 'the people who are to pay all . . . are glad to see a frugal court . . . which never fails to enrich a nation', though it is 'not so good for its followers' (vol. ii, 262–3). In brief, there are two types of people for Davenant: those who have 'the Prince's ear and favour' and those who demand a frugal court. This is precisely the political framework that Richelieu exploits.

As a country pamphleteer, however, Davenant also discusses 'frugality' in relation to the constitutional differences between absolute monarchies and trading nations 'ruled by laws'. In an absolute monarchy, the ruler 'rather lean[s] to munificence than thrift'; in nations ruled by law, frugality teaches people 'good husbandry in their domestic affairs, which never fails to enrich the whole body politic' (vol. ii, 263). Although Davenant thus ventures towards economic discussion of the private sector, he nevertheless relates his point to the framework of Richelieu's thoughts on politics and flatterers. The evil caused by flatterers thriving on the prince's favour is exactly that against which Richelieu warns, but in discussing it, Davenant speaks directly from his own soul:

> Much nobler it is to enjoy the praises of an universal people, living in plenty and at their ease, not burthened [*sic*] by taxes and duties, than to have the good words of a few flatterers, or those harpies which commonly haunt a court to gripe all they can; who, when they are gorged themselves, pollute all the remainder with their foul and obscene claws, so that no body else desires to touch it. Besides, we have hardly an instance of any Prince, that in time of need, was truly assisted and defended by his minions, and the creatures of his bounty and favour; but a King beloved for wise, just, and careful government, has been very seldom deserted by his people. (vol. ii, 263)

In Davenant's subsequent announcement that his aim in this section is to show 'how much the Balance of Trade may be affected by our Payments to the Public' (vol. ii, 265), the field seems unmistakeably to have shifted from Richelieu's politics to Davenant's mercantilist political economy. However, it has not. At least in regard to state finance, Richelieu remains the main source of Davenant's discourse. Delving in great detail into records on public revenues as presented by Gregory King, Davenant attempts to prove that frugality and thrift were the only principles of 'good management' available to lighten the burden of heavy taxes, which in their absence would end up causing the decline of trade. Davenant offers the familiar comparison of home economy and government to illustrate this idea:

> as in private instances, he who lives with economy, shall be richer, though his gains are but small, than a prodigal, let his gettings be never so large; so governments which manage their affairs thriftily, shall have more wealth than states which have the way to obtain never so large contributions from their people. (vol. ii, 290)

Davenant here turns once again to Richelieu for support: '[a] Venetian Ambassador once told Cardinal Richelieu, That there needed no more to make France happy, than wisely to lay out what was vainly dissipated' (vol. ii, 291).[46]

2.5 DAVENANT'S POLITICS AND RICHELIEU

Davenant further employs 'the authorities of two very able men' (1771, vol. ii, 356), Machiavelli and Richelieu, in his argument that a minister without foresight 'cannot consult safely for his Prince' and 'shall never give any sound advice'. Such safe consultation and sound advice derive rather from the virtues of wisdom and courage, in Davenant's view. Ministers lacking 'true wisdom' might too lightly involve their countries in war (vol. ii, 354). Davenant argues that such ministers, if appealing to people subsisting 'from hand to mouth', incline to advocate policy 'sufficient to live to-day, and to make provision for the present moment'. In private cases, this might reflect a 'good philosophy', Davenant allows, but applied to matters of state, such a philosophy is dangerous. To support his argument, Davenant quotes the words of Machiavelli: 'The Romans could never relish the saying that is so frequent in the mouths of our politicians; to enjoy the present benefits of time' (vol. ii, 355; Davenant's translation).[47] Although Davenant here argues that ministers must have the wisdom and foresight to avoid war, and Machiavelli that the Romans never postponed war because of 'the present benefits of time', Davenant refers to Machiavelli because of their shared conviction that able statesmen rely on virtue and prudence rather than on the short-term prospect of benefit.[48]

Machiavelli's warning against short-sightedness is fundamentally equivalent to Richelieu's emphasis on the necessity of *la prevoyance* (foresight) in ministers. To support his argument further, Davenant therefore turns to Richelieu following his discussion of Machiavelli, quoting Richelieu's arguments that: '[i]t is the duty of ministers of state to represent to their masters, that it is more necessary to consider the future, than the present' (vol. ii, 355; Davenant's translation);[49] and that 'ministers, who never consider tomorrow, live happily for themselves; but others live unhappily under them' (vol. ii, 356; Davenant's translation).[50]

Davenant here again applies the wisdom of these two 'very able men' to the question of how to manage public debt. If a country falls into the hands of ministers lacking foresight, who do 'not care with what debts and payments they load future times', it will suffer from high interest rates and duties, and subsequent damage to manufacturing and trade. Such ministers do 'not mind how profusely they waste the nation's treasure; negligence and prodigality being pleasant and easy for the present time' (vol. ii, 356).

In his argument that ministers should pursue public rather than private interests, Davenant again follows the lead of Machiavelli, quoting chapter 22 of *The Prince*, 'The secretaries of the rulers', discussed above along with chapter 23, 'How flatterers should be shunned': 'When you observe your officer more careful of himself than of you, and all his actions and designs pointing at his own interest and advantage, that man will never be a good minister' (vol. ii, 370; Davenant's translation).[51]

However, once again employing Richelieu to extend ideas originating in Machiavelli, Davenant makes use of the example of Spain that Richelieu cites in arguing for the primacy of public over private interests. Davenant observes that 'The Spaniards were in a flourishing condition in Richelieu's time' (vol. ii, 371), and footnotes the words 'Richelieu's time' with a reference to Part two, Chapter 3 of *Testament Politique*, the full title of which is: 'Chapter three which shows that the public interests must be the only aim of those who govern their countries, or at least that the public interests must be preferred to the particular interests' (Richelieu, 1995, 249).[52] In this chapter, Richelieu does indeed present Spain as a good example for France to follow, ascribing Spain's prosperity to its placement of the interests of the state before other interests, and France's misfortune to a government grounded in private interests.[53] The firmness of the Spanish council, in Richelieu's view, stands in stark contrast to the 'lightness' (*légèreté*) and 'fickleness' (*inconstance*) of that of the French.[54] To prevent such misfortune as befell France, Richelieu prescribes the simple measures of following 'prudence and reason' (p. 250) and 'reason and justice' (p. 251). As we have seen, reason is one of the fundamental principles of Richelieu's politics, playing the role that wisdom and virtue play for Davenant.

Davenant paraphrases Richelieu's views on Spain's admirable governance and France's 'great disorder' as follows: '[Richelieu] wholly attributes the prosperity of Spain to this principle . . . of preferring the public good to private interest; and the contrary obtaining in France . . . was the cause of all their disorders'. By Davenant's time, however, France was no longer in disorder, and Davenant therefore infers that 'the present greatness of the French has taken its rise from this noble principle' of preference for the public interest to the private. However, it should be noted that whereas Richelieu finally resorts to 'reason', Davenant does not. Rather he focuses on the character and performance of ministers. Ministers whose chief aim is 'their own greatness', Davenant maintains, 'can neither be good for prince nor people'. He elucidates as follows the disastrous outcomes that result from ministers who consult 'their private interest more than the public good': when ministers do not properly administer 'their Master's revenue', princes are plunged into 'debts and difficulties'; and when ministers take 'new and desperate counsels', they are 'ready to sacrifice his [the Prince's] safety to their own vanity or ambition' (vol. ii, 371). Davenant then presents once again the foundational idea of his political arithmetic,[55] which he earlier set forth in his *Discourses on the Public Revenues* (1698):

> When they [ministers] conceal from him [the prince] truths which he ought to know; when they do not acquaint him with the state of his affairs, nor with

> the true condition of the nation; when they do not endeavour to moderate his expences [sic]; and when they do not quit, when sound counsels cannot prevail, it is an evident proof that they prefer keeping their interest, as they call it, and holding their post and employments, to all other considerations whatsoever. (vol. ii, 372)

At the heart of Davenant's political arithmetic is a principle of governance: that ministers should give honest and sound advice to the prince and provide him with accurate information, and that doing so enables effective management of finance and trade. This passage shows that Davenant's political arithmetic constitutes a part of his politics, a politics that, without relying on reason, nonetheless largely reflects Richelieu's politics. Davenant's suggestion that bad ministers tend to 'consult more their own ease than the public good' was 'of Richelieu's mind' (vol. ii, 372–3).[56]

In a polemical pamphlet published in 1704, *Peace at Home, and War Abroad*, Davenant employs Richelieu's language to enrich the country-Tory character of his politics. In a section entitled 'Of the executive power', Davenant argues that 'our constitution lodges the executive power originally in princes', but he adds that its functions ultimately depend on 'ministers of state' (Davenant, 1771, vol. v, 1). While Davenant maintains his view that without virtue and wisdom, no country's prince can prosper, he also argues that 'right administration' is impossible unless a prince is 'served by honest and skilful ministers' (vol. v, 11). Davenant again considers the case of France, where ministers must play 'a very difficult game' when a prince is not sufficiently capable of ruling well. Such circumstances 'made Richlieu [*sic*] . . . say, that he found it harder to manage himself in the Ruelle, than to govern all the rest of France' (vol. v, 12). However, Davenant observed that the able statesman, Richelieu, handled the situation appropriately: 'it appears from this instance, that an able statesman could so work, as, under an obstinate and half-witted master, to compass a wise administration' (Davenant, 1771, vol. v, 12). Davenant here clearly invokes Richelieu's politics, in which ministers play an essential role in governance, to validate his own.

In the next section, however, Davenant admits that the case of France is unique, and argues for the fundamental necessity not only of wise ministers but also of wise princes: historically, Davenant argues, difficulties have been overcome 'by a wise and virtuous prince, assisted with a good and faithful council' (vol. v, 31). Borrowing an idea from his favourite chapter of Machiavelli's *The Prince*, that is, chapter 23 ('How flatterers should be shunned'), Davenant moreover asserts that ability is more important in a prince than in his council: 'it is an infallible rule, that a prince who has no wisdom of his own, can never be well advised, and that good councils proceed rather from the wisdom of the prince, than the prince's wisdom from the goodness of his councils' (vol. v, 32).[57] Significantly, Davenant does not frame this as a general 'rule'; it was 'truer in England than perhaps in other countries', for instance in France, where Davenant observes the opposite to hold. For Davenant, as discussed above, French statesmen compensated for the lack of wisdom of the prince. As Davenant argues: 'France had a steady and wise management of affairs under a weak prince, Lewis the thirteenth, who at last committed the whole administration, successively, to the cardinals Richlieu [*sic*] and Mazarine [*sic*], and these indeed ruled the kingdom' (vol. v, 32). In the following paragraph, Davenant explains why ministers in England cannot manage executive power as effectively: '[a] free country, and men jealous of their liberties, can never brook that [their] Prince should be engrossed by any one person'. Even 'the ablest man', such as Wolsey, 'sunk at last under the weight of being a single minister' (vol. v, 33). One may reasonably conjecture, moreover, that Davenant could imagine no statesman in England equal to Richelieu or Mazarin.

2.6 CONCLUSION

Careful consideration of what Davenant drew from Richelieu reveals that Davenant's focus on the abilities of statesmen and the counsellors around them did not come exclusively from his adoption of Machiavelli's politics, whether as a civic humanist or a Machiavellian, but was also a product of his keen reading of *Testament Politique*. For Davenant, the idea of a 'superhuman' legislator or statesman, the origins of whom Pocock found in Renaissance Florence, originated as well in Richelieu's France. Although Davenant doubted the validity of the French model for his own country, he was convinced that Richelieu's financial theory, inseparable from his political theory, applied to the challenge of restoring public credit and trade in England.

Waddell (1954; 1959) suggests that Davenant's objectivity and disinterestedness in making his arguments is questionable, given that he was a seeker after public office. The same may also be said of Richelieu, and indeed Richelieu's emphasis on the necessity of the able statesman is suspect in view of his comments that in choosing ministers, 'the ecclesiastical are often preferable to many others' (Richelieu, 1995, 278)[58] and that, 'because, having neither women nor children, they have much less [of private interest] than other men, they are free from the ties which attach others tightly' (p. 278).[59] That is to say, since Richelieu himself was a member of the ecclesiastical order, his argument seems self-serving.

Yet this does not mean that the arguments of Davenant and Richelieu are unreliable; on the contrary, their politics would have led them directly to claim that they would themselves make the best ministers. Both insisted that the best ministers are those who tell the truth, and in making such claims they would have been considering themselves to be telling the truth. To Davenant, Richelieu and their contemporaries, the question of what would comprise the most effective policies for recovery, and who would be the most able statesmen to implement these policies, were of the utmost importance. Rebuilding the state and restoring trade would require able statesmen with the skill to manage both the political reality and the chaotic economy of the times at once. Davenant and Richelieu each would have thought himself such a statesman.

NOTES

1. See Dickinson (1977), Feiling (1924), Kramnick (1968), and Waddell (1954, 1959). Kramnick counts Davenant among the 'Commonwealthmen' (1968, 239–41). Dickinson exploits the writings of Davenant as the evidential sources of the 'country ideology' (1977, 102–11, 330–31). Dickinson explains 'country ideology' as follows: 'The notion that civic virtue depended upon the possession of land and that political power was rooted in property was accepted by all the elements of the Country interest' (p. 103).
2. Concerning Davenant (1696), see Ito (2005).
3. Concerning the politico-economic thought of Davenant, see Hont (2005, 233–9), Ito (2005), Multamaki (1999) and Pocock (1975).
4. Pincus (1996) follows the course of the first and second Anglo-Dutch wars, revealing the role of the fear of universal monarchy as an essential factor in settling the second war. On Anglo-Dutch rivalry, also see Ormrod (2003).
5. Davenant explains the origins of political arithmetic as follows: 'The art itself is undoubtedly very ancient; but the application of it to the particular objects of revenue and trade, is what Sir William Petty first began' (Davenant, 1771, vol. 1, 128).
6. Buck (1977) and Deane (1987, 1989) trace the treatment of political arithmetic by Petty and Davenant.
7. These revisionist research programmes began with Pocock (1975), Hont and Ignatieff (1983) and Haakonsen (1981).
8. For example, Brenner (1993), Pincus (1996) and Ormrod (2003) show the impossibility of picturing the reality of early modern England without considering the international situation of the country, including the balance of power inside and outside Europe.
9. See Meinecke (1998 [1957]), Church (1972), Tuck (1993, 1999) and Hont (2005). Hont (2005) considers Davenant's political economy to be a typical product of the application of the principle of *raison d'état* to economic thinking, but he fails to see the importance of Richelieu for Davenant.
10. On the origins of and controversy surrounding the idea of universal monarchy, see Pincus (1996).
11. Both were published, together with one more essay, *An Essay on War, Peace, and Alliances,* as a set of collected essays by Davenant in 1701.
12. Even when Richelieu's political theory is not the direct subject, his age is discussed as 'the time of Richelieu' (Meinecke, 1998 [1957], chapter 6). Nevertheless, it should be noted that Richelieu has often been described as an active politician of reason of state

who allowed supportive pamphleteers such as Duke Henri de Rohan (Meinecke, 1998 [1957], chapter 6 [2]), François Langlois de Fancan, Jean Sirmond, Jérémie Ferrier, Mathieu de Morgues (Church, 1972, part II, part III), to write on his behalf. Richelieu's own arguments have themselves sometimes been omitted from the history of the concept of reason of state. For example, recent studies such as Tuck (1999) and Hont (2005) do not discuss the political thought of Richelieu or other early modern French thinkers. Tuck (1999) traces the idea of reason of state back through the humanist tradition beginning with Alberico Gentili, to roots found in ancient Rome. The only French writer whom Tuck considers is Rousseau. Though Tuck (1993) devotes 12 pages to 'the spread of the new humanism' in France, and Richelieu and his pamphleteers in particular, he relies here heavily on Church (1972).

13. 'Cette pièce verra le jour sous le titre de mon testament politique, parce qu'elle est faite pour servir, après ma mort, à la police e à la conduite de votre royaume' (Richelieu, 1995, 32).
14. On the authorship of *Testament politique*, see Hildesheimer (1995). Hildesheimer himself concludes that: 'On admet donc que la pensée est bien de Richelieu' (p. 16).
15. In his *Liberty before Liberalism*, Quentin Skinner shows that Algernon Sidney, a typical 'neo-Roman' thinker of the generation preceding Davenant, warned that flatterers were the people most dangerous to liberty. See Skinner (1998, 86–95). Davenant might also be considered a 'neo-Roman' theorist in the sense that he abhorred flatterers as dangerous to liberty. However, 'neo-Roman theory' does not sufficiently frame Davenant's description of the statesman. Guy (1995) argues that the political rhetoric of counsellors versus flatterers was 'feudal-baronial language, the origins of which lay in the attempts of the baronage in the reigns of Henry III and Edward II to render royal government accountable' (p. 297). Ito (2005) locates the origins of this language in the combined logic of the Ciceronian rhetorical tradition, which was explored by Skinner (1996), and by Pocock's civic humanism.
16. 'les meilleurs princes ont besoin d'un bon conseil', Richelieu (1995, 211), my translation. Unless noted, all quotations from Richelieu in English are in my translation.
17. As far as I have been able to determine, Richelieu does not name Machiavelli explicitly. During Richelieu's time Machiavelli's books were banned, and Machiavelli himself was often referred to as a symbol of evil (Meinecke, 1998 [1957], book one; Church, 1972, part I). On the other hand, writers advocated Machiavelli's notion of *r*ealpolitik in this period; they did so, however, in the names of Tacitus and Lipsius (Church, 1972, 58–62; Elliott, 1984, 26–7), neither of whom are mentioned in *Testament Politique*.
18. Richelieu (1995, 212).
19. Richelieu (1995, 212).
20. 'parfait accord entre l'entendement et la volontè' (p. 226).
21. 'De la probité et du courage naist une honneste hardiesse de dire aux roys ce qui leur est utile, bien qu'il ne leur soit pas toujours agréable' (p. 226).
22. Hildesheimer (2000, chapter 3) remarks that *raison* in Richelieu's *Testament politique* has multiple meanings, and is identical neither with the Cartesian *raison* nor with the *raison* of *raison d'état*' in the Machiavellian sense.
23. 'La lumière naturelle fait connoistre à un chacun que, l'homme ayant esté fait raisonnable, il ne doit rien faire que par raison, puisqu'autrement il feroit contre sa nature, et, par conséquent, contre celuy mesme qui en est l'autheur' (p. 245).
24. 'il est vray qu'ordinairement leur molesse les rend incapables d'une vertu masle, nécessaire à l'administration et qu'il est presque impossible que leur gouvernement soit exempt ou de la bassese ou de diminution, dont la foiblesse de leur sexe est la cause, ou d'injustice ou de cruauté, dont le dérèglement de leurs passions qui leur tient lieu de raison est la vraye source' (p. 248). Richelieu argues elsewhere: 'rien n'est plus capable de nuire aux Estats que ce sexe lorsque . . . il les fait souvent mouvoir comme bon luy semble, et mal par consequent, les pensées des femmes estant presque toujours mauvaises en celles qui se conduisent par leurs passions qui tiennent d'ordinaire lieu de raison dans leur esprit, au lieu que la raison est le seul et vray motif qui animer et

faire agir ceux qui son dans l'employ des affaires publiques' (pp. 224–5). Richelieu's condemnation of women for their purported lack of reason and inclination to passion is sustained throughout *Testament*.

25. See Multamäki (1999), section 2.4, 'Corruption: courts and hereditary monarchies as sources of evidence'.
26. See Hildesheimer (2004), and Church (1972, part III). Hildesheimer argues that the character of Richelieu was not unmarked by 'femininity' (*féminité*): 'la personnalité de Richelieu . . . juxtapose imprégnation féminine et refus de la féminité, sensibilitée, sexualité refoulée et exaltation intellectuelle de la raison' (p. 155). According to Church: 'in the factional strife that was so frequently directed against himself, Richelieu did not hesitate to accuse the followers of the Queen Mother and Gaston d'Orléans of *lése-majesté*' (Church, 1972, p. 179).
27. Moote (1992) characterizes the political scene in Europe in this period as the age of 'the minister-favourite'. Richelieu was a typical example.
28. 'c'est un sinistre augure pour un prince, lorsque celuy qui est le plus considérable pour son mérite n'est pas le plus considéré par la faveur . . . En tel cas, ny l'estime du souverain, ny l'amour qu'on luy porte, ny l'espérance de la récompense n'excitent plus à la vertu' (p. 275). Compare: 'Un prince qui veut estre aimé de ses sujets doit remplir les principales charges et les premières dignitez de son Estat de personnes si estimées de tout le monde qu'on puisse trouver la cause de son choix dans le mérite' (Richelieu, 1995, 275–6). Meinecke identifies the essence of Machiavelli's politics in three words, 'which keep on sounding again and again throughout his writings with a kind of brazen ring': *virtù, fortuna* and *necessità*. When *fortuna* is malicious in Machiavelli, Meinecke maintains, *virtù* must also be malicious; it is *necessità* which makes it possible to overcome such a 'struggle between *virtù* and *fortuna*' (Meinecke, *Machiavellism*, 1998 [1957], 37). Pocock adopts as the leitmotif of the 'Machiavellian Moment' this 'struggle between *virtù* and *fortuna*'. In contrast with Meinecke, however, Pocock describes this 'struggle' straightforwardly as a 'struggle' or simply as ambivalence, which is not susceptible to easy resolution, even if Machiavelli offers some slight hope, as Pocock maintains, in his idea of 'superhuman' virtue.
29. See Richelieu (1995, 276).
30. 'l'apétit de tells gens ou le dérèglement d'une femme' (p. 277).
31. See Richelieu (1995, 277): 'Plusieurs princes se sont perdus pour avoir préféré leur affection particulière aux intérêts publics. Tels malheurs sont arrivez à quelqu'uns par l'eccez des passions déréglées qu'ils ont eues pour les femmes.'
32. 'n'y a-t-il aucune raison qui puisse dessiller les yeux d'un prince qui les a couverts de faveur et de passion' (p. 277).
33. 'Il n'y a point de peste si capable de ruiner un Estat que les flateurs, mesdisans et certains esprits qui n'ont autre dessein que de former des cabales et des intrigues dans les cours' (p. 279).
34. According to Meinecke, Innocent Gentillet, in his *Discours sur les moyens de bien gouverner et maintenir en bonne paix un Royaume ou autre Principauté, divisez en trois parties: a savoir, du Conseil, de la Regiona et Police que doit tenir un Prince. Contre Nicolas Machiavel Florentin* (1576), hoped that François d'Alençon 'would put an end to the recent foreign tyranny'. By the 'foreign tyranny' Gentillet meant 'the rule in France of Italians and italianized Frenchmen, hence Catherine de Medici and her court and the new vicious doctrines of Machiavelli' (Meinecke, *Machiavellism*, 1998 [1957], 51). However, Meinecke was suspicious of Gentillet's assessment of 'the Massacre of St. Bartholemew in 1572' as an exercise of Machiavellian politics by Catherine de Medici. Meinecke himself suggested that it might have been caused by the 'passion and weakness' of women: 'her political views, which were so strongly tinged with petty feminine passion and weakness, in no way corresponded to the ideal of austere and consistent rationality, which Machiavelli had set up for princes'. On the other hand, Meinecke discerned a trace of Machiavellian policy in her Italian origins: 'in the native land where she had been born and brought up, she had caught the same disease which infected Machiavelli, and she had

no scruples about believing that a prince possessed the authority to kill'. And, finally, Meinecke disclaimed his own suggestion of feminine weakness on the part of Catherine de Medici, though with some qualification: 'it was not solely a feminine urge for rule and revenge that drove her on . . . The mean personal motive may perhaps have predominated in her; but it was inseparably mingled with the obscurely compelling motives of *raison d'ètat*. It was one of the most terrible examples of the unhappy combination that could exist between the principle of the pure assertion of national power and all the lower elemental forces' (Meinecke, *Machiavellism*, 1998 [1957], 52).

35. 'C'est un dire commun mais véritable qu'ainsy que les Estats augmentent souvent leur estendue par la guerre, ils s'enrichissent ordinairement dans la paix par le commerce' (p. 333).
36. 'nous tirerons l'argent de ceux qui voudront avoir nos marchandises qui leur sont si nécessaires et nous ne nous chargerons point beaucoup de leurs denrées qui nous son si peu utiles' (p. 335).
37. Church (1972, part III) shows that the scale of public expenses and the burden of taxation under Richelieu's government were issues among pamphleteers of the 1630s.
38. 'les finances sont les nerfs de l'Estat' (p. 343). Dickson (1967) and Brewer (1990) investigate the historical facts of seventeenth and eighteenth century England, with Dickson focusing on the development of the stock-market for long-term public debt, and Brewer on mechanisms of taxation. Brewer claims that, contrary to the general image of France's bureaucratic absolutism, the English system of taxation was much more comprehensive and efficient than that the French.
39. 'des flateurs et des vrayes pestes de l'Estat et de la cour de souffler aux oreilles des princes qu'ils peuvent exiger ce que bon leur semble' (p. 344).
40. 'absolument nécessaires pour la subsistance de l'Estat' (p. 344). Richelieu also said: 'je dis qu'il doit y avoir une proportion géométrique entre les subsides et les nécessitez de l'Estat, c'est-à-dire qu'on ne doit imposer que ce qui est du tout nécessaire pour la subsistance du royaume en sa grandeur et en sa gloire' (p. 349).
41. This essay comprised a section of *An essay upon the probable methods of making a people gainers in the balance of trade*, published in 1699 to disseminate the ideas in his magnum opus, *Discourses on the publick revenues, and on the trade of England.*
42. 'Je ne puis que je ne remarque à propos que la prospérité qui a toujours accompagné l'Espagne depuis quelque siècles n'a point d'autre cause que le soin que son conseil a eu de préférer les intérêts de l'Estat à tous autres, et que la plupart des malheurs qui sont arrivés à la France ont esté causez par le trop grand attachement que beaucoup de ceux qui ont esté employez à l'administration ont eu à leurs propres intérêts au préjudice du public' (p. 249).
43. Compare Price's translation, Machiavelli (1988, 56); and Machiavelli (1960, 67).
44. Price translated this word as both 'generosity' and 'open-handedness'. As in the preceding quotation, Davenant translated it as 'liberality'. See Machiavelli (1988, 55–8; 1960, 89–93).
45. Both are Price's translation. The original titles of the 1960 edition, on which Price's translation is based, are in Latin: 'De his quos a secretis principes habent' and 'Quomodo adulators sint fugiendi', respectively. See Machiavelli (1988, 80, 81; 1960, 93, 95).
46. Following this, Davenant quotes from Richelieu: 'Qu'elle scut aussi bien despenser ce qu'elle dissipoit sans raison que la republique scavoit bien n'employer pas un seul quadrain sans besoin, et sans beaucoup de menage' (vol. ii, 291). See Richelieu (1995, 345).
47. 'Nè piacque mai loro quello che tutto di è in bocca de' savi de' nostri tempi. *godere li beneficj del tempo*' (Machiavelli, *Il Principe*, 1960, 22).
48. Following the sentence in Davenant's quote above, Machiavelli continues, 'ma sibbene quello della virtù e prudenza loro' (Machiavelli, *Il Principe*, 1960, 22).
49. 'les ministres d'Estat doivent-ils souvent se remettre devant les yeux et représenter à leurs maistres qu'il est plus important de considerer l'avenir que le présent' (Richelieu, 1995, 253).

50. 'Ceux qui vivent au heureusement pour eux, mais on vit malheureusement sous leur conduite' (Richelieu, 1995, 253).
51. 'Quando tu vedi il ministro pensare piú a sé che a te, e che in tutte le azioni vi ricerca dentro l' utile suo, questo tale cosí fatto mai fia buono ministro' (Machiavelli, *Il Principe*, 1960, 94).
52. 'Chapitre 3e qui monstre que les intérêts publics doivent estre l'unique fin de ceux qui gouvernent les Estats, ou du moins qu'ils doivent estre préférés aux particuliers' (Richelieu, 1995, 249).
53. Richelieu (1995, 249).
54. Concerning the rivalry and contrast between Spain and France, and between the two representative statesmen of these countries, the Count-Duke of Olivares and Cardinal Richelieu, see Elliott (1984).
55. See Davenant, *Discourses on the Public Revenues, and Trade of England*, part I, Discourse 1, in Davenant (1771, vol. I). Also see Ito (2005).
56. Indeed, Davenant quotes here again from Part two, Chapter 4, of *Testament politique*. See Davenant (1771, vol. ii, 373).
57. Davenant did not employ direct quotation here. The original words of Machiavelli, in Price's translation, are as follows: 'it is an infallible rule that a prince who is not himself wise cannot be soundly advised, unless he happens to put himself in the hands of a man who is very able and controls everything . . . Therefore, it should be concluded that good advice, from whomsoever it may come, must have its source in the shrewdness of the ruler; the ruler's shrewdness cannot derive from sound advice' (1988, 82). This runs as follows in the original: 'questa è una regola generale che non falla mai: che uno principe, il quale non sia savio per sé stesso, non può essere consigliato bene, se già a sorte non si rimettessi in un solo che al tutto lo governassi, che fussi uomo prudentissimo . . . Però si conchiude che i buoni cousigli, da qualunque venghino, conviene naschino dalla prudenzia del principe, e non la prudenza del principe da' buoni consigli' (Machiavelli, *Il Principe*, 1960, 96).
58. 'les ecclésiastiques sont souvent préférables à beaucoup d'autre' (Richelieu, 1995, 278).
59. 'ils en ont beaucoup moins que les autres hommes, puisque n'ayant ny femmes ny enfans, ils sont libres des liens qui attachent davantage' (Richelieu, 1995, 278).

REFERENCES

Bonney, R. (1999), 'France, 1494–1815', in R. Bonney (ed.), *The Rise of the Fiscal State in Europe c.1200–1815*, Oxford: Oxford University Press, pp. 123–76.

Brenner, R. (1993), *Merchants and Revolution: Commercial Change, Political Conflict, and London's Overseas Traders, 1550–1653*. Princeton, NJ: Princeton University Press.

Brewer, J. (1990), *The Sinews of Power: War, Money, and the English State, 1688–1783*, New York: Knopf.

Buck, P. (1977), 'Seventeenth-century political arithmetic: civil strife and vital statistics', *Isis*, **68** (241), 67–84.

Church, W.F. (1972), *Richelieu and Reason of State*, Princeton, NJ: Princeton University Press.

Davenant, C. (1696), *Essay on Publick Virtue*, University of London Library, Manuscript No. 60.

Davenant, C. (1771), *The Political and Commercial Works of that Celebrated Writer Charles D'avenant, LL, D.; Relating to the Trade and Revenue of England, the Plantation Trade, the East-India Trade, and African Trade*, collected and revised by Sir C. Whitworth, 5 vols, London.

Deane, P. (1987), 'Political arithmetic', in J. Eatwell, M. Milgate and P. Newman (eds), *The New Palgrave: A Dictionary of Economics*, Vol. 4, London: Macmillan, pp. 900–903.
Deane, P. (1989), *State and the Economic System*, Oxford: Oxford University Press.
Dickinson, H.T. (1977), *Liberty and Property: Political Ideology in Eighteenth-century Britain*, New York: Holmes & Meier Publishers.
Dickson, P.G.M. (1967), *The Financial Revolution in England: A Study in the Development of Public Credit 1688–1756*, New York: Macmillan.
Elliott, J.K. (1984), *Richelieu and Olivares*, Cambridge: Cambridge University Press.
Feiling, K. (1924), *A History of the Tory Party*, Oxford: Clarendon Press.
Gelabert, J. (1995), 'The fiscal burden', in R. Bonney (ed.), *Economic Systems and State Finance*, Oxford: Clarendon Press, pp. 539–76.
Guy, J. (1995), 'The rhetoric of counsel in early modern England', in D. Hoak (ed.), *Tudor Political Culture*, Cambridge: Cambridge University Press.
Haakonsen, K. (1981), *The Science of a Legislator, the Natural Jurisprudence of David Hume & Adam Smith*, Cambridge: Cambridge University Press.
Hildesheimer, F. (1995), 'Introduction' in Richelieu, Armand Jean du Plessis, Due de, *Testament palitique de Richelieu*, Françoise Hildesheimer (ed.), Paris: Société de l'histoire de France, pp. 9–28.
Hildesheimer, F. (2000), *Relectures de Richelieu*, Paris: Éditions Publisud.
Hildesheimer, F. (2004), *Richelieu*, Paris: Flammarion.
Hont, I. (2005), *Jealousy of trade: International Competition and the Nation-State in Historical Perspective*, Cambridge, MA, USA and London, UK: Belknap Press of Harvard University Press.
Hont, I. and M. Ignatieff (ed.) (1983), *Wealth and Virtue: The Shaping of Political Economy in the Scottish Enlightenment*, Cambridge: Cambridge University Press.
Ito, S. (2005), 'Charles Davenant's politics and political arithmetic', *History of Economic Ideas*, **13** (1), 9–36.
Kramnick, I.F. (1968), 'The ambivalence of the Augustan Commonwealthman', *Bolingbroke and his Circle: The Politics of Nostalgia in the Age of Walpole*, Cambridge, MA: Harvard University Press, pp. 236–60.
Machiavelli, N. (1960) *Il principe e discorsi sopra la prima deca di Tito Livio*, Milan: Feltrinelli Editore.
Machiavelli, N. (1988), *The Prince*, Q. Skinner (ed.), R. Price (trans.), Cambridge: Cambridge University Press.
Meinecke, F. (1998 [1957]), *Machiavellism: The Doctrine of Raison d'etat and its Place in Modern History*, transl. D. Scott, New Brunswick, NJ: Transaction Publishers.
Moote, A.L. (1992), 'Richelieu as chief minister: a comparative study of the favourite in early seventeenth-century politics', in J. Bergin and L. Brockliss (eds), *Richelieu and his Age*, Oxford: Clarendon Press, pp. 13–43.
Multamaki, K. (1999), *Towards Great Britain, Commerce and Conquest in the Thought of Algernon Sidney and Charles Davenant*, Helsinki: Academia Scientiarum Fennica.
Ormrod, D. (2003), *The Rise of Commercial Empires: England and the Netherlands in the Age of Mercantilism, 1650–1770*, Cambridge: Cambridge University Press.
Pincus, S.C.A. (1996), *Protestantism and Patriotism: Ideologies and the Making of English Foreign Policy, 1650–1668*, Cambridge: Cambridge University Press.

Pocock, J.G.A. (1975), *The Machiavellian moment: Florentine Political Thought and the Atlantic Republican Tradition*, Princeton, NJ, USA and London, UK: Princeton University Press.
Richelieu, Armand Jean du Plessis, Duc de, (1995 [1688]), *Testament Politique de Richelieu*, Françoise Hildesheimer (ed.), Paris: Société de l'histoire de France.
Skinner Q. (1996), *Reason and Rhetoric in the Philosophy of Hobbes*, Cambridge: Cambridge University Press.
Skinner, Q. (1998), *Liberty before Liberalism*, Cambridge: Cambridge University Press.
Tuck, R. (1993), *Philosophy and Government, 1572–1651*, Cambridge: Cambridge University Press.
Tuck, R. (1999), *The Rights of War and Peace: Political Thought and the International Order from Grotius to Kand*, Oxford: Oxford University Press.
Waddell, D.A.G. (1954), 'The career and writings of Charles Davenant', unpublished DPhil thesis, Bodleian Library, Oxford.
Waddell, D.A.G. (1959), 'Charles Davenant: a biographical sketch', *Economic History Review*, 2nd ser. **11** (2), 279–88.

3. *Polizei* and the system of public finance: tracing the impact of Cameralism in eighteenth-century Portugal

Alexandre Mendes Cunha[1]

3.1 INTRODUCTION

It is necessary to say right at the very beginning that the role of the influence of Cameralism in Portuguese economic thought is not easy to define. For example, there is no trail of translations into Portuguese of the Cameralist literature which could be followed as evidence of the transfer of these ideas to the Portuguese world. However, in the economic policies of the Portuguese state during this period, and essentially in the process of centralization of the finances of the kingdom, there is a set of particularities that can be related to Cameralism, and more specifically to the 'science of police'.

The increasing attention given by the Crown to police matters during the second half of the eighteenth century offers an interesting instance where we might be able to trace the role of Cameralist doctrines in the formation of the Portuguese economic and political thought. It is possible, for example, to pursue the meaning of the term 'police' throughout the eighteenth century, showing how it gradually acquires a wider relevance and significance. This process reproduces the encompassing nature of the term 'police' (*Polizei*) in the Cameralist doctrinal tradition. Before 1750, there is clear evidence of a strict association of the term with the traditional idea of 'good order'. Nevertheless, from the second half of the century, the term has progressively assumed a new connotation associated with all sorts of themes regarding internal matters of the state related to the achievement of the 'common good'. Such themes included not only public security problems, but also much broader issues concerning economic and social life, population and natural resources, as well as the very organization of the state itself, thus enlarging what ought to be considered as police affairs.

The question of police enables us to reflect upon the transmission of Cameralist thought in continental Europe. If it is true that there is an evident centralization in the finances of the Portuguese state during the second half of the eighteenth century, and because of it a possible influence of the Cameralist conceptions in Portugal, it is also true that this influence is more in the field of practice than in theory. There is an absolute primacy of practice in this context. Nevertheless, it is in the specific field of 'police' that there is a degree of conceptual penetration and some level of theoretical elaboration. Thus it is also necessary to consider the term carefully in both Germanic and French traditions to establish its interaction with the theme of Cameralism itself.

The present chapter is divided as follows. Section 3.2 presents a conceptual discussion of 'police' and 'Cameralism'. Section 3.3 outlines the diffusion of economic ideas in the Iberian world. Section 3.4 articulates Cameralism and police with the centralization of the public finance system, paying special attention to the significance of the 1755 Lisbon Earthquake in this process.

3.2 *POLIZEI* AND CAMERALISM

Cameralism was a widespread phenomenon, not a specific and autonomous stage of economic thought. It principally involves an administrative concept of the state, systematically combining politics, economics and law, together with other specific knowledges. While this chapter is concerned with the history of economic thought, it avoids the presentation of Cameralism exclusively in terms of analytical economics, as for example Recktenwald does in his definition of the term for *The New Palgrave Dictionary of Economics* (Recktenwald, 2008). Fundamental to it is the lack of autonomy ascribed to the economic field. In this sense, Germanic and Austrian Cameralism does not represent an autonomous knowledge, but rather involves the systematization of the art of governing in new terms. This systematization combines politics, economics, administration and law, and thereby secures the affirmation of centralized power in the achievement of the prosperity of the state. Pierangelo Schiera suggests that the typical characteristics of Cameralism can be summarized as follows: 'globalism in its approach to the different themes of political experience'. And this was the foundation for a theoretical reconstruction which was consonant with the coherence and unity of the state imposed on some German territories: the police state (Schiera, 1995a [1976], 137).

It is interesting that the context in which the original formulation of Cameralism arose, often treated by historians as a variant form German mercantilism, is precisely that which directly confronted the unification of tax regimes in German territorial states. This is clearly discussed by Eli Heckscher (1955 [1931]). But this direct identification of Cameralism with mercantilism is not entirely appropriate, as Lars Magnusson notes. Magnusson insists on the idea that by treating Cameralism as a special form of mercantilism more coherence is given to the term than it really possesses. Cameralism emerged in the sixteenth and seventeenth centuries, but it was only in the eighteenth century that it really took the form of a 'system', articulating as a science 'police, Cameralism and economics' (Magnusson, 1994, 188–9). The key author behind this systematization was Johann Heinrich Gottlob von Justi (1717–68). Justi was the author of an extensive bibliography of 67 books and seven periodicals, a good part dedicated to economic and political themes. At least eight of his books were translated into different languages, including French, Spanish, Dutch, Russian and English, which indubitably attests to the wide circulation of his ideas (Reinert and Reinert, 2009; Adam 2006). Joseph von Sonnenfels (1733–1817) was another fundamental name in this systematization of Cameralism. His main book was *Grundsätze der Polizei, Handlung und Finanzwissenschaft*, in three volumes, each one about a specific theme (police, trade, finance), with the first of them appearing in 1765 and repeatedly reprinted until the start of the nineteenth century. Besides that, his work was translated into Russian, Italian and Latin, summed up in the form of manuals by other authors and widely spread throughout Central Europe (Tribe, 1988, chapter 4; Reinert and Reinert, 2009).

There is no doubt that the ideas of Justi and Sonnenfels (both officers of the Austrian Empire at different times), played an important role in the reforms promoted by the Empress Maria Teresa (Ingrao, 2000, 178–85).[2] Nevertheless, it is also important to stress the influence of Colbert's action on French finances, which also incorporated in part ideas related to Cameralism. And that Austria, even before Justi and Sonnenfels, already provided an interesting example of the influence of French mercantilism on Cameralism. This has been summarized as follows:

> Later on it was sustained by the desire to match the economic growth of Colbertine France and, ultimately, by the need to rebuilt Hungary. For the most part the monarchy was inspired by the contemporary German school of political economy know as cameralism. The emperor shared with his German vassals a compelling need to avert bankruptcy by a combination of economic reconstruction and the more efficient management of state finances. Most of the credit for the evolution of Austrian Cameralism has, in fact, gone to three German *émigré* political economists: Wilhelm von Schröder (1640–88), whose studies of the British economic system had familiarized him with western models of mercantilism; Johann Joachim Becher (1635–82), who was the most original and influential theorist; and his brother-in-law, Philipp Wilhelm von

> Hörnigk (1640–1714), a propagandist whose famous tract *Österreich über Alles, wann es nur will* (Austria above all others if it only wishes) strove to rebuilt the monarchy in to an economically self-sufficient great power in the aftermath of the siege of Vienna. (Ingrao, 2000, 92)

It is possible that the author who contributed the most, not to the formulation but to the diffusion of Cameralism, was Jakob Friedrich von Bielfeld (1717–70). His *Institutions politiques*, originally published in French in 1760, was reprinted 12 times, in addition to being translated into German, Russian, Spanish and Italian. This book became a kind of economics bestseller in its day, containing for example an extensive typology of the origins of the decadence of states. Divided by the author between external and intrinsic causes, he presents a wide variety of examples, among which are a reference to the danger of the loss of independence of Portugal in relation to England, and to the weakening of its authority with regards to the territory of Brazil (Bielfeld, 1762; Reinert and Reinert, 2009; Reinert, 2004, 19). Cameralism itself spread throughout continental Europe during the eighteenth century, including both the Germanic-Austrian as well as other traditions with similar approaches to the field of finances and state organization. Lars Magnusson comments on the Italian case that:

> both Beccaria in Milan and Genovesi in Naples had to lecture on such subjects as commerce, agriculture, taxation and public finance – certainly most useful for economic modernization and the formation of a strong public economy. However, such a discourse also had older lineages and cannot only be seen as a mere copy of Cameralism. (Magnusson, 1994, 200)

I need here to present a brief definition of what here has been generically referred to as Cameralism. The term 'Cameralism' (*Kameralien, Kameralwissenschaften*), as explained by Keith Tribe, comes from the Latin term *camera*, which originally meant the palace or the court of the prince, and which progressively evolved towards the specific designation for the place from where his domains were managed. The term *Kammermusik* has the same root, and served to describe the music played in this area of the court, as opposed to the music played in church, which was sacred music (Tribe, 1995, 9). The doctrine which emanates from there, however, is part of another term, *Polizei*, combining to cover what can be broadly called 'government science' (*Staatswissenschaft*).

It can be suggested that Cameralism elevates the administration of finances as the key to the organization and success of the state, while *Polizei* defines the composition and maintenance of internal order. This dimension of the internal order evokes another term, 'economics' (*Oeconomie*), derived from the idea of household administration (from *Oikos*). Tribe proposes the following set of meanings:

> Cameralism is principally concerned with the administration of a state; *Oeconomie* relates this activity of administration materially to the objective of happiness; and *Polizei* concerns itself with the general condition of order prevailing in the state. (Tribe, 1995, 11)

But he then notes that this separation only really becomes effective if we assume modern conceptions of economics and politics, not those which circulated in the eighteenth century. 'Police' (*Polizei*), by contrast, involves the idea of a non-legal form of regulation. During the eighteenth century these two terms were developed into areas of study and taught throughout the German states in faculties of philosophy, not of law (Tribe, 1995, 12–3).[3] This model was not imitated in Portugal, which is important for understanding the appropriation of this knowledge in Portuguese territories. The study of law was the most systematized field of knowledge in eighteenth-century Portugal, and the main means of access to the state bureaucracy. The extent to which law is critical to the diffusion of Cameralism will be made clear below, when discussing the direct legislative action of the King in Portugal during the second half of the eighteenth century.

It was in France, in the Dukedom of Burgundy, that the concept of 'police' first acquired an operative importance as an instrument used by the prince to achieve his political objectives. In this context the term 'police' would rapidly gain a specific technical meaning. From the seventeenth century, territorial unification was a reality in France, creating an emphasis upon the maintenance rather than the conquest of sovereignty. 'Police' became linked to the specific actions related to internal matters, focused on the security and tranquillity of the subjects and the command of the prince (Schiera, 1995b [1976], 410).

The term passed from France to Germany, but the role played by *Polizei* in the German territories was radically different to the development of the French *Police*. Within the Holy Roman Empire, *Polizei* became an instrument used by the territorial prince to impose his authority upon the traditional forces of imperial society. During the transition of imperial space in the course of the sixteenth century, power came to be centred on the territorial states, and the need to create his own autonomous and sovereign space became a central problem for the prince. *Polizei* would play a fundamental part in this process of reorganization, rationalization and centralization. This developed initially in Prussia, taking the following forms: (1) the formation of a consolidated body of sovereign prerogatives;

(2) indiscriminate regulatory intervention in the lives of the subjects; and (3) new administrative and bureaucratic instruments. By the end of the seventeenth century these were police matters: an entire internal system of state rule was created and, consequently, this became the apparatus destined to guarantee power to the monarch (Schiera, 1995b [1976], 410–1).

To understand the influence of the Cameralist tradition in Portugal it is necessary to consider the mediation of ideas relative to police in both the German and the French traditions. The difference between police (*Polizei*) and politics is a useful way to introduce this question. Politics specifically concerned the relationship between states, while 'police' was more focused on the internal context. In the German administrative thinking, the concept of 'police' gave shape to a specific form of 'police science' (*Polizeiwissenschaft*). Likewise, the practice of the officials of the prince's chamber, the coordinated organization of finances based on state centralization, became a 'chamber science' (*Kameralwissenschaften*). This is one of the most exact meanings of Cameralism itself.

Cameralism is effectively a set of discourses converging upon a specific administrative practice which permitted this literature to spread throughout Europe under the name of government science, or public administration science. Comparing Cameralism and *Polizei*, Keith Tribe's synthesis is once again useful to understand that the two terms are in fact dimensions of *Staatswissenschaft* or *Politik* in the 1700s:

> Cameralism can be generally defined as a set of discourses related to the maintenance of land and people which, if it turns to questions of trade, necessarily evaluates the benefits and drawbacks of relations with other states. *Polizei* on the other hand is confined to internal order, although an element of the maintenance of this good order and happiness necessarily involves evaluation of the internal consequences of objects treated by Cameralism. Or perhaps we can say: Cameralism assembles the objects which *Polizei* then orders for the good of the state and its subjects. Both of these belong in the eighteenth century to a *Politik* (or *Staatswissenschaft*), as is clear from Johann Georg Sulzer's *Kurzer Begriff aller Wissenschaften.* (Tribe, 1995, 19–20)

The government science referred to here is the point of convergence in the second half of the eighteenth century of a variety of ideas that had been developing since the sixteenth century. In the eighteenth century these conceptions take on a more academic shape, and the pedagogical function of these questions begins to be more important, as Andre Wakefield argues:

> Academic Cameralists, the propagandists of scholarly utility, promised to change the existing structures of knowledge to suit the needs of *Kammer*. They were ambitious dreamers who sought to remake society and the sciences. They envisioned new academies dedicated completely to useful sciences.

> At the same time, these Cameralist reformers sought to change the world of the *Kammer* itself. Older methods of apprenticeship and on-the-job training would be replaced by a formal education, complete with regular examinations to determine appointments and promotions. Practical Cameralists would be replaced by educated Cameralists, who would unlock vast treasures of hidden industriousness in the population. They would discover altogether unexpected sources of wealth in the thousands of improvements, large and small, facilitated by chemical, botanical and technological knowledge. (Wakefield, 2005, 318–9)

Wakefield has also written recently (2009) on the Mining Academy (Bergakademie) of Freiberg (Saxony) and its relation to the police matters and Cameralism; for anyone concerned with the history of economic ideas in Portugal there are suggestive insights here for further work.[4] The association between the mining (as well as mineral and metallurgical) sciences and Cameralism is relevant as an important source for the appropriation of Cameralism by Portuguese economic thought. But since this is not strictly related to public finances this point will not be further developed here.

We might finally note the widespread interest in the training of *Kammer* officials, who were essentially members of a specialized bureaucracy linked to the universe of finance. Hubert C. Johnson argues that:

> In the writings of the early Austrian Cameralists we find in turn a further development of a distinct bureaucratic ethos. Becher, Schröder, and Hornigk placed much greater emphasis on the prerogatives of the purely fiscal officialdom as opposed to the judiciary than did von Osse or Seckendorff. They placed considerably less emphasis on the semi-medieval side of princely authority and proclaimed in more daring terms the absolutism only vaguely expressed by their predecessors. Writing under the shadow of Luis XIV and of Colbert, they could comprehend the concept of the Leviathan State. At the same time that they hesitatingly outlined absolutism Bacher and his contemporaries tried to promote the new bureaucratic gospel. (Johnson, 1964, 384)

3.3 THE DIFFUSION OF ECONOMIC IDEAS

Tracing the influence of Cameralism upon Portuguese economic thought prompts reflection on the variety of patterns in the international diffusion of economic ideas and theory. As Cardoso points out:

> nationality or place of residence or publication are criteria regarded as necessary but not sufficient to determine the national character of economic thought. Diffusion and reception are uneven and selective, in accordance with the specific problems are faced and solved that innovative, genuinely national forms of economic thought may emerge. However, it should be noted that they are still an outcome of international diffusion phenomena. (Cardoso, 2003, 626)

Much of this perspective is based on the work of Ernest Lluch, who stressed the importance of the specificities of the national histories of economic thought to the analyses of the international transmission of economic ideas. Attention had to be paid to the constraints upon the process of adaptation and recreation of ideas, related for example to geography, language barriers, institutional and political factors.

Lluch's studies on the influence of Cameralism in Spain emphasized translations and editions of Germanic authors into the Spanish language, with particular attention to the work of Bielfeld. Another important aspect explored by Lluch in relation to the Spanish case was how those writings were used in practice, with particular attention given to the training of Treasury officials.

By comparison with Spain, understanding the Portuguese case is necessarily more indirect, given the absence of translations into Portuguese of any Cameralist author during the eighteenth century. Nonetheless, I can draw upon general understanding of these processes to illuminate my case. Thanks to the similarity between the Spanish and Portuguese languages, a book translated into Spanish is accessible to a Portuguese reader. And the same is also true, to a cultivated public, in relation to French. Hence the search for translations of Cameralist authors in eighteenth-century libraries and private collections in Portugal is also extremely important.

In spite of the difficulty in recovering these connections, it is in fact possible to affirm that there is substantial proximity between German Cameralism and other European traditions in the field of public finance and state policies, as Ernest Lluch insisted in his critique of Keith Tribe (Lluch, 1997; Tribe, 2006) and effectively demonstrated in relation to Spain (Lluch, 2000; Lluch and Argemí, 2000).

Lluch asserts that it is almost impossible to study the history of the political thought in Europe without a direct reference to Bielfeld's *Institutions politiques* (Lluch, 1996, 170). Analysis of that book, originally written in French, introduces a framework of cross-references that shows not only that Cameralism had influence beyond the German-speaking world, but also that it received and processed external influences, in particular from authors such as Melon, Forbonnais and Montesquieu (Lluch, 1996, 170).

Direct references to the political choices made by European countries are obviously one of the main reasons behind the interest in Bielfeld's work within the Spanish–Portuguese context. This appears in the title of a Spanish translation of Bielfeld's *Institutions politiques* (Bielfeld, 1762). Much of the text is dedicated to the administration of finances and praise for the centralization of these functions in the state, directly backing the work of the Royal Treasury, and possibly, as was noted by Ernest Lluch in the Spanish case, also influencing the training of public Treasury employees (Lluch, 2000, 726). The widespread availability of the book in important libraries of that time can also be traced. Bielfeld's book was also found in private collections, in Portugal and in distant corners of the Empire. For example, it was in the library confiscated from Cônego Luís Vieira da Silva, imprisoned following an important political uprising in the Portuguese colonial Empire, the *Inconfidência* of Minas Gerais (*ADIM*, 1976–83, vol. 6, 311; Frieiro, 1981).

Bielfeld's book was likewise prominently used by several authors within the Portuguese world. In his presentation of the economic works of José Joaquim da Cunha de Azeredo Coutinho (1794–1804), Sérgio Buarque de Holanda displays many similarities with Bielfeld's work. There is, for example, a coincidence in the presentation of topics as well as in the direct translation, without quotation marks or indication of source, of some paragraphs of Bielfeld's *Institutions* (Holanda, 1966, 45–6). Holanda suggests that there were links between this German author and Brazilian writers at the turn of the nineteenth century, among them José Bonifácio de Andrada e Silva, one of the most prominent names in the process of Brazilian political independence. He also mentions in a footnote a curious work by an anonymous author, published in 1823 in Rio de Janeiro as a 'summary of the political institutions of the Baron of Bielfeld', offered to 'the youth of Brazil'.[5] The author refers to himself simply as 'a compatriot from the state of Pernambuco'. Careful study at the National Library of Rio de Janeiro and in other writings of that time allowed me to determine that the author of these writings is Gervásio Pires Ferreira. It is of interest to add that it was published in the first year following the political independence of Brazil, and that the Brazilian translator introduced his work by mentioning the urgency and necessity for his country to learn the science of government.

3.4 THE 1755 LISBON EARTHQUAKE AND THE CENTRALIZATION OF THE PUBLIC FINANCE SYSTEM

The 1755 Lisbon Earthquake was a singular event having a great impact upon European history. Descriptions, political essays, plays, odes and poems, religious sermons, scientific treaties, and so on rapidly multiplied throughout Europe. Russel Dynes has argued that the 1755 earthquake can be read as the first modern disaster, in the sense that it was effectively the first time when the state was called upon to assume collective responsibility for the effects and consequences of a natural calamity, making a coordinated response to it (Dynes, 2005, 34–49). The earthquake was also a decisive event for the political importance of Sebastião José de Carvalho e Melo, future Count of Oeiras and Marquis of Pombal, the principal minister of King D. José I, and effectively head of the government.

The earthquake occurred on the morning of 1 November 1755 and was followed by a tsunami and many fires, causing nearly 30 000 deaths. It wrecked a large part of the city and brought about economic losses whose extent is hard to estimate, but whose impact on the economy of the kingdom was profound (Cardoso, 2007, 165–81). A greater part of the measures taken by Carvalho e Melo in the months that followed the disaster can be qualified as 'police matters', in the extended sense that the expression then had. They were measures related to the avoidance of epidemics and famine; caring for the wounded and the ill; controlling the flight of the population; guaranteeing security, justice and military defence; together with the early phases of reconstruction.

The impact of the earthquake was like that of a war. The administrative structure was suddenly destroyed, and this made clear the need for technical skills and for centralized decision-making and action. As an extreme event it permitted even the suppression of old rights of land ownership in the reconstruction of the destroyed areas of the city. It also produced a new sensitivity to public interest, and because of this represented an opportunity to reinforce the centralization of royal power and the administrative apparatus in general. The notion of public good was deployed in emphasizing the mechanisms of economic control in a manner favourable to mercantilism, but combined now with a new sense of discipline. All of this also represented an opening to new ideas and practical knowledge in solving the new, urgent and concrete problems of the kingdom, and it was in this context that the 'science of police' (*Polizeiwissenschaft*) attracted interest (Hespanha, 2007, 7; Subtil, 2007, 111–12).

The 1755 earthquake destroyed the Terreiro do Paço building, where the Casa dos Contos was located. This directly contributed to the disorder in the functions of this institution and precipitated its reorganization, which occurred with the creation of the Royal Treasury (Erário Régio). The earthquake created an opportunity to radicalize this centralization process, which would have otherwise probably been a more gradual transition.

The creation of the Royal Treasury, by a decree of December 1761, effectively changed the financial organization of the Portuguese state. Conceived as a unification of the revenue and expenditures for the kingdom and its domains, the Exchequer was a fundamental part of the political centralization process carried out by Carvalho e Melo. During the reign of D. José I in the mid-1700s a series of measures were introduced designed to improve the collection of royal rights and revenues, until then the prerogative of the Casa dos Contos and characterized by their dispersion over many government offices, by abuses on the part of the tax collectors and by delay in the deposits of revenues.

The Casa dos Contos, the prime institution responsible for organizing and inspecting the revenues and expenditures of the Portuguese state, probably goes back to the thirteenth century, during the reign of D. Dinis (1279–1325). Its creation was associated with increasing complexity in the accounts of the Crown and the establishment of the Royal Court in the city of Lisbon. The instition was made up of two separate departments, the Contos de Lisboa, to which the accounts of the entire kingdom deposits were linked, and the Contos d'El-Rei, which was responsible for the royal household accounts. During the reign of D. João I (1385–1433), several important reforms were made, restricting the responsibility of the Contos de Lisboa to the city accounts alone, leaving the accounts of the rest of the country under the control of the Treasury inspectors, as well as instituting a ruling (5 July 1389) which organized the routines, methods and hierarchies of the institution (Serrão, 1985, vol. 2, 174; Rau, 1951; Cruz, 2001).

It is essential to note that until the sixteenth century the Contos de Lisboa was responsible for the greater part of the collections, but as a result of the economic transformation caused by overseas expansion the Contos d'El-Rei began to assume a prominent position. For example, it was to Contos d'El-Rei that the accounts of the rights of the slave trade began to flow.

The establishment of the Royal Treasury occurred in this context, and can be seen as an attempt to address these challenges. If the Casa dos Contos did little more than compare the revenues received against the expenditures made by the tax collectors, the Royal Treasury was responsible for a substantial innovation. It was now the Treasury itself that paid and received, increasing control over the accounts as well as auditing the use of funds. The institution was internally structured in a very hierarchical fashion, and its head was the Marquis of Pombal himself. In other words, the principal minister of the King (Secretary of State of the Kingdom's Business) also held the position of General Inspector of the Treasury. After him in the internal hierarchy came the Treasurer-Major, the businessman José Francisco da Cruz, and a registrar, João Henrique de Souza, master from the School of Commerce (Aula de Comércio) and responsible for the key function of preparing a plan to introduce double-entry bookkeeping for the revenues account. Next in the hierarchy came four accounting departments, each one responsible for different parts of the Empire and headed by a general accountant aided by four registrars (Moreira, 1977, x–xii).

In the process of transforming the administration of the Treasury,

Carvalho e Melo took advantage of the vulnerability of private interests rooted in the collection structure consequent upon the economic losses caused by the earthquake. The holders of rights in that collection structure were especially sensitive to the prospect of compensation payments being made with the extinction of the Casa dos Contos. This was clearly an opportunity for the strengthening of the state. However, it lacked the existence of an official royal bureaucracy capable of implementing this administrative centralization. The importance that the Royal Treasury, placed by Carvalho e Melo under his personal command, would have in this process is undeniable. There is a persuasive link between Portugal's experience and the emergence of those new administrative principles in the European context. Among these new administrative principles was, for example, that finances be brought under a unitary adminsitration, together with a concern for the technical competence of the official royal bureaucracy. Both of these principles are clearly apparent in the institutions created by the Portuguese government at that time.

It is possible to suggest that this set of ideas, if only indirectly related to Cameralism, was important for the centralization of Portuguese finances and in the reordering of the state from the mid-eighteenth century. As noted in the introduction, it is difficult to reconstruct the detail of this process, since it is only hinted at by a few Portuguese historians. Unlike the Spanish case,[6] there are no Portuguese translations from German authors who originally wrote about this topic, or even a study of the presence of this literature in the Portuguese libraries of the period.

Another significant aspect is the importance of technical knowledge in financial administration. There is a convergence between the Cameralist perspective and the importance given to the training of the personnel of the public finance system. In the Portuguese experience, evidence can be found in the recruitment of experienced businessmen for the highest positions in the Royal Treasury. Even more important than this would be the creation of the School of Commerce (Aula de Comércio), which would be responsible over the years for providing staff for the Treasury.

The centralization of the Treasury administration within the Royal Treasury can be understood as one of the main actions of the Portuguese state during the second half of the eighteenth century. It is for this reason that it is important to go more deeply into the economic and administrative concept that guided, or at least informed, this moment. First of all, it is necessary to point to the fact that the fragmentation and dispersion of the centres of control and collection of the revenues of the kingdom within the context of the Casa dos Contos made it impossible for the royal administration to know the extent of expenditure and the implications that these had for the Royal Treasury, namely the limits on the indebtedness of the

Royal Treasury. This reflected an administration which conceived society as a set of private agents revolving around the figure of the monarch. To centralize public finances properly it would be necessary to break with corporatist ideas and conceptions proper to a financial administration based on the King's rewards and privileges. The serious consequences of the 1755 earthquake were thus crucial for the initiation of political modernity in Portugal. It can be argued that it represents the passage, as suggested by José Subtil, from a 'government of each' towards a 'government of all' (Subtil, 2006, 37–8).

The environment created by the cataclysm brought with it new problems. Immediate problems had to be resolved, and others forestalled through planning and anticipation. This was a key aspect of the task of urban reconstruction, together with problems related to safe housing, the circulation of people and products, safety, hygiene, health, supply of goods and defence. These were problems that required new demographic, social and economic knowledge, and at this time 'police science' (and also 'political arithmetic') had already registered, diagnosed and promised practical and effective solutions to these matters. This emergence of new administrative principles was essentially guided by the pursuit of public interest, necessarily in a sphere of a power that considered itself to be supra-individual. In other words, it is in fact a passage from a 'government of each' towards a 'government of all', to be supported by the power of the state rather than that of the Crown (Subtil, 2006, 38–9).

All these elements are closely related to another important question: the position of the ruler as a direct agent in the formulation of the law, or in other terms, the King as a legislator. This was one of the foundations of the centralization of political power, and the role played by police in this legislation would be an important part in the establishment of enlightened reformism in Portugal.

During the second half of the eighteenth century, 'police' affairs were central to the legislative activity of the King. They had an important role during the period under the administration of Carvalho e Melo (1750–77) and gave materiality to the administrative and economic changes of the time. This was the starting point for enlightened reformism in Portugal.

The proliferation of decrees, permits and laws during this period, dealing with themes related to police matters in general, reinforces this reformist perspective. Legislation combines themes like the creation of manufactures and the organization of commercial circuits, centralization of the public finance system, incentives for the production of knowledge related to natural resources, inducements for the increase of the population, educational reforms, security and public order, as well as issues related to political and economic reform of overseas administration.

It is possible to detect a progressive change in the meaning of the term 'police' from the mid-eighteenth century onwards. This change is a result of an attempt on the part of the crown to emulate advances in this field made in other parts of Europe. The decree of 25 June 1760 creating the General Intendancy of Police is a good example. This decree emphasizes the urgent need for the adoption of new measures, and contextualizes the Portuguese initiative with respect to similar initiatives in other parts of Europe.

This introduces a central aspect of the originality of the Portuguese case, and it is at the same time a key to the interpretation of the process of reception, assimilation and recreation of economic ideas in this country. During the second half of the eighteenth century, strongly related to the administrative transformations occurring after the 1755 earthquake initiated by the Marquis of Pombal, there is openness to new perspectives and ideas, marking the introduction of enlightened reformism to Portugal. This fits well with the concern about police matters. At a certain level we can detect here the assimilation of a Cameralist framework. However, this pragmatically oriented openness to new solutions for the economy and the administration of the Empire, with a particular emphasis on the question of the common good, is also suggestive of early elements of political economy. Ideas here become superimposed on each other. Political economy would have become more influential even without the practical exhaustion of mercantilist doctrine. In other words, in the administrative field pragmatic solutions would still form the focus of action, but not without generating new perceptions of the concrete challenges of the Empire's economy.

One last question to be highlighted is related to the specificity of the Portuguese case to the centralization of the public finance system. The post-earthquake context was responsible for the opening-up to new ideas, but more specifically for a concern with the practical application of this knowledge. In the case of public finances this would represent for Portugal a distinctive trajectory among other European nations, in particular in relation to Spain. The most representative example is the very early organization of the accounting apparatus of the fiscal domain, represented by the creation of the Royal Treasury, which took place before the organization of the political sphere of the treasury, the Secretary of State Department of the Treasury (Secretaria de Estado dos Negócios da Fazenda).

The centralization of finances in Portugal follows a concrete and persistent path throughout the eighteenth century prior to the earthquake, itself a specific conjuncture in the acceleration of the process. It is for instance possible to think that the discovery of gold in Brazil in the last years of the seventeenth century created a specific pathway for the collection of revenues related to royal rights. The fiscal organization of gold taxation was from the very first centralized and subject to direct and specific administration. It demanded administrative solutions as well as a mercantile organization reinforcing this centrality, as with the creation of the management of the fleets in 1720. The centralization of finances can here be read as a general element in a set of mercantilist ideas which could then take root due to the destabilization associated with the 1755 earthquake, together with the resolute action of Carvalho e Melo.

It is important to understand the way in which the accounting apparatus of the fiscal domain in Portugal functioned before the reorganization of the Treasury's political sphere of the treasury. Specifically, the modernization of the accounting–administrative organization of finance (with the creation of the Royal Treasury in 1761) came before the creation of the autonomous political entity that controlled it, the State Department of the Treasury, which came into existence in 1788, but which was only fully organized in 1801. In Spain, on the other hand, the opposite occurred. The reform began in the political arena, and only progressively extended to the accounting structure. There were different transformations in the central administrative structure in the first half of the eighteenth century, with the creation of a secretary dedicated to war and the Treasury in 1705, with alterations of its attributes in 1714 and 1716, finally giving rise in 1745 to a definitive structure called the State Department of the Treasury. This typifies the centralization of the political organization of Treasury affairs; it did not however supersede the previous accounting–administrative structure, inherited from the seventeenth century. For example, the principal element of this accounting structure, the General Superintendence of the Royal Treasury, coexisted autonomously and separated from the General Revenue Direction, which was responsible for the administration of the highest revenues of the Crown. To diminish potential conflicts over competence, the common solution was the attribution of the function of Superintendent of the Treasury to the person of the Secretary of State; nevertheless, the organizational problem persisted. The reorganization and effective centralization of public finances occurred only in 1795, with the suppression of the General Superintendence and the incorporation of its attributions by the Treasury Secretary (Griñán, 1993; Dedieu and Ruiz, 1994).

Moreover, an important qualification to the specificity of the Royal Treasury in Portugal can be seen in the extent of its powers within the accounting–administrative organization of revenues, not just within the kingdom, but also throughout the entire Portuguese Empire. Right from its inauguration, all of the monarchy's accounts were submitted to it in an integrated fashion. Kingdom and colonies were integrated within the four accounting departments in a strategy of fiscal subdivision, not necessarily of geographical proximity. The centralizing path taken in the administration of finances and taxes in Portugal is that of the centralization of the structures of direct management of the state taxes and revenues. The political structure and legal sphere aligned themselves to this centralized accounting institution, and not the reverse.

3.5 FINAL CONSIDERATIONS

The entrance of Cameralism into Portugal was in fact more a matter of practice than of theory, and this is basic to the understanding of the importance of mercantilist ideas to the centralization of the Treasury structure, and its connection to the development of enlightened reformism. This process varies according to national context, and takes account of the possibilities and imperatives of the monarchy, giving form to distinct paths of centralization in the area of finance. Hence we can better understand the circulation of ideas in this field by searching for an approximation between Cameralist doctrine, the sources of enlightened reformism and the 'imitation of solutions' to similar problems, developed in the administrative practice of each state.

It can be said that even though there was no trail of translations of Cameralist authors in Portugal as there was in Spain, there was indeed a practical appropriation of these themes, with emphasis on the centralization of finances. Even more important is that the use of German and French sources with respect to 'police' demands that we deal with the connection between these two traditions.

In the Portuguese case there is a connection between Cameralism, police science, enlightened reformism and the figure of the King as a legislator. All these dimensions are fundamental for understanding the change in Portuguese economic ideas during the second half of the eighteenth century, as well as for comprehension of the reception of emergent ideas from other parts of Europe.

NOTES

1. I am grateful to José Luís Cardoso and Stephen Meardon for their comments on a preliminary version of this chapter. I would also like to thank Keith Tribe and Tamotsu Nishizawa for their editorial support as well as an anonymous referee for their helpful comments. The usual disclaimer applies. I also like to acknowledge financial support from CNPq (Brazilian National Council of Research) and FAPEMIG (The State of Minas Gerais Research Foundation).
2. The role of Cameralism in the centralization of Austrian finances is important in understanding the transmission of economic ideas. Sebastião José de Carvalho e Melo served as a diplomatic envoy in Vienna between 1745 and 1749 and must have noted Austrian

administrative structure, influencing his work in the centralization of the Portuguese finances years later. The economic ideas of Carvalho e Melo undoubtedly retained influences from French mercantilism, especially from Colbert, on his work in the field of public finances (Pedreira, 2001, 272).

3. That is, in the generalist entry level of the university, the remaining three specialized faculties being Law, Medicine and Theology, training respectively lawyers, doctors and priests.
4. A very interesting illustration of this point is the time spent in the later 1700s by Manuel Ferreira da Câmara Bithencourt e Sá, José Bonifácio de Andrada and Joaquim Pedro Fragoso da Mota de Siqueira as students (and official envoys of the Portuguese government) in the Bergakademie. Their scientific journey, still a lesser-known event in the Luso-Brazilian historiography, took nearly ten years and included many other regions of Europe, including France, Austria, Bohemia, Hungary, Transylvania, Tirol, Piedmont, Tuscany, Naples, Sweden and Denmark.
5. The original title of the book is: *Resumo das instituiçoens politicas do barão de Bielfeld, parafraseadas e acommodadas à forma actual de governo no Imperio do Brasil, offerecido à mocidade brasiliense por hum seo compatriota pernambucano.*
6. From the general catalogue of the National Library of Spain and Historical Library 'Marqués de Valdecilla' of the Universidad Complutense de Madrid it was possible to recover some of these works, as, for example the following. Jacob Friedrich von Bielfeld (1781), *Instituciones políticas: Obra en que se trata de los Reynos de Portugal y España, de su situacion local, de sus posesiones, de sus Vecinos, y límites, de su clima, y producciones, de sus manufacturas, y fabricas, de su Comercio, de los habitantes, y de su número . . . del Soberano y de sus Títulos . . . de sus Exercitos, y Marina . . . Escrita en Francés . . . y Trad[a] . . . aumentada de muchas notas por Don Valentin de Foronda*, Burdéos, En casa de Francisco Mor. Jacob Friedrich von Bielfeld (1767–72), *Instituciones politicas obra . . . escrita en . . . frances por el Baron de Bielfeld; y traducida al castellano por D. Domingo de La Torre y Mollinedo*, Madrid, Gabriel Ramirez. Johann Heinrich Gottlob von Justi (1784), *Elementos generales de policia escritos por el Señor Juan Henrique Gottlobs de Justi . . . ; y del idioma francés traducidos al español, con varias noticas conducentes à España, añadidas por el mismo traductor D. Antonio Francisco Puig y Gelabert*, Barcelona, Eulalia Piferrer.

REFERENCES

Adam, U. (2006), *The Political Economy of J.H.G. von Justi*, Bern: Peter Lang.

ADIM (1976–83), *Autos de devassa da Inconfidência Mineira (1976–83)*. 2nd edn, 10 vols, Brasília: Câmara dos Deputados; Belo Horizonte: Governo do Estado de Minas Gerais.

Bielfeld, J.F. von (1762), *Institutions politiques: ouvrage oú l'ou traite de la societé civile; des loix, de la police, des finances, du commerce, des forces d'un état; et en general de tout ce quia rapport au gouvernement*, Paris: Duchesne.

Bielfeld, J.F. von (1767–72), *Instituciones politicas obra . . . escrita en . . . frances por el Baron de Bielfeld y traducida al castellano por D. Domingo de la Torre y Mollinedo*, Madrid: Gabriel Ramirez.

Bielfeld, J.F. von (1781), *Instituciones políticas: Obra en que se trata de los Reynos de Portugal y España, de su situacion local, de sus posesiones, de sus Vecinos, y límites, de su clima, y producciones, de sus manufacturas, y fabricas, de su Comercio, de los habitantes, y de su número . . . del Soberano y de sus Títulos . . . de sus Exercitos, y Marina . . . Escrita en Francés . . . y Trad[a] . . . aumentada de muchas notas por Don Valentin de Foronda*, Burdéos: Francisco Mor.

Cardoso, J.L. (2003), 'The international diffusion of economic thought', in W.J. Samuels, J.E. Biddle and J.B. Davis, *A Companion to the History of Economic Thought*, Oxford, Blackwell, pp. 662–33.
Cardoso, J.L. (2007), 'Pombal, o Terramoto e a Política de Regulação Económica', in A.C. Araújo, J.L. Cardoso, N.G. Monteiro, W. Rossa and J.V. Serrão (eds), *O Terramoto de 1755: impactos históricos*, Lisbon: Livros Horizonte, pp. 165–82.
Cruz, M.L.G. (2001), *A governação de D. João III: a fazenda real e os seus vedores*, Lisbon: Centro de História da Universidade.
Dedieu, J. and J.I. Ruiz (1994), 'Tres momentos de la historia de la Real Hacienda', *Cuadernos de Historia Moderna*, **15**, 77–98.
Dynes, R.R. (2005), 'The Lisbon earthquake of 1755: the first modern disaster', in T.E. Braun and J.B. Radner (eds), *The Lisbon Earthquake of 1755: Representations and Reactions*, Oxford: Voltaire Foundation, pp. 34–49.
Ferreira, G.P. (1823), *Resumo das instituiçoens politicas do barão de Bielfeld, parafraseadas e acommodadas à forma actual de governo no Imperio do Brasil, offerecido à mocidade brasiliense por hum seo compatriota pernambucano*. Rio de Janeiro: Typografia Nacional.
Frieiro, E. (1981), *O Diabo na livraria do cônego*, São Paulo: EDUSP and Belo Horizonte: Itatiaia.
Griñán, C.M.C (1993), 'El siglo XVIII e los intentos de reforma hacendística', *Cuadernos de Historia Moderna*, **14**, 29–37.
Heckscher, E.F. (1955 [1931]), *Mercantilism*, 2nd edn, London: George Allen & Unwin.
Hespanha, A.M. (2007), 'A note on two recent books on the patterns of Portuguese politics in the 18th century', *e-Journal of Portuguese History*, **5** (2), 1–9.
Holanda, S.B. (1966), 'Apresentação', in J.J.C.A. Coutinho, *Obras econômicas: 1794–1804*, São Paulo: Companhia Editora Nacional, pp. 13–53.
Ingrao, C.W. (2000), *The Habsbourg Monarchy: 1618–1815*, 2nd edn, Cambridge: Cambridge University Press.
Johnson, H.C. (1964), 'The concept of bureaucracy in Cameralism', *Political Science Quarterly*, **79** (3), 378–402.
Justi, J.H.G. von (1784), *Elementos generales de policia escritos por el Señor Juan Henrique Gottlobs de Justi . . . y del idioma francés traducidos al español, con varias noticas conducentes à España, añadidas por el mismo traductor D. Antonio Francisco Puig y Gelabert*, Barcelona: Eulalia Piferrer.
Lluch, E. (1996), '*El Cameralismo más allá del mundo gernánico', Revista de Economia Aplicada*, **10** (4), 163–75.
Lluch, E. (1997), 'Cameralism beyond the Germanic world: a note on Tribe', *History of Economic Ideas*, **5** (2), 85–99.
Lluch, E. (2000), 'El Cameralism en España', in E.F. Quintana (ed.), *Economia y Economistas Españoles: La Ilustración*, Vol. 3, Barcelona: Galáxia Gutenberg / Círculo de Lectores, pp. 721–8.
Lluch, E. and L. Argemí (2000), 'La influencia alemana en España (1800–1860): desde el Cameralism tardío a Jakob, Krause y List', in E.F. Quintana (ed.), *Economia y Economistas Españoles: La Ilustración*, Vol. 3, Barcelona: Galáxia Gutenberg / Círculo de Lectores, pp. 451–8.
Magnusson, L. (1994), *Mercantilism: The Shaping of an Economic Language*, London: Routledge.
Moreira, A.T.L. (1977), *Inventário do Fundo Geral do Erário Régio: Arquivo do Tribunal de Contas*, Lisbon: Tip. Minerva do Comércio.

Pedreira, J. (2001), 'Marquês de Pombal (1699–1782)', in J.L. Cardoso (ed.), *Dicionário Histórico de Economistas Portugueses*, Lisbon, Temas e Debates, pp. 269–72.

Rau, V. (1951), *A casa dos contos*, Coimbra, Faculdade de Letras / Instituto de Estudos Históricos Dr António de Vasconcelos.

Recktenwald, H.C. (2008), 'Cameralism', in S. Durlauf and L. Blume (eds), *The New Palgrave Dictionary of Economics*, 2nd edn, Basingstoke: Palgrave Macmillan, DOI:10.1057/9780230226203.2130.

Reinert, E.S. (2004), *Rich Nations Got Rich: Essays in the History of Economic Policy*, Oslo: Centre for Development and the Environment (SUM), University of Oslo.

Reinert, E.S. and H. Reinert (2009), 'A bibliography of J.H.G. von Justi', in J.G. Backhaus (ed.), *The Beginnings of Political Economy: Johann Heinrich Gottlob von Justi*, New York: Springer, pp. 19–32.

Schiera, P. (1995a [1976]), 'Cameralismo', in N. Bobbio, N. Matteucci and G. Pasquino (eds), *Dicionário de Política*, Trans. C. Varriale, 7th edn Brasília: UnB.

Schiera, P. (1995b [1976]), 'Estado de Polícia', in N. Bobbio, N. Matteucci and G. Pasquino (eds), *Dicionário de Política*, Trans. C. Varriale, 7th edn, Brasília: UnB.

Serrão, J. (1985), 'Contos', in J. Serrão (ed.), *Dicionário de história de Portugal*, Porto: Figueirinhas.

Sonnenfels, J. (1765–76), *Grundsätze der Polizei, Handlung und Finanzwissenschaft*, 3 vols, Wien.

Subtil, J.M. (2006), 'O governo da fazenda e das finanças (1750–1974)', in M.P. Cruz (ed.), *Dos Secretários de Estado dos Negócios da Fazenda aos Ministros das Finanças – 1788–2006: uma iconografia*, Lisbon: Secretaria-Geral do Ministério das Finanças e da Administração Pública, pp. 36–69.

Subtil, J.M. (2007), *O terramoto político (1755–1833): memória e poder*, Lisbon: UAL.

Tribe, K. (1988), *Governing Economy: The Reformation of German Economic Discourse 1750–1840*, Cambridge: Cambridge University Press.

Tribe, K. (1995), *Strategies of Economic Order: German Economic Discourse, 1750–1950*, Cambridge: Cambridge University Press.

Tribe, K. (2006), 'Cameralism and the Staatswissenschaften', in M. Goldie and R. Wokler (eds), *Cambridge History of Eighteenth Century Political Thought*, Cambridge: Cambridge University Press, pp. 525–46.

Wakefield, A. (2005), 'Books, bureaus, and the historiography of Cameralism', *European Journal of Law and Economics*, **19**, 311–20.

Wakefield, A. (2009), *The Disordered Police State: German Cameralism as Science and Practice*, Chicago, IL: University of Chicago Press.

PART II

European and American interactions

4. The development of economic theories in Germany: from Karl Heinrich Rau to Wilhelm Roscher

Yukihiro Ikeda

4.1 INTRODUCTION

Karl Heinrich Rau (1792–1870) and Wilhelm Roscher (1817–94) were leading German economists of the mid-nineteenth century, both of whom drew on English classical economics, but at different times in its development. Rau's three-volume textbook – *Grundsätzte der Volkswirtschaftslehre* (1826 [1997]), *Grundsätze der Volkswirtschaftspflege* (1828 [1997]), *Grundsätze der Finanzwissenschaft* (1837 [1997]) – was widely read, and among its readers was Carl Menger, the founder of the Austrian School of Economics.[1] Menger eagerly read and re-read Rau's *Grundsätze der Volkswirtschaftslehre* during the 1860s while preparing his own *Grundsätze* as a *Habilitationsschrift,* which he would later submit to Vienna University in support of his application for a lectureship. During this period he also studied Roscher's *Grundlagen*, which also exerted a powerful influence upon his thinking.[2]

Rau's work represents the earlier phase of the introduction of the English Classical School into German economic theory, before the work of John Stuart Mill was translated. Roscher's work was by contrast published after the introduction of Mill's economic doctrines into Germany. Both Rau and Roscher were to some extent lexicographic writers, gathering together whatever materials they thought to be important for their readers; making it difficult to identify their own positions. Nonetheless, *Grundsätze* and *Die Grundlagen* deserve scrutiny, as they represent an important phase within the development of economic thought in German, when the English Classical School became popular throughout German-speaking areas.

First, let us take a brief look at how Rau divided his work.[3] Rau begins with production, after which he deals with distribution, and finally consumption. This construction is reminiscent of the structure of the well-known economics book by Jean-Baptiste Say, who in the second edition of his *Traité* made the same tripartite division. It is therefore clear that Rau models his textbook on Say's structure. Another important figure who might be considered an influence is James Mill, who added an independent section on exchange to his book of 1821. See the following methodological justification by Mill himself:

> Though the Science of Political Economy in this manner divides itself into two grand inquiries, that which relates to Production, and that which relates to Consumption – it is evident that, before things are consumed, they require to be distributed. The laws of Distribution, therefore, constitute an intermediate inquiry between that which relates to Production and that which relates to Consumption. When commodities produced and distributed, it is highly convenient, for the sake both of re-production and consumption, that portions of them should be exchanged for one another. (James Mill, 1821)

It seems that Rau did not follow Mill's new division. Rau's textbook does not include an independent section on exchange; instead, this discussion is embedded in the section on distribution. Since Rau's textbook was published as early as 1826, it is not impossible that the German economist was an influence upon John Stuart Mill's 1848 book (Mill, 1965). See the following letter from J.S. Mill to Rau:[4]

> Your plan of separating the scientific inquiry into the production & distribution of wealth, as a branch of social science, from the consideration of the economic policy of governments, appears to me both logically and didactically the best, & I have made the same separation in my own treatise. (John Stuart Mill, 1972, 86)

It is clear that there are two levels of separation in the above quotation: first, there is the separation of economics into the parts of production and distribution; then, economic theories are separated from policy-making matters. In common with Shoken Mawatari's argument in his book on Mill, it seems almost certain that at issue here is a separation of economic theory from economic policies.[5] It is thus debatable whether the quotation indicates Mill's commitment to the notion that economic theory should always be divided between production and distribution.

We should not be too critical when reading Rau's work on economic theory. When regarded from within the narrow perspective of the development of economic theory, it is easy to see the limitations of his work. In his monograph on German economics discourse, Keith Tribe appropriately summarizes the characteristics of Rau's economics as follows:

> But Rau was something that neither Smith nor Ricardo were: a professor of economics at a major university whose task was to educate future administrators,

> lawyers, and teachers in the basic principles of economic life. Here it was not so important to develop a consistent argument on the proper conduct of national legislation as to impart some notion of the diversity of economic forms and the basic regularities that they reflected. Seen in this light, the theoretical achievements of a Smith and a Ricardo seem less significant; they may be admired for the elegance with which their principles systematically constructed arguments for legislative positions, but they lack the descriptive immediacy of Rau's treatment of economic life. (Tribe, 1988, 199)

Indeed, it was not necessary for Rau to give the students a detailed and sophisticated account of economic theory; rather, he attempted to teach them the fundamental concepts of economics, as can be seen in the basic structure of his work. It is important to bear this aspect of Rau's economics in mind when reading his texts. The identical tendency can also be seen in his follower in textbook writing, Wilhelm Roscher.

Roscher is generally recognized as the founder of the German Historical School; however, he was also the most distinguished writer of economic textbooks in the second half of the nineteenth century.[6] Among the five textbooks that he published – *Die Grundlagen der Nationaloekonomie* (1854), *Die Nationaloekonomik des Ackerbaues* (1859), *Die Nationaloekonomie des Handels* (1881), *System der Finanzwissenschaft* (1886), *System der Armenpflege* (1894) – *Grundlagen* was especially well read, and was republished many times. Roscher's *Grundlagen* does include an independent section on exchange, but the order of the sections is different from that of James Mill's book. Mill begins with a section on production, followed by one on distribution, then one on exchange phenomena, and he concludes with a section on consumption theory. In contrast, Roscher begins with a section on production, followed by a section on exchange, then one on distribution, concluding with a section on consumption.

Roscher was a passionate and erudite writer, gathering whatever materials he thought would be important for readers; this means that it is difficult to identify his own position from within his writings. For instance, he introduces a certain economic doctrine, say doctrine A, but soon after that he begins to introduce another doctrine, say doctrine B. Roscher fails to give us a detailed account of the relationship between doctrines A and B. Thus, the reader is rendered completely ignorant of Roscher's opinion of the relative merits of doctrines A and B. Anyone who attempts to analyse the influence of British, French, Italian or other writers on economics on Roscher's work are destined to face the same problem. Karl Marx even goes so far as to say that Roscher's economics was a form of professorial economics (*Professoralform*), implying that he regarded Roscher's work as the worst form of the vulgar economics. Marx was not entirely wrong (see his comments on Roscher in *Theorien über den Mehrwert*).[7] Indeed, Roscher's textbooks are a great melange of almost all the economic doctrines known his time. Nonetheless, since he was a prolific writer who absorbed many ideas from English-speaking economists, his work is an ideal way into the positive and negative influences of the English Classical School on German economic thought.

I propose the following hypothesis in this chapter. It is often said that the German concept of goods and the associated theory of value are relatively unique. However, the idea of the Robinson Crusoe economy was not entirely foreign to the mainstream economists of the English Classical School, such as John Stuart Mill. Furthermore, even if Roscher was inclined to the subjectivism of the later generation, he does nonetheless try to adhere to mainstream British political economy, such as the work of David Ricardo. I do not deny that the German influence added some new elements to mainstream British economics. One of these aspects that I am especially concerned with in this chapter is the new inclination they had toward normative economics.

I will proceed as follows. In the next section, I shall examine Rau's two concepts of value: abstract and concrete value. The concept of value plays a central role in the development of German economics in the nineteenth century. I then turn to Rau's price theory. In sections 4.4, 4.5 and 4.6 I focus on Roscherian economics, using his 1854 book as a reference point. Using the sections on Rau as a model, I first survey Roscher's value concept and then his price theory, both of which were developed in his *Grundlagen*. In the final section, I will give some concluding remarks, attempting to clarify the basic characteristics of the two great German economists. Despite the above-mentioned characteristics of Rau and Roscher's economics, I attempt to outline a basic theoretical interpretation of their economics discourses.

4.2 RAU'S TWO CONCEPTS OF VALUE: ABSTRACT VALUE AND CONCRETE VALUE[8]

Let me begin with Book 1 of Rau's *Grundsätze*. After a brief introduction and before Book 2, production theory per se, Rau inserted a part in which he examined various value concepts. In this section, the focus will be on Rau's concepts of value: abstract value and concrete value. However, before extrapolating the two concepts of value, it will be appropriate to explore the precise meaning of value theory, especially in German-speaking areas. The following explanation shows how important Rau regarded the concept of value in the evaluation of wealth:

> Property consists of material things, but the extent of the property economically observed cannot be measured only by relying upon the quantity of material. It depends on the benefits that the property gives to people, or rather the influence of that part of it under whose influence people are. (Rau, 1833, 53)

Wealth consists of material goods; services are not recognized as wealth. This definition is still embedded in the tradition of the English Classical School.

In the 1830s, F.B.W. von Hermann proposed that services and social relationships must be also included in the definition of wealth. However, Rau consistently retains the classical definition of wealth in his work. With this in mind, we might ask how wealth can then be validly measured. It is not enough to know the volume of each commodity and add them up, since each of them contributes to the well-being of the economic agent in a different way. Value is defined as the proportion of merit that each commodity brings to the person. It is important to recognize that the concept of value is necessitated by measuring wealth. It is possible neither to measure wealth by simply counting each commodity and then adding them up; nor to do so by using a market price of the goods.

Rau is critical of any attempt to measure national wealth simply by relying upon market prices. One of the reasons that he gives can be seen in the following quotation: 'Even when most commodities are bought and sold, there are still many things that are not exchanged and thus have no price. These things are evaluated only after value' (Rau, 1833, 64). It is often the case that there are goods that are generally not exchangeable. Naturally, they do not have any prices. Rau mentions two cases as examples. Often goods are not owned by specific people. These things are, in essence, free. Some commodities are not transferable due to legal restrictions. In both cases, the goods concerned are not exchangeable and cannot have prices. These examples suffice to show that measuring national wealth using prices is one-sided, to say the least. There are many goods in the world that are not exchangeable but which nonetheless play an important role in the activities of economic agents.

Next, we turn to the two concepts of value in Rau's economics. The following quotation illustrates Rau's definition of abstract value:

> If one looks at the situation more closely, it becomes clear that there are two ways to understand value: 1) concerning the certain group of goods, which have, generally speaking, abilities to satisfy human wants. This evaluation can be referred to as Group Value (*Gattungswerth*), for instance one hundredweight of wheat, iron, etc. (Rau, 1833, 57)

The first concept is known as *Gattungswerth* in the original German text, which might be roughly translated as 'group value'. This refers to the ability of certain group of goods to satisfy human wants. The alternative name for this concept is 'abstract value'. Wheat or iron of 50 or 100 kg is given as an example of goods that have group value. However, this is not the entire picture.

Rau continues his argument as follows: '2) A certain amount of goods in relation to the stock that a predetermined person already has, as well as the needs of the said person, is known as Concrete Value or Quantity Value (*concreter oder Quantitätswerth*)' (Rau, 1833, 57). As can been seen, the concept of concrete value can be only defined with respect to a specific person, considering the relationship between the stock of a commodity and their intensity of wants. The definition implies that the value of a commodity decreases as the existing amount increases, and that its value depends on the necessity of the goods given the initial amount. It is clear that the first implication is almost the equivalent of the law of decreasing marginal utility.

At this point, I will give a simple example to help illustrate the concept of measuring value. Suppose that there are two commodities: cars and suits. The family owns a car that is predominantly used by the husband. However, his wife urgently needs a car for her personal use. Thus, the demand value for cars in this family is two. Concrete value is based on the relationship between wants and the given amount. Let us say that the value in this case is calculated as two. On the other hand, the husband has three suits. However, he really needs only one suit, and the other two are superfluous. Thus, the demand value for suits is considered to be one in this family. If one is interested in the size of the wealth of the family, a possible way to make a guess is to calculate the value of each goods and aggregate them, using a suitable method.

It is worth noting that the value of wealth in this sense is not equal to the total utility brought by the total amount of a commodity. Rather, it is equivalent to the scarcity in relation to the demand. If there are more commodities, then total utility increases as the quantity increases, while the value in the above sense decreases.

The differences between the two concepts are obvious. Group value is concerned with a certain amount of goods, but gives no consideration to the relationship between wants and the existing amount of the commodity. Furthermore, group value does not refer to one specific person, while concrete value can be only be defined with reference to the predetermined subject.

In the following quotation, Rau provides three different value concepts, which are, to a certain extent, related to the two concepts of value we have examined above. The first one roughly corresponds to the concrete value, as can be seen from the following quotation:

> It is important to differentiate between the certain Group Values that economic subjects enjoy: 1) Individual value is the judgment of each person with regard to the usefulness of goods. Often, this differs from person to person. The value depends upon the particular situation of each person, his inclinations, habits, needs, intentions, etc. (Rau, 1833, 59)

Subjective value depends upon the individual situation of each person, his preferences, habits, and demands. It is obvious that different agents have different preferences. A loves apples, while B does not. A loves classical music, and B progressive rock.

The second concept can be outlined as follows: 'The evaluation of value is shared by many who experience similar situations, such as those in the same occupation or class, those having the same skill, etc.' (Rau, 1833, 59–60). Economic agents who are in similar situations are likely to have similar preferences, Rau argues. For instance, labourers go drinking with their friends on Saturday, while gentlemen of the upper middle class are likely to visit a museum on the same day. It cannot be denied that different social classes have a different preference structure. This is the second concept of value.

The third and final one is fundamentally a concept based on group value: 'The general or common value is shared at least by those who live within the same nation. They have uniform judgment' (Rau, 1833, 60). The terminology of the previous quotation indicates that this concept can be roughly translated as group value. Almost everyone is united in the feeling that owning certain goods is a necessity; this is independent of social class. In the quotation above, these are known as goods with general value. Perhaps to the reader this is reminiscent of basic needs in modern welfare state. In these cases the economist does not have to think about the difference of preferences among economic agents.

With these definitions of value in mind, the following explanation of how certain things become goods is a logical progression:

> For things to qualify as material goods, the following objective and subjective conditions are necessary: 1) It must be useful for human purposes. 2) It is necessary that this usefulness be recognized by the judgment of reasons . . . Only this judgment can ensure things are goods. Only once this judgment has been made should a certain position be adopted with regard to its identification as a part of property, even if it has been there having the same character for a long time (Rau, 1833, 79)

In Rau's opinion, two types of conditions must be satisfied for things to be goods: objective and subjective conditions. First, certain physical conditions must be fulfilled if things are to be used to meet human needs. This means that things must be deemed useful from a certain point of view. Second, this usefulness must be recognized in the context of human understanding. Things cannot be identified as goods if the second condition is not fulfilled. To understand the basic concept of Rau's idea let us look at the example of sugar. Sugar is sweet. As such, it satisfies a human need or purpose: sweetness. However, for sugar to be included in the world of goods, one must know that it is indeed sweet. Without this condition, sugar cannot be identified as a good, even if its objective character already exists and meets a human need. Rau's second condition shows how deeply he was committed to the tradition of subjective goods and value theories, which was a common trend in German-speaking areas, and the culmination of which can be seen in the economics discourses of the second half of the nineteenth century.

4.3 RAU'S PRICE THEORIES

I now turn to book 3, entitled 'Distribution of Property'. Bearing in mind that Rau's textbook was written after the publication of Ricardo's work but before the emergence of Mill's long-selling *Principles*, I examine Rau's price theory as well as its relationship with the disciplines of the English Classical School.

According to Rau there are three things which one must take account of when discussing the problem of price formation: 'In general, there are three situations to which all factors that help decide the price can be reduced: 1) the value of exchangeable goods, 2) the cost, 3) competition' (Rau, 1833, 137). Rau then examines these factors in the following way: he argues that the price of a commodity cannot go beyond the estimation of the buyer. Thus, the value is a deciding factor in the setting of a maximum price. In his own words: 'One can assume as the first rule that the price cannot go beyond the valuation of the demander' (Rau, 1833, 138). If a price goes beyond the value of the commodity, the demander shall certainly avoid making a deal. For him or her it is not worthwhile spending money on it. It is too expensive, considering his or her attachment to the commodity. Using modern terminology, we might outline this as follows: the decision of the consumer is based upon the relationship between price and utility, the latter being what Rau calls 'value'. This is what Rau refers to as 'the first rule' in the above quotation.

Also, the cost of a commodity plays an important role in price formation. It is important to note that 'cost' here has, in fact, two different meanings. First, it implies the 'cost' that is necessary to produce a commodity. The merchant endeavours to sell the commodity at a price that at least covers the production cost:

> They aim to have only such a price that exceeds the cost, ensuring that there is at least some profit. On the other hand, they must incur a loss if they cannot recover the basic cost. Therefore, it can be assumed as the second rule, that the goods cannot be alienated beyond the price corresponding to the cost level. (Rau, 1833, 140)

Thus, the second rule is that the price of a commodity must at least cover its cost of production. In other words, cost is interpreted as the minimum price of a good.

Interestingly, Rau offers us another definition of cost in the price formation, which can be neatly expressed as follows: 'Hence the third rule: Price cannot go beyond the level of cost, which should be defined as the amount that the demander needs to obtain the same goods from other sources' (Rau, 1833, 140–41). This quotation indicates that production cost influences the prices offered by other sellers. The price offered by one seller cannot go beyond those by his rivals; if it does, he loses his customer. This is the third rule.

When a certain commodity is produced by one producer only, the price level must fall somewhere between the lower and the upper limits, each of which correspond to value and cost respectively. This can be simply described as follows:

$$\textit{Value} > \textit{Price} > \textit{Cost}$$

Suppose that there is one competitive seller who sells his commodity for less than its value, say, *Price*(*r*), the price would be described as follows:

$$\textit{Value} > \textit{Price}(r) > \textit{Price} > \textit{Cost}$$

In this case, the price level would be lower in comparison to a case with no competitive sellers in the market. This is intuitively true.

After the above discussion, Rau introduces some price concepts which are in essence identical to his own concept of price, as determined by cost factor. These are called *natürlicher*, *notwendiger* or *angemessener* price respectively by Smith and Say; Sismondi and Storch; and Lotz. Jakob, Schlözer and Fulda call it *Kostenpreis* (Rau, 1833, 147). Cost is a factor in determining the price level, but it is only one factor among many, argues Rau. Furthermore, he shows that the market price continues to vary below and above the cost, due to various natural and human factors. It can be safely said that these arguments are more or less a recapitulation of the arguments made by Smith and his followers of the English Classical School.

4.4 ROSCHER ON THE DEFINITION OF GOODS[9]

There is a long tradition in German-speaking economic discourse of goods theory, the pinnacle of which can be seen in the four conditions of goods in Menger's *Grundsätze*. As a representative textbook writer from the latter part of the nineteenth century, it was quite natural for Roscher to give his definition of goods in the *Grundlagen*: 'Goods are anything which can be used, whether directly or indirectly, for the satisfaction of any true or legitimate human want, and whose utility, for this purpose, is recognized' (Roscher, 1882, 53).

Roscher asserts that anything that satisfies direct or indirect human wants can be regarded as a good. This means that goods include not only consumer goods but also those things that contribute to their making. In common with Rau, whose concept of goods we have examined already, Roscher thinks that to qualify as goods, things must satisfy a human purpose. This condition is an essential prerequisite if things are to be defined as goods. Furthermore, these wants must be true and legitimate. In other words, untrue wants are considered to be excluded from goods. The same can be said of illegitimate ones. This idea is unique; and it cannot be found in Rau's definition of goods above.

On the other hand, Roscher rightly points out that the concept of goods is essentially relative in the sense that the same goods can easily turn into non-goods, depending upon circumstances of time and space. Of course, the opposite is also true in that certain things become goods when recognized as such by human beings:

> Every change in man's wants, or knowledge, is accompanied by a rapid, corresponding change, either in the limits of the circle of goods, or in their relative importance. Thus, the tobacco plant has probably existed for thousands of years. It became a good, however, only from the time that man recognized its use for smoking, taking snuff, etc., and experienced the desire for it for these purposes. (Roscher, 1882, 53)

As can be seen in this quotation, Roscher believes that two conditions are necessary for things to be goods: human wants and the identification that certain things are capable of being used for the satisfaction of them. In the above quotation, two different interpretations are possible. Either Roscher thinks that smoking has become an enjoyable recreational activity only in recent history, or he thinks that tobacco was only recently recognized as meeting this desire, even if the pleasure of smoking had been already known in earlier years. Indeed, it is highly probable that smoking was recognized as enjoyable and relaxing when the Europeans first encountered tobacco in the New World. In any case, it is clear that in the same thing can becomes a good or can cease to be a good depending on the different preferences of the economic subjects in a specific time and place.

Roscher was deeply concerned with the ethics of economics. This can be easily seen in the following footnote, in which he emphasizes that only ethically plausible goods should be allowed to be included in the definition:

> The qualification 'true' excludes from the circle of goods not only all those things which might satisfy only irrational or immoral wants (compare *Mischer*, Grundsätze der Nationalökonomie, 1856, I, S. 187), but also vindicates the fundamental idea of the whole system of Political Economy, as a subject of moral as well as of psychological investigation. (Roscher, 1882, 53, n. 7)

Thus, only those things that satisfy rational and moral wants are considered to be goods. It is interesting to note that Roscher mentions Peter Mischler in this regard, well known as a strict Catholic and proponent of ethical economics. Here, Roscher is attempting to characterize economics as a moral subject, thus making clear his position as the founder of the German Historical School.

4.5 ROSCHER'S PRICE THEORIES

The plural ('price theories') is intentional here. Indeed, there are several price theories in Roscher's work, and they are not always consistent with each other. First, let us investigate his analysis based on demand and supply:

> As a rule, the price-relation of two commodities is determined by the relation of demand and supply – by the desire to possess something and the difficulty of obtaining that thing. It is important, therefore, to examine on what deeper relationships supply and demand themselves depend. In the case of the purchaser, the value given for the use of the commodity and the purchaser's own ability to pay constitute the maximum limit of its price, which may, however, be modified by the cost of producing it elsewhere or at another time. In the case of the seller, the cost of production is the minimum limit, which may, however, be extended by the cost of procuring the commodity by the purchaser at another time or place. (Roscher, 1882, 308–9)

As Roscher proposes, the price of two commodities is regulated by demand and supply. Furthermore, he investigates the various elements that determine these two factors. He finds first that demand is regulated by its value in terms of its use as a commodity and the budget of the consumer. These two elements set the maximum limit of the price, Roscher argues. Even if the commodity is worth the money that is being asked, the purchaser cannot purchase if the good is outside the limits of his budget.

The alternative is also possible, in a situation where the purchaser would rather refrain from buying the good even if the price is within the budget constraint. That is, it may be too expensive when it is considered in terms of the utility value it offers. Second, from the viewpoint of the seller, the cost of production plays an important role in setting the price level. If the price is below the cost of production, then the seller will refrain from selling and the latter is regarded as the minimum limit of the price. Thus, overall, the price is determined within these constraints which are decided upon by a demander and a seller, respectively.

However, these constraints can be modified by the competitive behaviour of economic agents. If the consumer can get the commodity at a lower price, then he or she is likely to lower the maximum price limit, formed by the constraints of his or her budget or the utility value of the commodity. In this case, the consumer could strengthen his bargaining power by making it clear that other sellers are offering a much lower price. On the other hand, the seller is likely to attempt to sell his goods at a higher price than the minimum limit if his competitors are also offering higher prices. The seller may then set the price under the level offered by other sellers, and still enjoy the possibility of excluding his competitors.

There is another price theory outlined in the *Grundlagen*, which looks like this:

> Goods whose cost of reproduction, that is the highest necessary cost of production, is the same, have uniformly the same value in exchange. Every deviation from this level immediately sets a process in motion that endeavors to restore the level, just as the water of the sea seeks its level, notwithstanding the mountains and abysses which the winds bring forth from its bosom. (Roscher, 1882, 319)

It is clear that the basic theory given in this quotation is different from the one we have seen above. This theory, the second theory in Roscher's work, is a price theory in the long run. Prices tend to converge with the cost of production, Roscher says. As we have seen, cost is only the limit of the price in the previous quote. This second theory is reminiscent of the cost theory that was proposed in the English Classical School. Roscher does not make clear the nature of the relationship between the two theories.

In the following quotation, Roscher further explains the movement of a market price and its convergence to the price in the long run:

> If the market price rises high above the cost of production, producers make a profit greater than the average profit made in the country. This induces them, by the appropriation of new land and the employment of new labour and capital, to increase their business. Other parties also engage in this profitable department of trade . . . If the market price sinks below the cost of production,

> the producer naturally suffers a loss, and diminishes his stock as soon as possible. That whole establishments engaged in industry should forsake a branch that is suffering from depression and replace it with a flourishing one, must ever remain a rare exception. But the discouraged manufacturer may delay renewing his stock on hand, replacing his machinery by new machinery; he may dismiss some of his workmen and diminish the number of days during which others shall work. (Roscher, 1882, 320, 323)

From this it is clear that this explanation is a recapitulation of the natural price theory of the English Classical School, going back at least to the well-known description found in *The Wealth of Nations*. If a market price is above the natural price level, then there is not only a motivation for existing entrepreneurs to expand their production using more land, labour and capital, but also an incentive for those capitalists that are engaged in other business to move to this sector and enjoy extra profit. On the other hand, if a market price is below the natural price level, entrepreneurs might reduce their workforce and shorten the working hours of those still remaining in the firm. In addition, they are likely to hesitate to renew their machines considering the market conditions. Thus a market price has a tendency to converge to the natural price, which is, in essence, equivalent to the cost necessary to produce the commodity. It can be safely said that the argument here has its origins in the long tradition of natural price theory.

To identify Roscher's own position in the history of economic thought, especially in the context of objective and subjective controversies, the following (very long) footnote deserves to be mentioned:[10]

> The English view, one very characteristic of the people, is that the equilibrium of prices depends on this: that all commodities should have a value equal to that of the labour they have cost. (Compare *Ariston.*, Eth. Nicoma., V, 5) The same doctrine is to be found in its germinal state in *Hobbes*, Leviathan, 24, 1651, and *Rice Vaughan*, Discourse of Coin and Coinage, 1675. More exhaustively in *Petty*, Treatise of Taxes and Contributions, 1679, 24, 31, 67. (Compare *Locke*, Civil Government, II, § 40ff.; *B. Franklin*, Inquiry into the Nature and Necessity of a paper Currency, 1729; Works, ed. Sparks, vol. II.) *Adam Smith* admits this to be true only of the first beginnings of society, before the origin of property in land in capital. (Wealth of Nations, I. ch. 5.) Most largely developed in *Ricardo*, Principles, ch. I, 4, 30. *Marx*, Zur Kritik der polit. Oekonomie, 1859, 6, endeavors to improve on this by calling all values in exchange 'a determinate quantity of thickly curdled working-time,' meaning by work an averaged *qualitätslose*, social work of production. (Roscher, 1882, 319)

In my view, this is a good summary of the development of the cost theory and the labour theory of value, which was prevalent mainly in English-speaking countries. This is a typically British way of looking at economic phenomena, Roscher says. Beginning with Hobbes, Vaughan, Petty and Locke, Roscher surveys the tradition of objective value theory. After mentioning Smith and

Ricardo – two representative personalities of the English Classical School – he even refers to the 1859 book by Marx. He rightly points out that what Marx had in mind when he discussed the determination of the value of each commodity was average working time, and not the working time of each worker. Here all the differences in quality of labour disappear. This seems to be a correct understanding of Marx's labour theory of value.

Now Roscher turns to subjective value theory:

> *Per contra*, compare *Hufeland*, N. Grundlegung, I, 134, 156 ff.; and *Malthus*, Principles ch. 2, secs. 2, 3, who claim very earnestly that price is not determined by the cost of production, but by the relation that exists between demand and supply. For a very marked case of reaction against Adam Smith and Ricardo, see *Macleod*, Elements, ch. 2, who, despite the fact that he is much too one-sided in considering only the amount necessary to the purchaser, and his means. Even Condillac has said: *une chose n'a pas une valeur, parcequ'elle coûte, mais elle coûte (du travail ou de l'argent), parcequ'elle a une valeur*. (Commerce et Gouvernement, 16.) (Roscher, 1882, 319–20)

First, Roscher introduces two economists, namely Hufeland and Malthus, who believe that price is regulated by the relation between demand and supply. It is clear that these thinkers dispute the cost theory of value. Then the work of Macleod is referred to as a reaction against the mainstream of the English Classical School, whose criticism was however not acceptable to Roscher. Indeed, he goes so far as to say that Macleod was 'much too one-sided'. Finally, the French economist Condillac is mentioned, who also disputed the objective value theory. Condillac was of the opinion that things are produced based on human wants and that this causal relationship is of vital importance in economic phenomena.

After the above quotation, Roscher emphasizes that '*Ricardo*'s doctrine is more tenable than appears at first blush', adding that '*Ricardo* does justice to value in use even *en passant*' (Roscher, 1882, 329). Now Roscher's position with regard to the controversies over value theory becomes clear. After scrutinizing both objective and subjective value theory, he concludes that Ricardo's argument is not entirely wrong. Thus, Roscher's standing point is typically Marshallian: the demand side of the economic phenomena is important, but the supply side should not be underestimated. Both sides contribute to the making of prices.

4.6 ROSCHER ON PRODUCTIVE LABOUR

Anyone who has even a passing interest in the history of economic thought knows well that the concept of productive labour is a crucial aspect of thought in the English Classical School, from the time of Adam Smith. In Book Two of his seminal work Smith extended the concept by emphasizing that manufacturing, and not only agriculture, should be considered productive. This is in contrast with physiocratic economists who believe that only the agricultural sector is truly productive. As is often said, Smith's concept is not always clear-cut, which has led to extensive debate. In this section, I hope to examine and identify Roscher's position in the history of economic thought, especially in terms of the concept of productive labour, which was a notoriously contentious issue in Britain, France, Germany and elsewhere for many years. Roscher's contribution to this debate is partly revealed in the *Grundlagen*.

For Roscher, the Smithian concept is not acceptable. He explained why in the following quotation, which is based upon the arguments of Garnier, a French translator of the *Wealth of Nations*; and Friedrich List, a famous critic of Smithian economics in general:

> Even Adam Smith called services – in the narrower sense of the term . . . that is, the grave and important ones of the statesman, clergyman, and physician, as well as the 'frivolous' ones of the opera singer, ballet-dancer, and buffoon, unproductive. The labour of none of these can be fixed or incorporated in any particular object. But how strange it is that the labour of a violin-maker is called productive, while that of the violin-player is called unproductive; although the product of the former has no other object than to be played on by the latter? (Garnier.) Is it not strange that the hog-raiser should be called productive, and the educator of man unproductive (List). (Roscher, 1882, 173–4)

Thus is formed a classical argument against the Smithian concept. The violin itself can be used many times without decreasing its value, while the violin music is consumed in a second, or at most in hours in which the music can be listened. The violinist offers a service, which can be deemed productive, at least according to Roscher's terminology.

Roscher then continues by explicating his notion of productive labour, which we can see from his own words, as follows:

> Every department of business for whose output has a rational demand, and who is remunerated in proportion to their demand, and who are remunerated in proportion to their deserts, has laboured productively. Actions are unproductive only when no one needs what has been brought forth, or when no one will pay for it; but in this case, what is true of the writer without readers – that he is unproductive – and of the singer without hearers, is equally true of the peasant whose corn rots in his granary, because he can find no sale for it. (Roscher, 1882, 178)

Thus, it seems clear that Roscher's notion is relatively simple: If there is final demand for the product, then the labour is said to be productive. It is not, if the product will suffer from a lack of demand. Hence, the concept is completely reduced to the final demand for the product. One cannot say that a certain type of labour is productive; instead, everything depends on the market, on the preference of each demander as well as the on individual budget constraints. To clarify then, this is a definition of productive labour from a social point of view. Regardless of whether the reader likes this definition or not, Roscher adds the following new element to the story discussed above:

> There is a great number of employments which are very remunerative to private individuals, but which are entirely unproductive, and even injurious, so far as mankind is concerned . . . Here belong, besides formal crimes against property, games of chance, usurious speculations . . . and measures taken to entice customers away from other competitors. Again, scientific experiments, means of communication etc., may be entirely unproductive in the individual economy of the undertaker, and yet be of more profit to mankind in general, than they have cost the former. (Roscher, 1882, 179–80)

This is indeed an about-turn. In the previous quotation Roscher makes clear that the productiveness of labour depends on the final demand, independently of whether the demand can be justified or not. Here, Roscher appears at odds with his own definition. According to the former definition, 'usurious speculations' must be accepted, since it allows the player to benefit from a large amount of money. However, in the new definition this is highly problematic from a social and moral point of view. Indeed, it should simply be rejected. In any case, these two definitions are not compatible with each other. Furthermore, it can be safely said that the new definition is, at least to a certain extent, a recapitulation of Roscher's normative economics, as we have already seen in section 4.5.

4.7 CONCLUDING REMARKS: GERMAN ECONOMIC DISCOURSE AND THE ENGLISH CLASSICAL SCHOOL

I have attempted to provide a succinct account of German economic discourse, concentrating on two great figures of the nineteenth century in Germany: Rau and Roscher. In this final section, an attempt is made to clarify the characteristics of German economics with special attention given to the relationship with the English Classical School.

Understanding the meanings of the concepts of value and the definition of goods that we have examined in the previous sections is crucial if we are to understand properly the forthcoming revolution of economics that occurred in the 1870s. In order to identify the importance of these concepts for a new generation of economists, I now turn to Carl Menger, one of the three leaders of the Marginal Revolution, and the founder of the Austrian School of Economics.

Menger's maximization problem can be reformulated as follows:[11]

$$\text{Max } U_1(x_1) + U_2(x_2) + \cdots + U_n(x_n)$$
$$\text{s.t.}$$
$$x_1 + x_2 + \cdots + x_n =$$

x_1, x_2, . . . and x_n are various ways to use a certain commodity x. The summation of the various uses must be equal to the total amount of the commodity, shown by ω. The consumer maximizes his utility function represented by the first equation. By using a simple utility function (which was presumably used by Menger himself), each part of the function can be interpreted as in terms of the utility of the way in which the commodity is used.

I believe it is worth mentioning that the economic agent of this model can be interpreted in various ways: the individual in the literal sense, the family or household, Robinson Crusoe (with or without Man Friday), a bureaucrat attempting to realize the concept of the welfare state, the central planning board of a socialist country, or even a merciful king. These are all possible interpretations of the above model.

One of the basic characteristics of German economics that is represented in this model is that economics is fundamentally a problem of resource allocation, and that this mechanism of resource allocation can function without relying upon prices. While price is a basic concept of the English Classical School, it is often unreliable in certain economic situations, as is illustrated by Rau's criticism. Rau was quite certain that the wealth of a country cannot be fully understood solely by using price indexes. The essential aspect for any proper evaluation of wealth is the value in use of each commodity, which is sometimes different from the exchangeable value.

While it might be said that the Robinson Crusoe way of thinking is typical in German economics, instead, it seems clear that this characterization has significant limitations. In the following quotation I turn to John Stuart Mill, who believed that there were many other options that could be examined before introducing the exchange model in economics:

> It is true that in the preceding Books we have not escaped the necessity of anticipating some small portion of the theory of Value, especially as to the value of labour and of land. It is nevertheless evident, that of the two great departments of

> Political Economy, the production of wealth and its distribution, the consideration of Value has to do with the latter alone; and with that, only so far as competition, and not usage or custom, is the distributing agency. The conditions and laws of Production would be the same as they are. The conditions and laws of society did not depend on Exchange, or did not admit it. (John Stuart Mill, 1965, 455)

Mill argues that the problem of production can be analysed without relying on the concept of value, that is, exchangeable value. Economics is not equivalent to an exchange theory that is based on prices; indeed, the latter is only a part of economics. Even distribution does not necessarily mean that the exchange model explicitly incorporates prices, since it is often the case that it can be reduced to the existence of custom. This opinion is in direct contradiction to those proposed by R. Whately and J.R. McCulloch, for whom the exchange model plays a pivotal role in economics; nonetheless, this contrary position would certainly have been acceptable for those German scholars who emphasized the importance of the Robinson Crusoe model, such as Roscher.[12]

Overall, British economic thought continued to be an important source for German economists. However, this does not mean that every aspect of the former was accepted, nor that German economists added nothing to the British orthodoxy. As my analysis of Roscherian economics shows, a relatively new method became a normative way of doing economics. Roscher did begin with the concept of productive labour in the English Classical School, but he added a completely new element to it. His claim is that there are products enjoying a large market, whose consumption, however, cannot be justified from a social point of view. This is indeed a new use of the old concept, which is difficult to find in the English orthodoxy at that time. As such, it shows a fascinating phase of the history German economics in the nineteenth century. It certainly is an aspect of what Birger Priddat called the *andere Ökonomie*.[13]

NOTES

1. In this chapter, all quotations from Rau come from the second edition of his works, published in 1833. All English translations are mine. A reprint of the first edition is available as Rau (1826 [1997]). Quotations from Roscher are from Lalor's English translation, based upon the 13th German edition, published in 1877. As has often been said, translation is indeed a difficult and challenging task. It is possible that misunderstandings may emerge during the process of translation. However, I believe that Lalor's translation is, at the very least, true to the basic messages of Roscher's original. Hence, I predominantly use Lalor's translations in my chapter.
2. Ikeda (1995a, 1997), Streissler (1990) and Yagi (1993) examined the formation of Menger's 1871 book (Menger, 1871 [1968]) using unpublished materials housed at Duke University, thus paving the way to further historical analyses of the *Grundsätze*.

3. For a survey of the structure of nineteenth-century economics textbooks see Schwartz (1972 [1968], 18–21) and Mawatari (1997).
4. This letter is well known among Mill scholars. See, for instance, Hollander (1985, 177), and Mawatari (1997, 102).
5. See Mawatari (1997, 100–103). Mawatari denies Rau's influence on Mill concerning the organization of the various parts of economics. Nevertheless, Mill was one of the few scholars in the English-speaking area during the first half of the nineteenth century who really read and understood Rau's economics. More detailed investigation of the relationship between the two will be an interesting task for the future.
6. The title of Streissler's paper (Streissler, 1994), is enough to indicate his intentions.
7. For Marx's critique of Roscher, see Ikeda (2001, 40–41). As I wrote there, this is by no means an inaccurate view.
8. On Rau's economics in general, see Priddat (1997), Rosner (1997) and Schefold (1997). Tribe (1988) deals with Rau in chapter 9 of his book. See also Streissler (1997), in which Rau plays an important role in the development of German economics. As for Rau's relationship with the English Classical School, I agree with the following characterization of Schefold: 'Trotz dieser vielfachen subjektivistischen Elemente enspringt die Rausche Preistheorie offensichtlich einem klassischen Rahmen, der erkennbar bleibt' (Schefold, 1997, XIV).
9. This and the following sections draw heavily on Ikeda (1995b). Those interested in Roscherian economics in general should consult the papers in the special volume of the *Journal of Economic Studies*, **22** (3–5), edited by Jürgen Backhaus (1995). For a normative aspect of Roscherian economics, see especially Priddat (1995) and Priddat (1997), upon which my analysis here draws heavily. Peukert examines the concept of productive labour in Roscher's *Grundriss zu Vorlesungen über die Staatswirthschaft* (see Peukert, 1998, 41).
10. See Streissler's remark on this footnote, upon which my analysis here is based. See Streissler (1994, 59–60).
11. This is a standard interpretation of Menger's table from the standpoint of neoclassical economics. See for instance Stigler (1950 [1965]).
12. I outline here an exception which cannot be totally ignored. Ricardo explicitly relied upon the exchange model in dealing with international trade.
13. See Priddat's remark: 'Die Frage, wie man die deutsche Nationalökonomie des 19. Jahrhunderts zu reinterpretieren habe, entscheidet sich an der Frage, ob man die sittliche Prädisposition für ein Element der ökonomischen Konzeption ansieht oder als externen Parameter exmatrikuliert. Abstrahiert man in der Theoriegeschichte von der sittlichen Prädisposition, erhält man Fragmente ökonomischer Theorieentwicklung, die – im Schatten der aufziehenden neuen englischen (und "österreichischen") Ökonomie des 19. Jahrhunderts – als längst verblaßt erscheinen. Nimmt man aber die sittliche Pädisposition der deutschen Nationalökonomie als Konstituante ihrer theoretischen Konzeption, erhält man den Rahmen einer *anderen Ökonomie*' (Priddat, 1997, S. 278). My chapter is a modest attempt to consider what the German economists imported from the British orthodoxy of the time, including objective value theory, without denying the existence of an *andere Ökonomie*.

REFERENCES

Backhaus, J. (1995), *Wilhelm Roscher and the 'Historical Method'* special volume of *Journal of Economic Studies*, **22** (3–5).

Hollander, S. (1985), *The Economics of John Stuart Mill*, Vol. 1, *Theory and Method*, Oxford: Basil Blackwell.

Ikeda, Y. (1995a), 'Carl Menger in the 1860s: Menger on Roscher's Grundlagen',

in G. Meijer (ed.), *New Perspectives on Austrian Economics*, London: Routledge, pp. 25–39.
Ikeda, Y. (1995b), 'Roscher's *Grundlagen* in the history of economic thought', *Journal of Economic Studies*, **22** (3–5), 209–20.
Ikeda, Y. (1997), *Die Entstehungsgeschichte der Grundsätze Carl Mengers*, St Katharinen: Scripta Mercaturae Verlag.
Ikeda, Y. (2001), 'A lecture notebook of Wilhelm Roscher with special reference to his published works', in Y. Shionoya (ed.), *The German Historical School: The Historical and Ethical Approach to Economics*, London: Routledge, pp. 35–53.
Mawatari, S. (1997), *Economics of J.S. Mill*, Tokyo: Ocha-no-Mizu-Shobo (in Japanese).
Menger, C. (1871), *Grundsätze der Volkswirthschaftslehre*, reprinted in F. Hayek (ed.) (1968), *Gesammelte Werke*, 2nd edn, Vol. 1, Tübingen: J.C.B. Mohr.
Mill, J. (1821), *Elements of Political Economy*, London: Baldwin, Cradock & Joy.
Mill, J.S. (1965), *Principles of Political Economy with Some of Their Applications to Social Philosophy, Collected Works of John Stuart Mill*, Vol. 3. Toronto: University of Toronto Press.
Mill, J.S. (1972), *The Later Letters of John Stuart Mill, 1849–1873, Collected Works of John Stuart Mill*, Vol. 14, Toronto: University of Toronto Press.
Peukert, H. (1998), *Das Handlungsparadigma in der Nationalökonomie*, Marburg: Metropolis Verlag.
Priddat, B. (1995), *Die andere Ökonomie*, Marburg: Metropolis Verlag.
Priddat, B. (1997), 'Der "Gattungswerth" oder die Moral der subjektiven Wertlehre in der deutschen Nationalökonomie. K.H. Rau, F.B.W. von Hermann, B. Hildebrand, G.W.F. Hegel und A. Wagner', in B. Priddat (ed.), *Wert, Meinung, Bedeutung*, Marburg: Metropolis-Verlag, pp. 241–85.
Rau, K.H. (1826), *Grundsätze der Volkswirtschaftlehre,* 1st edition (reprinted in B. Schefold (ed.) (1997), *Lehrbuch der politischen Oekonomie*, Band I, *Die Volkswirthschaftslehre*, Hildesheim: Olms-Weidmann.
Rau, K.H. (1828), *Grundsätze der Volkswirtschaftspflege*, reprinted in B. Schefold (ed.) (1997), *Lehrbuch der politischen Oekonomie*, Band 2, Hildesheim: Olms-Weidmann.
Rau, K.H. (1833), *Grundsätze der Volkswirtschaftlehre*, 2nd edn, Heidelberg: Universitätsbuchhandlung von F. Winter.
Rau, K.H. (1837), Grundsätze der Finanzwissenschaft, reprinted in B. Schefold (ed.) (1997), *Lehrbuch der politischen Oekonomie*, Band 3, Abt. 1, 2, Hildesheim: Olms-Weidmann.
Roscher, W. (1854), *Grundlagen der Nationaloekonomie, System der Volkswirthschaft*, Band 1, Stuttgart: J.G. Cotta'scher Verlag.
Roscher, W. (1859), *Die Nationaloekonmik des Ackerbaues, System der Volkswirthschaft*, Band 2, Stuttgart: J.G. Cotta'scher Verlag.
Roscher, W. (1881), *Nationalökonomik des Handels und Gewerbfleisses, System der Volkswirthschaft*, Bd. 3, Stuttgart: J.G. Cotta.
Roscher, W. (1882), *Principles of Political Economy*, Vol. 1, J. Lalor (trans.), Chicago, IL: Callaghan & Company.
Roscher, W. (1886), *System der Finanzwissenschaft, System der Volkswirthschaft*, Bd. 4, Stuttgart: J.G. Cotta.
Roscher, W. (1894), *System der Armenpflege, System der Volkswirthschaft*, Bd. 5, Stuttgart: J.G. Cotta.
Rosner, P. (1997), 'Reichtum und Wohlfart. Über einige Schwierigkeiten früher

deutschen Ökonoomie mit theoretischen Grundbegriffen', in B. Priddat (ed.), *Wert, Meinung, Bedeutung*, Marburg: Metropolis-Verlag, pp. 191–216.
Schefold, B. (1997), *Einleitung in Lehrbuch der politischen Oekonomie*, Band I, *Die Volkswirthschaftslehre*, Hildesheim: Olms-Weidmann.
Schwartz, P. (1972 [1968]), *The New Political Economy of J.S. Mill*, London: London School of Economics and Political Science.
Stigler, G. (1950), 'The development of utility theory', *Journal of Political Economy*, **58** (4–5), 307–27, 373–96; (1965) in, reprinted *Essays in the History of Economics*, Chicago, IL: University of Chicago Press, pp. 66–155.
Streissler, E. (1990), 'The influence of German economics on the work of Menger and Marshall', in B. Caldwell (ed.), *Carl Menger and His Legacy in Economics*, Durham, NC: Duke University Press, pp. 31–68.
Streissler, E. (1994), 'Wilhelm Roscher als führender Wirtschaftstheoretiker', in *Kommetarband zur Faksimilie-Ausgabe der 1861 erschienenen Erstausgabe von Wilhelm Roscher Ansichte der Volkswirtschaft aus dem geschichtlichen Standpunkte*, ed. B. Schefold, Düsseldorf: Verlag Wirtschaft und Finanzen, pp. 37–121.
Streissler, E. (1997), 'Carl Menger, der deutsche Nationalökonom', in B. Priddat (ed.), *Wert, Meinung, Bedeutung*, Marburg: Metropolis-Verlag, pp. 33–88.
Tribe, K. (1988), *Governing Economy: The Reformation of German Economic Discourse 1750–1840*, Cambridge: Cambridge University Press.
Yagi, K. (1993), 'Carl Menger's Grundsätze in the making', *History of Political Economy*, **25** (4), 697–724.

5. German influences in the making of American economics, 1885–1935

Bradley W. Bateman

5.1 INTRODUCTION

At the end of the American Civil War, before graduate education was available in the United States, Americans seeking a doctorate had to travel to Europe for their studies. Although the first American research university, Johns Hopkins, was founded in 1876, it would be another decade before the doctorate started to be regularly granted at American universities, and then only in small numbers.[1] Thus, the establishment of graduate education and the research university in America depended on the flow of individuals trained in Europe. Far and away the largest number of these individuals were trained in Germany.[2]

Economics was one of the disciplines that was affected deeply by the training of its graduate students in Germany. Economics had been a part of antebellum baccalaureate education in the United States, but only in a limited and narrow sense. During this time, colleges and universities in the United States had fixed curricula established on a classical model: Greek, Latin, mathematics and rhetoric. Although a few colleges offered a one-semester course in political economy, the topic was usually a part of the capstone course required of all seniors and taught by the college's president.[3] Thus, while the texts of both Say and Bastiat were popular in antebellum American colleges (in translation), the first generation of American textbook authors included college presidents and trustees who fashioned their texts explicitly for the purpose of teaching a capstone course to college seniors. Francis Wayland (president, Brown), Alonzo Potter (trustee, Penn), and Henry Vethake (trustee, Penn) all wrote economics texts that were widely used for teaching college economics. But while these three had differences in their analytical approaches to economics, they each offered a strong argument that the emerging capitalist economy of the Untied States represented the blessings of a benevolent God.[4]

This overtly religious message was a central theme of the economics taught in antebellum American colleges. Although there were rudimentary economic analyses on offer, usually drawn from European sources, the most important purpose of the economics that was taught was that it bolstered republicanism, capitalism and Christianity.[5]

By mid-century, American academic economics was almost entirely devoted to laissez-faire and the virtues of unregulated markets.[6] This was especially true as regards the rights of working men; the labour contract was seen as sacrosanct and this dictated that both organized labour and striking were anathema.

Perhaps more than anything else, after the Civil War the stance of the younger generation of German-trained economists on the rights and responsibilities of labour marked the place where they deviated from their older colleagues. On the one hand, many of the younger, German-trained economists had themselves faced daunting employment prospects upon their return from abroad, and some of them, like Richard T. Ely, had experienced unemployment in their own families during the decades following the Civil War. On the other hand, these young men had been influenced by their study in Germany, especially the work of the Verein für Socialpolitik, and they returned home with a belief that the government could make a difference in helping the economy to perform more equitably, and that labourers did not always fare well under capitalist market competition.

While in Germany, the young American doctoral candidates had learned the historical perspective on economics, and they therefore sought to explain the rapid industrialization that they observed upon their return in terms of the historical forces that had formed the contemporary situation. They did not accept the argument that all industrial economies operated according to the same natural laws that necessitated the acceptance of any and all market outcomes. Rather, they questioned the outcomes and asked questions about whether it was possible through culture, society and politics to obtain better outcomes.

This political difference between the older advocates of laissez-faire and the younger, German-trained economists is reasonably well known and is reinforced by many incidents in the history of late nineteenth-century American economics. Some of the more colourful incidents involve academic 'trials' through which several younger economists were put because of their support for labour unions and socialism. Perhaps the most well known of these involved Richard T. Ely, who was accused in the 1890s of entertaining a labour organizer in his home and of advocating socialism in his classroom.

But the most fundamental story about the clash between the older laissez-faire economists and the younger, German-trained economists is the story of the founding of the American Economic Association (AEA) in 1885.[7] This story points to many of the influences that the younger economists brought home with them from Germany. In the first instance, the organization of the AEA happened in Saratoga Springs, New York, at the second annual meeting of the American Historical Association; because so many of the young economists had been trained in Germany and advocated the importance of an historical approach to studying the economy, it seemed natural to meet together with the newly organized academic historians. Even more important than the connection with the historians, however, is the explicit political dimension in the founding of the AEA. The founders included in their charter a statement to the effect that the Association supported the principle that the state could play a positive role in the economy, a position that was anathema to the advocates of laissez-faire.

Because this statement so clearly marked the difference between the younger and older American economists, it also stood in the way of many of the other goals of the Association's founders. Among the founders' goals was to become the primary organization of American economists and so to help younger economists to establish their professional credentials and more easily find employment in academia. But while many of the older, laissez-faire economists were willing to join in forming a professional organization, they were opposed to the AEA's charter stating anything about a positive role for the state in the functioning of the economy. And so after a few years the statement was dropped; and the AEA quickly became the accepted professional organization for American economists.[8] The abandonment of the statement regarding the potential for a positive role for the state led to some anxiety among the members of the Association, however, as it was feared that Richard T. Ely, who had moved from Johns Hopkins to Wisconsin in the interim, would lead the younger economists out of the Association.

5.2 REACHING A DÉTENTE

But despite the worries that Ely would form a new rival organization to the AEA, the 1890s were actually marked less by turmoil than by calm. Ely's decision not to abandon the AEA may have been motivated in part by his own needs at Wisconsin, where following his academic trial, the president of the university, Charles Kendall Adams, encouraged Ely to keep a lower profile and work on building his programme; and there can be no doubt that the pressures that had led to the abandonment of the statement regarding the role of the state, such as the desire of young economists to find regular, full-time employment, were still in play and reduced the chances of a splinter movement.

The relative calm that came to prevail in the AEA during the 1890s suggests that our traditional picture of American economics at the end of the nineteenth century as a profession riven by methodological dispute is a distorted image, created by focusing on the political differences that existed between the older advocates of laissez-faire and the younger economists who had been trained in Germany. The most well-known distortion in the traditional interpretations of this period is the argument that it is best characterized by a *Methodenstreit* (war of methods) between younger and older economists, with the younger economists lined up as advocates of a historical method and the older economists as advocates of deductive, a priori theorizing. This American *Methodenstreit* is thought to reflect the one that occurred in Europe between the Younger German Historical School and the Austrian School in the late nineteenth century.[9]

This picture misrepresents the American scene at the end of the nineteenth century in several ways. As Yuval Yonay (1998) has pointed out, one of the most obvious distortions in the picture is that the leading American marginalist at this time, John Bates Clark, was a young, German-trained economist who had helped to found the AEA. Like Richard T. Ely and E.R.A. Seligman, Clark had studied at the University of Heidelberg under Professor Karl Knies. While it is true that Clark's politics became more moderate in the 1890s, he remained liberal; but more to the point, the leading lights among the laissez-faire school at the end of the nineteenth century were not themselves marginalists.[10] As Yonay (1998, 42) says: 'The profession of economics (in America) at the end of the 1880s can be divided into two main camps: the 'old school' of the conservative classical economists, and the 'new school' who supported both historical methods and marginal analysis, and who, in addition, favored a more active role of the state in the economy.' The primary mistake in the traditional picture of two warring camps of economists in late nineteenth-century economics, as Yonay points out, is that it was conceived many decades later after the success of modern Neoclassical economics and those who conceived it were conflating the interwar skirmishes (in the 1920s and 1930s) between Neoclassicism and Institutionalism with the earlier period in American economics.

John Bates Clark is not the only person in the traditional story who is depicted incorrectly. A careful reading of Clark's work, both his earlier *Philosophy of Wealth* (1886) and his later, more well-known *Distribution of Wealth* (1899), in which he first presented his marginalist theories regarding the distribution of income to factors of production, shows that Clark discusses the importance of institutions in understanding (and reforming) the economy in both books.

Like Clark, Ely also mixed his methods. Despite his traditional place as a leader of the historicist faction within American economics, the first edition of Ely's *Outline of Economics* (1893), which in subsequent editions was to become the best-selling economics text in the first three decades of the twentieth century, included a careful explanation of marginal utility theory. When Ely brought in three younger co-authors for the 1908 edition of the book to help him bring it up to date in theory, he kept the revision of the marginal utility chapters for himself. Likewise, E.R.A. Seligman incorporated both historical analysis and marginalist insights into his work on taxation and economic history.

Thus, by the middle of the 1890s, American economists in the academy had actually arrived at a kind of rapprochement, or détente. Although there were serious differences about the role of the government in the economy, as well as about the rights of labour to strike and organize, it was in this decade that professional status ceased to be defined solely by one's stand on these two issues. American politics in this decade were decidedly conservative, and the more liberal economists, such as Ely and Seligman, did not openly challenge this status quo in the same way that some had in the 1880s. The difference in the outcome of Ely's troubles at Johns Hopkins and at Wisconsin is instructive. When his senior colleague at Johns Hopkins, Simon Newcomb, attacked Ely in the *Nation* in 1884, this began a long process which eventually culminated in Ely leaving Johns Hopkins. His trial in Wisconsin, however, resulted in a credo on academic freedom at the university which is still central to its self-identity.

The most important element of the détente was at the national level, within the economics profession. As the decade of the 1890s progressed, people began in earnest to pursue their studies from eclectic points of view; for instance, Seligman's studies in taxation. Many economists would continue to work within a single framework, but the standard became not so much what one's politics were or which theoretical framework one worked within, but how well one could advance knowledge within the framework that was chosen. Thus, Henry Carter Adams, who received the first doctorate in economics from Johns Hopkins, would increasingly hone his skills as an inductive economist during the 1890s; while Frank Taussig, the defender of the Classical approach to laissez-faire at Harvard, would at the same time hone his skills as a Classical theorist. There was room for each of them in American academic economics by the mid-1890s.[11]

5.3 RE-FOCUSING THE GERMAN INFLUENCE ON LATE NINETEENTH-CENTURY AMERICAN ECONOMICS

In his account of this period in American economics, Yonay attributes the prevailing eclecticism to the influence of Alfred Marshall. Marshall's

Principles of Economics (1890 [1910]) was published in 1890 and Yonay is correct to point both to Marshall's eclectic approach to economics and to his iconic status in American economics at the end of the nineteenth century. Marshall speaks eloquently in the *Principles* of the importance to economics of inductive reasoning and historical study, despite the fact that the book is the first great Neoclassical synthesis and the book that more than any at the time conceived of marginal analysis as 'an engine of inquiry'; and the *Principles* did have a status in the United States in the 1890s as representing the frontier of economic analysis.

But it would be a mistake to credit Marshall with having created the eclecticism in American economics in the last decade of the nineteenth century. Marshall was eclectic and that made his work easily adoptable by Americans who were themselves already eclectic in their approaches to economics. But it was not the eclecticism alone that made Marshall's *Principles* attractive to *fin de siècle* Americans; rather, as Backhouse et al. (2011) have argued, Marshall was attractive to both camps of American economists because of his innovative uses of marginalist theory.

The older school of laissez-faire economists, who adhered to Classical English theory, had known for some time that they needed to find a new theoretical approach to reinvigorate American economics. On the occasion of the centennial of the United States in 1876, Charles F. Dunbar of Harvard had lamented the fact that American economics was not theoretically innovative.[12] Ricardian economics had been theoretically normative for many American economists since the 1820s, when the first American texts in economics were written; but land had never been scarce in the United States and so the American adaptations of Ricardian theory had never been very compelling. Thus, by the end of the century, and in the midst of a rapidly accelerating process of industrialization, marginalism offered the old laissez-faire school the possibility for the theoretical innovation they had been looking for (although none of them had embraced it themselves by 1890).[13] Thus, while many of them were uncertain about the details of emerging marginalism, Marshall made it seem palatable because he deliberately connected his own work to the Classical school, arguing that his work was a natural evolution from it, not a departure.[14]

At the same time, the young German-trained economists found in Marshall something very familiar when they encountered his marginalism. Although we have until recently imagined that these young Americans brought back a commitment to historicism, as against economic 'theory', we now know that they brought home with them both historicism and marginal analysis. All the leading Americans trained in Germany learned the importance of historical analysis in understanding contemporary economics, and with it a respect for the discipline of inductive work;

but those who studied in Germany in the 1860s and 1870s also learned about marginal utility analysis, as German economics had been suffused with marginal utility analysis for several decades by then.[15] Eric Streissler (1990) and John Chipman (2005) have been instrumental in helping us to understand more fully the history of marginal utility theorizing in mid-nineteenth-century German economics.

For several of the leading figures in late nineteenth-century American economics, this link came through their study in Heidelberg with Karl Knies. Although Knies has been best known in the English-speaking world for his work on money and credit (Knies, 1873, 1874, 1879), he was also the author in 1855 of one of the seminal pieces in the evolution of German thinking on marginal utility theory, the essay 'Die Nationalöekonomische Lehre vom Werth'.[16] In this essay, Knies seeks to link the marginal utility of goods to their various national contexts; it is a somewhat rambling work that offers a careful explanation of marginal utility as illustrated by the characteristics of goods as they are found to be valuable in different (national) situations. As might befit a good historical economist, Knies argues by analogy, compiling his argument by examining seemingly endless cases in which the additional consumption of simple goods yields increasingly less and less additional value as more of the goods are consumed.[17] It is a 'juridical' style of argument, based not on an a priori theory of how humans mean to satisfy their wants, but rather trying to build a theory of their actual behaviour from many case studies. Knies certainly understood the broad outlines of marginal utility theory from the work of the three other most prominent members of the Older German Historical School, Karl Rau (1847), Bruno Hildebrand (1848) and Wilhelm Roscher (1854). But his own treatment contains no mathematical formulations and is prefaced by no clear statement of the principles of marginal utility; rather he argues by analogy and case study to attempt an explanation of what a theory of value would look like within the historical (national) theory of economics.

Knies's sometimes ambiguous treatment was nonetheless fecund for the students in his Heidelberg seminar. Several of them recognized the nascent possibilities in his work and used it to develop some of the earliest and most influential work in marginalism. Eugen von Böhm-Bawerk and Friedrich von Wieser were students in the seminar; both returned to Austria and played important roles in the early Austrian school. John Bates Clark was a student in the seminar and returned to the United States to become the first great American marginalist. Richard T. Ely was a student in the seminar and became the first Amercian textbook author to include a chapter on marginal utility theory. In addition to those who participated in Knies's seminar at Heidelberg, Carl Menger engaged Knies's essay extensively in his early work.

Thus, it should be no surprise that the younger, German trained economists also found Marshall's work amenable to their purposes. Like the older advocates of laissez-faire, they saw in Marshall's work the synthesis of knowledge being created at what they took to be the frontier of economics. But they did not need Marshall to understand that marginal analysis did not have to be anathema to a good historical economist; many of them had learned that insight sitting in Karl Knies's seminar in Heidelberg and in reading the work of the Older German Historicists.

5.4 UNDERSTANDING INSTITUTIONALISM THROUGH A DIFFERENT LENS

If it is necessary to come to a new understanding of the role that German economics played in late nineteenth-century American economics, and to give up our older idea of a *Methodenstreit* between the German-trained Americans and the older Classically-oriented American economists who advocated laissez-faire, then American economics in the early decades of the twentieth century will also have to be reinterpreted. For like the 1890s, the first two decades of the twentieth century were a period of détente in which historical and marginalist economics were held in a creative tension. Many intellectual historians of this period have argued that Neoclassicism became triumphant in the early decades of the twentieth century (or even in the 1890s), but this interpretation involves two fundamental mistakes: first, it equates early marginalist thinking with Neoclassicism; and second, it conflates the prominence of Neoclassicism after the Second World War with the rise of marginalism at the end of the nineteenth century. However, as we have already seen, the eclectic use of marginalism by Americans in the late nineteenth and early twentieth centuries was not the same thing as Neoclassicism, nor was marginalism understood at the time as triumphant over all other forms of economic theorizing.[18]

Not until after the First World War did a real fissure appear in American economics on purely methodological grounds; there had been strong political differences between the older advocates of laissez-faire and the younger German-trained economists in the late nineteenth century, but their methodological differences had been largely mitigated in the détente of the 1890s. The fissure after the First World War was however more than a simple *Methodenstreit*. Just as mid-nineteenth century American economics had been suffused with moral arguments and Christian theology, so too was the American economics of the early twentieth century.[19] Following the political conservatism of the 1890s, American politics after the turn of the century had become progressive, and this progressivism was initially informed by a form of liberal Protestantism now termed the Social Gospel. Both Ely and J.B. Clark had written on Christian socialism after their return from Germany, and their work helped to form the Christian response to industrial capitalism by American Protestants at the end of the nineteenth century. Ultimately, however, the moral underpinnings of Christian progressivism were undercut by the repeated failure of real moral reform to take root during the first two decades of the twentieth century.

The ultimate break with the message of moral uplift came with the conclusion of the First World War. On the one hand, the awful reality of the war directly challenged the ideas of moral improvement and social 'progress' that many Protestant Americans had held before the war. On the other hand, many Protestant ministers had used their pulpits at the beginning of the war to promote America's entry into the war, and there was a direct and powerful revulsion against this abuse of the churches as a means to promote war. This revulsion manifested itself in popular culture as well as in a turn against reforming Christians, against progressivism, and against the social sciences that were closely associated with Christian progressivism: economics, sociology and political science. Immediately following the war, there was what Dorothy Ross has termed a turn to 'scientism' across all of these disciplines, as social scientists tried to distance themselves from the moral uplift and Christian progressivism that had defined them for much of the previous 30 years.[20]

This moment, then, marks the beginning of what would eventually become America's *Methodenstreit*. On the one hand, those marginalists who had never particularly embraced the moral uplift of the Social Gospel began to hone a hard-nosed body of analytical work. In figures such as Irving Fisher to Frank Knight, American economics began to evolve a distinctively Neoclassical school of thought. On the other hand, economists who rejected marginalist psychology and utilitarian ethics, embraced behaviouralist psychology and large-scale data collection and formed the emerging school of Institutionalist economics. Politics did not completely define this battle, as there were interventionists on both sides of this methodological divide; although those who forged the emerging neoclassicism, such as Knight, were largely laissez-faire in their economics, while those who formed Institutionalism were largely interventionists. The real battle, however, would eventually revolve around the question of how best to 'do' science. Were the a priori constructs of Neoclassicism sufficient grounds for a scientific economics, or did economics need a different psychological basis and more inductive work before it could achieve status as a science? The stakes in the battle ended up being quite high, as the resources available from research universities and philanthropic foundations would become the spoils for the winner.

Although we know the outcome of this battle, it was not clear to the participants who the winner(s) would be.[21] From the moment of the first use of the term 'Institutionalism' (in 1918), until the beginning of the Second World War, both Neoclassicists and Institutionalists thrived. Some leading institutions, such as Columbia and Wisconsin, remained bastions of Institutional thought until after the Second World War; Neoclassicism became well ensconced at other institutions, such as Chicago and Harvard.

During the decade of the 1920s, Neoclassicism and Institutionalism were competing paradigms, but initially there was not a pitched *Methodenstreit* between them. Not until the early 1930s, when Frank Knight attacked Sumner Schlicter's new Institutionalist textbook in his highly visible review in the *Journal of Political Economy* (1932) did the competition become aggressive and pointed. Thus, initially, more than one type of economic theorizing was respected. After Knight's attack, however, the battle became noticeably more pitched.[22]

Some have tried to depict the rise of Institutionalism as the ultimate expression of the inductive, historical method brought home by the young economists who had trained in Germany during the nineteenth century.[23] However, it is difficult to justify such an interpretation on the evidence. Of all the Americans who had received their doctorate in economics in Germany, the most vocal proponent of the historical methodology had probably been Richard T. Ely. His cry during the last two decades of the nineteenth century had been, 'Look and See!' which was meant to have a double meaning. On the one hand, he meant that if economists would look up from their abstract theorizing (even without the benefit of any historical perspective), they would see that markets did not always deliver good outcomes for the poor and unemployed. On the other hand, he meant it as a call for more empirical work.

But Ely was not among the Institutionalists. Of his students, the most well known to become an Institutionalist was John R. Commons, but Commons jumped on the Institutionalist bandwagon several years after the movement was started. And one of the best of the emerging new Neoclassicists was one of Ely's former graduate students at Wisconsin, Allyn Young, who was also one of Ely's co-authors in the later editions of his *Outlines of Economics* (1908). Frank Knight had, in turn, been Allyn Young's graduate student at Cornell.

Thus, it is difficult to find a strong, direct connection between those who had been trained in Germany and the Institutionalists. There was certainly a similarity in the interest in inductive work of each of these groups, and the Institutionalists' emphasis on data collection fit into this picture nicely. But it would be a mistake to interpret this similarity as deriving from a direct intellectual inheritance.[24] To the contrary, the Institutionalism of Walton Hamilton and Wesley Clair Michell represented a new movement that wanted to create a new empirically based economics that was completely secular.[25] The Institutionalists' desire to secularize economics made the older German-trained economists who had formed the early social science basis for Progressivism unlikely allies, since the older German trained economists had, almost to a person, embraced religious belief and/or religious institutions in their work.

The one possible legacy of the German-trained economists that we can imagine in the period after Institutionalism was founded might have occurred in the first ten or 12 years after Institutionalism was first introduced in 1918. During much of the 1920s, while emerging Neoclassicism and Institutionalism coexisted, there was a second détente in American economics which was not unlike the one that had formed in the 1890s. Although the emerging Neoclassicists and Institutionalists did not agree about how to do economics, they did speak with each other and read each other's work seriously in the early years. Ultimately, however, there is no evidence that this initial peaceful coexistence was a deliberate effort at imitating the kind of eclecticism that had existed in the Older German Historical School and which was replicated by many of its American students after they returned home.

What seems more likely is that the cultural influence of American Protestantism, which had played a large role in American economics since at least early in the nineteenth century, was still influential in the 1920s. American self-identity was still largely shaped at this time by the idea that America was a Protestant nation, and this was likely reflected in the genteel way that the different emerging factions coexisted relatively peacefully during the 1920s. Although they did not agree about how economics should be done, there was initially a kind of respect for the rights of others to do their work as they pleased. Since the participants on each side of this issue were predominantly Protestant, it seems likely that they held a basic respect for each other that helped foster this early attitude.

5.5 CONCLUSION

The central argument of this chapter is that the traditional picture of the influence of the generation of American economists who trained in Germany in the decades after the Civil War is distorted. That traditional picture includes the idea that there was a *Methodenstreit* between those young American economists and the emerging marginalists. In fact, there was a political dispute between the older advocates of laissez-faire and the younger German trained economists over the appropriate role of the government in the economy, but that split did not pit the marginalists against the German-trained economists.

The reason that the younger, German-trained economists were not averse to marginalism is that most of them had been exposed to marginalist ideas as a part of their training in Germany. The economists of the Older Historical School had considered marginal utility reasoning within their own theoretical frameworks for much of the nineteenth century, and so did not necessarily teach their students that it was abhorrent or *verboten*. Thus, these young Americans came home prepared to work with marginalist ideas as a part of their toolbox, even if they did not give them place of pride within that toolbox.[26] Just as the Older German Historical School had avoided the kind of all out *Methodenstreit* that the Younger Historical School embraced, so too did the Americans who studied with them avoid a *Methodenstreit* when they returned home.

The other traditional interpretation linking the rise of Institutionalism to the German training of the generation of Americans who had sought their doctorates in Germany is also incorrect. Although there is a similarity in their dedication to empirical, inductive work in economics, this similarity was not a direct influence of the generation of Americans trained in Germany. In fact, that generation had been largely responsible for the liberal Protestant influence in American economics that the Institutionalists were rebelling against.

Thus, both the nature and the timing of the influence of the Older German Historical School are quite different than has been imagined. The Older German Historical School was influential on American economics and that influence came through the young men who trained with them, but the influence was not what people have imagined it was.

NOTES

1. Johns Hopkins was founded on the German model of the university, which meant not only that graduate education was on offer, but also that it was conducted on the seminar model.
2. Approximately 9000 Americans studied in Germany in the second half of the nineteenth century. Jurgen Herbst (1965) is still the best study of the American scholarly diaspora to Germany in the nineteenth century, although his treatment of economics is thin.
3. See William J. Barber (1988) for a treatment of economics in the American undergraduate curriculum in the nineteenth century. See also Steven J. Meardon (2008).
4. Stewart Davenport (2008) contains an extended discussion of Wayland, Vethake and Potter, as expositors of the emerging 'market revolution' that took place in early nineteenth-century America. Following A.W. Coats (1992a), Davenport includes all three of these economists among the 'clerical economists'.

5. See Bateman (2005) for a discussion of how Republicanism, arguments for 'free labour', and laissez-faire were entwined before the American Civil War.
6. Francis Amasa Walker, who served as the first president of the American Economic Association, and who was older than many of the other founders, once observed that in his youth to be an economist meant that one was an advocate of laissez-faire. If one did not advocate laissez-faire, one could not be an economist.
7. There are good accounts of the founding of the AEA in Mary O. Furner (1975) and Dorothy Ross (1990). Ely (1938) is his own account at the time of the fiftieth anniversary of the founding of the AEA.
8. The standard accounts of the early decades of the AEA are the series of essays written by A.W. Coats and reprinted in Coats (1992a, 1992b).
9. It is important to understand that the German-trained economists who became pivotal in shaping American economics at the end of the nineteenth century all studied under members of the Older German Historical School, not under Gustav Schmoller or other members of the Younger German Historical School. The *Methodenstreit* was essentially a battle waged by the Younger German Historical School. Many Austrian economists looked favourably upon the work of Karl Knies, the last of the great figures in the Older School. The difference in tone and approach of the two schools of historical economists is noted in many places and also turns up in, for instance, Lionel Robbins's (1998) well-known lectures at the London School of Economics on the history of economic thought.
10. On Clark's ethics, see Mary S. Morgan (1994). For a more recent look at Clark's stand on policy issues, see Thomas Leonard (2003).
11. As Mary O. Furner has pointed out, questions of objectivity were central to the debates about method.
12. The perception of stagnation in American economics following the Civil War, and Dunbar's response to it, is recounted in William J. Barber (2003).
13. Arthur T. Hadley would represent someone whose loyalty lay with the classically oriented, laissez-faire economists who made some use of marginal analysis.
14. Frank Taussig is an interesting case in point of the interest on the part of the laissez-faire school in marginalism. Taussig (1893) was an early (positive) reviewer of Marshall's *Principles* and later in his life he became known as 'the American Marshall'. And yet, in his own textbook, he did not use marginalism as the unifying principle.
15. Hence Joseph Dorfman's (1955) statement about the 'Austrian influence' that the Americans who trained in Germany brought home with them. See note 9 above. It is important to note that those Americans who studied in Germany in the 1860s and 1870s studied under professors who were in the tradition of the Older Historical School, which while placing prime importance on historical analysis also worked with economic theory. It is the later members of the Younger Historical School who broke more fully from any serious consideration of theoretical work.
16. Papadopoulos and Bateman (2011a) have translated Knies's essay. Papadopoulos and Bateman (2011b) places the essay in historical context.
17. See Jun Kobayashi (2002) on Knies's style of arguing by analogy.
18. The essays in Morgan and Rutherford (1998), especially the introductory essay, make the best case that Neoclassicsm was not dominant until after the Second World War, and that it was a very different analytical organon than late nineteenth-century marginalism.
19. See Bateman (1998).
20. See Ross (1990), Bateman (2008a, 2008b).
21. Roger Backhouse (1998) shows nicely the ebb and flow of Institutionalist publication in top economic journals. Jeff Biddle (1998) argues persuasively that Institutionalism fell out of favour largely because of the paucity of Institutionalists who took positions at leading graduate schools. After the Great Depression hit, and following Franklin D. Roosevelt's election, the number of openings in government (both state and national) for those with graduate training in economics exploded, and Biddle documents that the

vast majority of those who received training as Institutionalists went on to fill those newly created jobs. Thus, the Institutionalists may not have lost the battle of ideas; they simply did not continue working in academia and so eventually failed to reproduce themselves.

22. Bateman (1998) treats Knight's attack on Schlicter in greater detail.
23. See, for instance, Geoffrey Hodgson (2001).
24. The issue of the commitment of the Institutionalists to data collection and inductive work brings up an interesting question in the historiography of American economics. For many decades, Institutionalism has been interpreted by some as an extension of Thorstein Veblen's work. But while some of the early Institutionalists did draw from Veblen's writing, they did not see themselves as primarily interested in furthering his ideas. The question of data collection and the potential for the use of large-scale data sets bears this out, for while it was central to the Institutionalists' project, it was not an idea that Veblen endorsed. See Malcolm Rutherford's series of recent essays (1997, 1999, 2000, 2002). See also Bateman (2004).
25. It is interesting that Wesley Clair Mitchell (1969) includes a long and laudatory chapter on 'The German Historical School: Gustav van Schmoller'. The chapter is interesting for my purposes not so much because Mitchell claims Schmoller as an influence, but because Mitchell's primary interest is in the Younger Historical School, not the Older Historical School (with whom Ely, Seligman, Clark and Patten had studied).
26. One important difference between the use of utility reasoning by the Americans trained in Germany and the Neoclassicists who emerged in the interwar years arises in the ethical frameworks of the two groups. Whereas the Neoclassicists were self-consciously developing a utilitarian ethics, the German-trained economists had no such intention; they saw marginalism as a technique, not an ethical framework. Richard T. Ely could not be called a utilitarian in any sense of the word. Nor, really, could John Bates Clark who, despite his ground-breaking work in marginal utility theory, offered many kinds of caveats in arguing about the best possible economic policies. One searches in vain for a late nineteenth-century American economist who was trained in Germany and who could be reasonably be labelled a utilitarian. Stewart Davenport (2008) demonstrates that the clerical economists earlier in the nineteenth century argued forcefully that they were not utilitarians when others tried to use this label for them. It would be interesting to know for how long 'utilitarian' remained a perjorative term for American economists.

REFERENCES

Backhouse, Roger E. (1998), 'The transformation of US economics, 1920–1960, viewed through the survey of journal articles', in Mary Morgan and Malcolm Rutherford (eds), *From Interwar Pluralism to Postwar Neoclassicism*, Durham, NC: Duke University Press, pp. 85–107.

Backhouse, Roger E., Bradley W. Bateman and Steven G. Medema (2011), 'The Reception of Marshall in the United States', in Tiziano Raffaelli, Giacomo Becattini, Katia Caldari and Marco Dardi (eds), *The Impact of Alfred Marshall's Ideas*, Cheltenham, UK and Northampton, MA, USA: Edward Elgar, pp. 59–80.

Barber, William J. (ed.) (1988), *Breaking the Academic Mould: Economists and American Higher Learning in the Nineteenth Century*, Middletown, CT: Wesleyan University Press.

Barber, William J. (2003), 'American economics to 1900', in Warren Samuels, Jeff Biddle and John Davis (eds), *A Companion to the History of Economic Thought*, Oxford: Blackwell, pp. 231–45.

Bateman, Bradley W. (1998), 'Clearing the ground: the demise of the Social Gospel Movement and the rise of neoclassicism in American economics', in Mary Morgan and Malcolm Rutherford (eds) *From Interwar Pluralism to Postwar Neoclassicism*, Durham, NC: Duke University Press, pp. 29–52.

Bateman, Bradley W. (2004), 'Why institutional economics matters as a category of historical analysis', *A Research Annual* (*Research in the History of Economic Thought and Methodology, Volume* 22), 193–201.

Bateman, Bradley W. (2005), 'Bringing in the state? The life and times of laissez-faire in the 19th century United States', in Steven Medema and Peter Boettke (eds), *The Role of Government in the History of Political Economy*, Durham, NC: Duke University Press, pp. 175–99.

Bateman, Bradley W. (2008a), 'Reflections on the secularization of American economics', *Journal of the History of Economic Thought*, **28** (1), 1–20.

Bateman, Bradley W. (2008b), 'American economics: 1885–1945', *New Palgrave Dictionary of Economics*, London: Palgrave.

Biddle, Jeff (1998), 'Institutional economics; a case of reproductive failure?' in Mary Morgan and Malcolm Rutherford (eds), *From Interwar Pluralism to Postwar Neoclassicism*, Durham, NC: Duke University Press, pp. 108–33.

Chipman, J.S. (2005), 'Contributions of the older German schools to the development of utility theory', in C. Scheer (ed.), *Studien zur Entwicklung der oekonomischen Theorie XX: Die aeletere historische Schule: Wirtschaftstheoretische Beitraege und wirtschaftpolitische Vorstellungen*, Berlin: Duncker & Humbolt, pp. 178–279.

Clark, John Bates (1886), *The Philosophy of Wealth: Economic Principles Newly Formulated*, Boston, MA: Ginn.

Clark, John Bates (1899), *The Distribution of Wealth: A Theory of Wages, Interest, and Profits*, New York: Macmillan.

Coats, A.W. (1992a), *On the History of Economic Thought*, British and American Economic Essays, Vol. 1, London: Routledge.

Coats, A.W. (1992b), *The Sociology and Professionalization of Economics*, British and American Economic Essays, Vol. 2, London: Routledge.

Davenport, Stewart (2008), *Friends of the Unrighteous Mammon*, Chicago, IL: University of Chicago Press.

Dorfman, J. (1955), *The Economic Mind in American Civilization*, 5 vols, New York: Viking.

Ely, Richard T. (1893), *Outlines of Economics*, New York: Flood & Vincent.

Ely, R.T. (1938), *Ground Under our Feet: An Autobiography*, New York: Macmillan.

Ely, R.T., T.S. Adams, M.O. Lorenz and A.A. Young (1908), *Outlines of Economics*, 2nd edn, New York: Macmillan.

Ely, Richard T., Thomas S. Adams, Allyn A. Young and Max O. Lorenz (1908), *Outlines of Economics*, 2nd edn, New York: Macmillan.

Furner, Mary O. (1975), *Advocacy and Objectivity: A Crisis in the Professionalization of American Social Science, 1865–1905*, Lexington, KY: University of Kentucky Press.

Herbst, Jurgen (1965), *The German Historical School in American Scholarship: A Study in the Transfer of Culture*, Ithaca, NY: Cornell University Press.

Hildebrand, Bruno (1848), *Die Nationalökonomie der Gegenwart und Zukunft. Erster Band*, Frankfurt am Main: Literarische Anstalt.

Hodgson, Geoffrey (2001), *How Economics Forgot History: The Problem of Historical Specificity in Social Science*, London: Routledge.

Knies, Karl (1855), 'Die nationalökonomische Lehre vom Werth', *Zeitschrift für die gesamte Staatswissenschaft*, 11.
Knies, Karl (1873), *Das Geld*, Berlin: Weidman.
Knies, Karl (1874), *Weldgeld und Weltmünze*, Berlin: Weidman.
Knies, Karl (1879), *Der Kredit*, Berlin: Weidman.
Knight, Frank H. (1932), 'The new economics and the control of economic activity', *Journal of Political Economy*, **40**, 433–76.
Kobayashi, Jun (2002), 'Karl Knies's conception of political economy: the logical status of Analogie and Sitte', in Yuichi Shionoya (ed.), *The German Historical School: The Historical and Ethical Approach to Economics*, London: Routledge, pp. 54–71.
Leonard, T. (2003), 'A certain rude honesty', John Bates Clark as a pioneering neoclassical economist', *History of Political Economy*, **35**, 521–58.
Marshall, A. (1890), *Principles of Economics*, London: Macmillan, 6th edn (1910).
Meardon, Steven (2008), 'American economics: before 1885', *New Palgrave Dictionary of Economics*, London: Palgrave.
Mitchell, Wesley C. (1969), *Types of Economic Theory: From Mercantilism to Institutionalism, Volume II*, Joseph Dorfman (ed.), New York: Augustus M. Kelley.
Morgan, M. (1994), 'Marketplace morals and the American economists: the case of John Bates Clark', in Neil De Marchi and Mary Morgan (eds), *Higgling: Transactors and Their Markets in the History of Economics*, Durham, NC: Duke University Press, pp. 229–52.
Morgan, M. and Malcolm Rutherford (eds) (1998), *From Interwar Pluralism to Postwar Neoclassicism*, *HOPE* supplement, Durham, NC: Duke University Press.
Newcomb, Simon (1886), 'Dr Ely on the labor movement', *Nation*, **43**, 293–4.
Papadopoulos, Kosmas and Bradley Bateman (2011a), 'Karl Knies and the Prehistory of Neoclassical Economics: Understanding the Importance of 'Die Nationaloekonomische Lehre vom Werth', *Journal of the History of Economic Thought*, **33**, 19–35.
Papadopoulos, Kosmas and Bradley Bateman (2011b), 'The theory of value in the national economy', translation of 'Die Nationaloekonomische Lehre vom Werth', 1855', *Journal of the History of Economic Thought*, **33**, 37–66.
Rau, Karl H. (1847), *Lehrbuch der politischen Oekonomie. Erster Band: Grundsätze der Volkswirthschaftslehre*, 5th edn, Heidelberg: Akadem.
Robbins, Lionel (1998), *A History of Economic Thought: The LSE Lectures,* Steven G. Medema and Warren J. Samuels (eds), Princeton, NJ: Princeton University Press.
Roscher, Wilhelm (1854), *System der Volkswirthschaft. Erster Band. Die Grundlagen der Nationalökonomie. Ein Hand- und Lesebuch für Geschäftmänner und Studierende*, Stuttgart and Tübingen: J.G. Cotta'scher Verlag.
Ross, D. (1990), *The Origins of American Social Science*, Cambridge: Cambridge University Press.
Rutherford, M. (1997), 'American Institutionalism and the history of economics', *Journal of the History of Economic Thought*, **19**, 178–95.
Rutherford, M. (1999), 'Instittuionalism as "scientific economics"', in R.E. Backhouse and J. Creedy (eds), *From Classical Economics to the Theory of the Firm: Essays in Honour of Dennis O'Brien*, Cheltenham, UK and Northampton, MA, USA: Edward Elgar, pp. 223–42.

Rutherford, M. (2000), 'Understanding Institutional economics, 1918–1929', *Journal of the History of Economic Thought*, **22**, 277–308.
Rutherford, M. (2002), 'Morris A. Copeland: a case study in the history of Institutional economics', *Journal of the History of Economic Thought*, **24**, 261–90.
Streissler, E.W. (1990), 'The influence of German economics on the work of Menger and Marshall', *History of Political Economy*, **22** (Annual Supplement), 31–68.
Taussig, F. (1893), 'Value and distribution as treated by Professor Marshall', *Publications of the American Economic Association*, **8**, 95–101.
Yonay, Yuval (1998), *The Struggle for the Soul of Economics: Institutionalist and Neoclassical Economics in America Between the Wars*, Princeton, NJ: Princeton University Press.

6. Marshall's ideas on progress: roots and diffusion

Katia Caldari and Tamotsu Nishizawa

6.1 INTRODUCTION

Recently it has been suggested that one of the main Marshallian concerns was economic development – 'the high theme of economic progress' as he called it. Progress, its ways and means, is the question that pervades all his writings, published and unpublished, his speeches, his private correspondence. Marshall was even going to publish a book on progress; this never materialized, although a number of annotations are still preserved in Cambridge. Those notes on progress are extremely interesting because they help to define the complex (and modern) idea that Marshall had of economic progress. Moreover, in those notes, Alfred Marshall effects a convergence of his principal long-lasting interests: the importance of education for the betterment of human character, the elevation of working classes and the consequent increase in national productivity; the attention given to industry and its relations (trade unions, industrial groups, non-competing groups) and to labour and its conditions (factory environment, level of wages, kinds of work); the conception of wealth and well-being, far from having an exclusively material meaning; the importance given to the quality of life, very close to the modern idea of sustainable development; the (possible) role of government in promoting national progress (not to be meant only as economic progress).

Progress is made up of several elements, all equally important: none of them can be missing to have real progress. Many of the characteristics underlined by Marshall were in fact widely shared in Cambridge and beyond. But the way in which Marshall considered and combined them is quite original. Nonetheless, a large part of his original and more interesting economic thought has been too long neglected. It was moreover neglected by those of his closer pupils who remained in Cambridge. The Marshallian idea of progress is present in their writings, but not fully and properly developed.

The term 'convergence' above is not used casually: we wish to underline that these topics were at the core of Marshall's reasoning, writings and teaching. In fact numerous references to them are scattered in Marshall's extensive published correspondence, (Whitaker, 1996) and some of them can be traced in the writings of his pupils and other contemporaries. By locating and identifying this use of 'progress' in the writings of his pupils we can constitute a 'Marshallian school'; we can also determine whether his ideas were diffused among his contemporaries.

The chapter is structured as follows. Section 6.2 summarizes the main contents of the manuscript notes on progress. Section 6.3 takes into consideration those who, in Marshall's time, shared his main ideas on progress (that is, the intellectual milieu of his ideas). Section 6.4 highlights the importance given by Marshall to industry and its relations (that is, the elimination of sectional interests). Section 6.5 underlines the ways in which Marshall's pupils and other contemporaries shared and developed the issues connected with progress; it also underlines which elements of that legacy, especially in Cambridge, were lost. Section 6.6 draws some final conclusions to show how his ideas could be rehabilitated, emphasizing the extreme modernity of Marshall's contributions, such as in the idea of sustainable development.

6.2 THE BOOK ON 'ECONOMIC PROGRESS'[1]

The archive of Cambridge University's Marshall Library holds notes that Marshall wrote for his last unfinished book. Keynes remarked: 'Up to his last illness, in spite of loss of memory and great feebleness of body, he [Marshall] struggled to piece together one more volume. It was to have been called *Progress: its economic conditions.* But the task was too great' (Keynes, 1972, 231). Unfortunately Keynes was right, the task was too great and the book never came out, but a substantial collection of notes fortunately remain which, although sketchy and unconnected, lend insight into the main structure of the book and its principal contents.

The provisional contents of the volume run as follows:

Book I: The nature of E.P.[2]
I. Introductory conditions of E.P.
II. Various tendencies of E.P.
III. Interactions among the tendencies of E.P (note or diagram)
IV. Sectional interests in E.P.

Book II: Functions & Resources of Govt in regard to E.P.
I. Intrody
II. Stability of credit
III. Taxes

IV I.T. Compn
V. Commercial policy

Book III: The economic future
I. Influence of E.P. on the quality of life
II. Retrospect & Prospect
III. Ideal & attainable Poverty

Some of these topics had always been of great interest to Marshall, and are developed in all of his writings. Moreover, these topics recur in his correspondence and the many speeches made during his career.

Progress was his prime interest, and it is not hard to understand why. Marshall had decided to devote himself to economics because his native country was confronted with a number of major economic problems. First among them was the grievous problem of poverty, the importance of which he described as follows: 'I have devoted myself . . . to the *problem of poverty*, and . . . very little of my work has been devoted to any inquiry which does not bear on that' (Keynes, 1926, 205).

Closely connected with poverty were the consequences for towns and the quality of life. In a letter to Ward Marshall recalls the reasons why he decided to end the study of mathematics, philosophy, and psychology and turn to economics: 'I spent a year in doubt: always preferring psychology for the pleasures of the chase; but economics grew and grew in practical urgency, not so much in relation to the growth of wealth as to the quality of life' (Whitaker, 1996, vol. II, 285).

Another problem that deeply worried Marshall was the economic decline of Britain, an issue that in the later nineteenth century came to the fore in public debate. If the problem of poverty could be resolved, the quality of life of Britain's population improved, and as a consequence, their 'character' ameliorated, then the country might once again become 'progressive', fostering its economic and social progress.

From the notes preserved in the archive we learn the meaning given to 'progress':

> Progress has many sides. It includes developments of mental and moral faculties, even when their exercise yields no material gain. The term 'economic progress' is narrow: and it is sometimes taken to imply merely an increase in mans [*sic*] command over the material requisites of physical mental and moral wellbeing; no special reference being made to the extent to which this command is turned to account in developing the higher life of mankind . . . True human progress is in the main an advance in capacity for feeling and for thought, yet it cannot be sustained without vigorous enterprise and energy.

This quotation echoes what Marshall had already written in *Principles*: 'the production of wealth is but a means to the sustenance of man; to the satisfaction of his wants; and to the development of his activities, physical, mental and moral' (1920, 173). Material wealth is of course a basic, necessary condition for progress, but it must not be confused with true progress, which involves many more elements. For Marshall, overall progress implies the development of human nature, together with the amelioration of human character. Accordingly we can have progress 'when increase of material wealth is united with solidity of character sufficient to turn it to good account'.

Increase in wealth is useless or even harmful if not coupled with the development of character, the latter being a much more difficult task: 'Improvement in the use of wealth needs more energy relatively to mere increase in its amount'. For this very reason, progress should proceed slowly: people must become 'ready' and prepared for each new step on the path of progress. Both manuscript notes and other writings emphasize this gradualist perspective. In a note we find that: 'Eagerness in listing progress is a duty: but the larger the measure, the more cogent is the rule Festina lente'. In the *Principles* the same idea is well expressed:

> In fact our new command over nature, while opening the door to much larger schemes for industrial organization than were physically possible even a short time ago, places greater responsibilities on those who would advocate new developments of social and industrial structure. For though institutions may be changed rapidly; yet if they are to endure they must be appropriate to man: they cannot retain their stability if they change very much faster than he does. Thus progress itself increases the urgency of the warning that in the economic world, Natura non facit saltum. Progress must be slow; but even from the merely material point of view it is to be remembered that changes, which add only a little to the immediate efficiency of production, may be worth having if they make mankind ready and fit for an organization, which will be more effective in the production of wealth and more equal in its distribution; and that every system, which allows the higher faculties of the lower grades of industry to go to waste, is open to grave suspicion (1920, 249).

The most important condition for progress is education, the chief purpose of which 'is to cause mental activities to be *thorough*'. Only through education can people, especially the lower classes, improve: the unskilled workers can become skilled and become better paid; people learn to appreciate a better life, refining their faculties, their homes, engaging in leisure pursuits; and it is only through education that people can learn how to use properly the increase in wealth resulting from economic development.[3]

Through education, people can improve their status as workers, while working conditions themselves and the nature of employment are themselves another important element of human progress. Marshall writes:

> Work is not a punishment for fault: it is a necessity for the formation of character and, therefore, for progress . . . work . . . [is] necessary for comfort and even for existence: that is it demanded serious strenuous work as a condition of race survival. Incidentally – though not by accident – it gave 'back bone' to the character of man.

And again: 'labour is needed for the making of a race that has enduring strength of character – the only material on which high aspirations and the pursuit of ideals has ever been sustained for a long time'.

Like Adam Smith, Marshall recognizes the important role of the state in assuring education to as many people as possible. An important sign of modern times is to be found in: 'participation of all classes of the people in those higher activities of mind & spirit, which used to belong almost exclusively to the ruling classes'. The key element is education: Marshall believes that at least an elementary standard should be available to all:

> Partly in order to widen the area from which capable governmental administration can be selected; partly in order that the votes of the masses of the people, who are to govern the government, may be well advised; partly it is a good thing in itself, popular education must be extended. It must be made more real: the Universities must (a) be more easily accessible to all & (b) more closely occupied with the problems of coming ages.

A substantial part of his notes on progress is devoted to the possible or plausible role of government and state. Although a liberal, in early twentieth-century Britain this by no means implied adherence to a free market ideology, but instead a commitment to 'social liberalism': 'Laissez Faire: . . . its true sense is let Govt do its own work; & not listen to what sectional interests who want to utilize it for appropriate work, or to prevent its working on behalf of the weak &c'. The complexities of modern times demand an increasing role for government: 'In a small isolated island, nearly everyone may be well acquainted with the contribution that each is making to the national resources. But in a large country much must be left to the discretion of authority.'

In reasoning about the role of the state, Marshall analyses one of its main instruments, taxation:

> If everyone's wealth was doubled by changes which obviated the necessity for personal exertion & self sacrifice, the world would be poorer . . . Thus it remains that wealth . . . is valued more for the power & distribution wh it gives . . . This is the logical basis for heavy taxation of private wealth, provided the proceeds of the tax can be well spent on building up noble forms of public wealth, wh will be turned to good account.

Marshall's point of view on state intervention is summarized in the following words:

> A beaver builds in view of coming storm: a fly is content with a good resting place for the night. An alert people must look far ahead.
>
> A father considers influences that will bear on his children when he has left this world: but seldom looks much further than a half century.
>
> National policy should be based on considerations relating to gradual evolution.
>
> National policy needs to fare forward . . .: it must be based on considerations that react far into the future. Patriotism is stupid if it does not look far ahead.
>
> National policy in taxation that does not consider distant future is as foolish as a man who builds a house on the back of a vagrant stream without caring whether a change in the course of the stream is likely to undermine its foundations.

Government is therefore a necessary element responsible for ensuring order and the coordination of people's different needs and aims; it can be absent only in an ideal, fanciful reality:

> Utopia does not absolutely require a Government. It relies on its wisest members to counsel the organization of work and the distribution of tasks among the citizens in accordance with their several abilities: each is willing to devote his energies to the work for which they are most appropriate; & to be rewarded in proportion to his needs.

In the ideal world that Marshall calls Utopia[4] we find that:

> each family is nearly self-sufficing, [and] Social Order may be maintained by mere goodwill, without any organization; each family holding its goods & its assistances at the service of its neighbours either gratuitously or in return for some definitely understood compensation.

On the contrary, in the real world state intervention is a necessary means of progress, as well as of the increase of wealth:

> the function of wealth and of order is to give full play to the free energies of faculties, in wh alone is the highest happiness. But wellbeing does no doubt demand some considerable measure of material comfort, especially in urban & even semi urban life

But, it is important to note, the Marshallian idea of state intervention is very close to that of Adam Smith, and quite removed from that of the socialists. Socialism was another topic that greatly occupied Marshall's mind over the years; although he shared much of the socialist perspective, he nonetheless parted company with them over the role of competition and trust in the capitalistic system:

> Private property is necessary. If it were not, it would be true that 'Property is theft' & the rich man would deserve only less consideration than the society which tolerated his existence . . . Economic rights are economic wrongs, justifiable only in order to prevent greater wrong . . . The use of the study of generals is to help us to see what particulars to look for: & the more difficult task of helping us to weigh the good against the evil when we have found out the quality of each effect. For this two classes of workers are wanted, professional students, & business men with a care for 'generals'

In part of his notes, Marshall outlines the chief features of the modern era and the conditions for further progress:

> Resources of the new age, which enable the great bulk of the people to share in high thoughts
>
> The intellectual opportunities, which were formerly confined to a few, are now open to all, through
>
> i) universal education
> ii) cheap print: various and adapted to all requirements especially to the special interests of the working classes as a whole
> iii) good and cheap artificial light
> iv) a relative abundance of fresh air after dark
> v) the shortening of hours of labour
> vi) the substitution (. . .) of artificial power for the strain of human muscles

Given these elements, he emphasizes a number of conditions that will bring reality as close as possible to Utopia:

> Cultured life for all who care for it. A world population considerably greater than the present: hours of work relatively short (reproduce previous suggestion as to break of main body of work for humans, machines to work all through). Educators to be real: the best thoughts of all past generations, as well as the present to be brought to bear on youth. These educators to be directed mainly to developing the faculties wh have always been in some degree specialized to them: ditto for women . . .
>
> Saving to be special duty of the State: A Council to control force, of which the chief function should be to make the population of each country, & each individual in each country to develop special faculties in their highest degrees. Work to be not only the means of life: but to be so as to direct the highest & fullest exercise of the faculties of each man & each woman.

6.3 THE INTELLECTUAL MILIEU OF MARSHALLIAN IDEAS ON PROGRESS

As noted above, in his extensive notes on *Progress* Alfred Marshall brings together his principal lifelong interests: the importance of education for the betterment of human character, the elevation of working classes, and the consequent increase in national productivity; the attention given to industry and its relations (trade unions, industrial groups, non competing groups), to labour and its conditions (factory environment; level of wages; kinds of work); the conception of wealth and well-being, far from having an exclusively material meaning; the importance given to the quality of life, very close to the modern idea of sustainable development (Caldari, 2004); the role of government in promoting national progress (not to be understood only as economic progress). These topics form the spine of Marshall's reasoning, writings and teaching. Such terms recur constantly in Marshall's rich correspondence (Whitaker, 1996) and in his writings and speeches.[5]

Marshall's position coincides with the general awareness of these issues in late Victorian and Edwardian Britain, manifested in a wide range of of movements and associations. Marshall himself was linked with some of these associations: the Eranus Club,[6] the Society for Promoting Industrial Villages, the Garden City Movement.[7] He was also closely involved with members of other movements: Christian Socialists,[8] the Charity Organization Society, the Co-operative Movement and trade unions.

It is not easy to distinguish cases where Marshall's thinking influenced these movements from those where he was influenced by them. We can however summarize contemporary opinion on the problem of poverty, which as we have seen was central to Marshall's thinking.

The issue of poverty was associated especially with large industrial towns and cities. The development of industrialization accentuated the problem, which developed into pauperism. The range of problems associated with poverty and pauperism was broad: labour conditions, especially for the lower ranks of the working classes; housing conditions and the more general problem of housing shortage; the heavy exploitation of children and women in the factories; the prevalence of drunkenness; the generally poor quality of life for the urban poor; and the high level of illiteracy.

One of those most deeply involved in the problem of poverty was Helen Bosanquet (1860–1925). She was 'Marshall's most distinguished woman student' (Whitaker, 1996, II, xii), a graduate of Newnham College, the leader of the Charity Organization Society (COS) and editor of its review, and a member of the Royal Commission on the Poor Laws and Relief and Distress in 1905–09. One of her main works is *The Strength of the People*,[9] first published in 1902. Marshall knew this work very well, his appreciative remarks being tempered however by some criticism, which was of course quite typical for Marshall (see the correspondence with Helen Bosanquet in Whitaker, 1996). Helen Bosanquet herself used part of her correspondence with Marshall in the Preface to the second edition of the book (1903, vii–xii).

Marshall and Bosanquet shared many common viewpoints, although there were points where their opinions diverged. In a letter dated 1902 Marshall wrote to Bosanquet:

> I think I agree with you in the main. I have always held that poverty & pain, disease & death are evils of much less importance than they appear, except in so far as they lead to weakness of life & character; & that a true philanthropy aims at increasing strength more than at diminishing poverty (Whitaker, 1996, II, 399)

Like Marshall, Bosanquet was convinced that the worst effect of poverty related to its impact on the individual character, and that education was the most important and effective means to overcome the problem. She also favoured wide access to educational opportunity regardless of class or gender. As she put it:

> What we aim at in all social work, the ideal which we set before ourselves, is, that both the whole community and every member of it shall be progressive, on the rising scale. We shall not be satisfied if the community as a whole can show a momentary increase in wealth, or learning, or culture, unless all classes within it are partaking intelligently in the social life, sharing in its progress, a source of strength and not of weakness. (1903, 5–6)

Moreover, poverty – as for Marshall[10] – did not have only a material dimension:

> And we shall not, of course, deny that in certain obvious but not very frequent cases poverty may be a vera causa, that it may prove an obstacle to progress, and prevent the individual from reaching certain kinds of culture. But we must distinguish. Poverty may be, and generally is, taken to mean merely a moderate degree of material wealth, a positive though, by implication, an insufficient possession of commodities, food, and clothing. This is the commonest use of the term. But there may also be poverty in a sense which covers the whole life; poverty of thought, of interests, of affections, of everything in short that is valuable in human beings; and to point to this as the cause of the phenomenon in question would be to commit the not uncommon fallacy of explaining a fact by giving it another name. (1903, 9–10)

Or again: 'The existence of people rich in material wealth, yet lacking the higher qualities, proves to us every day the insufficiency of material wealth alone to promote progress' (1903, 10).

For Marshall, an increase of material wealth did not mean genuine progress: together with the growth of wealth there had to be the development of character. The following passage from *The Strength of the People* is very close to Marshall's thinking:

> Increase of income, then, must be accompanied by the knowledge how to use it, if it is to bring with it any benefit. Nay, more, if it is not so accompanied it will be a curse. No man, and no class of men, can ever be raised, even from a purely economic point of view, by merely putting more money into their hands. It is true enough that it is the poverty of the poor which keeps them poor, but it is more often their poverty in interests and knowledge than lack of money. (1903, 94)

According to Bosanquet, the main characteristic of poverty was the lack of what she calls 'interests' in individuals: 'the limits fixed by our own vacant lack of interests is an infinitely more hopeless barrier to progress' (1903, 58).

Nonetheless, there are also some interesting points of difference. According to Marshall one main cause of misery and a sign of urban degradation was the problem of overcrowding. Bosanquet takes into consideration the problem of overcrowding, but almost exclusively referred to individual houses. In many parts of her book she enumerates the various evils that arise when a large family is forced to live in a single small room. Little reference is made to the problem of urban overcrowding.

Moreover, her perspective seems too optimistic and rather superficial when she writes:

> At present we must urge that the assumption is one which is seldom justified to the full. In these days of tram and train and cycle, men are not obliged even to live near their work; and, as a matter of fact, generally do live at some distance from it at any rate in the town. How far from it they will actually live depends mainly upon individual preferences: the weighing of a shilling a week spent in fares and fresher air, against a shilling a week higher rent and the proximity of a music hall (1903, 45).

Or again: 'A man's preferences not only influence his choice of home and locality; they will actively modify that home and locality to his liking if they are not already what he prefers' (1903, 46).

Marshall thought that people living in extremely poor conditions had no choice: the only possible way out for them (or better, for their children) was presented by education.[11] Bosanquet's point of view is very different:

> The best teaching will not be that which is professedly educational, but will come in three main ways. First, it will come from the interests naturally involved in a

man's own life, including that of his family. Secondly, it will come from the lives of those whom he emulates, and these will generally be those who, though living a wider life than his, are yet near enough to him for his comprehension. And finally, it will come to him in the best form from the claims which the community makes upon him . . . When a man's life is left in his own hands, it provides interests which will carry him far. If he realises his responsibility for his children, and is eager to give them a good start in life, and if he is interested in maintaining his independence through periods of sickness and old age, there is little fear that any moderate increase in income will be more than he can handle. (1903, 95)

Marshall thought that individuals should be first educated, following which in the long term they could do what, according to Bosanquet,[12] was better for them.

The problem of poverty attracted the attention of many of Marshall's contemporaries. One was Charles Stewart Loch (1849–1923), with whose major works Marshall was familiar[13] and who was a member of the Royal Commission on Poor Laws (1906–09). According to Loch: 'Pauperism is the social enemy of the modern State. The State wants citizens . . . Accordingly it becomes a duty of the State by some means to prevent pauperism, and of citizens to give their service to the State for the purpose' (1890, 4).

One aspect of the problem much discussed at the time concerned urban dirt and pollution and the lack of green spaces. Marshall was familiar with this and considered it as a sign of a lack of progress. Marshall was involved with the Society for Promoting Industrial Villages and the Garden Cities Movement. In his writings, speeches and private correspondence he repeatedly underlines the degree to which a lack of fresh air works on the character, productivity and progress of the nation. He discussed his ideas on this topic with two people in particular. One of them was Thomas Coglan Horsfall (1841–1932): 'a Manchester philanthropist who believed that the wealthy middle class had an obligation to supervise the leisure activities of the working class' (Kelvin, 1987: 12). Horsfall's major contribution is considered to be in relation to town planning (Reynolds, 1952). Marshall, in a letter to Horsfall dated 1900, refers to the following pamphlets: *Reforms in our System of Elementary Education, The Report of the Art Museum* and according to Whitaker, Marshall should have also known the pamphlets *The Study of Beauty, and Art in Large Towns* (London, 1883); *Art in Large Towns: In what Way can the influence of art be brought to bear on the masses of the population?* (London, 1882) and *The Relation of Art to the Welfare of the Inhabitants of English Towns* (Manchester, 1884).[14] In the letter Horsfall (1990) Marshall writes:

I am entirely in agreement with your claim that the community is bound to see to it that town dwellers have opportunities for knowing what a fully healthy

> life is. Country folk are less dependent on training & on inspiration derived from their fellow men. The fresh air & bright sunshine strengthen & stimulate, & at the same time soothe their nervous systems: & the beauty of ever changing nature offers an invitation to reverent & religious feeling, whether it be precipitated in theological form or not. But town life, with its ever-increasing density & extension, shrouds the individual away from himself, & from the infinite . . . The growth of towns makes it doubly urgent to supply wholesome thoughts & suggestions, lest unwholesome should prevail: & to turn music & painting &other fine arts to account in filling the void in man's life caused by the want of the free light & freshness & beauties of nature. The clatter & the bustle & the nervous strain of constant jostling against a multitude of others must impoverish some sides of his nature; & it is therefore imperatively necessary, if the child is to grow up in any fulness of life, that he should see & hear & read of the brightest ideals that have come to mankind. (Whitaker, 1996, II, 270–71).

When Marshall refers to education, he means a general education including technical, artistic,[15] and literary dimensions, although they are given different weights.[16]

In another letter to Horsfall from 1901, Marshall expresses his appreciation of the work of Octavia Hill (1838–1912), a woman deeply involved in housing and social reforms. She was also convinced of the important influence of environment on people, and in her writings often underlined the beneficial effects of gardens, green spaces and beautiful landscape. She was a founding member of the Society of Organizing Charitable Relief and Repressing Mendicity, which later became known as the Charity Organization Society; she was a member of the Royal Commission on the Poor Law (1905–90) together with, as we have already seen, Helen Bosanquet and C.S. Loch, and also Beatrice Webb and Charles Booth. Octavia Hill was influenced by Charles Kingsley and F.D. Maurice,[17] who had offered her the post of secretary to the women's classes at the Working Men's College. She also had a close connection to John Ruskin, who helped her buy a number of houses for the poor.

Octavia Hill was opposed to any large-scale intervention by the state in welfare, and 'had a horror of careless charity, which encouraged sloth and imprudence in the poor, and locked them into a condition of permanent dependency'[18] (Whelan, 1998, 6–7). Marshall likewise thought that charity alone could not solve the problem of poverty but, as we have seen, contrary to Octavia Hill he was in favour of state intervention whenever it was necessary.[19]

Marshall praised the broad outline of the rules Hill drew up after working among the poor of London. It was far better to give work than money or goods. It was essential that:

> each man has his own view of his life and must be free to fulfil it . . . The poor of London need the development of every power that can open to them '*noble sources of joy*'. In order to give them these sources of joy, we must bring them to judge rightly, not bring him into our own groove. We must regard a man as intelligent capital and try to make him productive. The ordinary way of shifting men about is as if a gardener should try to make trees grow by pulling them out by his own strength instead of digging and watering them and then letting them grow in their own way. We must make people feel pained to be a drag on society. We must teach them to love Beauty for its own sake. Of all the works of charity probably the greatest that has been done lately is the opening of the Bethnal Green Museum. (*Lectures to Women*, Marshall, 1995 [1873], 117–9)

The second person with whom Marshall exchanged ideas concerning progress is Brooke Foss Westcott (1825–1901), a theologian and churchman very deeply interested in the condition of the working classes, and in finding the means to progress. Education was considered the first and most important means. It was Westcott who founded the Eranus Club in 1872. At a conference held in London in 1888 by the London Society for the Extension of University Teaching, Westcott stated that:

> life is as the man is; that if the man is sordid, selfish, narrow, mean, his life, however affluent, will reflect his character; and, on the other hand . . . there is about us an inexhaustible store of unrealized possibilities, a treasure of spiritual wealth, open to the poorest, which grows with the using, if only we know how to use it. And we believe that true education opens the eyes of the soul; that it is a strength in the difficulties which we must face; a solace in the sorrows which we must bear; an inspiration in interpreting the new truths which claim to receive from us a harmonious place beside the old; that it offers to all a vision of a larger order, truly human and truly divine; that it is not, in the noble words of your motto, a means of livelihood, but a means of life. (Clayton, 1906, 66–7)

In November 1900 Westcott, speaking on education at the opening of a new Science Buildings at Barnard Castle, declared that:

> Education, as I understand it, is not a preparation for commerce or the professions, but the moulding of a noble character, a training for life – for life seen and unseen – a training of citizens of a heavenly as well as of an earthly kingdom, for generous service in Church and State. (Clayton, 1906, 117)

Or again, in his last address to the Christian Social Union at Leeds:

> Before we can determine whether a movement is really progress we must determine the end it is desired to reach. Progress is an advance towards an ideal. If we wish to estimate human progress we must fix the human ideal. (Clayton, 1906, 118)

At Bristol in 1896, in an address to the Christian Social Union on the 'Aim and Method of Education', he stated that the object of education is: 'To train for life, and not for a special occupation; to train the whole man for all life . . . to train men, in a word, and not craftsmen to train citizens for the Kingdom of GOD' (Clayton, 1906, 168).

In his correspondence with Westcott, Marshall became deeply engaged with the condition of the working classes, the possible helpful means to better their condition, and the importance of education. Through education it was possible to pursue 'the elevation of human life, the making it full and strong (life all around, individual and social, moral and religious, physical and intellectual, emotional and artistic)'. The elevation of human character would affect the quality of work, the level of jobs, the mode of living and use of spare time. It would bring about real progress in society. Since people only dedicate part of the day to work – although a large part – it is also important to take into consideration the way in which they spend the rest of their time. This explains the importance given by Marshall to the artistic, religious, physical and intellectual activities in which people may become involved when they are not working. His perspective is very close to that of Westcott when for instance he writes: 'The right use of leisure, is an object of education not second . . . even to the right fulfilment of work' (Clayton, 1906, 169).

6.4 THE WORKING CLASSES AND INDUSTRIAL RELATIONS IN ECONOMIC PROGRESS

Economic, social and human progress, with prospects for the betterment of industrial or human relations and the elimination of sectional interests, remained central to Marshall's economic ideas. In his notes on *Progress* there is a section entitled 'Sectional interest in E.P.' The importance of education for the elevation of the working classes, the attention given to industry and its relations (trade unions, industrial groups), to labour and its conditions, and the consequent increase in national productivity, all play a fundamental role in this important element of his economic thought.

In thanking Westcott for his address on progress to the annual meeting of the Christian Social Union (26 November 1900), Marshall wrote to him (20 January 1901) that: 'it will direct people's thoughts towards the true aims of life . . . the Christian Socialists did, I believe, a great deal more good than harm: but they did harm. Their authority has been used with great effect by those mean, lazy and selfish men who since 1860 have done so much to undermine the vigour and honest work of English industry, and have removed her from the honourable leadership which she used to hold among the nations' (Whitaker, 1996, II, 293). Marshall wrote to Westcott again on 23 January 1901 that trade unions should be treated 'as a special case of association in which the good of individual unselfishness is ever surrounded and apt to be vitiated by the evil of class selfishness' (ibid, 297). Marshall thought Westcott's address at Trinity 'one of the noblest and truest things ever said', which says:

> Looking back over the last fifty years I will even dare to say that the next century will witness serious endeavours to apply the principle of fellowship, of cooperation in the largest sense, to political, social, and industrial problems . . . Even now we are coming to see that the highest good of the body must be coincident with the highest good of all the members: that the work of every citizen is, if rightly regarded, a public service: that labour is a dominant element in the formation of character . . . (quoted in ibid, 298 [629.2])

In the final chapters of the *Principles of Economics* Marshall emphasized that progress was fast improving the condition of the great body of the working classes. Over time wages had risen and wages differentials narrowed: lower and middle incomes were increasing faster than those of the rich. Though it was impossible to raise all earnings beyond the level already reached by well-to-do artisan families, it was 'certainly desirable that those who are below that level should be raised, even at the expense of lowering those who are above it' (Marshall, 1920; 712, 714). In the added chapter called 'Progress in relation to standard of life', he stressed the links between the better earnings of labour and a rise in the 'standard of life'; that is, a rise in physical strength, mental ability and moral character, and therefore an increase of intelligence, energy and self-respect; which implied a rise in the quality, efficiency and productivity of labour, and the growth of national income.

Marshall seemed quite optimistic in regard to the future of the working classes and sectional interests. In *Industry and Trade*, Marshall drew attention to the fact that sectional interests in industry were

> changing their character and becoming increasingly plastic: but the chief change is the assimilation of the training, and consequently the capacity, of the working classes generally to those of the well-to-do. The spread of education is rapidly effacing those distinctions of mind and character between different social strata, which have prevailed in nearly all densely-peopled countries during several thousand years. (Marshall 1923 [1919], 4–5)

Marshall's evolutionary economics underpinned a theory of economic progress based on the rise and improvement of population quality and efficiency, and presented a striking alternative to the Malthusian spectre.

Ricardo and his followers spoke as though they regarded man's character and efficiency as a fixed quantity; their 'most vital fault was that they did not see how liable to change are the habits and institutions of industry' (Marshall, 1920, 763). While the older economists were pessimistic about the change in working men's moral character, Marshall personified 'a moralizing capitalism': people should have access to the 'necessaries for efficiency' so as to develop their potential capabilities. They would grow more mobile, more rational, more able to acquire and conserve property; in effect, the working man would increasingly seem a middle-class person in working-class dress. 'The sagacity and public spirit of the leading minds both among employers and employed are increasing fast; the recent improvement among the employed in particular is one of the most marvellous events in the history of the world' (Marshall, 1885 [1998], 64).

Edgeworth thought that 'Marshall's success in handling the theory of wages was largely due to his sympathy with the wage-earners' (1925, 70). Marshall enjoyed serving on the Royal Commission on Labour (1891–94), which put him into contact with many working-class leaders, trade unionists and co-operators, such as the Webbs, Henry Hyndman, Benn Tillett and Tom Mann, who saw Marshall as a 'very diligent commissioner, [who] gave close attention to all the evidence. It was obvious that his questions were carefully elaborated beforehand' (Mann, 1923; 101). The key issue in income distribution was that the cost of labour production could not be determined as definitely as that of a commodity; for the efficiency of labour depended on the its 'conventional necessaries'. Marshall concluded that: 'an increase of wages . . . almost always increases the strength, physical, mental and even moral of the coming generation', and that 'an increase in the earnings that are to be got by labour increases its rate of growth; or . . . a rise in its demand-price increases the supply of it' (Marshall, 1920, 532).

As Petridis (1973, 487) has pointed out, in 1892 Marshall prepared a paper on trade unions, to be part of the introduction to the Report of the Labour Commission. It was not published in this form, but he had a strong belief in the dual role of trade unions, that is, in their 'friendly benevolent purposes' as well as their 'trade purposes' connected with 'disputes and conflicts' (see ibid., 490–92).

Marshall called himself as 'an ardent Trade-Unionist' and 'wholly a trade-unionist of the old stamp' (Whitaker, 1996, II, 203, 216). For him, trade unions were 'modern representatives of a series of movements that have exercised great influence over the growth of the people of England' (Marshall and Marshall, 1879, 187). In his *Lectures to Women* (1995 [1873] he stated that:

> A member of a Trades Union has a definite aim put before him; he is taught to subordinate his own wishes to that aim. It is absolutely proved that no organization for exterminating humbug is so efficient as a Trades Union. In this way it does some good. But the great benefit of a Trades Union is that it gives the people a political education, and trains them in a habit of subordinating their own personal will to the good of the state. A Trades Union is equal to a Greek republic for imparting a political education to the people. (pp. 114–5)

They had benefited 'the nation as well as themselves by such uses of the Common Rule as make for a true standardization of work and wages', which was likely to make for social well-being. But when trade unions had not learnt full self-respect, forms of false standardization were common. Yet the services of the leading trade unionists who condemned this antisocial conduct were never to be forgotten. And though some partial relapse led up to the great dispute of 1897 in the engineering trade, 'the error was quickly purged of at least its worst features' (Marshall, 1920, 706–7).

In his letter to Edward Caird (22 October 1897) regarding the strikes of the Amalgamated Society of Engineering, Marshall wrote:

> Everywhere the tried men who had made trade-unionism the greatest of England's glories, have been pushed aside . . . For a time the Engineers adhered to moderate & unselfish courses. But lately they have used their grand prestige, I hold, for Englands ill . . . If the men sh[d] win, & I were an engineering employer, I would sell my works for anything I could get & emigrate to America. If I were a working man, I would wish for no better or more hopeful conditions of life than those wh I *understand* to prevail at the Carnegie works now. (Whitaker, 1996, ed. II; 204)

> I have often said that TU's are a greater glory to England than her wealth. But I thought then of TU's in which the minority, who wanted to compel others to put as little work as possible into the hour, were overruled. Latterly they have, I fear, completely dominated the Engineers' Union. I want these people to be beaten at all costs: the complete destruction of Unionism would be as heavy a price as it is possible to conceive: but I think not too high a price. (Letter of 5 December 1897 to Edward Caird, ibid. 214)

Marshall thought this 'the crisis of our industry' and 'a threat to national well-being' (ibid.)

> The extremist case of this sectional selfishness which has come under my notice is that of a glass worker in the Midlands, who boasted that his local union had mastered the wage problem . . . This 'Achilles' heel' of Britain's industries attracts as much attention abroad as it does at home. For instance, an American writer, quoted in *The Economist* of April 26, 1919, remarks: 'In England men are thoroughly wedded to the system of restricted output. In New York one man will run three gear-cutting machines, but an English working man will run only one'. (Marshall, 1923 [1919], 641, fn)

And he concluded a few pages later that: 'If Britain is to hold her place in the world', then this could only happen if a new spirit 'should rid her of her Achilles' heel' (ibid., 650).

The First World War brought rapid change in industrial organization. In 1917 the Whitley Report called for the establishment of Joint Works Committees as the lowest level of a structure leading up to Joint Industrial Councils. The main purpose of the Report was to raise the status and develop the self-respect of the working man, enabling him to form and express well-considered judgements on all aspects of the business with which he was involved and review its general policy. In all these matters 'frank talk heals'; and as the workman's knowledge and faculty expanded, growing self-respect would give firmness and moderation to his policy. Joint Industrial Councils and Workmen's Committees should include in their aims the better utilization of the knowledge and experience of the workers, together with determining general principles for fixing, paying and readjusting wages with a view to securing the workers a share in the increased prosperity of the industry. In other words, everyone should contribute, both as an individual and in association with his comrades, to the solution of such business problems as were of most direct interest to him and to them (Marshall, 1923 [1919], 643–4).

Marshall considered that in Britain industrial traditions were powerful, and class consciousness was cherished by the manual worker 'with an almost religious fervour':

> while Britain may derive great and almost unmixed gains from the technical adjustment of each worker's plant, methods of work, and auxiliary conditions to the highest standard which Scientific Management can devise; yet adjustments of a standard task and a standard wage can seldom be satisfactorily arranged by employers alone. Representatives of the manual workers must, as a rule, be able to take part in them. This cooperation may be facilitated by the present movement towards the setting up of joint committees of employers and employed for each industry as a whole; for each important branch of it; and, in appropriate cases, for individual works (ibid., 391–2).

Thus for Marshall, American methods of Scientific Management should be modified before they could obtain wide acceptance in British industry, where sectional solidarity had an intensity which did not exist amid the rapidly changing technical and racial conditions of American industry. The Whitley Report outlined a different path, developing some of the leading ideas of Scientific Management under the organized joint direction of employers and employed (ibid., 393).

In the final chapter of *Industry and Trade*, discussing 'The decline of exclusive class advantages in industry', Marshall stressed the importance of the movement to which the Whitley Report gave voice by extending the influence of employees. He was somewhat critical of G.D.H. Cole's collectivist scheme for National Guilds, suggesting that they only dealt superficially with business problems, and that: 'Mr Cole seems to follow closely in the paths of St Simon, Fourier, and other early socialists' (ibid., 660). Marshall then broached 'Possibilities of the future', stressing the extent to which industrial strength was being increased by broadening the basis of much of the higher administrative work which used to be the exclusive preserve of the well-to-do. The number of those who had the strength and the elasticity of mind and character needed for the larger responsibilities of industry was rapidly increasing. This change was emphasized by the Whitley Report, and would be promoted by Joint Industrial Councils (ibid., 661).

Thus for Marshall the future could be made better than the past by greater community of thought, action and sympathy; by a fuller recognition of the dignity of man, and cordial cooperation among all the various ranks of industry; and by a continued development of the fundamental principles of the Whitley Report. He thought that human nature had developed new possibilities in almost every generation, and that it had progressed very rapidly during the last 50 years (ibid., 650–51).

6.5 MARSHALL'S LEGACY: THE DEVELOPMENT OF HIS IDEAS ON PROGRESS

As is well known, the main theoretical contribution made by Marshall has long been considered to be Book V of *Principles*, especially its analytical apparatus. More recently, a 'new' and very different Alfred Marshall has been discovered, as testified by the papers collected in the book *The Elgar Companion to Alfred Marshall* (Raffaelli et al., 2006).

His ideas on progress are among those aspects of his work that have been neglected. In part this was because the book he planned was never published, but also because his principal pupils did not acknowledge, or insufficiently acknowledged, the importance of such ideas and did not build on them. Some of them did deal in their writings with 'progress', but mostly only in passing.

6.5.1 Arthur C. Pigou

First of these is Arthur Cecil Pigou, Marshall's favourite pupil, who succeeded him as Professor of Political Economy at Cambridge. Pigou, to a greater extent than any other student of Marshall, takes account of the properties of the Marshallian idea of progress, but does not consider them as essential to the whole, and does not deal with them in any detail.

Pigou's main contribution to economics is considered to be his works on economic welfare: *Wealth and Welfare* (1912) and *The Economics of Welfare* (1920). As noted elsewhere (Caldari, 2004), Pigou develops one important aspect of the modern concept of sustainable development to a greater degree than had Marshall: the exhaustion of natural resources. Pigou underlines the importance of the environment in general and of natural resources in particular, maintaining in *Economics of Welfare*: 'It is the clear duty of Government to watch over, and, if need be, by legislative enactment, to defend, the exhaustible natural resources of the country' (1920, 28). In addition to this, Pigou also takes into consideration other elements that form in Marshall the core idea of progress, although his view is much less comprehensive than that of Marshall.[20] The problem of poverty (and pauperism) is often referred to, together with its main connotations (the problem of housing, the brutalization of people, and so forth). As in Marshall, poverty is considered the foremost issue, behind which there lie are a number of different factors: 'The failure of poor persons to attain the level we deem to be satisfactory in the matter of nourishment, of education and of insurance, is frequently the result, not so much of poverty as of ignorance and mismanagement' (Pigou, 1914, 46).

Education is therefore lent emphasis as the fundamental means to better the condition of the poor. Recalling Marshall,[21] Pigou maintains:

> Investment in the education of children generally should be credited with the effect it produces in *these* children. This point and the implications of it are put with great force by Dr. Marshall in the following passage: 'There is no extravagance more prejudicial to the growth of national wealth than the wasteful negligence which allows genius that happens to be born of lowly parentage to expend itself in lowly work. No change would conduce so much to a rapid increase of national wealth as an improvement in our schools, and especially those of the middle grade, provided it be combined with an extensive system of scholarships, which will enable the clever son of a working man to rise gradually from school to school till he has the best theoretical and practical education which the age can give.' (Pigou, 1920, 781)

Through education people can ameliorate their character, and workers their skill and status:

> It follows from what has been said that the progress of education, physical, mental and moral, among the working-classes may truly be called a remedy, within limits, for unemployment. By developing general capacity, and sometimes also special technical capacity associated with some particular industry,

> education raises people, who would have been inefficient unskilled workers, into the ranks, if not of the skilled, at least of the efficient unskilled workers. (1924, 67)

Pigou devoted great attention to the aspects of this issue related to labour, writing a number of works on the subject (1905, 1916, 1924). He was mainly interested in the problems of unemployment and unskilled work, and during his life was engaged in exchanges with trade unionists, representatives of the working classes, and workers.[22]

Nonetheless, we may note an important difference here in comparison with Marshall. In Marshall's reasoning on progress and its mainsprings, education has a paramount role: it is only through education that people may better their character, and it is only through the betterment of human character that real progress may be attained. As we have seen in the above paragraph, with the enhancement of character, people aim at a higher quality of life, including a better and higher-paid job. In a letter to Westcott, Marshall refers to the necessity to improve people's education: 'we ought to expend more money, and with it more force, moral and physical, in cutting off the supply of people unable to do good work, and therefore unable to earn good wages' (Whitaker, 1996, II, 263). A general lack of education also explains in part the problem of unemployment:

> systematic unemployment is, I believe, caused by the existence of large numbers of people, who will not or can not work steadily or strongly enough to make it possible that they should be employed regularly. They are hunters for odd jobs, which are generally 'soft' jobs. A large part of the present unemployment seems to me of this kind: that is, it is a symptom of disease rather than a cause. (Letter to P. Alden, dated 28 January 1903, Whitaker, 1996, III, 3).

The other kind of unemployment considered by Marshall is occasional unemployment connected with trade fluctuations, due to 'the inability of beings of finite intelligence to forecast coming economic need and opportunities with perfect precision' (ibid.). In Pigou, education is important but, as we have seen, only 'within certain limits'. It is not considered – as in Marshall – the necessary, unavoidable starting point for removing unemployment and stimulating the growth and progress of a nation. It is considered a necessary prerequisite of progress, but insufficient for its realization.

In Pigou, as in Marshall, wealth and welfare do not only have a material, strictly economic meaning. An increase in material wealth is, of course, a necessary element, but it is not the sole factor guaranteeing complete welfare. Moreover, the increase in material wealth must go together with the development of other (qualitative) features.[23] This is clear in the concept of a minimum standard advanced in *Economics of Welfare*:

> [The minimum standard] must be conceived, not as a subjective minimum of satisfaction, but as an objective minimum of conditions. The conditions, too, must be conditions, not in respect of one aspect of life only, but in general. Thus, the minimum includes some defined quantity and quality of house accommodation, of medical care, of education, of food, of leisure, of the apparatus of sanitary convenience and safety where work is carried on, and so on. (1920, 788)

The problem of housing receives particular attention, since it is considered as 'one aspect of the general problem of poverty' (Pigou and Seebohm Rowntree, 1914, 35); and although Pigou acknowledges himself to be 'in no sense a housing expert', his analysis is of great interest. Pigou uses the concept 'of a minimum standard in its special application to housing'. Accordingly, the minimum standard concerns, first, 'the structure and repair of individual houses'; and second, 'the overcrowding of rooms'. These two factors, says Pigou, 'have long been recognized'. But the housing problem is much more complex, and implies other elements. Another important aspect is described with the following words:

> If one walks through an ordinary town to-day, and particularly if one walks through London . . . one sees, for instance, a great number of buildings frequently huddled together, stretching in long rows of dismal sameness, with narrow streets and no green spaces. The most conspicuous and most obvious imperfections are usually to be found in those congested districts inhabited by the poor, that exist in the central parts of some large towns. But even in the suburbs where towns are expanding in some of the out-lying parts of Cambridge, for example adjacent to open country, there are growing up with a terrible rapidity hideous unbroken tracts of undistinguishable, featureless, gardenless habitations. (Pigou and Seebohm Rowntree, 1914, 39–40)

Although, as Pigou notes, 'one becomes so permeated and soaked with the enervating squalor of these drab conditions, that one tends to regard it as an inevitable evil incident of town life', this should not be considered the rule. As proof, Pigou mentions the garden city experiments as Letchworth, or Hampstead Garden Suburb. As in Marshall, this aspect may have very important effects on people:

> It is not merely a matter of the aesthetic sense of a few superior persons. It is a matter of the character and of the health of the people as a whole a matter in a way even more significant than the internal arrangements of factories, because it affects not the workers only, but also their young children. Make your town sufficiently hideous, sufficiently congested, sufficiently void of open space and grass for children's play, and you go far to write, for character and for life, over the gate of it : 'All hope abandon ye who enter here.' (Pigou and Seebohm Rowntree, 1914, 41–2)

It is exactly the relevance of this element that justifies, for Pigou, state intervention:

> The recognition of this third element in satisfactory housing conditions leads inevitably to the granting of powers to some authority to limit the quantity of building permitted on a given area, and to control the building activities of individuals. It is as idle to expect a well-planned town to result from the independent activities of isolated speculators, as it would be to expect a satisfactory picture to result if each separate square inch were painted by an independent artist. No 'invisible hand' can be relied on to produce a good arrangement of the whole from a combination of separate treatments of the parts. It is necessary that an authority of wider reach should intervene and should tackle the collective problem of beauty, of air and of light, as those other collective problems of gas and water have been already tackled. (Pigou and Seebohm Rowntree, 1914, 42–43)

As in Marshall, although free competition is given a paramount role and importance, a number of factors justifying an active role for the state are recognized:

> It is the duty of a civilized State to lay down certain minimum conditions in every department of life, below which it refuses to allow any of its free citizens to fall. There must be a minimum standard of conditions in factories, a minimum standard (varying of course with the strain involved in different industries) of leisure, a minimum standard of dwelling accommodation, a minimum standard of education, of medical treatment in case of illness, and of wholesome food and clothing. Each one of these standards, so far as practicable, must be enforced separately. No such plea must be admitted as that, if a man is allowed to work excessive hours, or to live in a cheap and ruinous house, he will be able to attain independently to the required minima in all other departments of life. The standards must be upheld all along the line, and any man or family which fails to attain independently to any one of them must be regarded as a proper subject for State action. (Pigou and Seebohm Rowntree, 1914, 36)

6.5.2 Sydney J. Chapman

Sydney Chapman, one of Marshall's most distinguished pupils from his early years in Cambridge, described Marshall's method of economic thinking as follows: 'Marshall stressed the importance of taking evolution into account in Economics. This he had partly in mind in dwelling on "the many in the one, and the one in the many." And for an evolutionary study much realism is essential' (Chapman, n.d., 'Autobiography', 26). Chapman saw 'the economic world as a system of systems, each of which was in part a separate whole and in part a dependent portion of a larger whole . . . This was a biological idea . . . when the facts of growth were allowed for' (ibid., 63).

Chapman is best remembered for *The Lancashire Cotton Industry* (1904) and his *Work and Wages* (three volumes, 1904–14). The former is a case study in industrial economics of Marshallian style. *Work and Wages*, published in three volumes over a ten-year period, builds on the earlier work of Thomas Brassey and his son Earl Brassey in the 1870s. In his *Lectures to Women* (1873), Marshall provided summaries of Brassey's *Work and Wages* (1872). The main lesson was that high wages improved the physical condition of labour, and therefore workers' efficiency. In his later books *Economics of Industry* (co-authored, 1879) and *Principles of Economics* (1920), Marshall displayed a strong awareness of the links between wages and efficiency. Marshall's observations of the workings of industrial labour markets were reinforced by Brassey's observations.

In his *Work and Wages*, Part II 'Wages and Employment', Marshall's pupil Chapman summarized the law of wages as defined by Marshall, considering the organization of labour, trades unions, industrial peace and unemployment. Part III, 'Social Betterment', concludes with a treatment of social progress and improvements in housing, health and education for workers and their families. In the opening chapter, 'Aspects of social progress', he rejects eugenics in favour of a theory of environmental determinism; the human stock can be bettered most effectively by improving people's environment, housing, public health, education and training, and working conditions, concluding with a discussion of public aid.

Chapman argued that the productive characteristic of an ideal society was that: 'efficiency . . . is interwoven with the personal values . . . The physical and mental vigour of the workers is therefore a national concern . . . Housing, sanitation, and other things bearing on the health of the community, are consequently linked up with the problem of production. Connected with it also are the means of developing in each worker his highest potential value and securing that his task is appropriate to his cultivated powers' (1914, 5–6). In his view, 'the higher the average level of the vital stock of a community the better off is the community . . . Any circumstance which helps the realization of mind and purpose (for instance, a good social environment which includes a good system of education) encourages the selection which is good for the stock.' He maintained that: 'even if environment does not have a direct effect which is lasting (because acquired characteristics are not transmitted), yet an improved environment places a community more or less permanently in closer proximity to the perfect state' (ibid. 16, 18).

Chapman defines progress as an 'increasing demand for intelligence' that has the property of rendering 'employment of the least intelligent increasingly precarious' (p. 68). Skilled work is, according to Chapman, the real sign of progress, whereas unskilled work causes inefficiency and precariousness:

> The more precarious the work of the least efficient, the more rapidly is the army of unemployables recruited from their ranks. For as soon as they are out of work they are in distress, and the longer distress lasts the more physically incapable they become. (p. 68)

The means to transform unskilled into skilled work is considered to be education, technical education in particular, that as in Marshall has above all an effect on human character. Thus Chapman writes:

> Inefficiency is partly the result of insufficient or unsuitable education, even when it is immediately traceable to moral and physical deficiencies. Character and efficiency hang together. There can be no doubt but that improved and extended education and its closer adaptation to the needs of the scholars would be productive of a marked reduction in the numbers of those unfortunate people thronging the streets today who are only just fit for employment – and perhaps not for regular employment – when business is brisk, and of those who are so unimaginative and unadaptable that they struggle for the bare pittance which can be extracted from a sinking demand for their particular kind of skill. (Chapman and Hallsworth, 1909, 153)

6.5.3 D.H. MacGregor

Among those who studied in Cambridge under Marshall's supervision, D.H. MacGregor is distinguished by his studies of industrial economics. Marshall's influence is evident in his methodological approach, in the emphasis given to the organization of firm and industry, and in his concern for all those aspects that were connected with the progress of a nation. As with Marshall, his analysis is not limited to a static, abstract context; in inquiring into trusts, cartels and combinations MacGregor adopts an evolutionary view that allows him to depict critically the principal positive and negative characteristics of different industrial systems.

Economic and industrial progress is the main outcome of what MacGregor considers to be the most important influence: invention. As in Marshall, progress requires new and fresh knowledge, innovative contributions in terms of both new products and new processes (MacGregor, 1911). But as in Marshall, changes due to new inventions are slow, and necessarily so (MacGregor, 1911, 34–40).

In order to underline the dynamic, complex nature of economic problems, Marshall, in Principles, uses the metaphor of 'organic growth' (1920, 461). This is an image taken from biology that was at that time becoming increasingly fashionable. Marshall's preoccupation with biology is well known: biology is the only science capable of grasping the complexity of living organisms and, for this very reason, the only science that is of use in understanding the manifold nature of human beings and their institutions, economic relations included. MacGregor also – following on from Herbert Spencer as much as Marshall himself – refers to biology (the title *Evolution of Industry* for his 1911 book is a clear reference), and he uses the metaphor of organic growth.

In organisms, growth entails a passage from a lower to a higher form of life, characterized by a greater subdivisions and variety of parts and functions. A more developed organism is characterized by a unity made of several distinguished parts. In a certain measure, a similar change may be found in the industrial and economic systems. The growth of industry in time has been characterized by an increasing division of labour and specialization of parts, all comprehended in a greater unity. But there is an important difference between organic and industrial growth: while living organisms are characterized by circulation, their true principle of life, industrial organisms do not have an analogous principle. Labour must be considered for industrial organisms what blood is for living organisms; accordingly, MacGregor underlines that, contrary to blood, labour does not have a high degree of freedom, as it does not circulate inside the industrial organism. Labour is, indeed, characterized by class specialization that subdivides people into several different strata, among which movements are extremely difficult (1911, 58–9). It is a matter of what Marshall (and before him Mill) had already emphasized: the existence in society of the so-called non-competing groups, of different strata of people. It is for this very reason that 'economic evolution fails to correspond with organic evolution' (MacGregor, 1911, 58). This failure is due, according to MacGregor, to: 'the lateness of educational as compared with industrial development' (1911, 60).

Education, as in Marshall, is the key by means of which individuals can better their character and their position in the society. More precisely:

> the power of labour to move freely from rank to rank of the industrial systems depends upon educational change in two ways. In the first place, it depends upon the mere technical ability by which the workman is made competent to rise to a higher grade or to adapt himself to a changed but allied occupation, and in the second place, educational opportunity lays the basis of industrial aspiration itself. (MacGregor, 1911, 60–61)

Education is important both from a micro and a macro point of view. One of the most dangerous and detrimental problems for a nation is the problem of unemployment. Although it may be possible to reduce some of its severe effects (through insurance, regulation and so forth), the best solution is its prevention. The chief device to prevent unemployment is, according to MacGregor as well as Marshall, education: 'The health of the industrial system as a whole is here involved, depending on such influences as education, industrial peace, and such amendments of the industrial system itself as make for good relationships' (1922, 725).

The role of education is so important, its presence is so inalienable, that the state has to take responsibility for its provision:

> the full enforcement of the new Education Act is urgent, if a large amount of preventable unemployment is to be prevented. It is more urgent as a matter of mere economy, if the state intends in future to accept the recommendation of maintenance of adults under training. The addition of non-vocational education for juveniles up to a later age tends to open to their aspiration and competition other than the manual grades of industry. But faith in this entire idea is a most difficult thing to create. It requires that industry will itself march with educational preparation by the extension of opportunity to share in the government of industry. This reacts on the belief in education, and education will in turn react upon it. (1922, 748–9)

Although his main interest is not progress and its characteristics, but rather industrial economics, MacGregor adopts an evolutionary point of view: the economist, in describing the society as it is, tries to understand the elements that help improve human life and national well-being. A perspective which no doubt owes much to Marshall.

6.6 SOME CONCLUSIONS: THE MODERNITY OF MARSHALL'S IDEAS ON PROGRESS

Many aspects of the Marshallian idea of progress were deeply rooted in contemporary British culture. As we have seen, the importance given to the amelioration of the human character and education, the need to transform unskilled into skilled work, the urgency of providing good houses and green spaces to people, are all elements that belong to the culture of the late Victorian and Edwardian era. Undoubtedly, Marshall absorbed many ideas and suggestions scattered among the many articles, books and pamphlets that he read on these topics, and in the debates in which he participated. He also contributed to general awareness of these issues in Britain, and as we have seen he influenced the values and writings of some of his pupils, especially Pigou.

Nonetheless, it does appear that the manner in which Marshall elaborated and connected his ideas on social and economic progress is utterly original. As already emphasized elsewhere (Caldari and Masini, 2009),

Marshall absorbed ideas, opinions and suggestions, and then reworked them in a very idiosyncratic manner, rendering him an extremely modern economist and thinker.

With regard to progress, Marshall shares many ideas with Christian socialists, philanthropists, trade unionists and members of organizations such as the Charity Organization Society and the Garden City movement. But his perspective is not purely moral or political. For him, is a manifold science, with many different dimensions.

Furthermore, the Marshallian idea of progress still appears extremely modern. The first aspect to be noted is that progress is a really complex concept. It means economic development (that is, an increase in material wealth) but it also implies and requires moral, cultural and social improvement. The most important means for stimulating progress is education. Through education people can improve their character and can learn to do more and better things; and the quality of their work improves. Through education people can learn to appreciate good-quality housing, the possibility of having green open spaces for recreation and fresh air, and new opportunities for leisure-time pursuits. Through education, in short, people learn to value their quality of life. The state in this respect has an important responsibility, and must intervene to guarantee it. The quality of life is the real measure of progress. Given all the elements that are responsible for the betterment of the quality of life, the character of people would improve, and the nation could make progress.

If we look at the actual challenges we face today, from the problem of polluted towns to the critical situation of many economies, it is easy to realize that what are absent here are those elements of progress that Marshall outlined. This is a scenario that Marshall would have perhaps defined as 'in demand of progress'.

NOTES

1. All the quotations without references used in this paragraph are taken from the manuscript notes on progress (Marshall Library Archive, Cambridge).
2. That is, economic progress.
3. 'The dissemination of sound school education is enabling the children even of unskilled labourers to have some chance of rising to work that evokes faculties of a rather higher quality than those which his work gave exercise.'
4. Elements of the Marshallian idea of Utopia can be found in many of his writings, from the very early (the *Lectures to Women*, 1995 [1873]) to the 8th edition of *Principles* (1920). In substance, Utopia is close to the idea of Communism (also called Absolute Utopia) insofar as it depicts a world in which: 'every one renders the best service of which he is capable to the community. The return which he receives is not in proportion to the value of his work to the community: it is simply adjusted to his needs'. The important connection with the ideals of Communism (understood as the very ideal

state described by the previous quotation) and the important consequences following from Marshall having this background to his reasoning are underlined and developed by Becattini (1962, 1989). He also stresses that Marshall's idea of Utopia is strictly connected with Hegel's *Philosophy of History* and, more precisely, would correspond to Hegel's fully realized liberty, as a synthesis of both objective and subjective liberty.

5. See, for instance, those collected in Whitaker (1996).
6. The Eranus Club was founded in 1872 by B.F. Westcott, J.B. Lightfoot and F.J.A. Hort. It was an elite club for senior Apostles that 'included among its members: F.J.A. Hort, Henry Jackson, J.B. Lightfoot, Alfred Marshall, J. Clerk Maxwell, J.R. Seeley, Henry Sidgwick, Y.H. Stanton, G.G. Stokes, and Coutts Trotter. Any one familiar with Cambridge, or the world of learning, will recognise what a galaxy of talent here shines' (Westcott, 1903, I, 385). Its general intention is well synthesized in the following words: 'It has appeared to several resident members of the University [of Cambridge], who are actively engaged in different departments of academic work, that it would be a great advantage to have opportunities of meeting to consider questions of common interest in the light of their special studies. It is proposed, therefore, to form a small society for the purpose of hearing and discussing essays prepared by the members' (from a letter written by Westcott, quoted in Westcott, 1903, 385).
7. Marshall's involvement with the Society for Promoting Industrial Villages and the Garden City Movement was very strong and both movements (especially the latter) were deeply influenced by him and his writings (see Caldari, 2004).
8. A movement that sought to apply the principles of Christianity in solving urgent problems connected with the modern industrial life (for an account on this topic see Woodworth, 1903).
9. In *The Strength of the People*, there is an interesting reference to Chalmers's *Moral and Spiritual Influence of Parochial Associations* and *Christian and Civic Economy of Large Towns*. Although we have not found any mention of him by Marshall, and the books are not catalogued as either in the Marshall Library or in any other Cambridge libraries, some passages seem very close to Marshall's view: 'The remedy against the extension of pauperism does not lie in the liberalities of the rich. It lies in the hearts and habits of the poor. Plant in their bosoms a principle of independence. Give a higher tone of delicacy to their characters. Teach them to recoil from pauperism as a degradation' (Chalmers, *Moral and Spiritual Influence of Parochial Associations*, 150); 'if you wish to extinguish poverty, combat with it in its first elements. If you confine your beneficence to the relief of actual poverty, you do nothing. Dry up, if possible, the spring of poverty, for every attempt to intercept the running stream has totally failed' (ibid. 134).
10. According to Marshall, the poor are people with 'poor physique and feeble will, with no enterprise, no courage, no hope and scarcely any self-respect, whom misery drives them to work for lower wages than the same work gets in the country' (1884 [1952], 144–5).
11. According to Marshall: 'the best investment of the present capital of the country is to educate the next generation and make them all gentlemen' (1995 [1873]), 106).
12. Helen Bosanquet, like the other members of the Charity Organization Society (see below, the discussion of Octavia Hill, for instance) was strongly critical of state intervention in the field of education. This is, of course, clearly in contrast with Marshall's position.
13. In the Bound Volumes preserved in the Marshall Library (Caldari, 2000, 2003) there are, among others, the following articles: 'Old age pensions', *Economic Journal*, 1899; 'The statistics of metropolitan pauperism', *Charity Organization Review*, 1894; 'Methods of relief adopted in the metropolis during the winter 1895', *Charity Organization Review*, 1896. In a book edited by Loch (*Methods of Social Advance*, 1904) preserved in the Marshall Library we have found the following interesting passage: 'the best results will arise from an advance in the education and intelligence of the poor at large. Progress is necessarily slow and almost imperceptible in this direction, for the gradual dissemination of knowledge is a matter of years' 'Out-patient departments and the rearing of children', by Edmund Cautley in Loch, 1904, 15–16. Interestingly, this passage is very close to that quoted above from Marshall's *Principles*.

14. See Whitaker (1996). From the Bound Volumes we know that Marshall also had read 'Housing: lessons from Germany', *Independent Review*, 1904; 'The greater inquiry', *Independent Review*, 1904; 'Health and education', *Contemporary Review*, 1906; 'Art in everyday life', *Journal of Education*, 1900; *The Relation of Drawing to Healthy Life*, Manchester: J.E. Cornish, 1895.
15. In his notes on *Progress* there are many references to the importance of art. According to Horsfall, art should become: 'a teacher, an agent in the social reform and elevation of people' (in Frow and Frow, 1995, 1).
16. In his notes on *Progress* he maintains that all people should have a good early school education: 'all those who can profit by it, to have a (middle-age) 14–16 school education. A The rest of the children to be set to mechanical work, including writing, typewriting. B those who profit by A to [be] classified according to their special character of their abilities and tastes into . . . constructive studies [as] chemistry, electricity, biological sciences, [and] . . . especially pure mathematics'. Whereas literary studies 'should not be carried far in school'; and with regard to art, 'the class should be small. An artistic element should be present, as a secondary . . . element in all educations. But only exceptional natural genius for art' should be encouraged and helped: 'For the total number of people whose artistic work is of considerable value to others is small: those who enjoy artistic efforts, but have no special faculty for them should receive moderate assistance by various kinds of education: but not at very considerable expense to the public'.
17. Both of them were Christian Socialists.
18. Hill outlined her method (a term she preferred to 'system') in dealing with what she described as 'the destructive class of tenants' to the Royal Commission on the Housing of the Working Classes in 1884: 'The difficulty with these people is not financial, but moral; and, therefore, I know nothing for them but some individual power and watchfulness. They must be trained . . . You may have a destructive drunken man, whom neither Sir Sydney Waterlow's, nor any other society, would take into their buildings at all, for he will not conform to the rules; the only way that I know of getting hold of him is buying up the house in which he is, exactly as it is, and making him profit by his own care . . . I say to them, 'You must either do better or you must leave; which is it to be?' (quoted in Whelan, 1998, 5).
19. Marshall wrote a great deal about local and central taxation, free trade and other topics in his correspondence with John Llewelyn Davies (1826–1916), a theologian who was a friend of the movement for the higher education of women, a strong liberal and, in Cambridge, very close to Westcott (Whitaker 1996, II, 340–41).
20. Pigou's ideas are scattered throughout his writings, without converging on any precise idea of progress. He considers welfare, the importance of education, housing, environment, the problem of unemployment; but while in Marshall all these factors are aspects of the same whole (the idea of progress), in Pigou they remained somewhat isolated from each other.
21. In his writings Pigou refers also to Charles Booth, Octavia Hill, C.S. Loch, H. Bosanquet and many others.
22. For instance, in 1916 he participated in an Oxford Conference where the problem of the postwar reorganization of industry, commerce and finance was considered. At the conferences there were a large number of delegates representing trade unions, trades councils, co-operative societies, the Club and Institute Union, and other labour organizations. In the report of the Conference are included the papers presented (by A.C. Pigou, Sidney Webb, Arthur Greenwood and A.E. Zimmern) and the questions posed during the meeting.

    The report is very interesting and proves that many Marshallian conceptions were widely shared. For instance, a comment on the paper by Zimmern made by Mr W. Straker (Northumberland Miners' Association) runs: 'During this week we have heard a good deal about the necessity of greater power being in the hands of Trade Unions. I agree with that entirely, but power implies responsibility, and to discharge responsibility intelligently implies education. There can be no progress in the Labour or the Trade

Union movements without a greater knowledge and a better education. But when we come to think about the country's position we raise the question to a higher level than any mere class consideration. Then education becomes all the more imperative. When this war is ended the struggle of nations will not cease. Competition will still go on for a long time yet. An ignorant people is a weak people, and in that coming economic struggle, which may be as bitter in the future as ever it was, we must, in the interest of the country, have the best brains at the front, whether there be private money in combination with those brains or not' (pp. 81–2).

Or again in the paper presented by S. Webb we read: 'Finally, as to labour, which means, of course, the human beings who carry on the manual work. When we consider that we have something like 15 000 000 of these men and women who are manual working wage-earners, and that everything depends on their health and strength and training as to how effective they will be in industry, what a lesson that is to take care of the sanitation and education of the population, and especially of the generation which is growing up! We killed more babies last year wantonly in this country through our public neglect than all the lives that were lost in the war on our side! We can, if we choose, save as many babies in the coming twelve months as all the men's lives that will be lost to us in the coming twelve months of the war. This waste of infant and child life is going on from year to year' (p. 49).

23. More specifically, only if some qualities develop can the increase of material wealth be serviceable: 'The root of the matter is that, even when, under existing conditions, the mental constitution of poor persons is such that an enlarged income will at the moment yield them little benefit, yet, after a time more especially if the time is long enough to allow a new generation to grow up the possession of such an income will make possible the development in them, through education and otherwise, of capacities and faculties adapted for the enjoyment of the enlarged income. Thus, in the long run differences of temperament and taste between rich and poor are overcome by the very fact of a shifting of income between them. Plainly, therefore, they cannot be used as an argument to disprove the benefits of a transference' (1920, 54).

REFERENCES

Becattini, G. (1962), *Il Concetto di Industria e la Teoria del Valore*, Torino: Boringhieri.

Becattini, G. (1989), 'Sectors and/or districts: some remarks on the conceptual foundations of industrial economics', in E. Goodman and J. Bamford (eds), *Small Firms and Industrial Districts in Italy*, London: Routledge, pp. 123–35.

Becattini, G. (2000), 'Marshallian anomalies', *Marshall Studies Bulletin*, **7**, http://131.114.162.142/siti/marshall/marshall/7ndx.html.

Bosanquet, H. (1903), *The Strength of the People*, London: Macmillan.

Brassey, T. (1872), *Work and Wages Practically Illustrated*, London: Bell & Daldy.

Caldari, K. (2000), 'A list of the essays collected in bound volumes by Alfred Marshall: Part 1', *Marshall Studies Bulletin*, **7**, http://131.114.162.142/siti/marshall/marshall/7ndx.html.

Caldari, K. (2003), 'A list of the essays collected in bound volumes by Alfred Marshall: Part 2', *Marshall Studies Bulletin*, **8**, http://131.114.162.142/siti/marshall/marshall/8ndx.html.

Caldari, K. (2004), 'Alfred Marshall's idea of progress and sustainable development', *Journal of the History of Economic Thought*, **26** (4), 519–36.

Caldari, K. and F. Masini (2009), 'The limits to growth: Alfred Marshall and the British economic tradition', in Y. Shionoya and T. Nishizawa (eds), *Marshall and Schumpeter on Evolution: Economic Sociology of Capitalist Development*, Cheltenham, UK and Northampton, MA, USA: Edward Elgar, pp. 166–87.

Chapman, S.J. (n.d.), 'Unpublished autobiography of Sir Sydney John Chapman', Coll. Misc. 664, LSE Archives.

Chapman, S.J. (1904), *The Lancashire Cotton Industry: A Study in Economic Development*, Manchester: Manchester University Press.

Chapman, S.J. (1908), *Work and Wages. Part II: Wages and Employment*, London: Longmans, Green & Co.

Chapman, S.J. (1914), *Work and Wages. Part III: Social Betterment*, London: Longmans, Green & Co.

Chapman, S.J. and H.M. Hallsworth (1909), *Unemployment: The Results of an Investigation made in Lancashire and an Examination of the Report of the Poor Law Commission*, Manchester: University Press.

Clayton, J. (1906), 'Bishop Westcott', in G.W.E. Russell (ed.), *Leaders of the Church, 1800–1900*, London: A.R. Mowbray & Co.

Edgeworth, F.Y. (1925), 'Reminiscences', in A.C. Pigou (ed), *Memorials of Alfred Marshall*, London: Macmillan.

Frow, E. and R. Frow (1995), 'Morris's "working Folk and the future of Art"', *Journal of William Morris Studies*, **11** (3), 2–5.

Keynes, J.M. (1926), *Official Papers by Alfred Marshall*, London: Macmillan.

Keynes, J.M. (1972), *Essays in Biography*, The Collected Writings of John Maynard Keynes Vol. X, London: Macmillan.

Kelvin, N. (ed.) (1987), *The Collected Letters of William Morris*, Vol. II, Princeton, NJ: Princeton University Press.

Loch, C.S. (1890), *Charity Organization*, London: Swan Sonnenchein.

Loch, C.S. (ed.) (1904), *Methods of Social Advance*, London: Macmillan.

MacGregor, D.H. (1911), *The Evolution of Industry*, London: Thornton Butterworth.

MacGregor, D.H. (1922), 'British aspects of unemployment', *Journal of Political Economy*, **30** (6), 725–49.

Mann, Tom (1923) *Tom Mann's Memoirs*, London: Labour Publishing Company.

Marshall, A. (1873), *Lectures to Women*, reprinted (1995), T. Raffaelli, E. Biagini and R. McWilliams Tullberg (eds), *Alfred Marshall's Lectures to Women*, Aldershot, UK and Brookfield, USA: Edward Elgar, pp. 85–132.

Marshall, A. (1884), 'Where to house the London poor', *Contemporary Review*, reprinted in A.C. Pigou (ed). (1925) *Memorials of Alfred Marshall*, London: Macmillan, pp. 142–51.

Marshall, A. (1885), 'How far do remediable causes influence prejudicially (a) the continuity of Employment, (b) the rates of wages?' Industrial Remuneration Conference (1885), pp. 173–83; reprinted (1998) in *Alfred Marshall: Critical Responses*, P. Groenewegen (ed.), Vol. 2, London: Routledge.

Marshall, A. (1923 [1919]), *Industry and Trade. A Study of Industrial Technique and Business Organization; and of Their Influences on the Conditions of Various Classes and Nations*, 4th edn London: Macmillan.

Marshall, A. (1920), *Principles of Economics*, London: Macmillan.

Marshall, Alfred and Mary Marshall (1879), *Economics of Industry*, London: Macmillan.

Petridis, Ray (1973), 'Alfred Marshall's attitudes to and economic analysis of trade

unions', in J.C. Wood (ed.), *Alfred Marshall, Critical Assessments*, Vol. III, London: Croom Helm, 1982.
Pigou, A.C. (1905), *Principles and Methods of Industrial Peace*, London: Macmillan.
Pigou, A.C. (1912), *Wealth and Welfare*, London: Macmillan.
Pigou, A.C. (1914), *Lectures on Housing*, Manchester: Sherratt & Hughes.
Pigou, A.C. (1916), 'The disorganisation of industry, commerce and finance: the problems to be faced', in *The Reorganisation of Industry*, Oxford: The Council of Ruskin College.
Pigou, A.C. (1920), *Economics of Welfare*, London: Macmillan.
Pigou, A.C. (1924), *Unemployment*, London: Williams & Norgate.
Pigou, A.C. and B. Seebohm Rowntree (1914), *Lectures on Housing*, Manchester: Manchester University Press.
Raffaelli, T., G. Becattini and M. Dardi (eds) (2006), *The Elgar Companion to Alfred Marshall*, Cheltenham, UK and Northampton, MA, USA: Edward Elgar.
Reynolds, J.P. (1952), 'Thomas Coglan Horsfall and the town planning movement in England', *Town Planning Review*, **23**, 52–60.
Westcott, A. (1903), *Life and Letters of Brroke Foss Westcott*, 2 vols, London: Macmillan.
Whelan, R. (1998), *Octavia Hill and the Social Housing Debate: Essays and Letters by Octavia Hill*, London: St Edmundsbury Press.
Whitaker, K.K. (1996), *The Correspondence of Alfred Marshall Economist*, 3 vols, Cambridge: Cambridge University Press.
Woodworth, A.V. (1903), *Christian Socialism in England*, London: Swan Sonneschein.

PART III

The diffusion of economic ideas in South-Eastern Europe and beyond

7. The dissemination of economic thought in South-Eastern Europe in the nineteenth century

Michalis M. Psalidopoulos and Nicholas J. Theocarakis

7.1 INTRODUCTION

The renaissance of the history of political economy towards the end of the twentieth century has given rise to several national histories of economic thought, together with analysis of its international diffusion (Cardoso, 2003). Psalidopoulos and Mata (2002) have explored the relationship between economic thought and economic policy in Europe's less developed countries in the nineteenth century, while Augello and Guidi (2001, 2005) have examined the institutionalization and professionalization of economics and economists in European parliaments during the same period.

We here continue this work, seeking a better understanding of the dissemination of economic thought in South-Eastern Europe during the nineteenth century. This was the century of nation-building on the periphery of Europe, and was marked by the coming of age of liberalism, protectionism and socialism. Newborn states, especially those that became independent from the Ottoman Empire, like Greece, Serbia, Bulgaria and Rumania (Albania had to wait for the next century), absorbed economic ideas and theories from Europe's more developed countries. Striving to become rich and prosperous, they followed various routes into modernity. Doing so meant for them first and foremost building modern institutions, fighting illiteracy and spreading the use of their language in their territories. It also meant developing the nation economically. The economic interests of each South-Eastern European country therefore had to be defined, and a policy leading to growth and prosperity introduced. Intellectuals in these countries had travelled and studied abroad at a time when classical political economy had long defeated, ideologically and scientifically, the mercantilist doctrines of the past; it had achieved the status of a science, perceiving itself as a requirement for personal liberty, freedom and growth. As economic liberalism in its various forms disseminated from the core European countries to the periphery, the newly born national states of South-Eastern Europe at first adopted a liberal approach to economic management. Very soon, however, they encountered difficulties in seeking to raise standards of living. In fact a modern scholar has described economic life in the nineteenth-century Balkans as 'evolution without development' (Palairet, 1997). Historical statistics reveal that economic growth rates in South-Eastern Europe were considerably lower than those of Western Europe, with the income gap growing instead of closing (Maddison, 1995). Liberalism did not bring convergence. This led politicians and public opinion in South-Eastern Europe to become more nationalistic with regard to their economic policies. To date no great attention has been given to the role of nationalism in economics, and in economic thought in particular, as a driving force in this context; for the most part, the issue of nationalism has been linked to the study of protectionism.

The chapter comprises the following sections. Section 7.2 is devoted to the economic situation and the tradition of economic thought in the Ottoman Empire, out of which all South-Eastern European countries emerged. Here we review economic ideas shortly before its gradual dissolution. In section 7.3 we refer to the case of Greece, the first country to become independent, and especially the popularization of liberal economics in that country. In sections 7.4, 7.5 and 7.6 we discuss the case with developments in economic thought in other South-Eastern European countries. Finally, in section 7.7 we offer some preliminary conclusions that deal with the dissemination of economic thought in South-Eastern Europe in the nineteenth century.

7.2 THE OTTOMAN EMPIRE: THE DECLINE OF PROVISIONISM

Economic thought in the Ottoman state was organized in terms of three basic principles: (1) provisionism, that is, the uninterrupted supply of goods to the internal market, particularly the urban population; (2) traditionalism, a tendency to preserve existing conditions; and (3) fiscalism, the maximization of Treasury income (Genç, 1994, 60). The Ottoman state also pursued a policy of extensive accumulation, adding new territories. This policy came to an end in the late seventeenth century, leading to a fiscal crisis.

The Treaty of Küçük Kaynarca in 1774 resulted in loss of territory, but mainly loss of control of large areas of the Empire, strengthening the hand of the Great Powers and of non-Muslim minorities who held important positions in the economic sector. The state tried to regain control by modernizing first the army and then other sectors of society. After initial failed attempts, Reform (*Tanzimat*) was finally introduced through the promulgation of *Hatt-ı Şerif* of *Gülhane* in 1839, and consolidated through the *Hatt-ı Hümayun* of 1856. The principal effect of *Tanzimat* was increasing foreign intervention, resulting in the diffusion of liberal ideas in the Ottoman Empire.

In the Ottoman Empire the economy was 'embedded' in the social system, a fact reflected in Islamic economic thought (Özveren, 2002, 129). In the early period Islamic teaching dictated economic policy (Baeck, 1994, 1996; Tomass, 1996; Ghazanfar, 2003), being suspicious of markets, while the 'mirror of princes' literature advised rulers how to administer prices and strengthen central power (Tietze, 1979–82). According to Sayar[1] in the pre-*Tanzimat* period the basic channels that affected economic policy, and implicitly economic thought, were Ottoman merchants, ambassadorial letters and foreign officials (cited in Doğan, 2006, 154). Foreigners were particularly significant in importing liberal ideas into the Empire. The Frenchmen Charles Tricon and Alexandre Blacque diffused liberal economic ideas through the pages of *Le Spectateur Oriental*, published from 1826. Blacque was later responsible for the French version of the official journal *Le Moniteur Ottoman*, published during Mahmud II's reign (Bülbül, 2007; Doğan 2006). Blacque was succeeded in the *Moniteur* by an official at the British Embassy, David Urquhart, the person credited by most scholars as having a decisive influence on the diffusion of liberal ideas. He wrote a book on Turkey (Urquhart, 1833) and he was instrumental in the signing of the Anglo-Ottoman Commercial Treaty of 1838 which gave distinct trade privileges to Great Britain. Thus, even though French was the lingua franca of liberalism and of Ottoman intellectuals, free trade doctrine was imported through England. Nassau Senior even visited the Grand Vizier to discuss economic matters (Bülbül, 2007).

The *Tanzimat* introduced economic education to the Ottoman Empire. The failure of the initial reforms was partly attributed to a lack of appropriate education. There was also the fear that foreigners and, to a lesser extent non-Muslims, were knowledgeable, whereas loyal subjects were not. Economics entered the curriculum of secondary education, while new university-level schools were created where economics was taught. A committee was created to recommend foreign texts for translation.[2] Say's *Catéchisme d'économie politique* was chosen as a textbook of economics and Sehak (or Sahak) Abru, an Ottoman Armenian, was commissioned to translate it, the translation appearing in 1852 (Doganalp-Votzi, 2007). In 1869 Mehmet Midhat translated the *Petit manuel populaire d'économie politique* written by Otto Hübner and adapted into French by Charles Le Hardy de Beaulieu. As one scholar observed, translations of foreign economic texts offered improved economic knowledge, leading to the 'scientification of Urquhart's liberalism' (Berkes cited in Doğan, 2006, 159).[3] Professors at the Mekteb-i Mülkiye – a school of political science for training civil servants founded in 1859 – wrote liberal economic texts and supported liberal policy positions. They include Mehmed Şerif Efendi, the first Professor at the Mülkiye, who wrote a textbook in 1863 (*ilm-i emval-i milliye*, [Science of national wealth], cited in Bülbül, 2007, 5)[4] and Sakızlı Ohannes Pasha, an Ottoman Armenian and civil servant, who studied economics in France and taught for 20 years at the school. His textbook written in 1881 (*Mebadi-i ilm-i servet-i millel*, [Introduction to the wealth of nations]) remained for many years the standard introduction to political economy (Bülbül, 2007, 5; Doğan, 2006). Münif and Portakal Mikael Pashas, prominent Ottoman liberals, were also teachers at the Mülkiye and authors of liberal texts. The German trained Münif Pasha, while Minister of Education, was among the founders of the Society of Ottoman Science (Cemiyet-i İlmiye-i Osmaniye) and editor of its periodical the *Mecmua-i Fünun* [Review of sciences] founded in 1863. The Review was the first scientific journal in the Ottoman Empire and active in the diffusion of the sciences and liberal ideas through translations and original texts (Doğan, 2006; Budak, 2008; Seyitdanlioğlu, 1998). Ohannes Pasha and Cavit Bey, Minister of Finance of the Committee of Union and Progress, a teacher at the Mülkiye and author of an influential economics textbook in the early twentieth century, were contributors to the *Review*. The Armenian liberal Portakal Mikael Pasha became the first director of the Agricultural Bank (Gencer, 2002, 239).

Liberal views did not go unchallenged. The Anglo-Ottoman Commercial Treaty created economic problems that brought a protectionist backlash. The intervention of the Great Powers in the political and economic affairs of the Ottoman Empire, their tendency to treat the country as a colony, and the partial failure of liberal reforms despite much effort, all contributed to growing dissatisfaction with liberal policies. The Ottoman state declared itself bankrupt, and in 1881 the Administration de la Dette Publique Ottomane was created, a foreign-owned company that supervised and controlled state finances. After the disastrous results of the 1877–78 Ottoman-Russian War, liberal policies fell out of favour and the state opted for an etatism that would dilute Ottomanism and herald a more nationalist approach. The non-Muslim minorities that made up the Ottoman bourgeoisie had to be complemented with a Turkish middle class, an idea reflected in the economic thought of the period (Adanır, 2003).

The most popular and prolific writer of the times, Ahmet Midhat

Efendi, wrote a text called *Political Economy* in 1879 in which he argued that liberal policies in trade and tariffs were responsible for the decline of Ottoman industry, and that a nationalist and protectionist policy was called for (Doğan, 2006).[5] He popularized Friedrich List's ideas in the Empire. During the Hamidian period, the Armenian liberals Sakızlı Ohannes and Portakal Mikael were transferred from the Mülkiye to the Treasury so as not to exert influence over students. One of the most prominent authors of the period was Namık Kemal, who was trained in England in the 1860s, and who built on the notions of fatherland and freedom. Although nominally liberal in his economic views, he was opposed to the Anglo-Ottoman Commercial Treaty and suggested that liberalism could only be introduced once the economic problems of the state had been resolved. His approach was not theoretical but pragmatic, a common characteristic of Ottoman economic thought, especially of public officials. Economic policy remained liberal up until 1908, when a 'national economy' approach gained in popularity, personified by Ziya Gökalp (Parla, 1985). This teaching shifted the ethnic balance of power in favour of the Turks and against the other nationalities of the Ottoman Empire (Toprak, 1994). Liberalism thus lost its influence, and the appeal of liberal ideas was greatly diminished.

7.3 GREECE: THE DIFFICULTIES OF CLASSICAL POLITICAL ECONOMY

The Greek economy was severely dislocated by the Struggle for Independence. Political autonomy was achieved *de jure* in 1830. Large areas with Greek populations that had participated in the revolt remained outside its territory, and irredentist aspirations were to dominate the Greek political agenda throughout the nineteenth century, sparking a series of wars. A republican government led by Ioannis Kapodistrias was soon followed – after his assassination in 1831 and a brief regency – by the monarchy of the Bavarian King Otto. He was ousted in 1862, having conceded a constitution in the wake of a popular rebellion in 1843. He was succeeded in 1863 by King George I of the Danish house of Glücksburg.

Political stability after 1864 enabled gradual economic advance. In 1871 public lands were distributed to landless peasants, relieving some of the tension of the land question. In 1881 territorial expansion led to growth in the agricultural sector. Nevertheless, low import tariffs and a weak infrastructure made the development of a dynamic manufacturing sector impossible. After 1879 a huge wave of public lending and the introduction of a new tariff system in 1884 led to economic expansion. However, this period of expansion ended in bankruptcy in 1893, brought about by excessive lending and the Corinthian raisin crisis, the latter affecting revenues.

In pre-revolutionary Greece the diffusion of Enlightenment ideas and the introduction of 'Western' sciences was a major project of the Diaspora Greeks, living mainly in France, Austria and the Danubian Principalities. The most important figure of the Greek Enlightenment, Adamantios Koraes, propagated *metakenosis*, the 'transfusion', or 'decanting', of Western ideas of rationalism and liberal humanism into Ottoman Greece 'through translation of European books into modern Greek, so as to awaken her from her Ottoman slumber, "resuscitate" memories of Classical Hellenism, and, essentially, synchronize it with contemporary European culture' (Zacharia, 2008, 9–10). Koraes himself published a translation in 1802 of Cesare Beccaria's *Dei delitti e delle pene*. At the turn of the century there were translations published outside Greece of Fontenelle, Montesquieu, Locke, Condillac, Genovesi and Mably.

Books on economic matters before the creation of the Greek state were not books on political economy. Financed by rich merchants, they were commercial handbooks or books of commercial arithmetic, weights and measures, and tables for the conversion of foreign exchange[6] (Sklavenitis, 1990). The most interesting of them was N. Papadopoulos's *The Gainful Hermes: Encyclopaedia of Commerce* (five volumes, published in 1815 in Venice), where we find the first description in Greek of Adam Smith's pin factory and the division of labour (I, 131–2).

Books on political economy proper came after the independence of the Greek state, and were translations from the works of French liberal authors. The first such textbook was Jean-Baptiste Say's *Catéchisme d'économie politique* (1821). It was translated and published in 1828 by George Chrysêdis on the island of Aegina, the first capital of the not yet diplomatically recognized Greek state.[7] In 1833 Anastassios Polyzoides, a judge and politician, translated in a conscious act of *metakenosis* (p. xxii) Joseph Droz's *Économie politique: ou principes de la science des richesses* into Greek.

French liberal ideas did not influence the policy of Kapodistrias and the Bavarians, which was decidedly autocratic. The building of a 'model kingdom' run by the King along cameralist lines meant that civil liberties and freedom of trade had to be curtailed. This led to an almost complete standstill in translations, only resumed after 1865. Political economy was during this period an entirely academic discourse.

The most important academic figure of the nineteenth century was Ioannes Soutsos. He held the only academic position for political economy in Greece from 1837 to 1890 (Koundouris, 1998; Psalidopoulos and Stassinopoulos, 2009). He served in a number of positions in the administration and the judiciary, and became Rector of Athens University. A member of a prominent Phanariot family and a student of Pellegrino Rossi in Geneva, Soutsos was clearly influenced by the French liberal school, especially Jean-Baptiste Say and his own teacher Rossi. Soutsos published three major works on political economy: *Treatise on the Production and Distribution of Wealth* (1851), *Manual of Public Finance or Theory of the Budget* (1864) and *Plutology* (1868–69, 2nd edn 1882 and 1885). Soutsos argued that liberal principles must operate within a constitutional society and that: 'in practice, the application of these absolute theories is suspended or altered by the elements of nationality, time, distance etc.' (1851, 3; see also 1882, 12). Furthermore: 'we have to take into account these elements, and not claim the direct application of unconditional principles' (1851, 4). Nevertheless, he was a true liberal at heart; not very analytical but with a strong policy orientation.

A review of the books translated after 1864, when a change in the Royal House occurred, reveals that in Greece a total of ten books were translated between 1865 and 1903. With two exceptions, all translations were of francophone authors. The policy-oriented economic discourse in France (Schumpeter, 1954; cf. Mill, 1972 [1869]) was more suited to the needs of Greek society. These translations fall roughly into two categories. The first comprises books which are simple and elementary in style, liberal and anti-socialist, written as a dialogue or as a morality tale; these were popular throughout Europe, particularly on its periphery, and were translated into many languages. Greece was no exception. This category includes books by P.-H. Suzanne (1849), Jean-Jacques Rapet (1865, 1903), Jean Chaumeil (1882) and Maurice Block (1885).[8] The second category is that of books by liberal academic economists. These were not their more academic treatises, but comprehensive introductory texts. In this category we have the translations of Garnier (1869), Garrett Fawcett (1881), Leroy-Beaulieu (1889, 1902) and Laveleye (1894).[9]

Next to these translations, romantic reactions to commercial internationalism and anti-socialist literature were also present. Xenophon Zygouras, a student of Soutsos and an economics instructor in secondary education, is typical of this romantic stream of thought. In his books on home economics (Zygouras, 1878, 1892) he adopted a national and religious perspective, and recommending the thrifty and autarkic management of the household unit. A romantic author like Konstantinos Ramphos, in his 1868 theatre piece 'The economist's duck', denounced classical political economy, condemning Smith and Say and ridiculing the concepts of saving and accumulation (Psalidopoulos and Theocarakis, 2011).

Typical of the anti-socialist literature is the *Précis for the working people or advice for manual labourers* published in 1869 by the 'Society of the Friends of the People' and distributed free to workers in major industrial centres (Dragoumis, 1869; see Kordatos, 1931–32). Adapted by Nikolaos Dragoumis, a Greek journalist and public official, from Théodore-Henri Barrau's *Conseils aux ouvriers* (1850), it called on workers to be obedient, frugal, and churchgoing, admonishing them not to strike, to ignore socialist theories and to avoid becoming 'an instrument of dreamers, schemers and trouble-makers' (Dragoumis, 1869, 28). Socialist literature is scant in this period, the most notable exception being Platon Drakoules (1858–1942).[10] The first translation of a Marxist text had to wait until the twentieth century: *The Communist Manifesto* in 1908 (Marx and Engels, 1913 [1908]).

Among Soutsos's successors in the Athens Law Faculty's Chair of Political Economy was Nikolaos Gounarakis. German-influenced, his work *Elements of Political Economy* (1892) provides a less liberal approach than that of Soutsos, showing some sympathy for the predicament of the Greek working class (Koundouris, 1998). Neokles Kazazis, trained in Germany and France, was a staunch nationalist. Pro-business and anti-labour, he brought his contradictions to his work, which is a curious mixture of supposedly liberal ideas and a belief in the organic nature of the state (Kazazis, 1894). Ioannes Zografos trained in Heidelberg, was made Professor of Public Finance at the University of Athens and attempted to import aspects of the German Historical School into Greece. His policy recommendations introduced Listian arguments into Greek economic discourse, even though he remained formally liberal in his academic treatises, such as his *Dêmosionomikê* (Public finance) (1882).

Thus liberal economic ideas, disseminated through translations or works locally produced in academia, gave way in the last decade of the nineteenth century to romantic–organic ideas of state and society, together with protectionist ideas. This tendency was to intensify during the first decades of the twentieth century, when the influence of German thought became more pronounced.

7.4 RUMANIA: FROM ECLECTICISM TO STATIST LIBERALISM AND BEYOND

Even though Rumania's full independence came only in 1878, the relative independence of the country from the Ottoman Empire and its relationship with the Russian and the Austrian Empires made it more open to Western influences.[11] Enlightenment ideas were imported from the West mostly through French texts, French being a language which

– together with Greek – was spoken by the Rumanian elite (Hitchins, 1996; Pompiliu, 1980). The sons of many landlords (*boieri*) were educated abroad. Ideological, political and economic discussions took place in this atmosphere of partial independence, so that by the time of the 1866 constitution the two major currents of thought that would characterize Rumanian society until the end of the Second World War, liberalism and conservatism, were in place (Hitchins, 1994, 1996).

In Rumania, the defenders of liberalism were not bourgeois opponents of an absolutist state pursuing mercantilist policies, but members of the *boieri* landowning class who favoured liberalism as a means of opening markets for agricultural products and achieving full property rights to land (Love, 2002). Some of the smaller *boieri* supported liberal economic policies in order to develop an industrial base. Economic freedom was perceived as being in harmony with national rebirth, a key to Westernization and the road to civilization and economic progress. But this liberalism was limited. *Boieri* were unwilling to extend liberalism to the peasants, who even after independence remained in a state of quasi-serfdom, a situation which persisted until the early twentieth century.[12] Moreover, the independence of the country in 1878 coincided with the shift of economic policy in Europe's more developed countries to higher tariffs and protectionism. This led to 'statist liberalism', combining the use of liberal ideology with a strong nationalist state, hostile to those who were not ethnic Rumanians, especially Jews,[13] and to a lesser extent Greeks and other 'foreigners'.

In the first period of Rumanian liberalism (1820–78) economists were divided on the issue of the primacy of agriculture over industry. Many liberals were agrarianists believing that free trade would mean the development of agriculture, but that industry would remain underdeveloped, or at best an adjunct of agriculture. In this camp we have Nicolae Suțu (Soutzo), Alexandru D. Moruzi, Ion Strat and Ion Ghica. Suțu popularized the works of Smith, Ricardo, J.-B. Say and Michel Chevalier among the Rumanian elite (Love, 2002, 107). An important politician and man of letters, he believed that Rumania was essentially an agricultural nation, and that industry could develop only in relation to agriculture. Free trade, he thought, would guarantee high levels of grain exports, benefiting large-scale agriculture (Hitchins, 1994, 79–80).[14] Moruzi was even more liberal than Suțu. He believed that free trade would transform agricultural production and make Rumania the marketplace of Europe and the East. His books, in French like Suțu's, have telling titles: *L'abolition des monopoles et l'amélioration de l'état du paysan en Moldavie* (1860 [1941]) and *Progrès et liberté* (1861 [1941]). Ion Strat, a professor of economics at the University of Bucharest and also Minister of Finance, was another fervent free-trader who believed in agrarianism, and that industry would eventually develop if left unencumbered by artificial restrictions. He wrote *A Complete Treatise of Political Economy* in Rumanian in 1870 (Hitchins, 1994, 80). Ion Ghica, twice Prime Minister of Rumania and Bey of Samos, was the most influential free-trader of the second half of the nineteenth century. In his *Economic Conversations,* published in Rumanian in 1865, he treated agriculture as the principal activity of the Rumanian economy. Industry would eventually develop and help agriculture to modernize. He 'rejected state intervention in "natural" economic processes as unnecessary and harmful. "Laissez faire, laissez passer" was his motto' (Hitchins, 1994, 82).

Another strand of liberalism favoured industrial development. Enric Winterhalder, Austrian but a naturalized Rumanian citizen, believed in laissez-faire and admired the West. He thought that liberal policies would eventually bolster industry, which did not therefore need protectionism to establish itself. The influential economist Dionisie Pop Marţian was liberal in his views, but a protectionist in his recommendations – he had studied Law and Philosophy in Vienna and became the first Director of the Central Statistical Office in Bucharest. Even though he adhered to liberal principles, he believed that the Rumanian economy was doomed without a strong industrial base, so that the state should extend protection to industrial activity. He advanced an infant industry argument to strengthen the economy, state protection being removed only when industrial production had become fully established. In 1858 he wrote a book in Rumanian with the title *Social Economy*.

Liberalism, however, was not the only influence present in Rumanian society, especially after 1878. From mid-century another world view began to form that was critical of liberalism and Western influences. This current was centred on the Junimea (Youth) movement, founded in 1863, and in which Titu Maiorescu was the most important member. Maiorescu was German-trained (Hitchins, 1994, 58), as were most of the Junimists, providing a contrast to a society that had since the 1830s been influenced by French liberalism (Campbell, 1944, 1971). Their 'world-view was constructed in accordance with the principles of organic social development [and] it drew heavily upon the historicist theories of German romantic philosophy' (Hitchins, 1994, 60–61). They adopted an evolutionary, traditionalist, anti-revolutionary perspective, believing that change should be effected by moral and cultural means, thus leaving the economic structure of agriculture intact. They believed that industry lacked a national character, being the creation of foreigners (Hitchins, 1994, 64–5). This agrarianist current continued into the twentieth century with *Sămănătorism* (from *sămănător*, Rumanian for 'sower'), a romantic, anti-capitalist movement that turned its back on the importation of capitalism and sought to preserve existing social structures. Its main animator was the prolific historian and sociologist Nicolae Iorga (Oldson, 1973). This ultra-nationalist movement saw capitalism as an 'unnatural implantation' and offered 'education' as the only solution to the country's problems.

The economic conditions of the later nineteenth century did not help the diffusion of classical liberalism. In Rumania a tariff war with the Habsburg Empire developed, and in 1886 the adoption of a customs tariff ended the brief affair with classical liberalism (Love, 2002). The era of protectionist 'statist liberalism' dawned. Its main proponent, Alexandru D. Xenopol, gave theoretical substance to the doctrine. There were other reactions to classical liberalism from two different quarters: the first was populism, whose most important representative was Constantin Stere. The other was Marxism, developed theoretically in the works of Cristian Racovski and, most importantly, of Constantin Dobrogeanu-Gherea. We will examine them in turn.

Xenopol was a protectionist, and an exponent of industrialization. He had studied history, law and economics at the University of Berlin and became a professor of history at the University of Bucharest. Although he 'classified himself as an economic liberal' (Hitchins, 1994, 85), he was influenced by Friedrich List and Henry Carey, and introduced protectionist ideas into Rumanian economic discourse. His economic writings were published in 1879 as *Economic Studies*. He laid great emphasis on the importance of labour in society, clinging to the classical labour theory of value. He argued that the exchange of agricultural for manufactured goods constituted exploitation; that the international division of labour was a swindle; and that liberal economic theories were unscientific, serving the commercial interests of France and Britain (Love, 2002). He argued that the state should not only protect local industry, but also regulate economic life.

The statist liberalism of the industrializing protectionists of the Liberal Party and the free-trader agrarians of the Conservative Party bore little relation to social reality (Love, 2002, 110). This led to the rise of Marxism and Populism (*Poporanism*), doctrines that declared war on absentee landlords, a powerful social class in Rumania, and sought to improve the lot of the peasants.

Constantin Stere was born in Bessarabia, then part of the Russian Empire, and was was influenced by the Russian *narodniks*. Having served six years in Siberia for his revolutionary activities he moved to Rumania, where in 1906 he founded a journal, *Rumanian Life*, which served as the vehicle for his populist views. He later became a professor of constitutional law at the University of Jassy. His appeal to small property owners increased after 1895. He denounced the evils of landlordism in combination with capitalist production for international markets, resulting in peasant poverty. His writings were political rather than economic treatises, offering an analysis of and policy recommendations for the peasant problem. Stere distanced himself from Marxism, arguing that industrial workers were of negligible importance compared to peasants. He objected to protectionism as a means of development, pointing to its failure over the previous 30 years to induce growth, overcome illiteracy and ameliorate the poor living standards of the peasantry. Rumania should, according to Stere, develop its agriculture and its cooperative movement and found its own civilization, based on free peasant producers, bearers of a community-type anti-capitalist developmental spirit. His agrarian populism was known as *Poporanism*.

Opposed to *Poporanism* were two Marxist writers, Cristian Racovski and Constantin Dobrogeanu-Gherea. Both were born outside Rumania. Born in Bulgaria, Racovski was a prominent international revolutionary active in Bulgaria, Rumania, Russia and Ukraine. Always on the run from the authorities, he studied medicine in Berlin, Zurich, Nancy and Montpellier. He applied Marxist categories to the analysis of the Rumanian economy, arguing that capitalism in Rumania had begun to transform the agricultural sector, leading to the proletarianization of the peasants. He questioned the nature of the Rumanian economic formation, the theory of stages, the possibility of the emergence of a national bourgeoisie and whether capitalism was a necessary stage before the establishment of socialism. Racovski stressed the need for a political alliance between the urban and the rural proletariat, and in numerous publications he attacked Stere's agricultural populism and underlined the relevance of Marxism (Love, 2002).

Dobrogeanu-Gherea was the most original of Rumanian economic thinkers. Born Solomon Katz in Russia he studied at the University of Kharkov and, like Racovski, he was heavily involved in revolutionary activities. His analysis of Rumanian economy and society predated the centre–periphery and dependency theories debates of the later twentieth century. Dobrogeanu-Gherea argued in 1892 that as capitalism penetrated economically backward countries, existing traditional modes of production would be blocked in their development, causing production, income and growth imbalances. Changes in advanced capitalist countries necessarily affect developments in backward economies. In backward countries institutions, the superstructure, are developed in advance of the social and economic base, exactly the opposite trend from that in advanced countries. Thus Rumania had liberal institutions but a semi-feudal economy, its ruling class pretending to be a bourgeoisie. On the other hand, this inversion of the *Entsprechungsgesetz* has its benefits, since it would be easier for backward countries to adopt socialism. He argued, against the agrarians, that industrialization was a historical task for Rumania which socialists should wholeheartedly endorse. In his magnum opus, *Neoserfdom* (1910), he gave a penetrating analysis of economic and social relations in the countryside, dissecting the semi-feudal relations that prevailed (Trotsky, 1915; Love, 2002; Hitchins, 1994).

In Rumania, unlike Greece, liberalism was resisted by intellectuals after a brief period of success. In contrast to Greek intellectuals who were not involved in politics, most Rumanian economic thinkers combined their theoretical writings with active political involvement. In fact it was this involvement which gave rise to their theoretical analyses. In this respect, economic thinking in Rumania, following two centuries of partial independence, was much more original and appropriate to the circumstances of the society they sought to explain and change.

7.5 SERBIA: FROM LIBERALISM TO HISTORICISM

Serbia's road to independence started early. After the revolution in 1804 and a precarious independence, the Principality of Serbia was established in 1817 with Miloš Obrenović as its Prince. De facto independence was achieved in 1867 when the Ottoman troops left the Principality, while formal independence had to wait until the Congress of Berlin in 1878. In 1882 the Principality of Serbia was proclaimed a Kingdom. The period was characterized by the rivalry of the two royal houses, the Obrenović and the Karadjordjević, and problems relating to the constitution and the struggle between the three poles of government: the prince, the council and the legislative body (Jelavich and Jelavich, 1977).

The economy was primitive. Serbia first minted its own coins in 1869, and created a Central Bank in 1884 (Gnjatovic, 2006; Sojic and Djurdjevic, 2006). Enduring fiscal problems hindered the formation of infrastructure. The construction of roads and a telegraph network started only after 1855. Peasants lived in primitive conditions and did not see their lot improve after the departure of Ottoman landlords. Petrovich (1976, 187) remarks that whenever peasants entered towns they felt they were 'going into hostile territory'.

In education matters were also rudimentary. In 1810 only two schools existed in Serbia, and the language of instruction was Greek (Lederer, 1969, 401–2). Since there was a dearth of people to fill positions in the administration, the government had to rely on transriparian Serbs from the Austrian Empire to do the job, an unsatisfactory solution (see

Stoianovich, cited in Jelavich and Jelavich, 1977, 62–3). To solve this problem between 1839 and 1855 the state funded around 50 scholarships for young Serbians to acquire university education abroad, mostly in Germany (Petrovich, 1976, 283). These scholars eventually became the intelligentsia of the new state.

Up to the middle of the nineteenth century foreign trade was regarded as the engine of modernization. In the realm of ideas, 'a curious blend of western liberalism and a romantic native populism based on the idealisation of the Serbian folk' prevailed (Petrovich, 1976, 286), with especial emphasis on the self-sufficient agricultural unit, the *zadruga*. At first things did not change in the second half of the nineteenth century. From 1858 to 1868 'the government greatly neglected the economic progress of the country' (Petrovich, 1976, 344). A scarcity of capital persisted. The economy was primarily agrarian. By the turn of the century: 'almost 85% of the population was engaged in agriculture, only 7% worked in industry, around 5% in trade and the same percentage was affiliated with the government or working freelance' (Josifidis, 2002, 145). Demographically the population more than doubled in the last half of the nineteenth century from less than 1 million to 2.5 million, even though this partly reflects the addition of new territories after the war with the Ottoman Empire in 1878. The economy was monetized and capitalism penetrated economic relations; the *zadruga* was gradually dissolved. In the process many peasants became landless and small-scale cultivation prevailed (Petrovich, 1976, 526–9).

In the realm of political ideas, romantic thinking and socialist ideas made their appearance. The socialist Živojin Žujović, who studied in Munich, Zurich and St Petersburg, introduced Russian populists and Proudhon to the Serbs. Svetozar Marković studied abroad on a state scholarship in St Petersburg where he became acquainted with the ideas of the agrarian socialist and populist Nikolay Chernyshevsky. A formidable literary critic and editor of radical journals, Marković was the founder of Serbian socialism. In his short and troubled life he produced a systematic critique of Serbian society, authoring 46 books and pamphlets (Petrovich, 1976, 377–9). Ridiculing the notion of a Greater Serbia, he was a proponent of democratic federalism. His Western influences included J.S. Mill, Marx and Proudhon (Bataković, 2005, 173) even though he idealised the *zadruga*.

Despite hostile criticism from the Romantic Movement, liberal economic thought persisted within the political system. As in other South-Eastern European countries, intellectuals involved in the nationalist uprising embraced a paternalistic liberalism. Jevrem Grujić, diplomat and politician, who had studied law in Heidelberg and Paris on a state scholarship, was characteristic of this tradition (Stokes, 1975, 47), as were Stevča Mihailović, Prime Minister in 1876, and Milovan Janković, a German-trained professor of economics and statesman. In the mid-nineteenth century Dimitrije Matić, a law professor who had studied in Heidelberg and Berlin and had also lived in Paris, was a natural law theorist and a representative of the liberal order. His pupil Vladimir Jovanović, a leading figure of the Serbian uprising, had studied agriculture in Germany after his Belgrade degree (Stokes, 1975, 13; Tomasevich, 1955).

At the close of the nineteenth century three major thinkers put their mark in economic thought: Kosta Cukić (1826–79), an eclectic liberal, Čedomilj Mijatović (1842–1932), a follower of the German Historical School, and Mihailo Vujić (1853–1913), another eclectic economist (Josifidis, 2002). The economic thought of developed Europe was disseminated into Serbia at that time, and Serbian economists reworked and adapted economic ideas, fitting them into the framework of their country. [15]

Cukić, a student of Karl Heinrich Rau in Heidelberg, held many important posts including the governorship of the first State Bank, Minister of Education, and a professorship for state sciences. He was the author of the first textbook on economics in Serbia. Cukić was widely read, as was his liberal German mentor, and his work created a basis for discussion and debate. Following the German tradition he mixed classical, subjectivist and mercantilist concepts.

Mijatović, who studied economics in Munich, Zürich and Leipzig and became Minister of Finance, wrote for the young and the general public. A leading Anglophile among Serbs, his contributions are more original in the domain of economic history, with for example his *History of Trade* (1893). A prolific writer and follower of the historical method, he made an impact on economic discourse and strengthened the tendency among Serbian economists to follow the lead of the German Historical School. Vujić, the last of the great Serbian authors of the time, followed, as did his predecessors, the National School tradition and gave it new prominence. He was anti-Marxist and anti-classical, and tried to combine neoclassicism with the historical approach. Serbian economics of the second half of the nineteenth century can, therefore, be described as a mixture of liberal–neoclassical principles and of historical economics.[16]

7.6 BULGARIA: FROM LIBERALISM TO PROTECTIONISM

Amongst the states of South-Eastern Europe, Bulgaria was the last to become independent. The national awakening of the later nineteenth century moulded a national consciousness and led to an uprising whose major figures were Georgi Rakovski, Vasil Levski, Lyuben Karavelov and Hristo Botev. The last three of these formed the Bulgarian Revolutionary Central Committee which organized the 'April Uprising' of 1876. After a Russo-Turkish War and the treaties of San Stefano and Berlin in 1878, a Bulgarian Principality was created, and a Constituent Assembly was held in Tûrnovo in 1879.

Post-independence there were two major phases: (1) 1879–94, beginning with the creation of the new state and the constitutional order, and ending with the fall of the Stambolov regime; and (2) 1895–1918, during which there was major political restructuring, with new cleavages and conflicts becoming apparent, with the new bourgeoisie coming to terms with the working and agrarian classes. The Social Democratic Party was formed in 1891, and in 1899 the Bulgarian Agrarian People's Union (Karasimeonov, 1999, 40–41).

The leading ideas of the revolutionary leaders and of many educated Bulgarians were not for the most part imported from Western Europe. As Jelavich and Jelavich observe:

> whereas the Romanian youth had their views shaped by their French education, the Bulgarians were influenced by their studies in Greek schools, in Russian institutions and to some extent in the colleges of the American Protestant missionaries in Bulgaria and Constantinople. In all these places they were exposed to the liberal-national political ideology. (1977, 135–6)

In 1858 the Moscow Benevolent Society, a Panslavist organization, formed and provided scholarships for young Bulgarians to study in Russia, where they were exposed to the ideas of Herzen, Chernyshevsky, Dobroliubov and Pisarev, returning with a belief in a revolutionary social programme (ibid., see also MacDermott, 1962, 300; Rothschild, 1959, 10). The influence of populist Russian ideas, together with a strong nationalist attitude, is apparent in the first revolutionary leaders: Karavelov and Botev, who studied in Russia, were atheists and socialists, though not Marxists, influenced by Herzen and Chernyshevsky. Karavelov saw progress less through social and economic transformations and more through education, while Botev envisaged a 'Golden Age' of agrarian communities and opposed industrialization (MacDermott, 1962, 228). Rakovski, less clear in his social and economic views, was on the side of the 'people' against the *chorbadzhii*, and his vision was one of 'progress', there being a place for joint-stock companies in the promotion of economic development, but only if the shareholders were Bulgarian (MacDermott, 1962, 190).

In newly independent Bulgaria economic ideas were little influenced by French or English Liberalism. Of the 15 finance ministers during the nineteenth century, five were in part French-educated, three in economics. Ivan Geshov studied in Manchester, but he was no English liberal. Other places of study included Germany, Russia, the Austro-Hungarian Empire and Constantinople (Ministry of Finance of the Republic of Bulgaria, 2010). At university level, political economy, finance and statistics were included as part of the curriculum in the Faculty of Law that was established in 1892 in the First School of Higher Education. A separate Department of Political Economy had to wait until the twentieth century (University of Sofia, Faculty of Economics and Business Administration, 2010).

What differentiated Bulgaria from other South-Eastern European states was the fervent discussion of economic ideas. Following independence, the country failed to industrialize in the manner expected. International treaties imposed low tariffs. Gershenkron (1962, 221) remarked that all the causes were present, but effects did not materialize. Independence was followed by economic decline (Palairet, 1997). In agriculture, freedom from taxation benefited the peasantry, whose consumption and leisure increased. The emigration of Muslim populations and the decline of transhumant stockraising led to a fall in agricultural productivity and a reduction in domestic demand. Even though proto-industrial development was followed partly by factory production, industrialization did not happen and the economy stagnated. As Lampe notes:

> The issue of industrialization was more widely and hotly debated in Sofia than in any of the other Balkan capitals. In Athens, Bucharest and Belgrade, economic issues were secondary. Not so in Sofia. The key to national assertion seemed from the start to lie more with choosing the correct strategy for economic development than with pursuing the seemingly futile goals of parliamentary democracy or the claim to Macedonia . . . The start of the industrialization debate may be found in early issues of the journal of the Bulgarian Economic Society founded in 1895. [17] (1986, 38–9)

Educated Bulgarians looked to Germany or Russia, where the great majority of several thousand university graduates received their training. More of the country's political leaders appear to have been trained specifically in economics than their counterparts elsewhere in the Balkans, where lawyers or engineers predominated (Lampe, 1986, 40). Interestingly enough, no works by Western economists were translated into Bulgarian during this period.[18] Pragmatic economics dominated the agenda. It was only in the twentieth century that academic economics began to draw upon Western economic thought (Dimitrov, 2002).

The question of industrialization preoccupied both liberal and socialist economists. A related matter was the role of foreign capital in economic development. Among the most prominent liberal economists of the period was Ivan Evstratiev Geshov. Educated in Greek and Protestant institutions, he was trained as an economist in the heartland of English Liberalism, at Owens College Manchester, where his family was based. He served as Governor of the Bulgarian National Bank, Finance Minister and eventually Prime Minister in 1911–13 (Gueshoff, 1915; Ministry of Finance of the Republic of Bulgaria, 2010). His economic views, however, belied his training. He was a protectionist, a German National Liberal of Listian views and an ardent proponent of industrialization (Lampe, 1986, 39–40). There were two policy tools for industrialization: increased tariffs and encouragement to industry. Tariffs were restricted initially by the Berlin Treaty to import taxes of 8 per cent and export duty of 1 per cent (Weiss-Bartenstein, 1916). In the 1890s treaties were signed with the Great Powers and Serbia that increased tariffs. Geshov drafted the legislation that exempted private firms in textiles, heavy industry and sugar refining from import tariffs and certain other taxes, and reduced railway rates (Lampe, 1986; Gershenkron, 1962, 199). Nevertheless, Geshov argued that protection should apply only to those industries for which there were favourable conditions of production in Bulgaria. Higher tariffs would hurt consumers and help to maintain unviable industries. Moderate tariffs would provide room for free competition (Weiss-Bartenstein, 1916, 158). He believed: 'that a nation is politically independent only as long as it is economically so, and strenuously advocate[d] the idea of making Bulgaria as self- supporting as possible' (Logio, 1919, 219).

From the other side of the fence, the socialist politician Dimitûr Blagoev was an even more fervent supporter of industrialization. Blagoev was the main representative of Marxism in Bulgaria. Educated in Russia on a Benevolent Society scholarship he was soon involved in revolutionary politics and in the establishment of the first socialist organization in Russia in 1883 (Crampton, 1995). Expelled to Bulgaria in 1885, he founded the Bulgarian Workers' Social Democratic Party in 1891, and in 1919 he became the first leader of the Bulgarian Communist Party. Marxism came early to Bulgaria: translations of Marx appeared as early as 1886 (Rothschild, 1959, 14–16). In 1891 Blagoev wrote *Shto e sotsializûm i ima li toi pochva u nas?* [What is socialism and is there a basis for it here?]. The book, influenced by Plekhanov's *Our Differences* (1885), argued the same case: 'that the country must and will pass from the peasant economy into and through a capitalist phase to socialism, and that all hopes of avoiding this development through the resurrection of the largely defunct *zadruga* and of artisan industry are vain' (Rothschild, 1959, 15). Blagoev believed that an industrial revolution was already under way in Bulgaria (Lampe, 1986, 35). He believed that: 'the small peasant was destined to disappear as agriculture inevitably moved towards capitalization and larger units worked by wage-labourers; today's small peasants were therefore tomorrow's rural proletariat' (Crampton, 2007, 187).

Gerschenkron remarks that:

> In their positive attitude towards industrialization Bulgarian Marxians stood close to those relatively small group of Bulgarian intelligentsia which, influenced by List, thought in terms of 'national production' and 'development of the nation's productive forces,' and which published, in the late 1880s, the journal *Promishlenost* (Industry) and somewhat later accepted the leadership of I.E. Geshov. (1962, 218)

Blagoev praised Geshov for his policies, but criticized him for not going far enough.

The interests of the peasant class were consolidated politically with the creation of Alexandûr Stamboliĭski's Bulgarian Agrarians National Union at the end of the century (Bell, 1977). Peasant society in Bulgaria was in fact the major obstacle to a policy of industrialization. Geshov had to tread carefully lest his measures place a major burden on the small peasants. In fact, objections to Listian doctrines came not from English liberalism but from the pragmatic need to protect the peasants and the artisanal class from the effects of industrialization (Gerschenkron, 1962, 226). Xenophobia and a mistrust of foreign capital, partly necessary to protect domestic industry (Weiss-Bartenstein, 1916), were endemic in Bulgarian economic life. According to one economic historian (Palairet, 1997, 330–39) this was the principal reason for the absence of foreign investment in Bulgaria.

Liberalism was even more short-lived in Bulgaria than in the rest of the Balkans. Political rather than economic in orientation, it was soon eclipsed by advocates of industrialization, both bourgeois and Marxist, and it was only the interests of the peasant class that supported low tariffs, associated however with a non-liberal ideology.

7.7 CONCLUDING REMARKS

The European Enlightenment could gain no foothold during the later eighteenth century in a South-Eastern Europe that was still part of the Ottoman Empire. The Enlightenment project was instead taken up by the Diaspora and the leaders of the semi-independent principalities. The projects of progress, liberation and national rebirth, as well as the imagining of a national community, were developed together. A major intellectual force behind nationalist uprisings was the Enlightenment in general, and liberal economic and political thought in particular (Djorjevic and Fischer-Galati, 1981). These projects were financed by the merchant communities operating across the divide between the Ottoman Empire and Western Europe, and the first efforts at translating texts in European languages were possible only because of the financial support from 'conquering Balkan Orthodox merchants' (Stoianovich, 1960), who were also the mediators of the liberal ideas of the French Revolution.

Many independent states emerged in South-Eastern Europe during the nineteenth century. We have attempted to show that the political economy of nation-building in this region was dissimilar to that experienced in the core European countries two centuries earlier. British, French and German nation-building had their origins in mercantilist thought (Schmoller, 1884). Mercantilism advocated a positive balance of payments, an active population policy and a strong support for export trade, even using military means. The interests of a prospering commercial class had to be defended by the nation-state so that it might compete with its rivals.

South-Eastern nationalism on the contrary arose when liberal economic thought, either as classical political economy or as French liberal economics, had already replaced mercantilism as the leading policy doctrine in Western Europe. Most intellectuals in South-Eastern Europe were liberals. They considered that the substitution of Ottoman authority by a liberal national government would be the sole guarantee of economic progress. Even in the heart of the Ottoman Empire, liberalism, with a healthy dose of imperial pragmatism, was seen as a solution to the economic and social problems faced by state and society.

The failure of liberal policies to foster economic development generally coincided with the emergence of Germany as a European power, and German economic writings, from List to Schmoller, provided an attractive alternative. Towards the end of the century both Marxian socialism and romanticism provided further possibilities. But adherence to liberalism was never abandoned, if only as a pragmatic liberalism: modernizing, paternalistic and, paradoxically, statist. There were other approaches to economic policy alongside with liberalism. Agrarianists, socialists, romanticists, Slavophiles, interventionists and eclectic syntheses of the above blended with the liberal approach.

In the Balkan States before national independence the idea of a free citizenry was alien. A 'rational economic actor' was a distant prospect. Competition was not thought to play an important part in economic progress, although it did form part of contemporary rhetoric. The Orthodox Church played no positive part in the adoption of free market capitalism (Sugar, 1985, 1996). For various reasons the merchant class in the newly independent states could not assume a leading role in economic life. These were all agrarian economies with a very weak industrial base, reliant on a state whose intellectuals occasionally professed themselves 'liberal' in seeking to perform the duties of the modernizer. The key economic figure was the administrator, not the capitalist. The development of the state and territorial expansion had greater impact than business success. Successful national economic policy would follow the implementation of complete national independence, once the dust has settled and irredentist aspirations had reached their limit. While the limits of such liberal rhetoric became all too obvious throughout South-Eastern Europe, indigenous intellectual development was not sufficiently advanced to be able to produce original national economic thought of any importance. Such thinking came from the metropolis, and on the periphery it was simply adapted with a few cautionary words about making appropriate adjustments for national conditions, the political situation and the national psyche. Ruling political elites continued to make economic policy and create institutions almost without any reference to economics. In South-Eastern Europe the ruling political elite and economic interests became polarized. The spirit of capitalism was diffused; capitalism itself, however, could and did not flourish in this part of the world.

NOTES

1. A.G. Sayar (1986, 2000). This is the standard reference on Ottoman economic thought but is linguistically inaccessible to us.
2. Translation played an important role in a multi-ethnic society. In fact, the Translation Office became the major training ground of diplomats, bureaucrats and the new intelligentsia whose members were going to be the creators of the *Tanzimat* such as Sadık Rıfat, Mustafa Reşid, Ali and Fuad Pashas (Seyitdanlioğlu, 1998, 154).
3. Other translations of textbooks in French into Ottoman Turkish include Leroy-Beaulieu's *Traité de la science des finances* (1880), Maurice Block's *Petit manuel d'économie pratique* (1908), and Charles Gide's *Principes d'économic politique* (1909). We would like to thank our doctoral student Selcan Küçük for her help with the Turkish bibliography.
4. It was, however, an English orientalist, Charles Wells, who published before them in 1860 in London, the first book on economics in Turkish.
5. The diffusion of economic ideas was also effected through the columns of the Ottoman newspapers. Sayar (cited in Bülbül, 2007) writes that one newspaper was publishing both the lectures of Mehmed Şerif Efendi and the economic writings of Ahmed Midhat Efendi.
6. Thus, K. Kokkinakis published in Vienna in 1809 a Greek translation of Joseph Nowack (1799). There is an anonymous translation published in Jassy in 1817 of Johann Georg Büsch (1801). Panagiotis Spanopoulos had earlier published a book on *Commercial Arithmetic* in Trieste in 1803.
7. The fact that Say was the first economist to be translated was no accident. He was by far the most translated economist of the period (Tribe, 2003, 162). Not only was he well known for his Philhellenic sentiments, but his views and style suited the Greek intelligentsia (Sklavenitis, 1994).

8. The original texts were P.-H. Suzanne (1826), Jean-Jacques Rapet (1858), Jean Chaumeil (1882 [1881]) and Maurice Block (1872). Block's *Traité théorique et pratique de statistique* also appeared in Greek in 1895.
9. The original texts were Joseph Garnier (1846), Millicent Garrett Fawcett (1870), Paul Leroy-Beaulieu (1888), Emile de Laveleye, (1882). We have translations into Greek of two of Garnier's books: *Traité de finances* in 1887 and *Traité complet d'arithmétique théorique et appliquée au commerce, à la banque, aux finances et à l'industrie* in 1893. Moreover, two of Laveleye's books, on the future of the Catholic peoples and on contemporary socialism, were translated into Greek in 1875 and 1894 respectively. There is also another textbook in Greek, translated from the English without attribution to an author, published in 1901 with the title *Plutology for beginners*, by I. Marketis. Strangely enough, the language of the text is an extreme demotic Greek in a period when this linguistic form was associated with progressive and radical causes. The book, however, is as liberal as they come.
10. Platon E. Drakoules was born on the Ionian island of Zakynthos. He taught Modern Greek literature at Oxford. His socialism was a peculiar mixture incorporating anarchist, theosophical and utopian ideas. He published the first Greek Socialist magazine (*Ardên*). He translated Kropotkin in 1886, and he had written pamphlets and books such as *What Socialism Means*? (1886b), *The Worker's Manual, i.e., the Foundations of Socialism* (1893), *History of the French Revolution* (1890), *The Anti-plutocratic Spirit* (1910), and so on.
11. Nicolae Rosetti-Rosnovanu, 'well versed in the theories of J.B. Say, A Smith and D. Ricardo', visited Britain in 1818 (Georgescu, 1971, 73). Most intellectuals, however, knew English liberalism through France (Hitchins, 1996, 133).
12. Serfdom was formally abolished in 1864. Dobrogeanu-Gherea has coined the term 'neoserfdom' (*neoiobăgia*) to describe the peasants' predicament (in Hitchins, 1994, 77).
13. On the anti-Semitic ideology of Rumanian intellectuals in the nineteenth century see Oldson (1991).
14. His economic works include *Notions statistiques sur la Moldavie* (1849) (a Rumanian translation appeared in 1852) and *Quelques observations sur la statistique de la Roumanie* (1867). Nicolae Suţu was the older brother of Ioannes Soutsos, the Greek economist (Psalidopoulos and Stassinopoulos, 2009). Both were liberal, but with differing national allegiances: Nicolae with Romania, Ioannes with Greece. As common in the Balkans, there was no 'genetic' or cultural *Wahlverwandtschaft* with respect to national consciousness: choice and circumstance were stronger determining factors.
15. In terms of diffusion of economic ideas the production of translated of economic texts is really small. They include: Wilhelm Roscher's *Grundlagen der Nationalökonomie* (1863); Jean-Jacques Rapet's *Manuel de morale et d'économie politique* (1872); Joseph Garnier's *Premières notions d'économie politique, sociale ou industrielle* (1876); and Emile de Laveleye's *De la propriété et de ses formes primitives* (1899).
16. Perhaps an interesting contrast with Serbian economic thought is economic thought in Croatia, which is however beyond the scope of this chapter. Whereas in Serbia university education was non-existent, in Zagreb there had been a fully functioning tertiary educational institution since the middle of the seventeenth century. In Zagreb the first appointment of a Professor of Political-Cameral Studies was in 1769. He and his two successors taught from Joseph von Sonnenfels's *Grundsätze der Polizey, Handlung und Finanzwissenschaft* (1869–76). The fourth professor in line, Ivan Nepomuk Henfner, wrote a liberal textbook in 1831 in Latin: *Introductio in oeconomiam politicam alias nationalem*. The first professor in a chair entitled 'National Economy' was Blaž Lorković who translated Rapet in 1880 and wrote *Principles of Political Economy or General Economic Science* in Croatian in 1889. He was influenced by English liberal thinkers, especially Mill. It is only gradually that political economy differentiated itself from Cameralism to become a liberal discipline that could within the Empire be used as nationalist tool (University of Zagreb, 2010).
17. This was the first society of its kind in South-Eastern Europe.

18. Dimitrov (2002, §14) A translation of Friedrich List's *Das nationale System der politischen Oekonomie* appeared in Bulgarian only in 1926.

REFERENCES

Adanır, F. (2003), 'Religious communities and ethnic groups under imperial sway: Ottoman and Habsburg lands in comparison', in D. Hoerder, C. Harzig and A. Shubert (eds), *The Historical Practice of Diversity: Transcultural Interactions from the Early Modern Mediterranean to the Postcolonial World*, Oxford: Berghahn Books, pp. 54–86.

Augello, M.M. and M.E.L. Guidi (eds) (2001), *The Spread of Political Economy and the Professionalisation of Economists*, London: Routledge.

Augello, M.M. and M.E.L. Guidi (eds) (2005), *Economists in Parliament in the Liberal Age (1848–1920): A Comparative Perspective*, London: Ashgate.

Avramov, R. and Ş. Pamuk (eds) (2006), *Monetary and Fiscal Policies in South-east Europe: Historical and Comparative Perspectives*, First General Meeting of the South-east Europe Monetary History Network, 13–14 April, Sofia: Bulgarian National Bank.

Baeck, L. (1994), *The Mediterranean Tradition in Economic Thought*, London: Routledge.

Baeck, L. (1996), 'Ibn Khaldun's political and economic realism', in L.S. Moss (ed.), *Joseph A. Schumpeter: Historian of Economics*, London: Routledge, pp. 83–99.

Barrau, T.H. (1850), *Conseils aux ouvriers sur les moyens qu'ils ont d'être heureux* [Advice to workers on the ways by which they will be happy], Paris: Hachette.

Bataković, D.T. (2005), *Histoire du peuple serbe* [History of the Serbian people], Lausanne: L'Age d'homme.

Beccaria, C. (1802), *Peri amartematôn kai poinôn, politikôs theôroumenôn* [translation by Adamantios Koraês of *Dei delitti e delle pene* (On crimes and punishments)], Paris: Baudelot et Eberhart.

Bell, J. (1977), *Peasants in Power: Alexander Stamboliski and the Bulgarian Agrarian National Union, 1899–1923*, Princeton, NJ: Princeton University Press.

Blagoev, D. ['D. Bratanov'] (1891), *Shto e sotsializûm i ima li toi pochva u nas?* [What is socialism and is there a basis for it here?], Turnovo: P.H. Panaiotov.

Block, M. (1872), *Petit manuel d'économie pratique* [Little handbook of practical economics], Paris: J. Hetzel.

Block, M. (1882), *Mikron egcheiridion praktikês oikonomias* [translation by K.A. Kypriadis of Block, 1872], Athens: Enôsis.

Block, M. (1895), *Egcheiridion theôrêtikês kai praktikês statistikês* [translation by P.A. Sakellariou of *Traité théorique et pratique de statistique*], Athens: P.A. Sakellariou.

Block, M. (1908), *Ameli İktisadi dersleri* [translation by Ahmet Muhtar of Block, 1872], Istanbul: Mahmut Bey Matbaası.

Budak, A. (2008), 'The contributions of the Armenians over the constitution of a new social life and literature in 19th century', *Ozean Journal of Social Sciences*, **1**, 65–74.

Bülbül, Y. (2007), 'Transfer of political economy by a traditional society: Ilm-I tedbir-i menzil in the Ottoman Empire', paper presented at the XIII Jornadas de Epistemología de las Ciencias Económicas, Facultad de Ciencias Económicas

Universidad de Buenos Aires, 4-5 October, http://www.econ.uba.ar/www/institutos/epistemologia/marco_archivos/ponencias/Actas%20XIII/Trabajos%20Episte/BULBUL_paper.pdf.
Büsch, J.G. (1801), *Vollständiges systematisches Lehrbuch der gesammten Handlungswissenschaft* [Complete systematic textbook of the entire science of trade], Hamburg and Mainz: Gottfried Vollmer.
Büsch, J.G. (1817), *Didaskalia entelês sustêmatikê apasês tês emporikês epistêmês*, Jassy: Greek printing press [translation of Büsch, 1801].
Campbell, J. (1944), 'The influence of western political thought in the Rumanian principalities 1821–48', *Journal of Central European Affairs*, **4**, 262–73.
Campbell, J. (1971), *French Influence and the Rise of Rumanian Nationalism*, 2nd edn, New York: Arno.
Cardoso, J.L. (2003), 'The international diffusion of economic thought', in W.J. Samuels, J.E. Biddle and J.B. Davis (eds), *A Companion to the History of Economic Thought*, Malden, MA: Blackwell, pp. 622–33.
Chaumeil, J. (1882), *Mathêmata politikês oikonomias dia ton laon ek tou gallikou* [translation of (1881) *Leçons populaires d'économie politique, à l'usage des écoles et des familles* (Popular lessons of political economy for use by schools and families)], Athens: Aiôn.
Crampton, R.J. (1995), 'Blagoev, Dimitûr', in A.T. Lane (ed.), *Biographical Dictionary of European Labor Leaders*, Vol. I, Westport, CT: Greenwood Press, pp. 98–9.
Crampton, R.J. (2007), *Bulgaria*, Oxford: Oxford University Press.
Dimitrov, M. (2002), 'Economics – Bulgaria', in M. Kaase, V. Sparschuh and A. Wenninger (eds), *Three Social Science Disciplines in Central and Eastern Europe: Handbook on Economics, Political Science and Sociology (1989–2001)*, Berlin and Budapest: GESIS/Social Science Information Centre (IZ), Collegium Budapest Institute for Advanced Study, http://www.cee-socialscience.net/archive/economics/bulgaria/report1.html.
Djordjevic, D. and S. Fischer-Galati (1981), *The Balkan Revolutionary Tradition*. New York: Columbia University Press.
Dobrogeanu-Gherea, C. (1910), *Neoiobăgia; studiu economico-sociologic al problemei noastre agrare* [Neoserfdom: economic-sociological study of our agrarian problem], Bucharest: Editura Librăriei Socecu & Comp.
Doganalp-Votzi, H. (2007), 'Aspekte der Rezeptionsgeschichte der Theorien der Moderne im Osmanischen. Das erste osmanische Werk zur Nationalökonomie: Sehak Abrus' Übersetzung des *Catéchisme d'économie politique* von Jean Baptiste Say' [Aspects of the reception history of the theories of modernity in the Ottoman Empire. The first Ottoman work of political economy: Sehak Abrus's translation of Jean Baptiste Say's *Catéchisme d'économie politique*], in G. Neweklowsky (ed.), *Herrschaft, Staat und Gesellschaft in Südosteuropa aus sprach- und kulturhistorischer Sicht* [Government, state and society in South Eastern Europe in a linguistic and cultural-historical perspective] Vienna: Verlag der Österreichischen Akademie der Wissenschaften, pp. 239–56.
Doğan, Necmettin (2006), 'The origins of liberalism and Islamism in the Ottoman Empire (1908-1914): a sociological perspective', Doctoral dissertation, Freie Universität Berlin, Germany, http://www.diss.fu-berlin.de/diss/receive/FUDISS_thesis_000000002669.
Dragoumis, N. (1869), *Egkolpion tou ergatikou laou ê sumvoulai pros cheirônaktas* [Précis for the working people, or advice for manual labourers], (adaptation of

Barrau, 1850) Series: Vivliothêkê tês Etaireias tôn Philôn tou Laou, Athens: Vilaras.
Drakoules, P.E. (1886a), *Ekklêsis eis tous neous* [An appeal to the young] [translation of P.A. Kropotkin's 'Aux jeunes gens'], Athens: Tup. Enôseôs.
Drakoules, P.E. (1886b), *Ti sêmainei sosialismos* [What socialism means], Athens: Estia.
Drakoules, P.E. (1890), *Istoria tês Gallikês Epanastaseôs kai ta ex autês didagmata* [History of the French Revolution and the lessons from it]. Athens: Gabriêlidis.
Drakoules, P.E. (1893), *To egcheiridion tou ergatou êtoi ai baseis tou sosialismou* [The worker's manual, i.e., the foundations of socialism], Athens: Union of the Working Classes of Greece.
Drakoules, P.E. (1910), *To antiploutokratikon pneuma* [The anti-plutocratic spirit], parliamentary speech, Athens: [s.n.]
Droz, J. (1829), *Économie politique: ou principes de la science des richesses* [Political economy, or principles of the science of wealth], Paris: Jules Renouard.
Droz, J. (1833), *Politikê oikonomia êtoi archai tês epistêmês tou ploutou* [translated with many additions by A. Polyzoidis, translation of Droz, 1829], Nafplion: Tombras, Ioannidis & Athanasiadis.
Garnier, J. (1846), *Éléments de l'économie politique: Exposé des notions fondamentales de cette science* [Elements of Political Economy: presentation of the basic concepts of this science], Paris: Guillaumin.
Garnier, J. (1869), *Stoicheia politikês oikonomias* [translation of Garnier, 1846], Athens: Passaris.
Garnier, J. (1876), *Prvi pojmovi političke društvene ili industrijske ekonomije* [translation of *Premières notions d'économie politique, sociale ou industrielle* (First notions of political, social or industrial economy)], Belgrade: Državna štamparija.
Garnier, J. (1887), *Oikonomologikon egcheiridion* [translation by Ch. A. Zappas of *Traité de finances*], Bucharest: Tupografeion Ephêmeridos Sullogoi.
Garnier, J. (1893), *Arithmêtikê theôrêtikê kai efarmosmenê gia to emporion, tas trapezas ktl.* [Translation by I. Dyovouniôtis of *Traité complet d'arithmétique théorique et appliquée au commerce, à la banque, aux finances et à l'industrie* (Complete treatise of arithmetic theoretical and applied to banks, finance and industry)], Athens: [s.n.].
Garrett Fawcett, M. (1870), *Political Economy for Beginners*, series: Macmillan's School Class Books. London: Macmillan.
Garrett Fawcett, M. (1881), *Egcheiridion tês politikês oikonomias di'archarious* [translation by E.I. Mavrokordatos of Garret Fawcett, 1870 (4th edition of 1876)], Athens: Iasemidis.
Genç, M. (1994), 'Ottoman industry in the eighteenth century: general framework, characteristics and main trends', in D. Quataert (ed.), *Manufacturing in the Ottoman Empire and Turkey 1500–1950*, Albany, NY: State University of New York Press, pp. 59–86.
Gencer, Mustafa (2002), *Bildungspolitik, Modernisierung und kulturelle Interaktion: deutsch–türkische Beziehungen (1908–1918)* [Education policy, modernization and cultural interaction: German–Turkish relations (1908–1918)]. Münster: Lit.
Georgescu, V. (1971), *Political Ideas and the Enlightenment in the Romanian Principalities*, New York: Columbia University Press.
Gerschenkron, A. (1962), 'Some aspects of industrialization in Bulgaria,

1878–1939', in *Economic Backwardness in Historical Perspective*, Cambridge, MA: Harvard University Press, pp. 198–234.
Ghazanfar, S.M. (ed.) (2003), *Medieval Islamic Economic Thought: Filling the 'Great Gap' in European Economics*, London: Routledge.
Ghica, I. (1865), *Convorbiri economice* [Economic conversations], Bucharest: Tipografia Stefan Rassidescu.
Gide, C. (1909), *İlm-i iktisadi dersleri* [translation of *Principes d'économie politique*], Istanbul: Kadar Matbaası.
Gnjatovic, D. (2006), 'Introduction of limping gold standard in the principality of Serbia', in Avramov and Pamuk, op-cit., pp. 45–56.
Gounarakis, N.P. (1892), *Stoicheia politikês oikonomias* (Elements of political economy), Vol. 1, Athens: Paliggenesia.
Gueshoff, I.E. (1915), *The Balkan League*, London: John Murray.
Henfner, J. (1831), *Introductio in oeconomiam politicam alias nationalem* [Introduction to political, alias national, economy], Zagreb: Franciscus Suppan.
Hitchins, K.M. (1994), *Rumania, 1866–1947*, Oxford: Clarendon Press.
Hitchins, K.M. (1996), *The Romanians, 1774–1866*, Oxford: Clarendon Press.
Hübner, O. (1869), *Ekonomi tercümesi: Fenn-i idare* [translation by Mehmet Midhat of *Petit manuel populaire d'économie politique* (Little popular handbook of political economy) which in turn is the translation-adaptation by Charles Le Hardy de Beaulieu of Otto Hübner *Der kleine Ekonomist*], Istanbul: Cemiyet-i İlmiye Matbaası.
Jelavich, C. and B. Jelavich (1977), *The Establishment of the Balkan National States, 1804–1920*, Series: A History of East Central Europe, Vol. 8, Seattle, WA: University of Washington Press.
Josifidis, K. (2002), 'Aspects of economic thought and policy in Serbia, 1850–1900', in M. Psalidopoulos and M.E. Mata (eds), *Economic Thought and Policy in Less Developed Europe: The Nineteenth Century*, London: Routledge, pp. 145–71.
Karasimeonov, G. (1999), 'Between democracy and authoritarianism in Bulgaria', in K. Lawson, A. Römmele and G. Karasimeonov (eds.), *Cleavages, Parties, and Voters: Studies from Bulgaria, the Czech Republic, Hungary, Poland, and Romania*, Westport, CT: Praeger, pp. 37–45.
Kazazis, N. (1894), *Genikai archai tês politikês oikonomias* [General principles of political economy], Athens: Saliveros.
Kordatos, Y. (1931–32), *Istoria tou ellênikou ergatikou kinêmatos* [History of the Greek labour movement], Vols 1–2, Athens: Panepistêmiakon Vivliopôleion Alex N. Kololou.
Koundouris, M. (1998), 'Ê exelixê tês oikonomikês skepsês stên Ellada, 1837–1942' [The development of economic thought in Greece, 1837–1942], Unpublished doctoral dissertation, University of Athens, Greece.
Lampe, J.R. (1986), *The Bulgarian Economy in the Twentieth Century*, London: Croom Helm.
Laveleye, E. de (1882), *Éléments d'économie politique* [Elements of political economy], Paris: Hachette.
Laveleye, E. de (1875), *Peri tou mellontos tôn katholikôn laôn* [translation by S.A. Vlastos of *De l'avenir des peuples catholiques* (The future of Catholic peoples)], Marseilles: [s.n.].
Laveleye, E. de (1894), *Stoicheia politikês oikonomias* [translation by K. Vournazos of Laveleye, 1882 from the 3rd edn of 1890], Athens: Vlastos.

Laveleye, E. de (1894a), *O sugchronos sosialismos* [translation of *Le socialisme contemporain* (Contemporary socialism)], Athens: [s.n.].

Laveleye, E. de (1899), *Svojina i njeni prvobitni oblici* [translation of *De la propriété et de ses formes primitives* (On property and its primitive forms)], Belgrade: Državna štamparija.

Lederer, I.J. (1969), 'Nationalism and the Yugoslavs', in P.F. Sugar and I.J. Lederer (eds), *Nationalism in Eastern Europe*, Seattle, WA: University of Washington Press, pp. 396–438.

Leroy-Beaulieu, P. (1880), *İlm-i usul-i maliye* [translation by Hüseyin Kazım of *Traité de la science des finances* (Treatise of the science of finances)], Istanbul: [s.n.].

Leroy-Beaulieu, P. (1888), *Précis d'économie politique*, Paris: Librairie Ch. Delagrave.

Leroy-Beaulieu, P. (1889), *Egcheiridion ploutologias, ê tês oikonomikês epistêmês* [translation by K.A. Kypriadês of Leroy-Beaulieu, 1888], Athens: Estia.

List, F. (1926), *Sistema na narodno stopanstvo i mitnicheska politika* [translation by Racho P. Kosev of *Das nationale System der politischen Ökonomie* (The national system of political economy)], Sofia: Dŭrzh. Knigoizd.

Logio, G.C. (1919), *Bulgaria: Problems and Politics*, London: Heinemann.

Lorković, B. (1889), *Počela političke ekonomije ili nauke obćega gospodarstva* [Principles of political economy or general economic science], Zagreb: Družba 'Braća hrvatskog zmajar' [Society 'Brothers of the Croatian Dragon'].

Love, J.L. (2002), 'Resisting liberalism: theorizing backwardness and development in Rumania before 1914', in M. Psalidopoulos and M.E. Mata (eds), *Economic Thought and Policy in Less Developed Europe: The Nineteenth Century*, London: Routledge, pp. 105–28.

MacDermott, M. (1962), *A History of Bulgaria, 1393-1885*, London: Allen & Unwin.

Maddison, A. (1995), *Monitoring the World Economy, 1820–1992*, Paris: OECD.

Marketis, I. (1901), *Ploutologia gi'archarious* [Plutology for beginners] [translation from the English of an unidentified textbook], Athens: Estia.

Marţian, D.P. (1858), *Studii sistemice în Economia politică. Prima parte. Economia socială*, [Systematic studies in political economy; first part: social economy] in N. Marcu and Z. Ornea (eds), (1961) *D.P. Marţian Opere economice*, [Economic works], Bucharest: Editura Ştiinţifică.

Marx, K. and F. Engels (1913), *To koinônistiko manifesto* [translation by Konstantinos Chatzopoulos of *Manifest der Kommunistischen Partei* (Manifesto of the Communist Party)], Athens: Tupografeio efêmeridas tôn ergatôn [originally published in series in Volos in 1908 in the periodical *Ergatês* (Worker)].

Midhat, A. (1879), *Ekonomi politik* [Political economy], Istanbul: Kırk Anbar Matbaası.

Mijatović, Č. (1893), *Istorija trgovine* [History of Trade], Belgrade: D. M. Đorić.

Mill, J.S. (1972 [1869]), 'Letter no. 1497. To John Elliot Cairnes, Avignon, Nov. 16', in F.E. Mineka and D.N. Lindley (eds), *The Collected Works of John Stuart Mill, Volume XVII: The Later Letters of John Stuart Mill 1849–1873, Part IV*, Toronto: University of Toronto Press.

Ministry of Finance of the Republic of Bulgaria (2010), 'Ministers', http://www.minfin.bg/en/page/226.

Moruzi, A.D. (1860), *L'abolition des monopoles et l'amélioration de l'état du paysan en Moldavie* [The abolition of monopolies and the improvement of the

state of the peasant in Moldavia], Galatz: Frédéric Thiel [reprinted in Slăvescu, 1941].
Moruzi, A.D. (1861), *Progrès et liberté (Commerce, Finances, Agriculture dans les Principautés Unies)* [Progress and freedom: commerce, finances, agriculture in the United Principalities], Galatz: Frédéric Thiel [reprinted in Slăvescu, 1941].
Moss, L.S. (ed.) (1996), *Joseph A. Schumpeter: Historian of Economics*, London: Routledge.
Nowack, J. (1799), *Grundriß der Handlungsgeschichte* [Outline of the history of trade], Vienna: widow of J. Alberti.
Nowack, J. (1809), *Istorias tou emporiou epitomê* [translation by K. Kokkinakis of Nowack, 1799], Vienna: Georgios Vendotis.
Oldson, W.O. (1973), *The Historical and Nationalistic Thought of Nicolae Iorga*, New York: Columbia University Press.
Oldson, W.O. (1991), *A Providential Anti-Semitism: Nationalism and Polity in Nineteenth Century Romania*, Philadephia, PA: American Philosophical Society.
Özveren, E. (2002), 'Ottoman economic thought and economic policy in transition: rethinking the nineteenth century', in M. Psalidopoulos and M.E. Mata (eds), *Economic Thought and Policy in Less Developed Europe: The Nineteenth Century*, London: Routledge, pp. 129–44.
Palairet, M. (1997), *The Balkan Economies, c. 1800–1914: Evolution without Development*, Cambridge: Cambridge University Press.
Papadopoulos, N. (1815), *Ermês o Kerdôos, êtoi Emporikê Egkyklopaideia* [The gainful Hermes, i.e., encyclopaedia of commerce], 5 vols, Venice: Nikolaos Glukus.
Parla, T. (1985), *The Social and Political Thought of Ziya Gökalp, 1876–1924*, Leiden: Brill.
Petrovich, M.B. (1976), *A History of Modern Serbia, 1804–1918*, New York: Harcourt Brace Jovanovic.
Plekhanov, G.V. (1885), *Nashi raznoglasiya* [Our differences], Geneva: Osvobozhdenie truda [Emancipation of labour], [English version, http://www.marxists.org/archive/plekhanov/1885/ourdiff/index.html].
Pompiliu, T. (ed.) (1980), *Enlightenment and Romanian Society*, Cluj: Editura Dacia.
Psalidopoulos, M. and M.E. Mata (eds) (2002), *Economic Thought and Policy in Less Developed Europe: The Nineteenth Century*, London: Routledge.
Psalidopoulos, M. and Y. Stassinopoulos (2009), 'A liberal economist and economic policy reform in nineteenth-century Greece: the case of Ioannes Soutsos', *History of Political Economy*, **41**, 491–517.
Psalidopoulos, M. and N.J. Theocarakis (2011), '"The economist's duck": an anti-economist theatrical play of the nineteenth century', unpublished manuscript, University of Athens.
Rapet, J.J. (1858), *Manuel de morale et d'économie politique à l'usage des classes ouvrières*, [Manual of moral and political economy for the use of the working classes], Paris: Guillaumin.
Rapet, J.J. (1865), *Dêmodes egcheiridion êthikês kai politikês oikonomias* [translation by M. Kanellopoulos and A. Skalidês of Rapet, 1858], Athens: Filomousos Leschê.
Rapet, J.J. (1872), *Narodna ekonomija; u prostu izvodu* [translation of Rapet, 1858], Novi Sad: Fuks.

Rapet, J.J. (1880), *Razgovori o narodnog gospodarstvu* [translation by Blaž Lorković of Rapet, 1858], Zagreb: Matica hrvatska.

Rapet, J.J. (1903), *Egcheiridion êthikês kai politikês oikonomias* [translation by E. Fotiadou of Rapet, 1858], Athens: Raftanis-Papageôrgiou.

Roscher, W. (1863), *Sistema narodne privrede: prvi deo; Osnovi narodne privrede* [translation by Vladimir Jovanović of *System der Volkswirthschaft; Erster Band, die Grundlagen der Nationalökonomie* (System of political economy; first volume; the foundations of national economy)]. Belgrade: Državna štamparija.

Rothschild, J. (1959), *The Communist Party of Bulgaria: Origins and Development, 1883–1936*, New York: Columbia University Press.

Say, J.-B. (1821), *Catéchisme d'économie politique, ou, Instruction familière qui montre de quelle façon les richesses sont produites, distribuées et consommées dans la société* [Catechism of political economy, or, familiar instruction that shows the way in which wealth is produced, distributed and consumed in society], 2nd edn, Paris: Bossange père.

Say, J.-B. (1828), *Politikês oikonomias katêchêsis* [translation by G. Chrysêidis of Say, 1821], Aegina: [s.n.].

Say, J.-B. (1852), *ilm-i tedbir-i menzil* [translation by Sahak Abru of Say, 1821], Istanbul: Mühendisoğlu Tabıhanesi.

Sayar, A.G. (1986, 2000), *Osmanlı İktisadi Düşüncesinin Çağdaşlaşması* [The contemporization of Ottoman economic thought], Istanbul: Ötüken.

Schmoller, G. (1884), 'Das Merkantilsystem in seiner historischen Bedeutung: städtische, territoriale und staatliche Wirtschaftspolitik', *Jahrbuch für Gesetzgebung, Verwaltung und Volkswirtschaft im Deutschen Reich*, **8**, 15–61.

Schumpeter, J.A. (1954), *History of Economic Analysis*, New York: Oxford University Press.

Seyitdanlioğlu, M. (1998), 'The rise and development of the liberal thought in Turkey', *Hacettepe Üniversitesi Edebiyat Fakültesi Dergisi Cumhuriyetimizin 75. Yılı Özel Sayısı* [Special annual issue], 151–62, http://www.edebiyatdergisi.hacettepe.edu.tr/75ozelMehmetSeyitdanlioglu.pdf.

Sklavenitis, T. (1990), 'Ta emporika egcheiridia tês Venetokratias kai tês Tourkokratias kai ê Emporikê Egkyklopaideia tou Nikolaou Papadopoulou' [The commercial handbooks of the Venetian and Turkish occupation and the Commercial Encyclopaedia of Nikolaos Papadopoulos], *Mnêmôn*, Appendix 5, pp. 1–178.

Sklavenitis, T. (1994), 'O Spyridôn Valetas kai ê metaphrasê tês *Politikês Oikonomias* tou J. B. Say' [Spyridon Valetas and the translation of J.B. Say's *Political Economy*], *Mnêmôn*, Appendix 9, pp. 107–56.

Slavĕscu, V. (1941), *Viata şi opera economistului Alexandru D. Moruzi, 1815–1878* [Life and Works of the Economist Alexandru D. Moruzi], Bucharest: Academia Română Studii Şi Cercetări, Imprimeria Nationala.

Sojic, M. and L. Djurdjevic (2006), 'National Bank of Serbia 1884–2006: establishment and beginning of operation', in Avramov and Pamuk, op. cit., pp. 141–56.

Sonnenfels, J. von (1769–76), *Grundsätze der Polizey, Handlung, und Finanzwissenschaft* [Principles of policy, trade and the science of finance], 3 vols, Vienna: Joseph Kurzböck.

Soutsos, I.A. (1851), *Pragmateia peri paragôgês kai dianomês tou ploutou* [Treatise on the production and distribution of wealth], Athens: A. Koromilas.

Soutsos, I.A. (1864), *Egcheiridion dêmosiologias, ê theôria peri proüpologismou* [Manual of public finance, or theory of the budget], Athens: N.G. Passaris.

Soutsos, I.A. (1868–69), *Ploutologia* [Plutology], 2 vols, Athens: N.G. Passaris.
Soutsos, I.A. (1882 and 1885), *Ploutologia* [Plutology], 2 vols, 2nd edn, Athens: N.G. Passaris.
Spanopoulos, P. (1803), *Emporikê arithmêtikê* [Commercial arithmetic], Trieste: Katzatis printing press.
Strat, I. (1870), *Tractat complectu de economie politică* [A complete treatise of political economy], Bucharest: Imprimeriile statului.
Stoianovich, T. (1960), 'The conquering Balkan Orthodox merchant', *Journal of Economic History*, **20**, 234–313.
Stokes, G. (1975), *Legitimacy through Liberalism: Vladimir Jovanovic and the Transformation of Serbian Politics*, Seattle: University of Washington Press.
Strat, L. (1870), Tractat complectu de economie politiça [A Complete Treatise of Political Economy], Bucharest: Imprimeriile statului.
Sugar, P.F. (1985), 'The Enlightenment in the Balkans: some basic considerations', *East European Quarterly*, **9**, 499–507.
Sugar, P.F. (1996), *Nationalism and Religion in the Balkans since the 19th Century*, the Donald W. Treadgold papers in Russian, East European, and Central Asian studies, paper no. 8, Seattle, WA: Henry M. Jackson School of International Studies, University of Washington.
Suțu, N. (1849), *Notions statistiques sur la Moldavie* [Statistical data on Moldavia] Jassy: Henning.
Suțu, N. (1852), *Noțiuni statistice asupra Moldaviei* [translation of Suțu, 1849], Jassy: Buciumul român.
Suțu, N. (1867), *Quelques observations sur la statistique de la Roumanie* [Certain observations on the statistics of Rumania], Focşani: [s.n.]
Suzanne, P.H. (1826), *Principes généraux d'économie publique et industrielle, en forme d'entretiens* [General principles of public and industrial economics in the form of interviews], Paris: L. Colas.
Suzanne, P.-H. (1849), *Genikai archai tês dêmosias kai viomêchanikês oikonomias en eidei syndialexeôs metaxu patros kai uiou* [translation by M. Vernardos of Suzanne, 1826], Athens: Antoniadis.
Tietze, A. (ed., transl.) (1979–82), *Mustafa Ali's Counsel for Sultans of 1581*, Vienna: Verlag der Österreichischen Akademie der Wissenschaften.
Tomasevich, J. (1955), *Peasants, Politics and Economic Development in Yugoslavia*, Palo Alto, CA: Stanford University Press.
Tomass, M. (1996), 'Al-Maqrizi's Book of aiding the nation by investigating the depression of 1406: translation and commentary', in L.S. Moss (ed.) *Joseph A. Schumpeter: Historian of Economics*, London: Routledge, pp. 110–52.
Toprak, Z. (1994), 'Nationalism and economics in the Young Turk era (1908–1918)', in J. Thobie and S. Kançal (eds), *Industrialisation, Communication et Rapports Sociaux en Turquie et en Méditerranée Orientale*, Paris: L'Harmattan, pp. 260–66
Tribe, K. (2003), 'Continental political economy from the physiocrats to the marginal revolution', in T.M. Porter and D. Ross (eds), *The Cambridge History of Science Volume 7: The Modern Social Sciences*, Cambridge: Cambridge University Press, pp. 154–70.
Trotsky, L. (1915), 'Political profiles: Dobrogeanu-Gherea', *Nashe Slovo*, **100**, 29 May, http://www.marxists.org/archive/trotsky/profiles/gherea.htm.
University of Sofia, Faculty of Economics and Business Administration (2010),

'History', Retrieved from http://www.uni-sofia.bg/index.php/eng/faculties/faculty_of_economics_and_business_administration/history.

University of Zagreb, Faculty of Law, Department of political economy (2010), 'The teachers who taught the subject of Political Economy' [Sveučilište u Zagrebu: Pravni Fakultet: Katedra za političku ekonomiju, 'O nastavnicima koji su predavali predmet Politička ekonomija'], http://www.pravo.hr/PE/onkp.

Urquhart, D. (1833), *Turkey and its resources*. . . London: Saunders & Otley.

Weiss-Bartenstein, W.K. (1916), 'Bulgariens handelspolitische Entwicklung und das Auslandskapital' [Bulgaria's trade development and foreign capital], *Zeitschrift für Volkswirtschaft, Sozialpolitik und Verwaltung*, **25**, 141–208.

Wells, C. (1860), *Ilm tedbiri milk = The Science of the Administration of a State', or, An Essay on Political Economy, in Turkish: Being the First ever Written in that Language*, London: Williams & Norgate.

Xenopol, A.D. (1879), *Studii economice* [Economic studies], Jassy: Steaua României.

Zacharia, K. (2008), 'Introduction', in K. Zacharia (ed.), *Hellenisms: Culture, Identity, and Ethnicity from Antiquity to Modernity*, Aldershot: Ashgate, pp. 1–18.

Zografos, I. (1892), *Dêmosionomikê: êtoi episteme tês tôn dêmosiôn chrêmatôn dioikêseôs* [Public finance, i.e., the science of managing public money], Athens: Perris Bros.

Zygouras, X.D. (1878), *Epitomê oikiakês oikonomias* [Compendium of home economics], Athens: Kouvelos & Trimis.

Zygouras, X.D. (1892), *Egcheiridion oikonomikês, êtoi mathêmata oikiakês oikonomias epistêmonikôs ektethenta, pros chrêsin tôn anôterôn Parthenagôgeiôn kai Didaskaleiôn tôn thêleôn* [Manual of economics, i.e., lessons of home economics scientifically exposed, for use by girls' high schools], Athens: Kouvelos & Delis.

8. Adventures of an Austrian trio abroad: the influence of Schumpeter, Polanyi and Hayek in Turkey and the dissemination of their work

Eyüp Özveren

8.1 INTRODUCTION

A significant number of the more active Turkish economists have in recent years diverged from conventional neoclassical or Marxian economics and become influenced by some of the major names of heterodox economics. They may not yet outnumber their rivals, but they certainly outperform them in terms of publication. Moreover, there is a snowball effect at work as regards their influence upon students. The purpose of this chapter is to trace, evaluate and interpret the influences of Joseph A. Schumpeter (1883–1950), Karl Polanyi (1886–1964) and Friedrich A. von Hayek (1899–1992) in Turkey, illuminating the dissemination of economic ideas across national and cultural boundaries in the *longue durée*.

Turkey has always occupied a middle ground between the East and West, and has served as a bridge for the transfer of ideas and technologies. Turkish intellectual life has always been characterized by a relatively high degree of complexity and heterogeneity. Bearing this in mind, I first present a brief survey of the careers and major positions of these three scholars. Their growing influence in Turkey will then be shown to be characterized by two successive waves: the first during the Keynesian epoch, and the second during the neoliberal era. To trace this influence, I will first focus on the Turkish translators of the trio's major works, many of whom also happened to be academics. Extensive tape-recorded interviews[1] with major academics involved in this process of dissemination are then exploited. Finally, use is made of a questionnaire directed to the Turkish community of historians of economic thought. A distinction will be made between the strength of worldwide intellectual trends and the degree of structural openness to national reception. While in the short term it is the first that counts, in the long term the outcome is determined by structural and historical factors. To illustrate this point a comparison will be made with the influence of the same three scholars in Japan. While globalization has certainly played a role, differences in historical and institutional background create path-dependencies in Turkey and Japan that are responsible for the differential reception and ultimate effect of ideas.

8.2 THE PROGRESSION OF THE TRIO

Schumpeter and Hayek are often classified as Austrian economists, irrespective of some of the major theoretical differences that set them apart in important respects. For example, it is well known that Schumpeter was first and foremost a supply-side, production-first economist, much in the spirit of classical political economists; whereas Hayek adhered closely to the neoclassical and Austrian commitment to the 'sovereignty' of consumers insofar as their preferences dictated the main course of events in a market economy. Nevertheless, because both Schumpeter (Haberler, 1950; Streissler, 1981) and Hayek were products of the same Viennese intellectual atmosphere (Johnston, 1972, 76–87; Grassl and Smith, 1986), and because both moved in more or less the same circles, they shared an intellectual common denominator as representatives of an 'Austrian School' (Ekelund, Jr and Hébert, 1997, 507–30). On the other hand, Polanyi, known for his polemical criticisms of the Austrian economics of his time, was nevertheless also an offshoot of the same intellectual climate that characterized the *fin-de-siècle* Austro-Hungarian Empire and interwar Central Europe (Gábor, 1999; Schaffer, 1999). Notwithstanding their political and theoretical differences, these three men probably had more in common with one another, given their intellectual background, than with the various schools and scholars with whom they have in retrospect been affiliated.

Each of the Austrian trio left his country during the interwar period to live abroad until the end of his life. Schumpeter left as early as 1925, when he took up a post at the University of Bonn in Germany. After a year-long visit to Harvard University (1927–28) he returned briefly to Germany, only to emigrate finally to the United States and teach at the same university from 1932 until his death. Hayek took up a post at London School of Economics upon the invitation of Lionel Robbins in 1931, but decided to stay for good, becoming a British citizen in the wake of the infamous *Anschluss* of 1938. Hayek moved to the United States in 1950 and affiliated himself with the University of Chicago. Polanyi, like Hayek born in

Vienna, was nevertheless Budapest-based until 1924. It was there that he became active in the creation of Club Galilei while being a student at the University of Budapest. He helped found the Radical Party in 1914, but fled to Vienna when Bela Kun toppled the government and formed the Hungarian Soviet Republic. Between 1924 and 1925 Polanyi worked as a journalist for *Der Oesterreichische Volkswirt*. However, he fled to London in 1933 as the fragile republican regime began to collapse under increasing Nazi pressure. He worked as a journalist, and became a lecturer for the Workers' Educational Association. He went to the United States first in 1940 to take up a year-long position at Bennington College in Vermont, only to return to London. After the war, he joined Columbia University, where he taught from 1947 to 1953. He then settled in Canada, where he died.

All three were uprooted from their native soil, caught up by the strong winds of the interwar period, only to become *citoyens du monde*, as their contemporary countryman Stefan Zweig would put it. They were however only world citizens as far as the term 'world' connoted Old Europe and its extension in the New World. The lengthy process by which they became such citizens led to a growing divergence between them in respect of their intellectual trajectories. Theirs was in many ways almost a lifelong exile[2] – voluntary or otherwise – in the most general sense of the term. As with most exiles with whom we are familiar in the history of thought in general, and in the history of economic thought in particular, their exile was instrumental in both the growing differentiation of their ideas and their dissemination. This Austrian trio is no exception, indeed they are quite representative of a more general trend in the contours and sociology of the dissemination of ideas. The fact that every one of them exerted an influence on the course of economic thought and history, their legacy enduring to this day, makes their case all the more deserving of closer investigation.

All three members of the Austrian trio were overshadowed by the Keynesian Revolution, albeit to different degrees. Even their common misfortune was not compelling enough to bring them together, since by the 1930s each had already made critical theoretical choices that would distinguish him in the long run from his counterparts. Of the three, Hayek became the most outspoken critic of Keynesian economics, reinforced by his location at the London School of Economics which represented at the time an intellectual and academic counterweight to the University of Cambridge. It is no coincidence that Hayek became involved in exchanges, controversies and polemics with Cambridge economists such as John Maynard Keynes, Piero Sraffa and Joan Robinson. These only served to make his differences, such as his shift as of 1928[3] to the idea of an intertemporal equilibrium, all the more pointed (Faber, 1980; Desai, 1982; Lawlor and Horn, 1992). Even in the mid-1970s he wrote a critique entitled *Full Employment at Any Price*? a fully fledged and timely assault on Keynesian economics that came at the right moment of sustained stagflation (Hayek, 1975).

In retrospect, Schumpeter is perhaps less well known for his criticism of Keynesian economics, but he was certainly no less sharp (Schumpeter, 1942, 390n, 392, 396n) or determined (Schefold, 1986).[4] The difference was in part due to the fact that he was not living in Keynes's homeland but in the United States, while teaching at Harvard University. Keynes's influence in the USA came via Alvin Hansen, who domesticated Keynes's propositions and introduced them to the American scene.[5]

Of the three, Polanyi was probably the most receptive to Keynesian ideas, both because of the policies Keynes advocated, and because Keynes's diagnosis in *The End of Laissez-Faire* (Keynes, 1926) confirmed Polanyi's anticipation of the fall of 'nineteenth century civilization', 'the fount and matrix' of which was the self-regulating market system (Polanyi, 1944, 3). Moreover, the Keynesian instruments of active economic policy seeking full employment indicated a shift of balance from 'market exchange' to 'redistribution' in Polanyi's classificatory scheme of the forms of economic integration (Polanyi, 1957, 250–56, 270).[6] In light of this fact, it seems ironic at first sight that of all the three, Polanyi, despite his affinities with Keynesian economics noted above, should in fact be the one most overshadowed by the Keynesian Revolution. This was first and foremost because Keynesian economics was myopically short term in orientation, the explicit emphasis being on capacity utilization at the expense of capacity creation. Moreover, it also favoured policy over institutions, and chose to work with policies formulated within the context of existing institutions. As long as institutional context and change are ignored, it is only natural that the analytical potential of Polanyi's work for institutional economics, and its implications for the specification of the institutional and social conditions of a market economy, should also be overlooked – as was the case with mainstream Keynesianism.[7]

The respective fortunes of the now further differentiated members of the Austrian trio were nevertheless revived as of the 1970s; there was renewed interest in their work as plausible alternatives to the once-dominant Keynesian 'synthesis'. Suddenly reappearing on the scene, Hayek inspired the initial pro-market liberal revival. Some prominent members of the Thatcher and Reagan administrations looked upon him as a mentor. In a far more gradual but sustained manner, Schumpeter, then long dead, became a source of inspiration for those who emphasized the primacy of the supply side, together with an eye to the critical role of innovation in engendering economic development. This was so much the case that he became the major influence behind widely shared European technological policies. As for Polanyi, he became the guiding spirit of those disillusioned by the dismantling of the welfare state at the behest of the neoliberal processes of globalization cultivated by Hayekian and Schumpeterian approaches.[8] In short, during this second phase the influence of the members of the Austrian trio spread fast and far, well beyond the boundaries of Europe and North America. As such, they became true *citoyens du monde*, as far as intellectual affinity is concerned. However, the relative fortunes of these three figures differed, depending on the specific circumstances of the individual countries in which their ideas were received. By 'specific circumstances', I have in mind a host of factors such as social and economic structure, but also culture and, more importantly, the nature of the institutions of higher learning, research and policy design.

Each of these Austrians produced a major characteristic work. These works amount to what the French call *vulgarisation*, in the positive sense of the term which gets lost when translated literally into English. This positive sense involves making sophisticated state-of-the-art ideas available to the reading public. Schumpeter's *Capitalism, Socialism and Democracy* was first published in 1942. Then came Polanyi's *The Great Transformation*, and Hayek's *The Road to Serfdom*, both in 1944. There was no cross-referencing among these works, and the authors remained virtually cut off from one another. Nevertheless, while these three books were rooted in the intellectual atmosphere of the interwar period, they reflected in particular a concern about the post-war order that came to the fore during the closing phases of the Second World War.

8.3 FIRST WAVE OF INFLUENCE: HESITANT BEGINNINGS CAUGHT IN THE KEYNESIAN LANDSLIDE

Of the three scholars and their now classic works, the first one to be translated into Turkish, albeit incompletely, was Hayek's. At the behest of Aydın Yalçın (1920–94), a professor of economics with strong Anglo-American leanings and connections in the wake of the Cold War, Turhan Feyzioğlu (1922–88), a later professor of law, translated the first eight chapters and published it in the journal of the Faculty of Political Sciences of Ankara University in 1947–48 (Yayla, 1995). Several observations ought to be made for the benefit of the reader. Whereas Hayek's book was intended for the public at large, in Turkey only part of it was published, in a highly academic journal with limited circulation. Both Yalçın and Feyzioğlu belonged to the same institution, which had been founded to train modern-minded civil servants for the republican regime. They both studied as graduates in London, where Yalçın obtained his degree in 1951 and Feyzioğlu gained his shortly afterwards. Yalçin became the youngest full professor in Turkey in 1955, and it would be many years before an even younger appointment was made. Whereas one would have expected an economist of Yalçın's calibre to undertake the translation, he did not do so; instead it was translated by a specialist in law. Furthermore, though one would have expected Feyzioğlu to develop a genuine scholarly interest in Hayek's other works relating to law, he did not do so. In 1954, Yalçın led a coalition of academics and intellectuals that included Feyzioğlu – but also certain Marxists – in publishing a journal, *Forum*, which served as a medium for high-level extra-academic debates. What united the contributors to this journal was their disillusionment with, and common opposition to, the authoritarian tendencies of the Democratic Party government that came to power in 1950, and which was ultimately overthrown by the coup d'état of 1960. Later on in their careers both tried their fortunes in major as well as minority political parties, without however accomplishing a great deal. In short, there is good reason to suspect that the translation of Hayek's *The Road to Serfdom* was encouraged by the favourable Cold War climate, and that it was deliberately promoted by particular Anglo-American agencies. The channel of diffusion is also no surprise. But Turkey was far from ready for its reception. The translation had no discernable impact in the short and medium term, except by contributing to the social scientific knowledge of Turkish academics. This tentative beginning would remain as truncated as the translation, at least until the second wave came along.

Schumpeter's *Capitalism, Socialism and Democracy* was the second text of the three writers to be translated into Turkish. This was first done in 1966 by Tunay Akoğlu,[9] and then in 1971 by Rasin Tınaz, both being non-academic professionals who translated fiction as well as occasional titles in the social sciences. It is quite obvious that the book was commissioned by the publishing house (Varlık), committed to improving the quality of learning. It is perhaps significant that it appeared only two years before the worldwide unrest of 1968, and five years before the 1971 Turkish military *pronunciamento* against leftist movements inspired by the events of 1968. The concepts referred to in the title were already familiar to the public, but the publisher's attention must also have been caught by Schumpeter's original and quite 'un-Austrian' proof of the theoretical feasibility of socialism. Given Schumpeter's conservative ideological stance, this proof must have appeared all the more convincing, hence scientific and so escaping prosecution under martial law. This emphasis clearly distinguished Schumpeter from Hayek for a reading public unfamiliar with their common roots in Austrian economics.

More can be said about the penetration of Schumpeter's influence into Turkey. Whereas the translation of his most popular work into Turkish came somewhat belatedly and through non-academic channels, there had existed a strong line of potential dissemination long before this publication. Sabri Ülgener (1911–83), a reputable Turkish academic affiliated with the Faculty of Economics of Istanbul University, was sent to the United States shortly after the war in order to pursue postdoctoral research at Harvard University. He arrived in Boston in December 1946, staying there until the summer of 1948. He later wrote of his delight at being at Harvard where academics such as Schumpeter, Gottfried Haberler, Wassily Leontief, Edward H. Chamberlin and Alvin Hansen were assembled. Thanks to his having been taught German at the Istanbul Erkek Lisesi (Istanbul High School for Boys) and his further interaction with German-speaking scholars employed by Istanbul University, Ülgener was fairly fluent in German and well versed in the German academic tradition. Even before the arrival of German emigrés, he had been acquainted with the works of Werner Sombart, and especially those of Max Weber (Neumark, 2008 [1980], 125). Prior to his departure for the United States Ülgener had taught a course, 'Theory of Conjunctures', in which he made extensive use of Schumpeter's *Business Cycles.* Hence it is no surprise that upon arrival he headed directly for Schumpeter. However, the real surprise was twofold. Firstly, how excited Schumpeter was with one of the two gifts Ülgener had brought him. Seeing in a volume that was given to him the Saint Sophia church-turned-mosque-turned-museum, Schumpeter recalled from memory the three architects of this monument. The second real surprise was that he was entirely unmoved when Ülgener presented him with the recent German translation of his *Capitalism, Socialism and Democracy*, which Schumpeter had not yet seen (Sayar, 1998, 96).

Ülgener attended Schumpeter's graduate seminar, as well as meeting him regularly to converse in German. He was impressed with Schumpeter's command of English in his course on the history of economic thought.[10] Ülgener records that Schumpeter once asked him about German academics at the Faculty of Economics of Istanbul University.[11] Upon hearing the names of Wilhelm Röpke, Alexander Rüstow, Fritz Neumark,[12] Gerhard Kessler and Josef Dobretsberger, he reacted condescendingly, for he saw them as influenced by Werner Sombart, whom he despised.[13] When Schumpeter asked who else was there, Ülgener added Umberto Ricci, the Italian. Schumpeter then got really excited and commented that Ricci was a great man, in the tradition of Walras-Pareto-Panteleoni (Sayar, 1998, 98–9). In short, Ülgener had close connections with Schumpeter, who also impressed him greatly on the personal level.

Under the above circumstances, it is not surprising that Ülgener's intellectual formation bore the heavy mark of Schumpeter to the very end of his life. However, he never became a Schumpeterian economist per se. To understand the reason for this, we need to look at the evolution of Ülgener's equally strong Keynesian affinity. Before his arrival at Harvard Ülgener was already no stranger to the Keynesian ideas that had been introduced at Istanbul University. He was obviously acquainted with Osman Okyar as a colleague, the first Turkish economist to devote himself to the study of Keynesian economics. Okyar was the son of the former Prime Minister Fethi Okyar, who had translated Keynes's *The Economic Consequences of the Peace* (1971 [1920]) into Turkish shortly after it had been published in 1920. Fethi Okyar then served as Ambassador in London and his son studied at King's College, Cambridge from 1936 until 1940. Osman Okyar's supervisor was Arthur C. Pigou, but he also took Keynes's course, 'How to Pay for the War', during his last year. Upon his return to Turkey, he pursued a doctoral degree under Neumark's supervision in Istanbul University. He earned his degree in 1947 with a thesis on the transition from neoclassical to Keynesian theory. Okyar thus became the first Turkish scholar to pursue a graduate degree on Keynes at Istanbul University. He first became acquainted with the Keynesian approach while at Cambridge (Neumark, 2008, 140), but once he joined Istanbul University he found a receptive environment among the economics faculty, where he was able to pursue this interest further. Nor was the appointment of Neumark as supervisor for Okyar's Keynes-inspired thesis mere coincidence. Neumark had replaced Schumpeter at the University of Bonn during the winter semester 1932–33 after Schumpeter's move to Harvard (Neumark, 2008, 177). Generally quite open-minded, Neumark was receptive to Keynesian ideas during the 'years of high theory'. After a brief visiting professorship in 1950, he returned to Goethe University in Frankfurt for good in 1952, as Professor of Public Finance, and also served twice as Rector of the university (Hoss, 2008 [2007], 202). He became the leading German expert on public finance, with a strongly Keynesian flavour. While during the interwar period Ülgener himself was not as deeply involved in this new approach as Okyar, he was certainly acquainted with it.

With this background, once at Harvard, Ülgener also interacted closely with Hansen, the author of the influential *A Guide to Keynes* (1953), and whose seminar on Keynesian economics he followed enthusiastically. Ülgener thought highly of Hansen, as second only to Keynes himself. When he returned home he began teaching a macroeconomic theory course along the Keynes–Hansen line during the academic year of 1948–49. Ülgener thus became instrumental in the dissemination not of Schumpeterian, but of Keynesian economics among the Istanbul-based faction of Turkish academia. In 1962 he published a book in Turkish, the title of which can be translated as 'National income, employment and economic growth' (*Milli Gelir, İstihdam ve İktisadi Büyüme*), revealing the author's Keynesian affinity.

Ultimately, Ülgener is now in retrospect identified as one of the two major channels through which Keynesian economics penetrated into the Turkish academic establishment during the 1950s. The other channel was based in Ankara and operated through Yalçın's journal, *Forum*, which included among its regular contributors members of the Faculty of Political Sciences of the Ankara University. Ironically, the Hayek-oriented Yalçın and his colleagues – one of whom was Osman Okyar – thus became promoters of Keynesian economics. Among their contributors was Sadun Aren, a leading Marxist figure on the Turkish left who had been to Cambridge for postgraduate research, and who is now identified as Ülgener's Ankara-based counterpart in this respect. Whereas Aren's Keynesianism is understandable, Ülgener has always possessed a wider range of interests that included economic sociology as well as history of economic thought. He wrote extensively on the question of economic mentality, so much so as to be dubbed the 'Turkish Weber'. As a matter of fact, his PhD thesis, defended in 1937 at Istanbul University, was on economic ethics and mentality in the Near Eastern Turco-Islamic world. His *Habilitation* thesis, completed in 1941, was on the crises of provisioning during the pre-capitalist era (Ayan, 2000, 163). All these concerns derive from his upbringing in the German tradition.

In short, Ülgener had one foot in Schumpeter's camp and the other in Keynes's (Sayar, 1998, 339),[14] not to mention Weber, who was always on his mind. If one person upheld Schumpeterian economics among this generation of Turkish scholars, it was Ülgener who was most qualified for the task. But there was at that time no such camp of Schumpeterian economists. At best there was a nascent camp of Keynesian economists. Under these circumstances, the role of being the standard-bearer of Keynesian economics fell upon him, much to his dislike. The fact that the straitjacket of Keynesian economics was forced upon him can be taken as a direct indication of the strength of the Keynesian landslide in the post-war world.

Somewhat differently from the fortunes of Hayek and Schumpeter in Turkey, Polanyi's initial reception is more difficult to detect and would have remained negligible had it not been for its slow, gradual but cumulative effect that would culminate during the second wave. Polanyi was probably known first to Şerif Mardin (1927–), a Turkish academic specializing in political science who studied at Stanford and Johns Hopkins University, and who later became a visiting scholar at Columbia University, where Polanyi had once taught. It was Mardin who brought

Polanyi to the attention of Yahya Sezai Tezel, a professor of economics now retired from the Faculty of Political Sciences of Ankara University. Tezel had studied at Cambridge. Upon his return he started a politico-academic journal the title of which translates as 'Socialist thought for democracy' (*Demokrasi İçin Toplumcu Düşün*). It was in this journal that Polanyi was first translated into Turkish (by Etyen Mahcupyan). His 1957 article, 'The economy as instituted process', was published in 1978, long before *The Great Transformation.* As a matter of fact, students of the Middle East Technical University became familiar with Polanyi's name in the 1970s through the Turkish as well as visiting faculty. The visitors were Chicago scholars who came to teach at the Department of Sociology, the Turks including Fikret Görün and Çağlar Keyder at the Department of Economics, both of whom had been abroad either to study or to conduct postgraduate research. The emphasis fell at first on Polanyi's later writings, belonging to the subfield of economic anthropology. These articles overshadowed *The Great Transformation*, although this would be rediscovered during the second wave.

8.4 SECOND WAVE: PARADOXICAL PROLIFERATION OF INFLUENCES IN THE NEOLIBERAL PERIOD

The year of the military takeover, 1980, found Turkey at an economic and political impasse. The economy was then a strongly state-regulated mixed economy, committed to industrialization through import substitution. It was thus at odds with the emergent neoliberal trend of reducing the scale of the state in combination with 'private sector first' export-oriented policies. The military regime decided to readjust the economy towards this trend, foreshadowing the rise of 'globalization'. With the opposition virtually silenced, a 'consensus' was imposed regarding the primacy of markets in economic regulation. This economic transition was coupled with political authoritarianism, as in Latin America. The role of the government in the political system was strengthened at the expense of civil liberties. The military interregnum was fairly short, but the institutional reforms it introduced left a lasting legacy. Pro-market and politically anti-liberal forces remained dominant for at least a decade, if not longer.

It would seem that there was here ample room for a Hayekian agenda. First of all, Hayek and Milton Friedman had inspired the economic policies first adopted in Chile, New Zealand, Britain and the USA, which were then diffused to the rest of the world under the auspices of international organizations such as the International Monetary Fund and the World

Bank, not to mention the World Trade Organization (Gray, 1998, 28). Whereas there was an 'imposed' consensus on the primacy of markets in Turkey, this was not of itself sufficient to generate academic interest in Hayek. Hayek was at that time more frequently mentioned than anyone else by influential columnists of popular newspapers and magazines (excepting perhaps Friedman), but academic interest in Hayek was conspicuously lacking. Hayek's commitment to a 'liberal' politics made him unpalatable for people seeking a compromise with the newly regimented constitutional system. As such, political scientists and social philosophers steered clear of Hayek. On the other hand, economists who conformed to the regime's new economic policy were far too practically minded and intellectually shallow to seek inspiration and legitimacy in Hayek's work. The legitimacy they needed was generously provided by the international economic institutions on whose support they counted. In contrast, economists with a stronger bent for intellectual and theoretical causes resisted Hayek's influence, because they considered him to be identified too greatly with a status quo that they felt they should oppose. Hence Hayek's name circulated widely in the media, but he was shunned in academia.

It was only over the 1990s, when Turkey finally sloughed off the legacy of the military regime, that an interest in Hayek finally developed among both journalists and academics. Interestingly enough, this was now not among economists, but among political scientists and lawyers of a liberal persuasion (Erdoğan, 1993; Aktaş, 2001). Hayek's *The Road to Serfdom* was finally published as a book in 1995 with the addition of a new translation of the latter seven chapters (with a summary of supposedly irrelevant sections). The translation was done by Yıldıray Arsan (Hayek, 1995), a professor. An introduction was written for this edition by Atilla Yayla (1957–), a somewhat eccentric liberal professor of public administration at Gazi University in Ankara, who also wrote a book on Hayek's social theory (Yayla, 2000), and who additionally leads a self-professed liberal think-tank of academics, including Arsan, organized around the Liberté publishing house. Needless to say, *The Road to Serfdom* is gospel for those involved in this network.

Had it not been for the current financial world economic crisis, Schumpeter's name could not have found its way into the Turkish press. Rightly or wrongly, some journalists consider there to be a strong connection between the current crisis and Schumpeter's successive waves of creative destruction. I do not share this view. Nevertheless, the crisis has served to make Schumpeter's name familiar to a broader section of the reading public. It could be said in retrospect that, with the shift in economic policy towards the private sector and its quest for increasing regional and worldwide competitiveness, there was more room for Schumpeterian influence during the 1980s. This was even more apparent when Turkey began exporting entrepreneurship to former Soviet bloc countries in the 1990s. Last but not least, a policy focus on innovation and technological renewal came into prominence, with attempts to fine-tune the Turkish economy with European policies of a similar kind. Even so, interest in Schumpeter remained relatively limited, except for a young generation of economists who were educated abroad and/or had connections with neo-Schumpeterian economists elsewhere, and who pursued mostly empirical research and model-building in the spirit of of evolutionary economics (Ballot and Taymaz, 1998; Eliasson et al., 2005; Erbil, 2007).

This neo-Schumpeterian approach is far from representing Schumpeter's legacy comprehensively. As such, Schumpeter's influence in Turkey exists – unlike that of Hayek – among economists of a certain bent; however, it has only come into the picture obliquely via his influence on neo-Schumpeterians abroad, and the transmission of this to Turkey. There is good reason to expect that this stratum of economists and their works will over the next decade or so increase in prominence. We should remind ourselves here that, in contrast with Hayek, Schumpeter does not provide a potential umbrella for any political cause, be that liberal or otherwise, and therefore is more likely to be read for purely intellectual and academic reasons. A new translation of *Capitalism, Socialism and Democracy* has been published in 2007 by a different publishing house (Schumpeter, 2007). As such, Schumpeter has caught up with Hayek as far as translation goes. It would not be surprising to see Schumpeter outrank Hayek in terms of overall influence in the near future, given the highly productive group of research-oriented neo-Schumpeterian economists mentioned above, as well as the nascent graduate and research programmes in science and technology policy fostered by the challenges of a global economy on the one hand, and the European integration process on the other.

Concerning the available translations and their circulation in Turkey, Polanyi's *The Great Transformation* outdistances by a wide margin either *The Road to Serfdom* or *Capitalism, Socialism and Democracy*. It was the first major work to be translated into Turkish during the neoliberal era. It was translated in 1986 by a respectable academic, Ayşe Buğra, a professor of economics at Boğaziçi University in Istanbul (Polanyi, 2007 [1986]). Buğra is committed personally to Polanyi's approach and has done her best to introduce it to her students as well as to academia. Buğra's dedication has been central to the success and reception of this work in Turkey. We may infer that, had it not been for the favourable environment that this book created, subsequent translators and publishers may have been more reluctant to undertake the translation of either Hayek's or Schumpeter's classics. As a matter of fact, among the members of the Austrian trio, the greatest impact among the Turkish community of economists has been exerted by Polanyi at a time when the dominant trend in economics worldwide has been in favour of standardization and formalization. This is somewhat paradoxical because Polanyi himself, while being quite well versed in the economics of his time, was not an economist by training. This requires an explanation that goes beyond Buğra's personal dedication to the Polanyian cause.

Among the three members of the Austrian trio, Polanyi is the only one who offers a critical counterpoint to the neoliberal trend, as manifest in the globalization of the last few decades. Hayek and Schumpeter may offer us much to understand the processes at work, but little to criticize or oppose, or to overturn them, if indeed we sought to and could. Here lies Polanyi's great attraction. But this attraction would not work on just any community of economists to the same degree. A particular characteristic of the Turkish community of economists enters into the picture at this stage. As with most other communities of economists in academia, the greater part of this body consists of mainstream economists who are oriented to modelling and prediction with a narrow focus. What one eminent historian has termed 'the tyranny of here and now' (Tilly, 1986), and what another had long before referred to as 'the myopia of the moment' (Huizinga, 1955, 195), prevails strongly among them. Furthermore, these economists are more hypothesis- and technique-conscious than theory-conscious. Setting aside this greater part of the community of economists, there is however a considerable population of heterodox economists. These are obviously fewer in number but greater in impact because they teach, publish and influence the reading public at large.

Many elder members of this – far from united – camp come from a Marxian background dating back to the 1970s. During the 1980s they looked to other sources of inspiration. Some of them did so because they were disillusioned by the more vulgar versions of Marxism and/or the misfortunes of the Soviet Union and its satellites. Others did so because they thought they had to make their stance more acceptable in a rapidly changing Turkey. Whatever the initial cause, they wished to remain in opposition to the existing state of affairs. Many of them found Marx and Polanyi in potential agreement, awaiting a complementary synthetic treatment. Others who delved more deeply into Polanyi's work realized certain irreconcilable differences. In either case, there occurred a pooling of critical academic energies in favour of Polanyi. The route from Marx to Polanyi was easier to take than, say, a route from Marx to Schumpeter, if we give greater priority to the politics associated with such a transition over its purely economic aspects. For the Turkish economists, politics came first. Schumpeter, given his conservative politics, was not thought worth reviving; hence his economics was not examined that closely. In fact, had this second chance been granted it would have become clear that Schumpeter was in general much more compatible with the Marxian research agenda in economics than are either Hayek or Polanyi.[15]

On the one hand, in contrast to Hayek, Schumpeter was a supply-side, production-first economist in the spirit of the classical approach. He had been much influenced by the emphasis Marx placed on the role of capital accumulation and technical progress in the long-run development of the capitalist economy (Schumpeter, 1989 [1937], 166). On the other hand, in contrast to Polanyi, who did not have a notion of economic dynamics, Schumpeter elaborated a theory of economic process based on the successive innovations carried out by members of entrepreneurial strata. Blind to the attraction of such factors, given the dominant mainstream economic trend in favour of formalization and abstraction, these critical economists were further intrigued by the interdisciplinary openings a Polanyi-esque perspective offered.[16] While employed as economists, they nevertheless resisted more of the same economics as propagated by the mainstream. Polanyi's work thus provided them with a basis upon which they could elaborate a new theoretical synthesis. It is no coincidence that some recent openings to the works of Schumpeter and even Hayek in Turkey originate from among these economists who are, first and foremost, inspired by Polanyi. There was no prospect of a similar rapprochement with Polanyi on the part of those economists inspired by Hayek or Schumpeter. Hence the asymmetric distribution of the influences of the three members of the Austrian trio in Turkey is far from accidental.

8.5 A COMPARISON WITH JAPAN: DISPARATE REALITIES YET CONVERGING TRAJECTORIES?

We have seen above how the influence of the Austrian trio in Turkey came in two major waves and how the ranking of the three members changed over time. However, when one is dealing with a small number of cases, as is the case especially when one looks at the first wave, it becomes almost impossible to distinguish between what is accidental and what is structural. The picture gets all the more complicated because, as time unfolds, chance occurrences serve to cultivate structural consequences that lead to path-dependencies and even occasional lock-ins. Any account of the Turkish case is inevitably biased in favour of the most evident features, thereby blurring the more important structural context.

We can avoid some of these problems by attempting a comparison with a different national case, if not several cases. The second case has to be relatively independent of the first. Furthermore, the more instances the second case contains, the better; the size of the population compensating for the distortion due to accidental factors, as well as outlier effects. The Japanese case as a potential candidate for such a comparison would fulfill both conditions, given that: (1) the two countries have little interaction in this respect; and (2) Japan has had a rich tradition of economic thought with a significantly higher number of economists. Therefore, such a comparison and contrast could serve as a check on the conclusions inferred from the Turkish case. Moreover, it would serve to foreground structural factors at work. Last but not least, one could then see if the primacy of structural factors has a tendency to yield their place to the primacy of international context over time. I will therefore attempt an outline comparison and contrast with Japan. Unfortunately, whereas I relied on original interviews and questionnaires for the elaboration of the Turkish case, I will have to be content with the existing literature in English for its Japanese counterpart. Even so, there is utility in such an attempt. This is not the first time that the histories of the Ottoman Empire or Turkey and Japan have been the basis for a comparative study. As such, the choice of Japan is not random, but based on a scholarly tradition that I will first of all briefly summarize.

Ottoman statesmen and the intelligentsia turned to Japan as a source for inspiration ever since the Japanese victory in the Russo-Japanese War (1904–05) over the arch-enemy Russia. Here, they thought, was an Oriental power that proved Russia in particular, and the West in general, were not invincible. This historic conjuncture thus directed Ottoman interest to Japan in the early twentieth century. The more closely one studied Japan, the more there seemed to be a basis for comparing the fortunes of the two empires so that policy implications might be derived. After all, in addition to their cultural differences from the West, Japan had embarked on a deliberate path of modernization from above, typified by Barrington Moore as 'revolution from above' in 'the absence of a peasant revolution' (Moore Jr., 1967). The Meiji Restoration seemed to mirror the course of the Ottoman Empire in the hands of enlightened bureaucrats, officials and intelligentsia, culminating with the Young Turks in the revolution of Kemal Atatürk. To this day, this comparison (Timberger, 1972), with an emphasis on the conscious import of elite knowledge and modern technology from the West by the active intermediation of a political and intellectual elite, remains popular among academics. However, in contrast to this line of thought, shared by both Turkish and Western scholars, a second line of argument has persisted among Turkish conservatives. According to this line of thought, particularly strengthened after the 1960s, Japan has successfully combined a traditional culture with modern technology,[17] whereas Turkey has wrongly departed from its own culture and values to achieve economic development which remains unrealized. In short, Turkey has failed in its pursuit of economic development because it has not held fast to its traditional culture, an imperative for economic development which is illustrated by the miraculous example of Japan. By deploying the Japanese example in this way, Turkish conservatives can justify what was until recently a covert critique of the reformist Young Turk and revolutionary Kemalist past of their country. The corollary follows: if only the Turks had clung to their traditional culture, they would have fared better during a century of economic development.

Both of the above lines of thought assume that the Turkish and Japanese cases lend themselves to comparison. The advocates of both positions dwell almost exclusively on the superficial similarities of the two cases, traceable to a historical convergence forced upon them by circumstance, and factors such as incorporation into the modern world system. Had one focused instead on the structural attributes of the two cases one would have been able to identify reasons for the Ottoman and Japanese Empires, together with their contemporary successors, remaining so far apart. The convergence of a traditional Japanese system with European feudalism has been much noted as a reason for the rapid development of capitalism on this receptive soil (Anderson, 1974). On the other hand, the Ottoman land system cannot be described as feudal and fits better Max Weber's concept of prebendalism, or Marx's much-criticized concept of the Asiatic mode of production. One further example will illustrate the implications of this. The Ottoman Empire in the nineteenth century, and Turkey in the first half of the twentieth century, remained for the most part chronically underpopulated. As a consequence, there has never been either a 'Land Question' or a 'Peasant Question'. The clear contrast with Japan should here be obvious. The existence of an agrarian question provides not only a root cause of political mobilization, but also much ammunition for an intellectual debate over the nature of landholding and rural transformation. It is no coincidence that much of early Japanese Marxism was stimulated by this problem. On the other hand, the non-existence of this problem in Turkey made Turkish Marxism a pretentious import from outside well into the 1960s. It is argued here that whereas there are superficial similarities for comparison, structural dissimilarities instead demand a contrast.[18] Economic thought in many instances starts off from transcultural influences. Here a focus on seeming superficial similarities is initially of great importance. Once imported, economic ideas acquire a momentum of their own in interaction with the structural attributes of the context in which they are now cultivated. At this stage, structure has precedence over conjuncture in the determination of the prospects of further economic thought.

With the above point in mind, I will briefly survey the leading points of Japanese economic thought vis-à-vis its Turkish counterpart. For the sake of brevity, I will ignore the richness of traditional economic thought in Japan (Sugiyama, 1994) and in the Ottoman Empire (Özveren, 2002), and refrain from assessing their relative openness to the reception of an external 'modernity'. In Japan as well as in Turkey, Marxism played a prominent role by comparison with neoclassical orthodoxy well into the last quarter of the twentieth century. Marxism filled a vacuum, whereas neoclassicism appeared neither attractive nor successful.[19] Hence the apparent strength of Marxism was a reflection of the weakness of neoclassical economics. Japanese Marxism arrived on the scene in advance of its Ottoman counterpart. It set up its academic headquarters in a respectable institution, Tokyo Imperial University. Because it addressed the pressing problems of land and labour and nascent imperialism, it became dynamic and highly creative. As it developed divisions appeared, giving rise to rival factions that engaged in debates of substantial importance. In 1927 the Koza faction adhered to the orthodoxy of Comintern that lent priority to the defeat of feudalism, whereas the Rono faction insisted that Japanese capitalism was already mature enough to be assaulted directly (Ando, 1998). From the First World War to the Great Depression, Marxism was 'perhaps the greatest new influence on economic ideas' (Morris-Suzuki, 1991, 73) at a time when it was virtually non-existent in the Ottoman–Turkish intellectual and academic scene. With the advent of the military dictatorship, Japanese economic thought entered into a period of intellectual isolation and endured a counterproductive freeze that lasted until the end of the Second World War (Morris-Suzuki, 1991, 94).[20] Marxist economics was not unaffected; some of its advocates, such as Arisawa Hiromi, accommodated themselves to the viewpoint of the military dictatorship:

> Arisawa Hiromi's version had a strong nationalist orientation; it emphasized ways to strengthen Japan in competition among nation states, especially between Western and non-Western countries . . . Arisawa's version of Marxism moreover prescribed the avoidance of class conflict and advocated cooperation between management and labor especially when the nation was in a crisis. (Gao, 1997, 63)

During the very same period Turkish economic thought lived through one of its most dynamic, original and varied phases. It was in the 1930s that the Turkish Kadro movement emerged as a conglomeration of

Arisawa-like Marxist renegades. Many of their writings echoed the line taken by Arisawa. They elaborated a theory of unequal exchange with asymmetric developmental implications. The very same concept of 'unequal exchange' emerged on the Japanese scene at about the same time, with the Osaka-based Nawa Toichi (Morris-Suzuki, 1991, 114). This temporal coincidence was however a unique exception rather than the rule, and was largely the outcome of world-economic pressures to which both countries were then exposed.[21] There was also a significant chronological difference between the two national experiences; Turkish economic thought followed its Japanese counterpart with a lag, notwithstanding further substantial differences.

After the Second World War, both traditions came under the impact of similar international pressures. The winds of change blew from the same direction. Their effects were quite different in degree. In principle, economic growth shakes and thereby destabilizes socio-economic structures irrespective of its fundamental characteristics. This process unleashes forces that generate new debates. In Japan, the high growth rates associated with structural transformation forced economists of all kinds to adapt to new domestic circumstances. In Turkey, lagging economic growth meant that external influences continued to matter more than domestic developments well into the 1960s. By the time the Japanese 'economic miracle' had been identified, the nature of the economic problems that the economists in Japan confronted had significantly changed. The country's profile called for cross-fertilization between the two rival traditions of Marxism and neoclassicism, which however remained as far apart as in Turkey. One Japanese author noted, with a touch of sarcasm, that: 'the percentage of enthusiastic admirers of Marx was, and is, noticeably higher in Japan than elsewhere, except of course in Soviet Russia and her satellites, and Red China' (Komatsu, 1961, 14). Another estimated that more than half the economists in Japan were Marxists (Bronfenbrenner, 1956, 390). Yet another authority identifies in retrospect the golden age of Japanese Marxian economics as the period 1967–83 (Akama, 2000, 128). In spite of this observation, Marxism in Japan might nevertheless during the 1970s have been losing ground relatively (Morris-Suzuki, 1991, 130), whereas in this period its prestige reached an all-time high in Turkey, thanks to the impetus given by the 1968 movement.

In Turkey, the borderline between Marxists and their neoclassical counterparts was reinforced. Orthodoxy ruled supreme in both camps. There was little room for either originality or dialogue, and no incentive for them. Japanese economic thought was prompted by structural circumstances to develop in terms of indigenous theoretical achievement:

> By the beginning of the 1970's, however, the basis not only of high growth, but also of this comfortable intellectual edifice was crumbling. Japanese economists were therefore forced to redirect their attention to the most essential and fundamental questions of economic theory – even to the meaning of the term 'economics' itself. Just as Japan was finding it increasingly hard to rely on imported technology, so there came to be a growing sense that Japanese economics, rather than accepting and adapting imported theories, would need to contribute to the generation of new paradigms to meet the problems of a changing economic environment. (Morris-Suzuki, 1991, 163)

Whereas intellectual arrogance was the rule of the day in Turkey, in Japan there was a self-confident and open-minded search for a new opening. It was during the last quarter of the twentieth century that heterodox economists in both countries, disillusioned by the economics practised on their own national scene, would look increasingly for inspiration to figures like Polanyi, Schumpeter and Hayek, seeking a new way out of an intellectual impasse. Consequently the second wave in the dissemination and elaboration of the work of the Austrian trio more or less coincided in both countries. The differences in trajectory created by historical circumstances were no more.

Vigorous debates and the academic environment of Japan during the 1930s had already attracted the attention of leading economists. Keynes wrote a special preface dated 4 December 1936 for the Japanese translation of his *The General Theory of Employment, Interest and Money* (1973 [1936]). Keynes expected to find a more favourable hearing in Japan, which he thought would be receptive to his arguments. Keynes made two points clear. First, the dissemination of economic ideas into Japan was strong, yet one-sided; and second, the Japanese audience was less burdened with the legacy of a dominant tradition in economic thought, and therefore more open to new ideas:

> Perhaps Japanese readers, however, will neither require nor resist my assaults against the English tradition. We are well aware of the large scale on which English economic writings are read in Japan, but we are not so well informed as to how Japanese opinions regard them. The recent praiseworthy enterprise on the part of the International Economic Circle of Tokyo in reprinting Malthus's 'Principles of Political Economy' as the first volume in the Tokyo Series of Reprints encourages me to think that a book which traces its decent from Malthus rather than Ricardo may be received with sympathy in some quarters at least. (Keynes, 1973 [1936], xxix)

Ichiro Nakayama, a prominent post-war economist, used it as a textbook in his undergraduate course at Hitotsubashi University the very same year (Hamada, 1986, 451).

Implicit in Keynes's effort was an attempt to capture Japanese opinion in the global competition for influence among his peers. In 1931 Schumpeter had made a well-publicized lecture tour of Japan. He had previously been invited to teach at Tokyo University in 1924 (Gao, 1997, 206). In the wake of the Great Depression Schumpeter's theory of economic cycles was well received. In addition, Schumpeter's mix of neoclassical analysis with economic history and empirical research must have offered a plausible alternative for many Japanese economists. Last but not least, Schumpeter was first and foremost oriented to the supply side and production, and in a country that had been experiencing sustained economic growth this may have seemed a favourable aspect of his work. Nakayama Ichiro – together with Tobata Seiichi, another influential economist – had studied with Schumpeter at the University of Bonn in the late 1920s and then returned to teach in Tokyo, where he helped introduce marginalism and general equilibrium analysis (Morris-Suzuki, 1991, 92). The two economists translated Schumpeter's *Theory of Economic Development* in 1937. Schumpeter wrote a preface for the Japanese edition in which he referred to himself as: 'so ardent an admirer of the Japanese nation and its culture' (Schumpeter, 1989, 165). Whether this was genuine or intended to please the reading public is not immediately relevant. This preface is where Schumpeter best articulated Marx's formative influence on his conceptualization of the economic dynamics of capitalism in a deliberate departure from the Walrasian scheme of a stationary state (Schumpeter, 1989 [1937], 106–7); a point that would strike a chord in a country noted for its tradition of Marxian economics. Nakayama also took part in a study group of Keynes's book in the very same year of its publication and their discussions resulted in the publication in 1941 of a critical commentary on it (Morris-Suzuki, 1991, 93). *Capitalism, Socialism and Democracy* was published in Japan in 1951–52. Japanese economists were thus well ahead of their Turkish counterparts. Moreover, even when they fell under the spell of Keynesian economics, many such as Sabura Okita and Osamu Shimamura nevertheless also managed to benefit from Schumpeterian economics (Cömert, 2005, 29). The 1956 government White Paper transmitted Schumpeter's idea of technological innovation from theory into a lasting policy (Gao, 1997, 207–8).

Schumpeter's influence was undermined by the Keynesian landslide, but would remain a strong undercurrent for the rest of the century. For example, Shinohara Miyohei's comparative work dating from the 1960s on the phenomenon of high growth expressed the point that: 'the greater the destruction, the faster was the rate of recovery' (Morris-Suzuki, 1991, 142). Perhaps implicit in this statement was an echo of Schumpeter's concept of 'creative destruction'.[22] In yet another example, in Morris-Suzuki's account of Nagasu Kazuji's ideas dating from the mid-1960s, it is possible to discern the echo of Schumpeter's point concerning the evolutionary transition to socialism from within capitalism:

> For an increasingly socialized production system and its growing reliance on state intervention has created the very structures that will be required by socialism. Nationalized enterprises, government control of trade and exchange, large-scale managerially-run enterprises – all of these will be the necessary elements in the socialist future. (Morris-Suzuki, 1991, 128)

Among influential Japanese economists with an affinity to Schumpeter, Tsuru Shigeto holds a special place. Tsuru was at Harvard studying with Schumpeter (as well as others) from 1933 until his return to Japan in 1942 following the outbreak of the Pacific War (Morris-Suzuki, 1991, 159). As such, he predated his Turkish counterpart, Ülgener, who went to Harvard after the war. Tsuru maintained a Marx-inspired yet Schumpeter-like flexible and eclectic approach (within which he also brought together Schumpeter and Keynes, just like Hans Singer who had done so in a different context); he eventually launched a critique of high growth and moved towards institutional economics. Murakami Yasusuke dwelt on the interaction of social values and industrial growth much along the lines of Max Weber and Schumpeter, reversing the terms however by insisting that Japanese values are more amenable to twentieth-century industrialization than their Western counterparts (Morris-Suzuki, 1991, 185). The best indicator of the strength of the persistent Schumpeterian undercurrent in Japan is the scholarly achievement of Yuichi Shionoya. In contrast to many who work under the influence of Schumpeterian ideas, he is the one economist who has become a leading scholar working and publishing extensively on Schumpeter himself (Shionoya, 1990, 1992).[23]

Hayek's name is not mentioned once in Morris-Suzuki's survey of Japanese economic thought. The fact that the Friedmans are cited at least once suggests that Hayek may have been eclipsed by them. Later, during the material prosperity of the 1980s in Japan coincident with the neoliberal surge, Hayek did become very popular (along with Karl Popper):

> Incidentally, in Japan, the 1980's saw the prestige of economic liberalism at its height. Especially, Hayek was evaluated because of his more well-balanced market view than Milton Friedman and because of his reference to 'the limit of human knowledge' and the 'spontaneous order'. (Wakamori, 1999, 9)

Nevertheless, *The Road to Serfdom* was first translated into Japanese as late as 1954. Hayek's collected works became available during the second half of the 1980s in ten volumes. It is highly likely that he had a greater impact upon popular economists in Japan as well as an indirect influence on those academics who concentrate on problems of knowledge and communication in a post-industrial stage. Imai Kenichi's work focusing on an information network society with its Hayekian projection for a future in which we will finally be liberated is a case in point: 'we may perhaps escape from the existing dominance of the visible hand, and move towards a world where a new invisible hand is supported by that imperceptible substance, information' (Imai, 1984, quoted in Morris-Suzuki, 1991, 191). In summary, however, if my overall impression concerning Hayek is correct, then we could conclude that the ranking in importance of Schumpeter and Hayek is the reverse of that which has been unearthed in the Turkish case.

But before concluding I will briefly consider the contours of Polanyi's influence in Japan. We are told that Shiro Nagao was the first scholar to refer to Polanyi, as late as 1973, and was one of the three people who translated *The Great Transformation*, published in 1975 (Wakamori, 1999, 10, 13). This is more or less comparable to Polanyi's introduction into the Turkish scene, albeit with a lag. But it is extremely late when the comparison is made with the fortunes of Schumpeter and Hayek in Japan. Wakamori uses Polanyi's own words to qualify the scholarly hopes he has raised:

> Polanyi's life and work is, perhaps, 'the fount of our strength and new hope' to tide over the crisis of liberal market utopia, fascistic nationalism as countermovement of social protection, constructivist central planning and mechanization of human society, which will lead us to the following condition: the precariousness of existence and the loss of freedom. (Wakamori, 1999, 12)

As of the 1990s, Polanyi-inspired studies flourished in Japan. Once introduced, Polanyi found a very favourable reception in Japan. The social and environmental problems of a highly industrialized society made the Polanyi thesis of the urgent need for social and natural re-embeddedness all the more attractive. For example, the theory of social capital put forward by Miyamoto Kenichi in the 1980s places special emphasis on land, water, transport and communications as items 'ill-adapted to private ownership' (Morris-Suzuki, 1991, 178–9), recalling Polanyi's concept of 'fictitious commodities'. The same theme can be identified in the work of Uzawa Hirofumi, who distinguishes among natural capital (air, water, and so on), social capital (roads, bridges, and so on) and institutional capital (laws, administrative systems, and so on) (Morris-Suzuki, 1991, 181–2). Furthermore, Murakami Yasusuke's perception of traditional Japanese collectivism as a positive and desirable value (Morris-Suzuki, 1991, 187) implies a potentially nostalgic quest for Polanyi-type re-embeddedness. Moreover, there was in Japan an indigenous tradition of thought that could easily be linked with Polanyi.

Perhaps the delay in introducing Polanyi was in part because of the strength of the local substitute. Instrumental in introducing Polanyi were economists of the Uno School, named after the highly original scholar, Kozo Uno (1897–1977). Uno, renowned for his 'level analysis' of capitalism, singled out nineteenth-century capitalism as the model for a pure theory (Morris-Suzuki, 1991, 120–21), while Polanyi based his theory of the self-regulating market system on the evidence of the very same epoch. As long as this Marx-inspired school had an uncontested alternative there was presumably little need for Polanyi, whose economics seemed weaker. However, with the crisis of Marxism, the Uno School also was in need of new openings and turned to Polanyi, whose international standing was high and in the ascendant. According to the impression of Japanese advocates of Polanyi, the theories of Marx and Polanyi seem complementary rather than contradictory, thanks to the legacy of the labour theory of value that Uno favoured (Sekine, 1999, 54–5). In time, the balance between Uno and Polanyi may increasingly tilt in favour of the latter.

In short, it seems that Schumpeter might, after all, cede priority to Polanyi, if recent trends continue in Japan. If this happens, this would reflect the position in Turkey, and in this way prove the strength of global influence. In other words, the structural differences of the two countries may erode in the face of external pressures in favour of theoretical uniformity. However, this is only a possibility and one should refrain from further unwarranted speculation.

NOTES

1. I would like to thank A. Yücel Özden, Gülşah Gülen and Damla Özdemir for recording these face-to-face interviews.
2. Of the three, only Hayek had an opportunity of returning to Europe. He moved from Chicago to Germany in 1962 to become Professor at the University of Freiburg until his retirement in 1968. Upon retirement, he spent several years in his home country, Austria, as a Guest Professor of Philosophy at the University of Salzburg until moving back to Freiburg in 1977, where he died in 1992.
3. 'Intertemporal price equilibrium and movements in the value of money' (Hayek, 1984 [1928]).
4. In fact, Schumpeter wrote a review article on Keynes's *The General Theory of Employment, Interest and Money* in which he launched an intemperate assault on the theory of effective demand. He ended with a sarcastic comment: 'Let him who accepts the message there expounded rewrite the history of the French *ancien régime* in some such terms as these: Louis XV was a most enlightened monarch. Feeling the necessity of stimulating expenditure he secured the services of such expert spenders as Madame de Pompadour and Madame du Berry. They went to work with unsurpassable efficiency. Full employment, a maximum of resulting output, and general well-being ought to have been the consequence. It is true that instead we find misery, shame and, at the end of it all, a stream of blood. But that was a chance coincidence' (Schumpeter, 1936, 795).

5. In addition, Schumpeter's pre-existing theoretical scheme of economic development, given its high level of abstraction, did not explicitly preclude a Keynesian perspective if we leave his fiscal sociology aside, which is really the basis for his critique of what he called stagnationism.
6. 'Redistribution, the ruling method in tribal and archaic society beside which Exchange plays only a minor part, grew to great importance in the later Roman Empire and is actually gaining ground today in some modern industrial states. The Soviet Union is an extreme instance' (Polanyi, 1957, 256).
7. An awareness of a possible rapprochement between the Keynesian approach and institutional economics (Hodgson, 1989) emerged much later in the era of Post-Keynesianism, when the institutional pillars and ideological hegemony of Keynesian economics had already been removed, and in response the search for a more solid theoretical foundation had begun.
8. It is no coincidence that a critical study of the neoliberal era takes as its theoretical point of departure the sharp contrast between the analytical scheme of Hayek on the one hand, and that of Schumpeter and Polanyi on the other (Gray, 1998).
9. It was first translated from French into Turkish by Tunay Akoğlu, who claims that he compared his translation with the original in English, as well as with the German translation of the text (Schumpeter, 1974 [1966]).
10. Meanwhile Ülgener was working hard to improve his English by private tutoring. At one point, he had an opportunity to tell Schumpeter that he found it difficult to follow his English, to which Schumpeter responded: '*Herr Doktor*! Girl friend!' (that is, if you want to improve your English, get an English girlfriend) (Sayar, 1998, 97).
11. The reform of İstanbul University was initiated by the government in 1933. What was at issue was more than a reform; it was in fact a thorough transformation of a traditional institute of higher learning into a modern university. To effect this some of the faculty was dismissed, making the recruitment of new faculty an urgent matter. German-speaking academics persecuted by the Nazi regime were contracted to join the university staff. Albert Einstein corresponded with President Atatürk to this effect. In the course of this process the Faculty of Economics was also formed.
12. Fritz Neumark (1900–1991) exerted a formative influence during his tenure (1933–51) on the development of the discipline of economics in this institutional context. In contrast to the then better known Wilhelm Röpke (1899–1966) who felt culturally alienated and moved to Switzerland in 1937 (Neumark, 2008 [1980], 75), or Alexander Rüstow (1885–1963) who never felt quite at ease with either Turkey or with spoken Turkish (Hoss, 2008, 213–15, 219), Neumark mastered Turkish, interacted with his students and stayed for a considerable time even after the war ended. Neumark maintained his ties in Turkey even after his return to Germany, and published his memoirs in 1980 (Neumark, 2008 [1980]). Thus it was Neumark, and not Röpke, who helped to shape the minds of many Turkish economists of the coming generations.
13. The impression Schumpeter gave by assuming that all these economists belonged to the same camp is grossly misleading. For example, Röpke was an outspoken liberal who became a staunch anti-Keynesian and a leading figure in Hayek's Mont Pelerin Society formed after the Second World War. Moreover, Rüstow was a hardcore classical liberal, Kessler and Neumark, were social liberals, and Dobretsberger a left-wing Catholic (Neumark, 2008 [1980], 27, 76–9). Among them, Kessler was mostly influenced by the German Historical School (Neumark, 2008 [1980], 79).
14. In this respect, Ülgener reminds one of the influential development economist, Hans Singer (1910–2006) – of the famous Prebisch–Singer thesis – who is also known to have two heroes, Schumpeter and Keynes. Singer had started his PhD with Schumpeter at Bonn in 1931 and finished with Kahn and Keynes at Cambridge in 1936. He was briefly a German emigré in Turkey in 1933 before moving to Cambridge. Singer's case illustrates that one could combine Schumpeterian and Keynesian ideas up to a certain point. Ülgener's thought also reflects elements from both sources of inspiration, even though he did not commit himself to exploring such

middle ground. In contrast to Singer, who concentrated his energies in exploring the possibilities of synthesis within the given boundaries of economics as a discipline, Ülgener shied away from such an attempt and retreated to a much broader interdisciplinary approach.

15. In this context, we should remind ourselves of Paul M. Sweezy, a student of Schumpeter at Harvard who made a genuine contribution to Marxian economics in North America with his *Theory of Capitalist Development* (1970 [1942]).
16. It goes without saying that Hayek and Schumpeter could have served this purpose equally well, if only other factors also obtained.
17. There has always been a strong scholarly tradition in Japan that dwells on the uniquely cultural parameters of Japanese capitalism, but especially the importance of a Confucian ethic *pace* Max Weber's Protestant ethic. There were many studies of this kind during the 1960s and 1970s (Bellah, 1968; Vogel, 1979), when the Japanese economic miracle appeared to demand an exceptionalist explanation. Michio Morishima, otherwise a mathematical economist in the Marxian tradition, adopted this position in his later writings (1982).
18. Whereas the lessons of the Japanese case highlight the importance of the mode-of-production debate and the emergence of a market in land, for which there were no counterparts for a long time in Turkey, the Ottoman Turkish case emphasizes concentration on the nature of economic dependency, a fate that Japan first narrowly escaped in the nineteenth century, and then promoted to its own advantage in its Far Eastern sphere of influence.
19. The German Historical School also had an important role early on.
20. The very same isolation brought about a very different outcome in the sphere of Japanese film art (Burch, 1979).
21. Even so, the analysis of unequal exchange soon yielded to Akamatsu Kaname, whose 'flying geese' theory combined a product-cycle approach to industrialization and trade with the lessons and prospects of Japanese imperialism in East Asia during the 1940s (Morris-Suzuki, 1991, 151). Turkey was remote from both issues at the time, and unequal exchange theory, far from leading to something new, was soon forgotten. Again, structural factors caused the two national experiences to diverge.
22. In any case, there is a broader convergence with the Austrian approach to production that unites Schumpeter with Hayek. Hayek persistently emphasized the importance of the structure of production and therefore of the capital structure.
23. Interestingly enough, Shionoya has also been deeply influenced by Weber, like Schumpeter himself, but also like Ülgener in Turkey.

REFERENCES

Akama, M. (2000), 'Marxian Economics', in A. Ikeo (ed.), *Japanese Economics and Economists since 1945*, London: Routledge, pp. 123–41.

Aktaş, S. (2001), *Hayek'in Hukuk ve Adalet Teorisi*, Ankara: Liberte.

Anderson, P. (1974), *Lineages of the Absolutist State*, London: New Left Books.

Ando, T. (1998), 'The debate on Japanese capitalism: the Koza faction and its perception of society', in S. Sugiharo and T. Tanaka (eds), *Economic Thought and Modernization in Japan*, Cheltenham, UK and Lyme, NH, USA: Edward Elgar, pp. 78–96.

Ayan, D. (2000), 'Sabri F. Ülgener'in Türk Düşünce Kültüründeki Yeri', *Doğu Batı*, **3** (12), 157–91.

Ballot, G. and E. Taymaz (1998), 'Human capital, technological lock-in and evolutionary dynamics', in G. Eliasson and C. Green (eds), *Microfoundations of*

Economic Growth: A Schumpeterian Perspective, Ann Arbor, MI: University of Michigan Press, pp. 301–30.

Bellah, R. (1968), 'Reflections on the Protestant ethic analogy in Asia', in S.N. Eisenstadt (ed.), *The Protestant Ethic and Modernization: A Comparative View*, New York: Basic Books, pp. 243–51.

Bronfenbrenner, M. (1956), 'The state of Japanese economics', *American Economic Review*, **46** (1–2), 389–98.

Burch, N. (1979), *To the Distant Observer: Form and Meaning in the Japanese Cinema*, Los Angeles, CA: University of California Press.

Cömert, H. (2005), 'Japan's development and economic theory', unpublished Master's thesis submitted to the Graduate School of Social Sciences, Middle East Technical University.

Desai, M. (1982), 'The task of monetary theory: the Hayek–Sraffa debate in a modern perspective', in M. Baranzini (ed.), *Advances in Economic Theory*, Oxford: Basil Blackwell, pp. 149–70.

Ekelund Jr., R.B. and Hébert, R.F. (1997), *A History of Economic Theory and Method*, New York: McGraw-Hill.

Eliasson, G., D. Johansson and E. Taymaz (2005), 'Firm turnover and the rate of macro economic growth – simulating the macroeconomic effects of Schumpeterian creative destruction', in G. Eliasson (ed.), *The Birth, the Life and the Death of Firms*, Stockholm: Ratio Institute, pp. 305–56.

Erbil, T. (2007), 'The limits of the national innovation systems model: the case of Turkey', PhD Thesis, Faculty of the Graduate School of Cornell University, Ithaca, NY.

Erdoğan, M. (1993), 'Liberal Anayasacılık ve Hayek', *Türkiye Günlüğü*, **22**, 95–102.

Faber, M. (1980), 'Relationships between modern Austrian and Sraffa's capital theory', *Journal of Institutional and Theoretical Economics*, **136** (4), 617–29.

Gábor, É. (1999), 'The early formation of Karl Polanyi's ideas', in K. McRobbie and K. Polanyi Levitt (eds), *Karl Polanyi in Vienna*, Montreal: Black Rose Books, pp. 295–301.

Gao, B. (1997), *Economic Ideology and Japanese Industrial Policy: Developmentalism from 1931 to 1965*, Cambridge: Cambridge University Press.

Grassl, W. and B. Smith (1986), *Austrian Economics: Historical and Philosophical Background*, London: Croom Helm.

Gray, John (1998), *False Down: The Delusions of Global Capitalism*, New York: New Press.

Haberler, G. (1950), 'Joseph Alois Schumpeter: 1883–1950', *Quarterly Journal of Economics*, **64** (3), 333–72.

Hamada, K. (1986), 'The impact of general theory in Japan', *Eastern Economic Journal*, **12** (4), 451–86.

Hansen, A. (1953), *A Guide to Keynes*, New York: McGraw-Hill.

Hayek, F.A. von (1975), *Full Employment at Any Price?* London: Institute of Economic Affairs.

Hayek, F.A. von (1984 [1928]), 'Intertemporal price equilibrium and movements in the value of money', in R. Cloughry (ed.), *Money Capital and Fluctuations: Early Essays*, Chicago, IL: University of Chicago Press, pp. 71–117.

Hayek, F.A. von (1994 [1944]), *The Road to Serfdom*, Chicago, IL: University of Chicago Press.

Hayek, F.A. von (2004 [1995]), *Kölelik Yolu*, T. Feyzioğlu and Y. Arsan (trans.), Ankara: Liberte.
Hodgson, G.M. (1989), 'Post-Keynesianism and institutionalism: the missing link', in John Pheby (ed.), *New Directions in Post-Keynesian Economics*, Aldershot: Edward Elgar, pp. 94–123.
Hoss, C. (2008 [2007]), 'Sürgün Yolları', in Faruk Şen (ed.), *Ayyıldız Altında Sürgün* [*Exil unter Halbmond und Stern*], Istanbul: Günizi.
Huizinga, J. (1955), *Homo Ludens: A Study of the Play-Element in Culture*, Boston, MA: Beacon.
Imai, K. (1984), *Jōhō Nettowāku Shakai*, Tokyo: Iwanami Shinsho.
Johnston, W.M. (1972), *The Austrian Mind: An Intellectual and Social History, 1848–1938*, Berkeley, CA: University of California Press.
Keynes, J.M. (1926), *The End of Laissez-Faire*, London: Hogarth Press.
Keynes, J.M. (1971 [1920]), *The Economic Consequences of the Peace*, New York: Harper & Row.
Keynes, J.M. (1973 [1936]), 'Preface to the Japanese edition', *The General Theory of Employment, Interest and Money*, London: Macmillan, pp. xxix–xxx.
Komatsu, Y. (1961), 'The study of economic history in Japan', *Economic History Review*, **14** (1), 115–21.
Lawlor, M.S. and B.L. Horn (1992), 'Notes on the Sraffa–Hayek Exchange', *Review of Political Economy*, **4** (3), 317–40.
Moore Jr., B. (1967), *Social Origins of Dictatorship and Democracy*, Harmondsworth: Penguin.
Morishima, M. (1982), *Why Has Japan Succeeded?* Cambridge: Cambridge University Press.
Morris-Suzuki, T. (1991), *A History of Japanese Economic Thought*, London: Routledge.
Neumark, F. (2008 [1980]), *Boğaziçi'ne Sığınanlar: Türkiye'ye İltica Eden Alman Bilim, Siyaset ve Sanat Adamları, 1933–1953* [*Zuflucht am Bosphorus* in Turkish], Istanbul: Neden.
Özveren, E. (2002), 'Ottoman economic thought and economic policy in transition: rethinking the nineteenth century', in M. Psalidopoulos and M.E. Mata (eds), *Economic Thought and Policy in Less Developed Europe: The Nineteenth Century*, London: Routledge, pp. 129–44.
Polanyi, K. (1944), *The Great Transformation*, Boston, MA: Beacon.
Polanyi, K. (1957), 'The economy as instituted process', in K. Polanyi, C. Arensberg and H. Pearson (eds), *Trade and Market in the Early Empires*, New York: Free Press, pp. 243–70.
Polanyi, K. (1978), 'Kurumlaşmış Bir Süreç Olarak Ekonomi', E. Mahcupyan (trans.), *Demokrasi İçin Toplumcu Düşün*, **4**, 279–99.
Polanyi, K. (2007 [1986]), *Büyük Dönüşüm*, A. Buğra (trans.), Istanbul: İletişim.
Sayar, A.G. (1998), *Bir İktisatçının Entellektüel Portresi: Sabri F. Ülgener*, Istanbul: Eren.
Schaffer, F. (1999), 'Vorgartenstrasse 203: Extracts from a Memoir', in K. McRobbie and K. Polanyi Levitt (eds), *Karl Polanyi in Vienna*, Montreal: Black Rose Books, pp. 328–46.
Schefold, B. (1986), 'Schumpeter as a Walrasian Austrian and Keynes as a Classical Marshallian', in H.J. Wagner and J.W. Drukker (eds), *The Economic Law of Motion of Modern Society: A Marx–Keynes–Schumpeter Centennial*, Cambridge: Cambridge University Press, pp. 93–111.

Schumpeter, J.A. (1936), 'Review: *The General Theory of Employment, Interest and Money*, by John Maynard Keynes', *Journal of the American Statistical Association*, **31** (196), 791–5.

Schumpeter, J.A. (1942), *Capitalism, Socialism and Democracy*, New York: Harper.

Schumpeter, J.A. (1971), *Kapitalizm, Sosyalizm ve Demokrasi I*, Rasin Tinaz (trans.), Istanbul: Varlık.

Schumpeter, J.A. (1989 [1937]), 'Preface to Japanese edition of "Theorie der Wirtschaftlichen Entwicklung"', in R.V. Clemence (ed.), *Essays on Entrepeneurs, Innovations, Business Cycles, and the Evolution of Capitalism*, New Brunswick, NJ: Transaction Publishers, pp. 165–8.

Schumpeter, J.A. (2007), *Kapitalizm Sosyalizm ve Demokrasi*, Ankara: Alter.

Sekine, T.T. (1999), 'Polanyi, Marx, et Uno', unpublished working paper.

Shionoya, Y. (1990), 'The origin of the Schumpeterian research program: a chapter omitted from Schumpeter's *Theory of Economic Development*', *Journal of Institutional and Theoretical Economics*, **146** (2), 314–27.

Shionoya, Y. (1992), 'Taking Schumpeter's methodology seriously', in F.M. Scherer and M. Perlman (eds), *Entrepreneurship, Technological Innovation, and Economic Growth: Studies in the Schumpeterian Tradition*, Ann Arbor, MI: University of Michigan Press, pp. 343–62.

Streissler, E. (1981), 'Schumpeter's Vienna and the role of credit in innovation', in H. Frisch (ed.), *Schumpeterian Economics*, New York: Praeger, pp. 60–83.

Sugiyama, C. (1994), *Origins of Economic Thought in Modern Japan*, London: Routledge.

Sweezy, P. (1970 [1942]), *The Theory of Capitalist Development*, New York: Modern Reader Paperbacks.

Tilly, C. (1986), 'The tyranny of here and now', *Sociological Forum*, **1**, 179–88.

Timberger, E.K. (1972), 'A theory of elite revolution', *Studies on Comparative International Development*, **7**, 191–207.

Ülgener, S. (1962), *Milli Gelir, İstihdam ve İktisadi Büyüme*, Istanbul: Istanbul Üniversitesi Yayınları.

Vogel, F.E. (1979), *Japan as Number One: Lessons for America*, Cambridge, MA: Harvard University Press.

Wakamori, M. (1999), 'The reception of Karl Polanyi in Japan', paper presented at the Seventh International Karl Polanyi Conference 'Re-Thinking Human Needs', Centre Auguste et Léon Walras, Université Lumiére-Lyon II, 26–28 May.

Yayla, A. (2000), *Özgürlük Yolu: Hayek'in Sosyal Teorisi*, Ankara: Liberte.

Yayla, A. (2004 [1995]), 'Takdim2', in F.A. von Hayek, *Kölelik Yolu*, Ankara: Liberte, pp. iii–vi.

PART IV

The exchange of ideas between Japan and the rest of the world

9. The diffusion of economic ideas: Lionel Robbins in Italy and Japan

Atsushi Komine and Fabio Masini[1]

9.1 INTRODUCTION

In a famous article on the international transmission of culture, Joseph J. Spengler (1970, 133) complained that: 'historians of ideas have devoted little attention to the social processes underlying the transmission of ideas from culture to culture and from nation to nation'. Since then, Colander and Coats (1989) have pioneered a series of books and papers enquiring into several aspects concerning what they called 'the dissemination of economic ideas'.

As products or services, economic ideas can in fact be studied as the output of a production process, where several ingredients are needed. Specific events or urgent policy decisions may stimulate intellectual debate; the institutional and political environment can ease, postpone or provide incentives for specific productions. And ingredients, by-products or final products may come from or move to production processes which take place somewhere else.

Sometimes, as with material goods, a culture can undergo a process of import substitution, and in those cases the attempt to hinder the diffusion of particular ideas deemed dangerous to the domestic dominating paradigm can have a major impact on the reception of foreign debates. This usually happens under established totalitarian regimes.

This was the situation of Italy and Japan between the two World Wars. But the degree of 'openness' of these countries differed. In 1949 Kanetaro Nomura, in *A History of Japanese Economic Theory*, underlined the enormous importance of the 'import and assimilation of foreign economics'. But as one of his reviewer stressed, he had a negative view of this process:

> The effects cut deep; particularly the exposure to English classical writings . . . There then arose a theoretical lag, for imported economics explained a situation quite different from that in Japan. One of the results, in Japanese theory, has been a highly theoretical discussion of economics, with little relation to the real Japanese economic scene. (Burks, 1953, 228)

In Italy the situation was rather more complex. For example, Biagini (2007, 223) claims that the reception of Keynes in Italy in the 1930s demonstrates the 'Italian openness to foreign economic culture, an openness which was also confirmed by the extent to which the works of other liberal economists . . . were reviewed and discussed'. As concerns Hayek, Matteucci (2001, 145) argues that 'in Italian culture the [reception of the] thought of Friedrich von Hayek was unfortunate', although Noto (2007, 160) observes that this was not true of the interwar years, when 'his name had some resonance and prompted profound respect among Italian economists'. Both Biagini and Noto conclude that there was some intellectual freedom in economic ideas 'under a regime that, despite being authoritarian, tolerated a strictly limited amount of academic freedom' (Biagini, 2007, 224).

The chapter aims at comparing means and outcomes in the transmission of economic ideas during the interwar years for Italy and Japan through a systematic enquiry into the reception of Lionel Robbins's works. Lionel Robbins provides an interesting case study because of his classical liberalism and his 'orthodox' approach (as Robbins himself defined it) to economic theory and policy in the 1930s. This presented an obstacle to the diffusion of his writings in Italy and Japan, where liberal thought was in difficulty (Italy) or almost entirely absent (Japan).

Furthermore, his writings were controversial even in English-speaking countries. Joan Robinson (1972, 1) wrote of Robbins's *Essay* and his definition of economics:

> No doubt this was the expression of a long tradition but the date of publication was unlucky. By the time the book came out there were three million workers unemployed in Great Britain . . . It was just a coincidence that the book appeared when means for any end at all had rarely been less scarce.

And when Robbins's second book, *The Great Depression*, appeared in 1934, providing an orthodox reading of and remedies for the crisis, this publication date was even worse, prompting irritation and a vivid critical debate. This promoted a negative attitude towards Robbins himself and his later writings.

Recently it has been suggested (Komine, 2007; Masini, 2009a, 2009b; Colander, 2009) that much of this criticism in Britain and the USA arose not only from the unfortunate timing of Robbins's books, but also from a misunderstanding of what he in fact wrote. Contrary to the views expressed in most of the reactions to his early writings in English-speaking countries, Robbins was opposed to determinism and in favour of complexity in the study of economics; he was opposed to social atomism, and considered the role of the economist both as social scientist and as political economist. An additional aim of this chapter is to assess whether such biased representation of Robbins also affected the Italian and Japanese reception process.

We will examine the reviews devoted to Robbins's works, their translations and the principal debates on his contributions to economics in Italy and Japan from the publication of the *Essay* to the end of the Second World War. Although Robbins's most important writings were published in the 1930s, the timing of his reception in these two countries diverged. A comparison between the two cases will also suggest reasons for Robbins's reception in the economic literature being so negative, shedding light on the attitude of Italian and Japanese cultures towards foreign literature during the interwar years.

9.2 THE CULTURAL CLIMATE IN ITALY AND THE RECEPTION OF ROBBINS

During the later 1920s and 1930s, Italian economic debates were dominated by three major questions. The first concerned epistemology, the nature of economics and the role of the economist in society. The second concerned the maintenance of the exchange-rate target of 90 liras to the pound sterling. The third, which would increasingly gather momentum after the 1929 Crash, related to the nature of crises and the strategies for recovering from the Great Depression.

Superimposed on this was the increasing politicization of culture by the Fascist regime. From the late 1920s the Italian economic system was dominated by 'corporatism', a socio-economic and political approach seeking to do away 'with the traditional and artificial antagonism between economics on one side, politics and ethics on the other' (Arias, 1927 [1934], 269). Italian corporatism presumes a social ontology in which the main subjects are not single individuals but corporate groups[2] whose collective interests have to be managed in the higher interest of the nation (De Stefani and Amoroso, 1933; Resta, 1935; Carli, 1937).

On 14 November 1933, before the General Assembly of the National Council of Corporations, Benito Mussolini emphatically stated: 'today we bury economic liberalism' (Mussolini, 1933 [1934], 264). But Mussolini was only able to 'bury' economic liberalism in November because its death had already been announced: the first article of 1933 in the journal *L'economia italiana* was entitled 'Liberalism is dead' (Anonymous, 1933a).

If in 1933 liberalism was dead and buried, the gradual poisoning of liberal culture in Italy had started long before. At the beginning of the century critical reassessment of liberal neoclassical orthodoxy (Vilfredo Pareto, Maffeo Pantaleoni, Benedetto Croce) had accompanied and paralleled revisionism of Marxist theory (Arturo Labriola). During the 1920s, both these streams appeared to converge on similar new, common values: 'nationalism, idealism, the stress on the importance of authority and force, the concept of an ethical State and . . . the top-down pacification of capital and labour' (Zagari, 2004, 61). Such values replaced those on which the old liberal tradition had been based.

Corporatism, therefore, was not only the pathological degeneration of a political malady, but also gathered and embodied several reform projects for society, even for economic theory, seeking to save economics from its flaws (Almodovar and Cardoso, 2005).[3] Whatever one thinks of the original motive underlying the birth of corporatism, by the 1930s it had become a significant social force controlling many aspects of social life; in August 1931 university professors were obliged to swear an oath of loyalty to Fascism. The relative importance of the principal scientific journals also reflected the increasing difficulty of representing a theoretical alternative to corporatism. The leading economic journals of the early 1930s,[4] the primary source for our study, can be differentiated according to their differing orientations to the directorship.[5] Public academic and scientific debate was divided between corporatist, liberal and Catholic approaches. During the second half of the 1930s liberals increasingly succumbed to political pressure. The Catholic tendency survived, thanks to their apparent support for corporatism. This was the cultural and theoretical background against which Robbins's works, epistemological and theoretical, were read in Italy.

9.2.1 The Debates on Epistemology and the Impact of Robbins's Works

Italian economists already had a strong interest in methodology and the nature of economics when Robbins published *An Essay on the Nature and Significance of Economic Science* in 1932. Benedetto Croce (1983 [1896]) had sought to convince economists to 'avoid trespassing too much on neighbouring domains', and in 1900 he even accused Pareto of trying to 'introduce metaphysical hypotheses into economic science' (Einaudi, 1950 [1980], 95). According to Einaudi Croce's argument gained acceptance, for subsequently 'economists stopped dealing with matters outside their specific field' (1950, 97). Or at least they did so explicitly, adopting a different disciplinary stance, as for example with Pareto and sociology.

Nonetheless, during the 1930s, with the rise of corporatism and the collapse of 1929, there was a new wave of interest in economic epistemology. An extensive debate took place among Italian economists on the nature of economics (Galli, 1935; Vito, 1938), on its relationship with ethics (Marsili-Libelli, 1933; Einaudi, 1936; Vito, 1937) and politics (Amoroso, 1932), on the degree of realism of economic studies, and on the nature of *Homo economicus*[6] (Contento, 1931, 1932; Amoroso, 1932; Consiglio, 1932a, 1932c; Fanfani, 1932; Costanza, 1933; Lorenzoni, 1933). And, aligned with these questions, political circumstances demanded serious consideration of the role of the economist in society (Lanzillo, 1935).

Apart from one early brief note,[7] the first important review of Robbins is the article on his *Essay* written by Francesco Vito (1932a) and published in *Rivista internazionale di scienze sociali* at the end of 1932. Vito agrees with Robbins as regards his refusal to accept Cannan's idea that economics should direct itself to the causes of material wealth. But he also underlines how Robbins's definition concerning the 'relationship between alternative ends and scarce means . . . seems to be completely detached from the idea of needs, and relates to a more extensive domain than that which economists usually consider their field' (Vito, 1932a, 565). Given Vito's Catholicism, we might also note here his restrained critique of the demarcation of economics from ethics. In conclusion he writes:

> the conflict between the author and those (Hobson, Hawtrey, etc) who affirm that economics cannot be dissociated from ethics seems to us more apparent than real. These two approaches refer, in our opinion, to two different stages in the study of economic problems, and it is only in the initial stages of the study of economics that a dissociation from ethics can exist. (Vito, 1932a, 566)

Four years later, in a review article devoted to the second edition of the *Essay* (Robbins, 1935a), Vito reaffirmed more strongly this demarcation of ethics as the central critique of Robbins.[8] He states that Robbins's clarification of the relationship between economics and ethics 'does not seem satisfactory' (Vito, 1936, 533). He argues that:

> it is not possible to construct economic science – as a science of means – without referring to social ends; and social ends are essentially of an ethical nature; therefore the economist cannot avoid expressing his opinions as regards ethics. This means that the economist, consciously on unconsciously but unavoidably, will end up assuming a particular set of ethical ends. In Robbins' case this set of ethical ends is represented by the individualistic vision of society. (Vito, 1936, 533)

Vito recognizes that Robbins himself denies such a perspective, and rejects the charge of social atomism (Robbins, 1935a, 128), but Vito does not consider that Robbins is convincing on this point: 'in fact, he reasons exactly according to such an assumption' (Vito, 1936, 533).

The second review article dedicated to Robbins's *Essay* was published anonymously in 1933 in *La riforma sociale* (Anonymous, 1933b). It is very likely that the review can be attributed to Ernesto Rossi.[9] The reviewer explains at length the principal questions considered in the *Essay*, underlining the following points.

The first is the role of *Homo economicus* as 'a mere expository device and not – as many believe – a necessary assumption to establish the law of value'; this is considered to be 'one of the most convincing parts of the book' (Anonymous, 1933b, 219). The second point is the return to the central role of subjective evaluations in the definition of value, as opposed to the classical 'dualism, still supported by Marshall', concerning both 'marginal utility and the cost of production' (Anonymous, 1933b, 220). Thirdly, the writer agrees with Robbins in his distinction of economics from ethics and value judgements:

> The entire theory of *social utility* is interesting as a development of an ethical postulate, but lies entirely outside the realm of scientific economics . . . There are still some who affirm that economics should somehow maintain a connection with ethics. But such a connection has always led to, and is bound to lead to, unfortunate results. Economics is about ascertainable facts; ethics is about evaluations and obligations. (Anonymous, 1933b, 221)

A further element is the question of the complexity of society. Regarding the 'practical relevance of economic studies', it would be misleading to 'look only at the immediate and apparent results' of economic policies, ignoring the 'indirect and hidden' effects. He concludes: 'Those aware of the great complexity of modern society can easily understand the importance of economic analysis in providing a technique for rational action' (Anonymous, 1933b, 222). This very much resembles Robbins's arguments (1932, 1935a). The reviewer also points to the innovative nature of Robbins's work in the Italian context, noting some similarities (but also differences) with Pantaleoni,[10] who it is suggested was wedded to the hedonistic postulate and ambiguous on the role of material wealth in the study of economics.

In the final pages the reviewer tries to explain why he nonetheless does not agree with Robbins: scarcity cannot be related only to time or goods, but must also be related to the psychological disposition of man, implying a need to enquire into his psychological nature. According to the reviewer, this would permit 'analysis to comprehend the most complex problems . . . assuming first of all scarcity of time, then the scarcity of goods in the external world, coming later step by step to represent a world closer to that in which we live' (Anonymous, 1933b, 226).

The comparison with Pantaleoni is also a central feature of another paper, published in 1933 in *L'economia italiana*. This paper, 'Le economie non-euclidee e l'economia corporativa' by Giuseppe Palomba,[11] focussed on the role of *Homo economicus* for the explanation of economic reality. Palomba seeks to extend the hedonistic postulate to society through the idea of 'species hedonism' according to which 'each has a motive for action, which is the maximum happiness of his species' (Palomba, 1933, 457). Hence Palomba, quoting from Carli (1931), defines a 'homo corporativus' as an 'experimental concept', a man who considers utility not only in its individualistic terms but also as it concerns the effects on the corporation in which he works 'and on the entire Nation' (Palomba, 1933, 458). This article is important because one year later, in May 1934, another contribution by Palomba was published in *Rivista di politica economica*, where Robbins is referred to and directly cited.

In this later article, Palomba (1934, 1011) tries to defend the necessity of substituting a *Homo sociologicus* for *Homo economicus* in the study of economics: 'man, from this point of view, is not an atom but a molecule' (1934, 1011), meaning that men are all different because they are the result of different combinations (molecules) of very different constituting elements (atoms). And in this respect he quotes Robbins's definition of economics from 1932, arguing that it is too narrow and that:

> it is only one aspect of economic science. A complete definition should on the contrary be: political economy studies the composition (static part) and transformations (dynamic part) of the equilibrium of the social body, therefore the laws governing both, and the means of achieving such equilibrium. As one can see, definitions like that of Robbins are limited to the second part of the preceding definition, and so study only the logical actions of man. (Palomba, 1934, 1014)

Palomba also underlines how his approach is more similar to 'the Marshallian biological conception', already invoked in the Italian debate by Vito in his book on *La concezione biologica dell'economia* (1934).

Some months later in January 1935, a third brief review article of Robbins's *Essay* was published by Gustavo Del Vecchio[12] in the *Giornale degli economisti*. Del Vecchio reviewed the first edition of Robbins's *Essay* together with Mises's *Grundprobleme der Nationalökonomie*, published in 1933 and Conrad's *Die Todsünde der Nationalöconomie*, published in 1934. He quickly dismisses Robbins's book as mainly based on Mises's arguments, which is equally 'short on concrete meaning both in its practical aspect and as regards knowledge' (Gustavo Del Vecchio, 1935, 52).

Del Vecchio has some positive things to say about the works by Mises and Robbins, but underlines their inadequacy and irrelevance to the explanation of concrete phenomena: 'economic studies have real tasks too important and too difficult to be scattered . . . in a literature which is unavoidably boring, as the economic theory of [theoretical economic] Schools almost always is' (p. 52). Economic theory cannot avoid:

> competing with economic history, economic statistics and with the philosophical critique of economic doctrines, [if] confronted with the enormous problems faced by our society . . . it wishes to maintain that eminent place as a system of thought and within political life which was in the past occupied by the political doctrines of the mercantilists, by classical economists, by the theorists of an optimistic liberalism, by socialist critics of various tendencies, and even by early general equilibrium theory. (pp. 52–3)

While the definition of economics according to scientific relevance and abstract generalizations was for Robbins a way of lending it an autonomous status, for Del Vecchio economics had a relevant autonomous status only if able to explain and change real economic phenomena in a more ready way than other disciplines. But in his opinion economists lost this capacity after the first generation of the marginal revolution (p. 52).

These contributions would remain the only reviews of Robbins's *Essay* published in Italy. Nonetheless, the issues that Robbins had raised were widely debated at this time, both in the main Italian journals and in the *Revue d'économie politique* which, after the closure of *La Riforma Sociale*, became the main location of discussion among non-corporatist Italian economists. Robbins was hardly ever cited in these discussions. But it might be worth recalling the main elements of that debate, since they testify to the reception of Robbins's arguments among Italian economists.

The initial contribution to the *Revue d'économie politique* in 1935 is the article 'Droit et économie' by Giorgio Del Vecchio[13] (1935) who mainly rejects a purely hedonistic conception of economics, the employment of *Homo economicus* and any pretension of refraining from value judgements. De Vecchio never quotes Robbins; his targets are Pantaleoni and Croce. In particular, the hedonistic principle implies that the *Homo economicus* is a conceptual abstraction and therefore irrelevant to economics in concrete terms.

In his reply, 'Morale et économique', Luigi Einaudi (1936) quotes Robbins in paragraph 15. He not only cites Robbins's 1932 *Essay*, 'which is the best exposition of the present state of economic methodology' (p. 298) but also his 'Introduction' to Wicksteed's *Common Sense of Political Economy* (Robbins, 1933). Einaudi makes two points. The first is that economics is not strictly dependent on the Benthamite hedonistic postulate. According to Einaudi:

> there is not one economist who has thought about the foundations of his problems who does not consider as immoral or (to express it in a way more in tune

with a science without preconceptions) as absurd the proposition: you must act as though your sole motive for action is personal interest. (Einaudi, 1936, 308)

The second element is a refusal of a pure, mechanical association of economic science with the concept of a simple maximizing *homo economicus*. It is in this respect that Einaudi recalls what Robbins says about Wicksteed. Einaudi (1936, 297–8) quotes Robbins as follows:

> Before Wicksteed wrote, it was still possible for intelligent men to give countenance to the belief that the whole structure of Economics depends upon the assumption of a world of economic men, each actuated by egocentric or hedonistic motives. For anyone who has read the *Common Sense*, the expression of such a view is no longer consistent with intellectual honesty. (Robbins, 1933, xxi)

In replying to Einaudi, Vito wonders: 'Is it possible to formulate the laws of social economy ignoring ethics?' (Vito, 1937, 45). Refusing any conception of social atomism, but also the corporatist elision of society with the nation-state, he states:

> The object of economic science is neither individual economics, nor domestic economics, but social economics . . . The relationship between economics and ethics becomes evident in the choice of the system of social goals, and it is in these terms that the coordination of scarce means has to be studied. This can only imply a relationship of subordination of economics to ethics [but] this does not imply surrendering of the scientific autonomy of economics. (Vito, 1937, 46–7)

In 1938 Vito returned to these questions, citing the same passage in Robbins concerning the distinction between technical and economic problems, but without quoting him directly.

9.2.2 The Nature of Crises and the Role of Public Authorities

Einaudi drew on the *Essay* to write the preface to the translations of Robbins's *The Great Depression*, published by Giulio Einaudi in 1935. In that book Robbins states that he provides an 'orthodox' explanation of the causes of, and remedies for, the 1929 collapse (Robbins 1935b [1934], 15).

In his introductory comments Einaudi refers explicitly to Robbins as an exponent of the 'Viennese economic school' (Einaudi, 1935, 10). He also sympathizes with Robbins's arguments against the prophets of 'managed money' (Keynes), saying that until they are 'defeated' and the gold standard restored, 'there is no hope that the crisis will end' (Einaudi, 1935,

10–11). But Einaudi does not find the explanation of, and remedies for, the crisis the most interesting part of the book. Instead, he raises the 'nexus between the abstract and the concrete, between theory and reality' (p. 11):

> These young economists . . . seem to be saying: we are of no significance, prophets neither of conviction nor creed, we accept those ideals that you, the powerful of this world, impose on your peoples: capitalism where it persists, communism in Russia, corporatism in Italy, National Socialism in Germany. It is not our concern, as humble technicians of an economic instrumentalism, to lecture people on the ideals they should voluntarily or compulsorily adopt. (p. 13)

Echoing Robbins's definition of economics, he writes: 'Life is a continuous choice between ideals and means to achieve them. We economists accept the ideals and direct our efforts to the analysis of the means chosen to achieve them' (13). But there is a special reason for this: the 'optimum use of scarce means . . . is the condition necessary to achieve not the economic ideal, which is the most trivial of all the goals of life, but the supreme ideal which, conforming to the moral categorical imperative, rules both people and rulers' (p. 14). The truth of economic doctrine, says Einaudi,[14] is the only instrument of freedom that can be wielded against political extremism, against totalitarianism. For Einaudi, the recovery and diffusion of orthodox economic theory is a way of confronting corporatism and the increasingly pervasive intervention of the fascist state into the economy. It is for this reason that Einaudi decided to publish a translation of Robbins's book.

The review essay written by Ernesto D'Albergo in *Giornale degli economisti* in April 1935[15] takes a much softer line. D'Albergo (1935, 348) is positive in his appraisal, but for the fact that Robbins was too inclined to accept the confrontation of political ideologies, something that was definitely inappropriate for the contemporary Italian situation. He further states that Robbins, in respect of the remedies offered, 'is not very original [suggesting the restoration of] trust and exchange rates stabilization', and that in 'proposing to restrict as much as possible the intervention of political organisms' he is too much 'attached to prejudice'.

In this respect it is interesting to see how the book was received by one of the main exponents of corporatism. In August 1935 Gino Arias[16] published in *Economia* a long review article on the Italian translation of *The Great Depression*. Arias stressed the distinction, to which Einaudi himself refers in his 'Introduction' to Robbins, between the 'original Classical school' and the proponents of a 'marginalist equilibrism'[17] (Arias, 1935, 141), suggesting therefore that Robbins's book represented a return to the classics. The abstractions of classical economics had some capacity to explain reality, whereas marginalism had completely lost any contact with it: 'Marginalism and equilibrium . . . is a denial of human nature and rudely introduces mechanics into the study of the moral life of man, of which economic life is only one aspect' (Arias, 1935, 141). Arias also values Robbins's critique of any socialist approach (Arias, 1935, 149ff).

He also agrees with Robbins's 'credit-based interpretation of crisis': dear money implies a greater attention given to investments and provides incentives to save. In this respect, Arias – echoing the official line of the Fascist Party (on similar lines, see also Consiglio, 1932b, 285; La Torre, 1932) – is against any expansionary monetary policy, since: 'it increases prices in a way that increases the scarcity of gold [while budgetary policy] like deficit financing and major expenditure on public works have an inflationary effect that facilitates production in other fields, thus creating an increase in prices that would presumably be followed by deflation and collapse' (Arias, 1935, 146).

According to Arias, the irresponsible maintenance of bank rate below the market rate of interest testifies to the need to alter the distortions of a perverted capitalism. He concludes by stating that such a change 'is not possible . . . without the profound spiritual and political work that Fascism is doing. It is imperative to prevent particularistic, selfish individuals making use of their freedom, simply waiting for the outcome of spontaneous forces!' (Arias, 1935, 145).

Arias is favourable to Robbins's analyses, but contests vigorously his policy prescriptions: competition is no solution. It merely implies its denial, the 'creation of agreements, trade-unions, trusts, the hatred monopolies' (p. 148). The lines 'written as an exaltation of unfettered, lawless capitalism are contrary to reason and the most vivid, recent and painful experience' (p. 150).

It is clear that Arias's criticism of some parts of Robbins's book is in fact a direct attack on Einaudi (who had published the volume), a veiled response to Einaudi's refusal to yield to corporatism and Fascism. Only in this regard is it possible to understand the following: 'the book, in its Italian edition . . . silently illuminates the Fascist corporate economy as the solution to the crisis. We can attribute this insight . . . to the editor' (Arias, 1935, 149).

Just to complete the picture, it might be of interest to note the reception of Robbins's *The Great Depression* among Catholics and socialists. With respect to the first, at the end of 1935 Vito wrote a review of both the Italian and French translations, published in *Rivista Internazionale di Scienze Sociali*. This is a short note in which Vito underlines that the analysis adheres to Hayek's view of the business cycle, about which he is lukewarm, having already labelled similar accounts as 'outdated' (Vito, 1932b, 638). Vito is more sceptical of the efficacy of simply restoring freedom. He believes that the erroneous economic policy choices leading to the crisis are not 'purely arbitrary', but are the result of 'necessary measures, although not correctly implemented'. In such a case, the solution 'cannot be anticipated from a restoration of freedom, but from the revision and improvement of interventions which have hitherto been disorderly and poorly co-ordinated' (Vito, 1935, 783).

From the socialist camp the only reference we have found to Robbins's (1935b) book is by Altiero Spinelli. He was unsympathetic to Robbins's account of the Great Depression and the remedies proposed for recovery. There is in fact a lengthy manuscript note by Spinelli to the Italian translation, dated June 1940, in which he echoes Vito in his criticisms of the book: both analysis of the Great Depression, and the exit strategy prescribed, are faulty. The mere restoration of the conditions of the free market and the gold standard are no longer relevant to a profoundly altered economic context, in which cartels prevail (Spinelli, 1993, 522–4).

9.2.3 International Economic Planning and Constitutional Federalism

Although their conceptualization dates back to the early 1930s,[18] the most important texts by Robbins on the design of a new international order based on federalist principles were published in Britain in the later 1930s (Robbins, 1937a, 1937b, 1939a, 1939b, 1940). We have already suggested (Masini, 2007a) that the great influence of these writings in Italy is attributable to the years that Altiero Spinelli[19] spent imprisoned on the Island of Ventotene. During this period Spinelli read several books by Italian and foreign economists, which he borrowed from Ernesto Rossi who, being an economist, was given permission to correspond with, and also receive books from, Luigi Einaudi. Einaudi is therefore once more the figure who facilitated the circulation of Robbins's writings. Spinelli translated *The Economic Causes of War* in June 1940 and Einaudi saw to its publication by UTET in 1944.[20] There is a reason why Einaudi was particularly sympathetic towards such writings: he had written many articles on the possibilities for European Federation soon after the First World War, published under the pen-name 'Junius' in *Corriere della Sera* (Einaudi, 1920).

Thanks to Einaudi and Spinelli, Robbins's federalist ideas were positively received by many leading intellectuals during the years of the Italian Resistance (economists like Wilhelm Röpke,[21] Rodolfo Morandi and Ernesto Rossi, but also politicians like Sandro Pertini, Ugo La Malfa and others). Robbins's ideas were incorporated into Spinelli's political project for the reconstruction of post-war Europe: his well-known *Manifesto for a United Europe* (Spinelli and Rossi, 1941) (implicitly) made extensive use of Robbins's thinking, while he was more explicit in other political documents.

Robbins considers that the cause of war is the existence of exclusive national sovereignties which will inevitably come into conflict. A confederation of national states, as shown by many international conferences of the 1930s, would not be capable of creating the collective public goods necessary for the harmonious regulation of global market forces. Instead a constitutional architecture based on a multilevel federal system was required, permitting decentralized decisions but, at the same time, a central strategic unity.

Spinelli thought this to be the best way to build a new European polity in which the relationships among the single nation-states could be prevented from degenerating into permanent conflict. In his memoirs, published in the 1980s Spinelli (1984) points to Robbins and 'the British federalists' as the primary source of inspiration for his federalist activities throughout his life.[22]

But, apart from this back story, Robbins's book *National Planning and International Order* was reviewed twice, and both were published in *Giornale degli economisti* in 1939. The first review was by Giuseppe Di Nardi,[23] in the September–October issue. Di Nardi summarizes the main questions of the book: the dilemma between economic nationalism and internationalism; the unavoidability of planning, even involving a liberal approach to economics; the necessity of a coordinating authority to manage any plan, even if liberal; and the necessity of establishing such an authority at the international level, given the international dimension of economic activity.

Di Nardi is favourable to Robbins's proposals, but considers his message weak and utopian. Referring to the resurgence of national routes to economic policy, he writes:

> We cannot condemn the considerable efforts being made in the contemporary world. Nobody can deny the economic cost implied and the enormous sacrifice of welfare for all of mankind they cause; but the historical fatality from which they arise cannot be superseded by the contemplation of an ideal which has for centuries proved unattainable . . . This artificial construction can provide only a modest contribution to solving the most serious current problems. (Di Nardi, 1939, 781–2)

The second review of *Economic Planning and International Order* was published two months later by Luigi Federici, dealing with the French translation of the book. The criticism by Federici is the same as Di Nardi's: its 'practical ineffectiveness and [hence] the sterility of the book' (Federici, 1939, 918). Federici further accuses Robbins of envisaging a society of mere:

> *homines oeconomici* for whom it is obvious that the only reasonable political goal is the highest material welfare, understood as the maximum net social

> product (in value) . . . The necessary premise to economic revolution is political revolution. Therefore national states should surrender some of their rights to an international authority . . . But will the day ever come when men will decide to act in such a rational economic, although hardly natural, way? (Federici, 1939, 918)

This is a surprising conclusion: Robbins is accused of being excessively normative. Federici concludes that: 'Robbins blames politicians for pretending to have a tailor-made economics. But he makes the same mistake, assuming that politics follows the requirements of economics' (Federici, 1939, 920).

No other review of Robbins (1937a) has been found in Italian journals, but it is worth briefly underlining another aspect of the book which seems to have had some influence on Italian economic literature. In 1944 Giuseppe Ugo Papi[24] published *Preliminary Notes on Post-War Planning*, in which he cites Robbins[25] with respect to the negative effects of duties on national income. He does not cite Robbins again, but there are many passages on the concept of planning (Papi, 1944, 229ff) which very much resemble Robbins's arguments. Papi denies the viability of socialist planning (1944, vi, 66) and supports instead 'liberal' planning based upon cooperation between public authorities and individuals, consumers and enterprises.[26]

The final work by Robbins reviewed in Italy before the war was *The Economic Basis of Class Conflict and Other Essays in Political Economy*, published in 1939. This was reviewed by Libero Lenti in the *Giornale degli economisti* at the end of 1939. In a short note Lenti observed how Robbins, 'once a trade-unionist',[27] had developed a strong aversion to corporative interests. While his 'arguments are undoubtedly interesting', Lenti notes that he also emphasizes that: 'organization into groups is not necessarily an agent of disharmony, especially within a political and economic power like Italy' (Lenti, 1939, 913).

9.2.4 Robbins in the Italian Context: A Summary

Given the cultural and political context, Robbins's arguments would not be met with widespread sympathy in pre-war Italy, but his first and most important works were picked up and reviewed. The debate on methodology divided into three camps. Vito, from the Catholic point of view, tried to defend the close connection of economics and ethics, contrary to Robbins's *Essay* on the issue of demarcation. Palomba, advancing the idea of a *Homo corporativus*, attacked Robbins's ontology, which he thought was based upon rational maximizing *Homines economici*. Both of them misunderstood Robbins's distinction between economic science and political economy, although it must be said that knowing only the *Essay*, and prior to the publication of *Economic Planning and International Order* in 1937, his view on this issue was not so clear. Rossi and Einaudi (both liberals, although very different in their liberalism), understood Robbins rather better and propagated the content of Robbins's *Essay*: cultural and political empathy count.

As regards *The Great Depression*, its analysis was shared by many writers, given a widespread consensus on an 'excess credit' explanation of the crisis. But his underlying message seemed to go against the stream, at odds with corporatist, socialist and Catholic cultures. The books on the importance of federalism to the international economic order were read in Italy during the war and contributed only to some of the utopian plans for the post-war European recovery. Nevertheless, over time their stock rose with the translation of utopian projects into a real process of European integration from the early 1950s.

The reception of Robbins's work in Italy does not however allow us to conclude that this represents a case of theoretical import substitution compared to the condition of Italian economics under the Fascist regime. New approaches to economic governance were actively sought, and this became more urgent when faced with the need to recover from the economic crisis of the later 1920s and at the same time prepare domestic resources for a possible future war. This never resulted in the advocacy of protectionist policy, mainly because autarchy quickly proved utopian, orthodox neoclassical theories maintaining a central role in economic analysis.

9.3 ROBBINS'S RECEPTION IN JAPAN

This section turns to the way in which Robbins's ideas were introduced into Japan from the 1930s onwards. We first examine the development of economics as an independent academic discipline, looking at six tendencies of economic thought which responded to similar ideas in the West. Some of these arguments explain why, in Japan, Robbins was in some areas not picked up in the way he was in Italy or in other countries. We then deal with the work of five leading academics in two specific areas – general equilibrium theory and economic regimes theory – and group them into three patterns of reception (or rejection).

Three political periods between 1868 and 1945 coincided with three social and academic periods. First, the Meiji Era (1868–1912). Japan's social structure developed rapidly along Western lines. The ruling class wanted Japan to modernize quickly, to catch up with more advanced nations. A new education system, including new universities, was established. Economics was first studied from about 1900, but was seen as a subject of secondary importance. Second, the Taisho Era (1912–26). Democracy grew but was at the mercy of social chaos. Academic societies and journals developed. Some faculties of economics became independent, and for the first time people were trained as academic economists. Third, the Showa Era I (1926–45). Japan's leaders relied on a controlled economy, and academics were no longer free to discuss controversial issues. Marxism was banned from the mid-1920s onwards.

9.3.1 Six Tendencies of Economic Thought

To explain Robbins's reception in Japan during the 1930s and early 1940s we first need to examine six tendencies of economic thought influenced by the West.

Tendency I (1868–1940s)

The first predominant influence came from British liberalism, which was expected to sweep away the last vestiges of Japan's feudal system. Japanese scholars studied Smith and J.S. Mill in the light of not only the approval of individualism and hedonism, but also the coexistence of commercial society and ethics. Robbins's importance also lay in his reassessment of classical economists. Oka (1958) and Minami (1970) reviewed Robbins's books on the classical school favourably. However, in this chapter we pay little attention to the period after 1945.

Tendency II (1881–1940s)

The second influence was a wide-ranging set of German ideas: the Historical or Social Policy Schools and Idealism. Although this tendency was at its peak from the late 1890s to the 1920s, it lasted until the 1940s and even into the post-war era as the basis of Japanese ideas on economics. The German Historical School relied on an ethical, historical and national (or political) oriented basis for economic study (see Pyle, 1974, 132). It was considered important to look beyond simple self-interest and to 'explain the reality in terms of broader human motives' (Shionoya, 2001, 13). The German way of thinking encouraged another trend in Japan: the philosophy of economics, based on idealism. Kiichiro Soda and Kozo Sugimura's originality lay in the connection between neo-Kantian ideas and economics. The influences of German economic theory explains why almost no Japanese scholars[28] referred to the methodological or epistemological aspects of Robbins's *Essay* for at least two decades after its publication.

Tendency III (mid-1910s to 1930s)

By the mid-1910s Marxism had become mainstream as a theoretical tool. German ideas gave academics easy access to ideological and dialectical ways of thinking. In reality, rapid industrialization since the mid-1910s and the birth of the working class gave an air of authenticity to Marxist doctrines. A large number of scholars, students and social reformers had been much involved in controversies on how Marxism should be applied to various stages of Japan's development. In fact, at least 67 scholars, among which the leading figures were in their thirties (Cho, 1984, 100), participated in the 'debate on Japanese capitalism' (1927–37) that was the climax of the theoretical development of social sciences in Japan. The debate brought out in Japanese intellectuals not only strengths but also flaws: the former were evident in the deeper and original style of development of theoretical as well as empirical arguments; the latter was a tendency to degenerate into dogmatism. Robbins's ideas contributed little to discussions in Japan about Tendency III, as Yasui (1933, 128) made clear: 'Robbins examines the materialistic view of history, but we shall omit his examination because his understanding is poor'.

Tendency IV (1920s–1930s)

Marginalist economics and general equilibrium theory arrived. It was Tokuzo Fukuda (1874–1930) in the 1910s who championed neoclassical economics in Japan: he encouraged Yasuma Takata (1883–1972) indirectly and Ichiro Nakayama (1898–1980) directly to study Walrasian economics; they both took the initiative in studying general equilibrium theory from their own viewpoints. Both had an impact on the younger Takuma Yasui (1909–95), a leading figure in mathematical economics from the 1930s onwards.

Various factors may explain why this school was introduced at that time: in the early 1920s Fukuda insisted that his pupil Nakayama should read Cournot, Gossen and Walras; Alfred Amon, a Czech who lectured (1926–29) at the University of Tokyo, taught economics based on Cassel; and when Schumpeter visited Japan in 1931 his exhortation to 'begin with Walras' made a lasting impression on Yasui. The core of general equilibrium theory did not resemble that of the Historical School, German Idealism or Marxism. It was a delicate, objective and mechanical set of interdependent elements and variables. Once the economic way of thinking became too practical, too abstract or too politically dangerous, Walrasian economics seemed to fill the gap.

Robbins mattered in this context. In contrast to later views that his contributions could be defined as epistemology, methodology, advocacy of the scarcity definition of economics, and criticism of Pigou's interpersonal comparison of utility, for Nakayama and Yasui he was primarily an evangelist of the equilibrium concept. As the majority of economic academia had argued over every other topic mentioned above (except criticism of Pigou), they felt that they had no need for Robbins's arguments. This is why very few economists paid special attention to Robbins's *Essay*. However, the few who did so were also eminent. Nakayama and Yasui consolidated the foundations of the theoretical development of non-Marxian economics during and after the Second World War. Another great theorist, Takata, relied on the simpler Cassel, and not Walras. He and his pupil Kei Shibata did not refer to Robbins.

Tendency V (mid-1930s)

Even before Keynes's *General Theory* (1936), monetary disturbances and fluctuations were important topics. Among them, the 'return to gold' controversy in the late 1920s was the most important event in the history of economic debates in Japan. The questions were: should we restore the prewar parity? Should we tolerate domestic deflation to protect the international legacy? In this context, economists tended to rely on Cassel, Fisher and Keynes. Robbins, together with Gregory, was notoriously against reflationary policies, but in our investigation of the controversy we found no articles which referred to Robbins. *The General Theory* might have been a solution, but there was not enough time for the essence of Keynes's theory to be absorbed before militarism and nationalism spread through the whole country.

Tendency VI (late 1930s to 1945)

This last trend came in the late 1930s and became the basis of Japanese economics, but while is quickly flourished it was soon extinct. Although this kind of economics was known at that time as either economics for life, economics for national defence, *Kodo* (or the Imperial Way) economics, or Japanese economics, they could all be called 'political economy', that is, a synthesis of economic ideas with which to consider the relationship between, on the one hand, the economy and, on the other, society, politics and ethics, based on the 'Japanese pure spirit'. Numerous eminent scholars contributed to the study of political economy. They hoped to overcome the economic, social and political crisis by drastically reforming social structures and by raising the population's consciousness.

Political economy in this period was a genuine synthesis of economic thinking, seeking to establish an original Japanese school of economics through the absorption and transformation of Western ideas from the viewpoints of ontology, epistemology and methodology. Examination of the relationship between economics and politics, sociology and ethics continues in many countries. However, political economy could also be a dangerous driving force for war. Nakayama and Yasui were harsh critics of the whole idea of political economy and thought that it did not contribute towards solving economic problems.

In this period, Yamada, Kiga and Kitagawa paid attention to Robbins's *Economic Planning and International Order* (1937a). Robbins also developed his arguments on political economy, or applied economics, a device he used to convert pure economic science into realistic policies by using value judgements. The three economists mentioned above, who were not part of the mainstream, had a high regard for Robbins since, as a liberal, he provided models of economic regimes based on a rigorous version of equilibrium theory.

The next subsections deal with Tendency IV and, in part, Tendency VI. Robbins's works were discussed in Japan in three contexts: general equilibrium theory, economic regime theory, and that of methodology and epistemology. There is little literature on this third topic, and as a result we concentrate on the first and second, which characterize the Japanese approach to Robbins.[29]

9.3.2 The General Equilibrium Theory

Nakayama

By the 1910s, marginalist economists such as Jevons, Marshall, Gossen, Cournot and Walras were becoming known in Japan, through partial translations or direct personal connections. Fukuda, a most eminent pioneer of modern economics, played among others an important role in introducing their ideas. He delivered lectures at Keio based on Marshall's *Principles of Economics* (1890), and involved his students by getting each of them to translate the work of a famous economist from the classical or neoclassical school.

Nakayama was greatly influenced by Fukuda's approach to his works. He once mentioned that his master's motto was: 'The significant thing may be to pursue a theoretical framework for the sake of my own economics' (Nakayama, 1979, 48). Clearly, this was Nakayama's motto too.

Nakayama referred to Robbins's *Essay* in his memorial paper to Fukuda of 21 September 1932. As far as we can see, this is the first response to the *Essay* in Japan, only three months after its publication. He had a high regard for general equilibrium theory, the essence of which was: 'to describe economic phenomena as having mutual relationships' (Nakayama, 1933a, 84). The *Essay* was referred to in the context of both a sharp distinction between a theory and a given condition, and the usefulness of the theory of equilibrium. Although he valued Walras's formal approach, Nakayama (1933b, 11) went beyond him when he said: 'Economy should be understood through cause and effect . . . A simple summation of individual behaviour cannot constitute a society'.

In 1938, after the Keynes–Robertson controversy, he developed his own position, which he called 'stability and progress'. It was to an extent a mixture of Walrasian microeconomics and Keynesian macroeconomics, or pure theory and practical policy.

Nakayama's position becomes clearer when we look at the words he used later, in an introduction to the Japanese translation of the *Essay* in 1957.[30] When he talked to Robbins in Rome in 1956, two things occurred to him: first, a fundamental matter that Robbins had tackled was still relevant in spite of the new Keynesian approach; second, as he said:

> Robbins and Schumpeter shared the view that methodology did not precede its theoretical content . . . However, Robbins's *Essay* is more substantial than Schumpeter's *Wesen* . . . [While Schumpeter had] both the statics and the dynamics, Robbins's view differed. The principle of scarcity was the kernel of his theories. There was no essential distinction in principle between the theories of statics and dynamics . . . This single theoretical weapon would make us grasp the essence of complex and fluctuating economic phenomena. (Nakayama, 1957, iii–iv)

Nakayama respected Robbins in two respects: first, he agreed with his proposition that the theory of equilibrium should be a means of understanding the substance of human economic behaviour; second, by emphasizing scarcity, theories of statics and dynamics should be continuous, a kind of monism.

Nakayama (1933a, 1933b) did not focus on all the arguments in the *Essay*. Rather, he was sympathetic to the way in which Robbins developed his arguments, using the concept of scarcity and equilibrium in order to grasp the nature of economies through focusing on human behaviour. Nakayama's books and the Japanese translation of the *Essay* were so popular that for other economists in Japan they served as reliable guides to Robbins's methodological arguments. On the other hand, Nakayama himself needed the *Essay* to develop his own economics. In fact, his ultimate aim was to explicate human behaviour at the micro level, and stability and progress at the macro level.

Yasui

Takuma Yasui (1909–95) was one of the most eminent mathematical economists in Japan. His way of absorbing European ideas was very new: it was not only through personal connections (Schumpeter, Nakayama, Yasuma Takata, Alfred Amon), reading translations and treatises, but also through international academic journals, which Ikeo (2006, 11) called 'the rise of an international forum of economists'.

Yasui's book review on the *Essay* was the second-earliest, following Nakayama's response (1933a). Very familiar with German literature, he seemed slightly to despise British economic methodology, including that of Robbins. Therefore, he felt that Robbins's *Essay* was a surprise and an object worthy of attention because of its 'scarcity'. But Robbins had introduced the argument that economic science should be based on marginal utility and rationality in choice (Yasui, 1933, 125, 128). Yasui read almost all Robbins's papers, such as those on the representative firm of 1928, on the stationary state of 1930, and on the works of Wicksteed of 1930. Unlike Nakayama's eclecticism, Yasui studied general equilibrium theory exclusively and eventually, in the 1940s, he discovered the stability condition of equilibrium. Robbins's book and papers were catalysts in the development of his own research programme. Yasui's position is clarified in his later writing, after he met Robbins in Tokyo in 1973:

> I read the work of Schumpeter [*Wesen*] and your *Essay* when I was a new assistant . . . I remember I was touched to a great degree by your book, so you were my master, in a sense . . . Besides, I became very interested in the London School of the early 1930s. (Yasui, 1980, 212)

He was not that interested in interpersonal comparison between individuals and in Marshallian partial equilibrium theory. Rather: 'the central theme of the *Essay* was to regard the rational allocation of resources as a fundamental issue of economics' (Yasui, 1980, 52). This viewpoint was exactly the same as Nakayama's. In fact, Yasui once compared Nakayama to Robbins, saying: 'his status as an elder in academia and his numerous government posts made me regard him as the Lionel Robbins of Japan' (Yasui, 1981, 266). This quotation indicates that two leading theorists were closely connected through Robbins's influence.

Yasuo Kumagai (1914–96), Yasui's famous disciple, made clear his recognition of the significance of the *Essay*, describing it as: 'a must-read for anyone studying the methodology of modern economics' (Kumagai and Ohishi, 1970, 21), and 'a definite, essential viewpoint' (Kumagai, 1972, 13). Since the 1950s this evaluation has been firmly established as a standard image of Robbins. Thus Yasui played an important role in ensuring that Robbins's ideas prevailed and took root in Japan.

Sugimoto and Suenaga

The work of Eiichi Sugimoto (1901–52), Fukuda's disciple, contrasted with that of the above two leading economists. He criticized general equilibrium theory on the grounds that it was impossible to use a static equilibrium theory to consider dynamic phenomena in the real world. He preferred the Marshallian approach, not only because of its tendency towards biological evolution, but also because it assumed the concept of British civil society. Marshall and Pigou, he explained, presumed that in economic life men and women were social beings, not just individuals. In this context 'social beings' means those who respect others as being totally independent, even though as members of society they also consider the greater good (Sugimoto, 1960 [1950], vol. 1, 207). Conversely, for him the economics of the Austrian School and of Robbins was too individualistic and lacked social considerations (ibid., 208).

After the Second World War, absorbing a Marxian approach, Sugimoto began to prevail upon students to appreciate the importance of studying the history of economic thought and econometrics. His slogan was 'Marxian and modern economics are in friendly rivalry'. He published some very popular books, such as *Explications of Modern Economics* (1950) and *A History of Modern Economics* (1953). Through those books, Sugimoto's assessment of Robbins became very influential and engendered two opposing attitudes: first, Marxian economists tended to criticize Robbins's ideas as typical bourgeois economics, requiring that economists should not think about value judgements (1960 [1950], vol. 1, 156); second, non-Marxian economists were apt to follow Robbins unquestioningly, judging that his methodology was the only way to make economics more scientific.

Takasuke Suenaga (1928–2004), influenced by his mentor Sugimoto, went further: he criticized Robbins much more strongly than Sugimoto:

> It appears that Robbins, the leader of the London School, regarded general equilibrium theory as the only scientific subject, rejecting all introduction of value judgements; nevertheless, he did take a firm stand on extreme liberalism when he considered real economic problems . . . It was a Tory view, and it coincided with the interests of the financial sector, not with those of industrialists. (Suenaga, 1953, 420)

Suenaga's aggressive criticism of Robbins created a different image of him. As Uzawa (1970) once said, Robbins's values were: 'to pursue efficiency solely and to ignore justice and equality'. In summary, Sugimoto and Suenaga sowed the seeds of a more critical view of Robbins.

9.3.3 The Economic Regimes

From the mid-1930s onwards, Robbins published numerous works on political or applied economy, seeking to transform economic analysis into policy. These were occasional works rather than considered contributions to economic science. In Japan, as total war approached, academics were restricted in what they were permitted to study, and were forced to confine their interests to the national polity. One of the permitted subjects was the behaviour of political and industrial leaders, some of whom were entrepreneurs, including an examination of the direct connection between economy and politics or ethics.

Yuzo Yamada (1902–96) was, between 1938 and 1942, an enthusiast in introducing Robbins's political economy, and particularly his *Economic Planning and International Order* (1937a). He focused on Robbins's economic regime theory, based on the theoretical price mechanism. In price theory, the concept of equilibrium was so important, however, that: 'there were natural equilibria as well as agreed or artificial ones' (Yamada, 1938, 38). Yamada searched for the latter:

> In conclusion, the best economic regime is a kind of corporatism whose mechanism is to restrain speculation and to plan effective cooperation. The regime exists between unstable liberal economy and arbitrary socialist economy. (Yamada, 1942, 3)

In the regime, individual consumers and producers based their actions on price indicators, whereas a state had to direct and control the economy as a whole. This concept was very near to that of German organic economy and of Italian corporatism (Yamada, 1942, 277).

Yamada agreed with Robbins in that he developed an argument about various economic regimes, but he disagreed with his international liberalism. Robbins approved of free trade, on the assumption that there were merits in the international division of labour and the free movement of goods, capital and labour. However, Yamada explored the possibilities of autarky, taking the merits of trade into consideration. In summary, although he had a high regard for economic planning as a basis for further arguments, Yamada distanced himself from Robbins's international liberalism. He believed in a mixed economy. This is why he also devoted himself after the war to Beveridge and Myrdal's ideas on the welfare state, and the coexistence of social security and capitalism.

Kenzo Kiga (1908–2002), who had studied under von Mises, valued Robbins's *Economic Planning* and Yamada's review articles and books. He regarded *Economic Planning* as 'typically orthodox, in the British tradition of economics, because of Robbins's strong support for liberalism' (Kiga, 1937, 131). Judging from his later statements, he ought to have empathized deeply with Robbins's stance on liberalism. However, he posed a question: 'How could international liberalism, which Robbins proposed, resist the general tendency of the times (an international economy based on blocs), whereas he understood that it could contribute to world peace and happiness?' (ibid., 135). In other words, Robbins could not explain how international liberalism could be guaranteed and prevent war. Kiga concluded that: 'although his commentary on types of economic structure was tremendously useful, Robbins's idea was a utopia' (ibid., 136).

At that time, numerous economists in Japan were forced to consider an economic system appropriate to wartime, or a controlled economy. In contrast, Kiga pursued his original interest: orthodox liberalism. Thus he read Robbins's book as one which was fighting for classical liberalism. Nevertheless, while he admired Robbins's sincere faith in liberalism and his analytical viewpoints, he did not share his optimistic view that free trade would have averted the risk of war.

9.3.4 Observations on the Japanese Case

In the 1930s and the 1940s, Robbins did not have major influence in Japan. But this does not mean that he was ignored. In fact, a few eminent young scholars were interested in his two main arguments, and saw them as significant opportunities to promote their own research programmes.

First, general equilibrium theory was introduced to Japanese economists through Robbins's *Essay*. Of course, it was already known to some extent, thanks to Cassel and Walras, but Nakayama and Yasui, who had a good understanding of Walras, made the *Essay* more widely known. They needed an analysis of the conditions of equilibrium between various economic elements, given certain initial data. They regarded this objective approach as a fundamental core of economics, and used it as a springboard in the development of their own economics.

Second, economic system or regime theory was closely connected with Robbins's *Economic Planning*. Almost all European economic thinking had been suppressed in Japan since the mid-1930s, and regime theory was virtually the only way to consider deeper academic arguments based on price theory. The main theme was a combination of economic and political or ethical considerations, so it could be applied realistically to the controlled economy during the war.

The above two topics were received by different academics in one of three ways. Acceptance A (total acceptance) was the most assertive pattern, and was adopted by Yasui. He respected the *Essay* as a great work that clearly declares that the nature of economics is the rational distribution of resources. He simply expanded the Walrasian approach, paving the way for later work by younger London School of Economics (LSE) economists. In this regard, Robbins had exactly same effect on Yasui as he did on the 'Robbins School' composed of Hicks, Lerner, Kaldor and others. This pattern of acceptance had a universal form and occurred at the same time in London and Japan, irrespective of the physical distance between them. Furthermore, with the help of his apprentice, Kumagai, Yasui continued to promulgate the standard image of 'scarcity Robbins' after the 1950s.

Acceptance B (Japanese-style compromise) shows limited assertiveness, and is seen in the responses of Nakayama, Yamada and Kiga. This pattern is seen hardly at all in the West. Nakayama inherited Fukuda's way of thinking and recognized the brilliance of the underlying foresight of *Essay*, with its question: what is the nature of economics? The mutual dependence of various elements within an economy, based on individual behaviour, was very important as a tool. However, at the outset, Nakayama used a concept that went beyond Walras. This was an understanding of macroeconomics oriented towards public policy and the capital theory. Robbins was useful as a way of understanding economic phenomena as part of a one-dimensional, unified theory. Nakayama, however, needed another dimension, that is to say, Keynesian concepts or theories applied to policy. Yamada, much like Nakayama, had a great affinity for Robbins's basic frameworks: an economic system based on price theory. However, the Yamada of this period did not choose Robbins's liberalism (the free movement of production elements), but rather strongly controlled cooperatism. Kiga shares the same position as Robbins as regards liberalism, but he was ultimately incapable of accepting its ideals. Although the above three scholars had made a thorough study of Robbins's arguments, they did so only as a way of developing and articulating their own economics or economic thought. Thus, this style of acceptance is limited, and should be called the Japanese compromise pattern.

Rejections included a thorough critique, as with Sugimoto and Suenaga. In the West, they would be close to Harrod, Dobb (Backhouse and Medema, 2007, 6–7) or Keynes, who advocated a moral science. From the outset, Sugimoto fundamentally criticized the static timelessness of the Lausanne School and conversely had a strong affinity with the Cambridge School, which embodied various concepts such as representative firms, elasticity, welfare and historical time. In the 1950s, Suenaga denounced Robbins as representing conservatism. Their critical attitude is yet another image that endured in Japan.

By exploring the patterns of reaction among a few pre-eminent economists, it is possible to identify the various ways in which Lionel Robbins's ideas were received. In the 1930s he raised various issues such as: the definition of economics (methodology); what economists deem to be truth (epistemology); the development of pure theory (from general equilibrium theory to welfare economics); liberalism and the controlled, wartime economy; and the polarization of the LSE against the traditional Cambridge School.

9.4 CONCLUDING REMARKS

We have surveyed the reception of Lionel Robbins's works in two culturally very different countries, but in a period when they shared some similar characteristics. Before the two World Wars, both Italy and Japan were developing rapidly. During the 1930s – when the first books by Robbins arrived in these countries – Japanese intellectuals were eager to absorb new institutions and ideas, including the most important contributions of the British debates in the 'years of high theory', while seeking to retain their own tradition and culture. And most Italian economists, not just the liberals who rejected the dominance of new corporatist ideas, looked at the major exponents of British liberal orthodoxy in search of intellectual support.

Even more importantly, both countries experienced a period of political and cultural dictatorship, creating a very special context that made the discussion and diffusion, acceptance or rejection of Robbins's messages particularly difficult. As we have pointed out, these peculiarities induced in some cases underestimation and misrepresentation of his thoughts in the 1930s, which also would be perpetuated in the following decades.

The comparison between the two national cases is suggestive. Firstly, in both countries Robbins's message was used as an instrument in domestic theoretical and policy debates. Corporatism in Italy and the economics of von Gottl-Ottlilienfeld in Japan obstructed the reception of the liberal Robbins, whose ideas were definitely not in tune with totalitarian regimes. Nevertheless, and notwithstanding some attempts at import substitution in economic thinking, in both countries most economists paid close attention to the ongoing international debate. In both national cases, the will to find and defend some national and characteristic approaches to economic analysis and policy never turned to autarchy, and actually benefited from continuous confrontation with foreign views, even when these were apparently hostile.

An important difference between the two cases concerns the fact that in Japan we can trace both positive and negative caricatures of Robbins back to specific authors: Yasui and Sugimoto. On the one hand, Robbins is a hero in the promotion of economic science. On the other, Robbins represents the bourgeois economist who exiles value judgements from economics. Such simplistic views of Robbins have been common knowledge in Japan until recently.

Another important difference concerns the peculiar role that Robbins has occupied in Japan concerning general equilibrium theory. Robbins's contributions to this system of thought, almost completely neglected in other countries, was a crucial feature of the theoretical debates in Japan. A minor role was on the contrary attributed to the specifically epistemological content of his *Essay*.

Apart from such differences, the reception of Robbins shows that – although to different degrees – most Italian and Japanese economists grasped the complexity of his work, from ontology and methodology to economic policies, from general equilibrium to economic regimes, from international economics to federalism. Despite the geographical distance between Japan and Italy, and the differences in politics and culture of their totalitarian regimes of the 1930s and 1940s, there is a striking consistency and openness in the manner in which the work of this British economist was received.

NOTES

1. Sections 9.1 and 9.2 were written by Masini and sections 9.3 and 9.4 by Komine. All the translations from Italian, French and Japanese texts into English are our own.
2. The economic movement was named after the corporations of the Middle Ages representing professions and/or groups of collective interests within society and the economic system. It is also widely recognized that the starting point of modern corporatism is Pope Leone XIII's 1891 encyclical, *Rerum Novarum*, in which he established the foundations for social reform based on a strategic agreement between workers and entrepreneurs.
3. Corporatism has usually been considered an exogenous (ideological and political, not economic) construction intended to undermine the political and economic ontology of liberalism (Zagari, 1982). But it has also been an endogenous response of orthodox economic theory to the ever-increasing faults of its underlying marginalist assumptions (perfect competition, the sovereignty of individual choices, and so on) and to the search for both a new framework of analysis and a new, effective system of economic governance (Finoia, 1983).
4. For reviews of the principal economic debates among such journals during Fascism, see Bini (1981, 2004).
5. The most renowned journal, *Giornale degli economisti e annali di statistica*, bought in 1890 by Antonio de Viti de Marco and Maffeo Pantaleoni, defended the traditional Italian marginalist tradition. *La Riforma Sociale*, directed by Luigi Einaudi and Pasquale Jannaccone until 1935 (when it would be closed by the Fascist regime, and from 1936 replaced by the *Rivista di storia economica*), was the defender of liberal orthodoxy, although open to scientific contributions from other approaches. Also the French *Revue d'économie politique* – founded in Paris by Charles Gide, Alfred Jourdan and Edmond Villey (all the three were dead by the mid-1930s) and edited by Charles Rist and Gaëtan Pirou – should be mentioned among these journals, as it would print many contributions from Italian economists during the 1930s, where they could express their opinions more freely. The *Rivista internazionale di scienze sociali*, edited by the Università Cattolica del Sacro Cuore in Milan, represented Catholic economists. The *Rivista italiana di statistica, economia e finanza*, from 1933 *Rivista italiana di scienze economiche*, was edited by Alberto De Stefani, Luigi Amoroso and Felice Vinci, and

it too soon became a medium for corporatism, as did the *Rivista di politica economica*, edited by Felice Guarneri and *Economia. L'economia italiana* was an official journal of the Fascist Party; its subtitle was *Rassegna fascista mensile di politica ed economia* and it was edited by Luigi Lojacono and Umberto Klinger. Journals oriented to socialism had already been closed during the 1920s.

6. A Manifesto against the specific question of the *Homo economicus* had been launched in March 1928 by Bottai (1928) in *Critica Fascista*. See Zagari (1982, 27).
7. The first mention of Robbins in the journals we have examined is an article by Bruno Foà (1932), published in *Giornale degli economisti* in February 1932, where Robbins is cited twice for his participation in the debate on 'empty boxes' in the *Economic Journal* (Robbins, 1930).
8. On this point see the contribution by Duchini (1972, 463ff).
9. We agree with Cressati (1992, 65), who claims that the article should be attributed to Ernesto Rossi. Rossi (1897–1967) was a political activist, founder of the Giustizia e libertà movement (based on a peculiar compromise between socialist and liberal ideals), later a teacher of economics in a high school, and imprisoned in the late 1930s for anti-Fascist propaganda. In 1941 he wrote, together with Spinelli, the *Manifesto for a United Europe* (Spinelli and Rossi, 1941) and was among the founders of the political party Partito d'azione. In his writings he often refers to Robbins's books on the international order as the best expositions of how to build a new economic and political order after the end of the Second World War. Cressati notes that Einaudi included some of Rossi's writings in his journal *La riforma sociale*, which were published anonymously since he had already been condemned by the Fascist regime.
10. The author cites the essay on 'the economic act' within *Erotemi di economia*, (Pantaleoni, 1925).
11. Giuseppe Palomba (1908–86) was Professor of Political Economy at the University of Naples, but he published studies in philosophy, mathematics, biology and thermodynamics.
12. Gustavo Del Vecchio (1883–1972) was a very idiosyncratic scholar. Professor of Economics in Trieste, Bologna, Milan and Rome, after the Second World War he was Treasury Minister in the Italian government and Governor of the International Monetary Fund. He engaged in questions of epistemology (he denied the existence of contrasting theories, stating that each is valid in specific contexts) and economic dynamics (see Faucci, 2000, 293–6).
13. Professor of Law and Dean at the University of Rome.
14. The defence of 'economic dogma' which Einaudi (1932a, 1932b) attempts against less academic and somewhat questionable approaches to the history of economic theories (Michels, 1932) sounds extremely and irritatingly fundamentalist if it is not understood within this context.
15. It might be interesting to note that another review article of the book was published in 1938 in *Giornale degli economisti*, where the author, Ghetti, ignoring or forgetting the previous review written by D'Albergo, apologizes to the reader for having to wait so long to be informed about Robbins's book. Although the work is praised for its analysis of the crisis, the remedies are considered 'inapplicable' in 'a world afflicted with political instability' (Ghetti, 1938, 270).
16. Gino Arias (1879–1940), Professor of Political Economy at the University of Rome, was among the leading economists of corporatism until the Fascist regime imposed the Racial Laws in 1938. As a Jew, and although a strong supporter of the regime, he had to leave the country for Argentina, where he began to teach at the University of Cordoba, but died some months later.
17. *Equilibrismo* in the original, a negative neologism; by coining this term Arias disparaged treatment of the concept of equilibrium as if it were the key tenet of a new faith.
18. Especially as regards the main contribution, *Economic Planning and International Order* (1937a), which was made up of lectures that Robbins had been invited to give at the Institute des Haute Etudes Internationales of Geneva in 1935.

19. Born in Rome, August 1907, and arrested in 1927 for anti-Fascist activity, he remained imprisoned until 1943, when he founded the European Federalist Movement. This was based on the strategy outlined in the document *For a Free and United Europe. Project of a Manifesto*, later widely known as the *Ventotene Manifesto*, written by Spinelli himself with the help of the economist Ernesto Rossi (Spinelli and Rossi, 1941). Spinelli would later become a leading figure of the European integration process; founder of the Istituto Affari Internazionali in the 1960s, Commissioner for Industry at the European Commission from 1970 to 1976, later member of the Italian Chamber of Deputies and of the European Parliament until his death in 1986. On the role of Spinelli in the diffusion of the economic thought, see Masini (2008).
20. *National Planning and International Order* would be published by Rizzoli only in 1948, with a translation by Ruggero Haardt, who had also translated two Marxist texts, both published by Editore Fasiani, Milan, in 1946. In 1948, under the title *Aspetti economici della federazione*, in a collection of writings on the European Federation, a translation was published of 'Economic aspects of federation', one of Robbins's contributions to the debates of the association Federal Union (on whose activities we can refer to Chaning Pearce (1940).
21. Many important members of the Italian Resistance based themselves in Switzerland, where they found shelter from the Fascist regime, together with many other intellectuals from all over Europe. Röpke was a reference point for many Italian economists, such as Einaudi, Rossi and Ricci (the uncle of Spinelli), and had an interesting correspondence with Spinelli.
22. When, after the war, the European Federation project was progressively displaced by the slow advance of economic integration, the entire federalist culture became the utopia of a marginalized intellectual elite. Only in the second half of the 1980s, when the European integration project had a new impetus and monetary union was envisaged as an explicit first step towards a federal Europe, were Robbins's contributions rediscovered, thanks to some federalist writers. In 1987, Il Mulino published an anthology of Robbins's writings on federalism, with an introduction by Guido Montani (1985); and some years later the journal *Storia del pensiero economico* published an article on the role of Robbins in the federalist liberal tradition in Britain (Masini, 1994).
23. Giuseppe Di Nardi (1911–92) was Professor of Political Economy at the universities of Bari, Naples and Rome. He worked for the Cassa per il Mezzogiorno, the Bank of Italy, the Consiglio Nazionale dell'Economica e il Lavoro (CNEL) and was a member of the Academy of Lincei.
24. Giuseppe Ugo Papi (1893–1989) was Professor of Economics and Provost at the University of Rome 'La Sapienza'. He was also responsible for several governmental commissions of enquiry into many aspects of the Italian economic system.
25. He quotes an edition of 1938, which either was a mistake or might refer to an English reprint of whose existence we are unaware, or (most probably) to the first French edition, *L'économie pianifiée et l'ordre internationale*, Paris.
26. Papi would also play a role in the diffusion of Robbins's thought after the war. He would in fact invite Robbins to his faculty in Rome to give a lecture on 'The present position of economics' in April 1959. The speech was published (accompanied by an Italian translation) in *Rivista di Politica Economica*. Robbins's (1959) contribution had some effect, as the following year an article by Mario Talamona (1960) was published in the journal *L'Industria*, edited by Ferdinando di Fenizio, on 'The methodological evolution of Lionel Robbins' (published in Italian). The group of di Fenizio was engaged in the spreading of Keynesianism in Italy and Robbins's interest in Keynesian arguments during the 1950s was probably thought to be a good opportunity to get Robbins's support. Talamona maintained that Robbins had undergone a radical shift in his reflections on method: from pure deductivism to a more tolerant attitude towards inductivism (Talamona, 1960). Di Fenizio himself spoke of an alleged 'conversion' on the part of Robbins in a review essay of *The Economic Problem in Peace and War* (London, Macmillan, 1947) published in *L'Industria*, 3, 1947: 499–504.

27. This is Lenti's definition but, in fact only Robbins's father was a trade unionist.
28. In our investigation, Nomura (1939) was the only exception. In the paper Nomura, of Keio University, reviewed the methodological controversy provoked by the *Essay* in Britain and America.
29. The table below (divided by topics, dates and universities) shows who introduced Robbins and the year they first referred to him. An asterisk indicates that the person is mentioned in this chapter.

	Tokyo	Kyoto	Hitotsubashi	Keio	Others
General equilibrium	*Yasui (1933) *Kumagai (1948)	Takata Shibata	*Nakayama (1933) *Sugimoto (1950)		Toyosaki (1937) *Suenaga (1950)
Regime			Ohkuma *Yamada (1938)	*Kiga (1937) Takemura	Kitagawa (1938)
Methodology			*Sugimoto (1950) Baba (1956)	Nomura (1937) Tomita (1950)	Toyosaki (1937) *Suenaga (1950) Kashiwara (1953) Tsuji (1958)

30. Nakayama supervised the translation. The translator was one of his pupils, Rokubei Tsuji (1916–?).

BIBLIOGRAPHY

Almodovar, A. and J.L. Cardoso (2005), 'Corporatism and the economic role of government', *History of Political Economy*, **37** (s1), 333–54.

Anonymous (1933a), 'Il liberalismo è morto', *L'economia italiana*, **18** (1), 3–4.

Anonymous (1933b), 'Che cosa è la scienza economica?' [Review article: Lionel Robbins, *An Essay on the Nature and Significance of Economic Science*, 1932], *La Riforma Sociale*, **44**, 218–26.

Anonymous (1948), 'Trakhtenberg's critique on economics of Hayek and Robbins: a bourgeois economics which opposes to state intervention', *Sekai Keizai*, or *Journal of World Economy*, **3** (10), 45–51.

Amoroso, Luigi (1932), 'Economia e politica', *Rivista italiana di statistica, economia e finanza*, **4**, 627–44.

Arias, Gino (1927), 'Economia corporativa', *Il Diritto del Lavoro*, marzo; reprinted in A. Montemaggiori (ed.) (1934), *Dizionario della dottrina fascista*, Torino: Paravia, p. 269.

Arias, Gino (1935), 'Rassegna di economia corporativa [Review article: Lionel Robbins, *Di chi la colpa della grande crisi*, 1935]', *Economia. Rivista di economia corporativa e di scienze sociali*, **16** (2), 140–50.

Baba, Keinosuke (1956), *The Methodology of Economics: A Form of Society and Economic Theory*, Tokyo: Shunjusha Publishing Company.

Backhouse, R.E. and S.G. Medema (2007), 'Defining economics: Robbins' *Essay* in theory and practice', Discussion Paper, Social Science Research Network, id=969994.

Balisciano, M.L. and S.G. Medema (1999), 'Positive science, normative man: Lionel Robbins and the political economy of art', *History of Political Economy. Annual Supplement. Economists and Art, Historically Considered*, **31**, 256–84.

Barshay, A.E. (2004), *The Social Sciences in Modern Japan: The Marxian and Modernist Traditions*, Berkeley, CA: University of California Press.

Biagini, Eugenio (2007), 'Keynesian ideas and Italian democracy, 1945–1953', in E.H.H. Green and D. Tanner (eds), *The Strange Survival of Liberal England: Political Leaders, Moral Values and the Reception of Economic Debate*, Cambridge: Cambridge University Press, pp. 212–44.

Bini, P. (1981), 'Il dibattito attraverso le "riviste di regime"'. In AA.VV. *Banca e industria tra le due guerre. L'economia e il pensiero economico*, Bologna: Il Mulino, pp. 245–98.

Bini, P. (1982), 'Il salario "corporativo" negli studi economici tra le due guerre', in R. Faucci (ed.). *Gli italiani e Bentham. Dalla 'felicità pubblica' all'economia del benessere*, Vol. 2, Milano: Angeli, pp. 255–83.

Bini, P. (2000), 'The making of economic policy in Italy in the inter-war years', *Storia del pensiero economico*, **40**, 5–30.

Bini, P. (2004), 'Gli anni del fascismo 1921–1943', in P. Bini (ed.), *I novant'anni della Rivista di Politica Economica (1911–2000). Teorie economiche, scelte politiche e cultura d'impresa nell'Italia del Novecento, Rivista di politica economica, XCIV*(fascicolo speciale), 77–132.

Bottai, G. (1928), 'Editoriale', *Critica fascista*, 15 marzo.

Bronfenbrenner, M. (1956), 'The state of Japanese economics', *American Economic Review*, **46** (2), *Papers and Proceedings of the Sixty-eighth Annual Meeting of the American Economic Association*, May, pp. 389–98.

Burks, A.W. (1953), Review article of Nomura Kanetaro, *A History of Japanese Economic Theory*, *Far Eastern Quarterly*, **12** (2), 226–8.

Carli, Filippo (1931), *Teoria generale dell'economia politica nazionale*, Milano: Hoepli.

Carli, Filippo (1937), 'Ethique, économie pure et économie corporatives, *Revue d'économie politique*, **51** (6), 1538–58.

Chaning Pearce, M. (ed.) (1940), *Federal Union: A Symposium*, London: Jonathan Cape.

Cho, Yukio (1984), 'Economic thought in interwar Japan', in Japanese Society for the History of Economic Thought (ed.), *Economics in Japan*, Tokyo: Toyo Keizai, pp. 93–135.

Colander, David (2009), 'What was "It" that Robbins was defining?' *Journal of the History of Economic Thought*, **31** (4), 21–32.

Colander, David and Alfred William Coats (eds) (1989), *The Spread of Economic Ideas*, Cambridge: Cambridge University Press.

Consiglio, Vincenzo (1932a), 'Homo œconomicus e scienza economica', *L'economia italiana*, **17** (1), 16–19.

Consiglio, Vincenzo (1932b), 'Le crisi nella teoria e nella storia', *L'economia italiana*, **17** (5–6), 285–91.

Consiglio, Vincenzo (1932c), 'Ancora sull'homo œconomicus', *L'economia italiana*, **17** (7–8), 393–5.

Contento, Aldo (1931), 'Difesa dell'*homo œconomicus*', *Giornale degli economisti e annali di economia*, luglio.
Contento, Aldo (1932), 'Ancora sulla realtà dell'homo oeconomicus', *Giornale degli economisti e annali di economia*, apr., 265–85.
Costanza, Michele (1933), 'Nascita e funzione dell'homo economicus', *Rivista Internazionale di Scienze Sociali*, **4** (5), 605–15.
Cressati, C. (1992), *L'Europa necessaria. Il federalismo liberale di Luigi Einaudi* [The necessity of Europe. The liberal federalism of Luigi Einaudi], Torino: Giappichelli.
Croce, Benedetto (1983 [1896]), 'Le teorie storiche del prof. Loria', *Materialismo storico ed economia marxista*, Bari: Laterza, pp. 21–51.
D'Albergo, Ernesto (1935), Review article, Lionel Robbins, *The Great Depression*, 1934, *Giornale degli Economisti*, apr., 347–8.
De Finetti, Bruno (1935), 'Il tragico sofisma', *Rivista italiana di scienze economiche*, **7**, 362–82.
De Stefani, Alberto and Luigi Amoroso (1933), 'La logica del sistema corporativo', *Rivista Internazionale di Scienze Sociali*, **4** (4), 393–411.
Deguchi, Yuzo (ed.) (1953), *A History of Economic Thought*, Kyoto: Minerva Publishing Co.
Del Vecchio, Giorgio (1935), 'Droit et économie', *Revue d'économie politique*, **49** (5), 1457–94.
Del Vecchio, Gustavo (1935), Review article, 'Lionel Robbins, *An Essay on the Nature and Significance of Economic Science*, 1932', *Giornale degli Economisti*, gennaio, 51–3.
Di Nardi, Giuseppe (1939), Review article, 'Lionel Robbins, *Economic Planning and International Order*, 1937', *Giornale degli Economisti*, set.–ott., 779–82.
Duchini, Francesca (1972), 'Scienza economica e giudizi di valore nella storia del pensiero economico', *Rivista internazionale di scienze sociali*, set–dic, 462–508.
Einaudi, L. (1920), *Lettere politiche di Junius*, Bari: Laterza.
Einaudi, Luigi (1932a), 'Del modo di scrivere la storia del dogma economico', *La Riforma Sociale*, **43**, 207–19.
Einaudi, Luigi (1932b), 'Ancora intorno al modo di scrivere la storia del dogma economico', *La Riforma Sociale*, **43**, 308–13.
Einaudi, Luigi (1935), 'Prefazione', in Lionel Robbins, *Di chi la colpa della grande crisi? E la via d'uscita*, Torino: Einaudi, pp. 9–14.
Einaudi, Luigi (1936), 'Morale et économique', *Revue d'économie politique*, **50** (2), 289–311.
Einaudi, Luigi (1950), 'La scienza economica. Reminescenze. 1896–1946', reprinted in Massimo Finoia (1980); *Il pensiero economico italiano 1850–1950*, Bologna: Cappelli, pp. 94–115.
Fanfani, Amintore (1932), 'Natura e concetto di bisogno in una visione integrale della realtà economica', *Economia. Rivista di economia corporativa e di scienze sociali*, **10** (3), 238–52.
Faucci, Riccardo (2000), *L'economia politica in Italia. Dal Cinquecento ai nostri giorni*, Torino: Utet.
Federici, Luigi (1939), Review article, 'Lionel Robbins, *L'économie planifiée et l'ordre international*, 1938', *Giornale degli Economisti*, nov.–dic., 917–20.
Finoia, Massimo (1980), *Il pensiero economico italiano 1850–1950*, Bologna: Cappelli.

Finoia, Massimo (1983), 'Il Pensiero economico italiano negli anni '30', *Rassegna Economica*, **3** (maggio–giugno), 565–91.

Foà, Bruno (1932), 'Sul metodo della scienza economica', *Giornale degli Economisti*, Feb., 59–70.

Galli, Renato (1935), 'Questioni di metodologia negli studi economici', *Rivista di Politica Economica*, **6**, 692–700.

Ghetti, E. (1938), Review article, 'Lionel Robbins, *Di chi la colpa della grande crisi? E la via d'uscita*, 1935', *Giornale degli Economisti*, mar.: 268–70.

Guidi, M.E.L. (2000), 'Corporative economics and the Italian tradition of economic thought: a survey', *Storia del pensiero economico*, **40**, 31–58.

Hawtrey, Ralph G. (1926), *The Economic Problem*, London: Longmans Green.

Hayasaka, Tadashi (1971), 'Modern economics and Lionel Robbins', *Keizai Seminar* (Nippon-Hyoron-sha Co.), **192** (September), 46–52.

Howson, S. (2004), 'The origins of Lionel Robbins's essay on the nature and significance of economic science', *History of Political Economy*, **36** (3), 413–43.

Ikema, Makoto, Yoshio Inoue, Tamotsu Nishizawa and Susumu Yamauchi (eds) (2000), *Hitotsubashi University 1875–2000: A Hundred and Twenty-Five Years of Higher Education in Japan*, London: Macmillan.

Ikeo, Aiko (1993), 'Japanese modern economics, 1930–1945', in Robert F. Hebert (ed.), *Themes on Economic Discourse, Method, Money and Trade, Perspectives on the History of Economic Thought*, Vol. 9, Aldershot, UK and Brookfield, VT, USA: Edward Elgar, pp. 192–202.

Ikeo, Aiko (ed.) (2000), *Japanese Economics and Economists since 1945*, London: Routledge.

Ikeo, Aiko (2006), *Economics in Japan: The Internationalization of Economics in the Twentieth Century*, Nagoya: University of Nagoya Press.

Kashiwara, Keizo (1953–54), 'Lionel Robbins and the methodology of economics', part 1 & 2, *Review of Kumamoto Junior College*, **8** and **9**, November 1953 and March 1954, 1–33 and 1–36.

Keio University Study Group on Humanities (ed.) (1933), *The Methodology of Economics*, Tokyo: Okura Shoten.

Keynes, John N. (1890), *The Scope and Method of Political Economy*, London: Macmillan. 1897.

Keynes, J.M. (1936), *The General Theory of Employment, Interest and Money*, London: Macmillan.

Kiga, Kenzo (1937), Book review, 'L. Robbins; *Economic Planning and International Order*, London 1937, pp. 330', *Mita Journal of Economics*, **31** (11), 131–7.

Kiga, Kenzo (2000), 'Anti-socialism economy and freedom: seeking for moral in community', *Reformer*, **41** (12), 10–13.

Komine, Atsushi (2007), *W.H. Beveridge in Economic Thought: A Collaboration with J. M. Keynes et al.*, Kyoto: Showa-do.

Kumagai, Hisao (1972), *Modern Economics*, new edn, Tokyo: Nihon Hyoron Sha.

Kumagai, Hisao and Yasuhiko Ohishi (eds) (1970), *A Basic Theory of Modern Economics*, Tokyo: Yuhikaku Publishing Co.

La Torre, Michele (1932), 'Crisi economiche e risparmio', *L'economia italiana*, **17** (9), 456–8.

Lange, O. (1935), 'Marxian economics and modern economic theory', *Review of Economic Studies*, **2** (3), 189–201.

Lanzillo, Agostino (1935), 'L'economico e l'extraeconomico. Compito dell'economista nel nostro tempo', *Rivista di Politica Economica*, **1**, 24–8.

Lenti, Libero (1939), Review article, 'Lionel Robbins, *The Economic Basis of Class Conflict and Other Essays in Political Economy*, 1939', *Giornale degli Economisti*, nov.–dic., 912–13.
Lorenzoni, Giovanni (1933), 'Economia ed etica', *La Riforma Sociale*, **44**, 160–69.
Mancini, Ombretta, Francesco D. Perillo and Eugenio Zagari (eds) (1982), *La teoria economica del corporativismo*, 2 vols, Napoli: ESI.
Marshall, Alfred (1890), *Principles of Economics*, London: Macmillan.
Marsili-Libelli, Mario (1933), 'Spunti di morale economica', *Rivista Internazionale di Scienze Sociali*, **4** (4), 420–29.
Masini, Fabio (1994), 'Lionel Robbins e la svolta federalista nella tradizione liberale inglese', *Storia del pensiero economico*, **28,** 69–92.
Masini, Fabio (2007), 'Money, business cycle, public goods: British economists and peace in Europe, 1919–1941', in Marta Petricioli and Donatella Cherubini (eds), *Pour la Paix en Europe. Institutions et société civile dans l'entre-deux-guerre – For Peace in Europe. Institutions and Civil Society between the World Wars*, Bruxelles: Peter Lang, pp. 169–90.
Masini, F. (2008), 'Umberto Ricci e la cultura economica di Altiero Spinelli' [Umberto Ricci and the economic culture of Altiero Spinelli], *Eurostudium 3W*, **3**, 46–67.
Masini, F. (2009a), 'Robbins' epistemology and the role of the economist in society', in F. Cowell and A. Witzum (eds), *Lionel Robbins' Essay on the Nature and Significance of Economic Science. 75th Anniversary Conference Proceedings*, London: Sunctory and Toyota International Centres for Economic Research and Development, pp. 343–65.
Masini, Fabio (2009b), '*Economics* and *Political Economy* in Lionel Robbins's writings', *Journal of the History of Economic Thought*, **31** (4), 421–36.
Matteucci, Nicola (2001), 'Friedrich von Hayek alla ricerca di un ordine spontaneo' [Friedrich von Hayek in search of a spontaneous order], *Filosofi politici Contemporanei* [Contemporary political philosophers], Bologna: Il Mulino.
Mazzei, Jacopo (1936), 'La tesi liberista e la tesi protezionista nell'800', *Rivista italiana di scienze economiche*, **2**, 96–131.
Michels, Roberto (1932), 'Ancora intorno al modo di scrivere la storia del dogma economico', *La Riforma Sociale*, **43**, 303–8.
Minami, Ryozaburo (1970), 'Robbins's theory of economic development', *Economic Review of Komazawa University*, **1** (3), 48–60.
Montani, Guido (1985), 'Introduzione', in Lionel Robbins (ed.), *Il federalismo e l'ordine economico internazionale* [Federalism and the international economic order], Bologna: Il Mulino.
Montani, Guido (1987), 'Introduzione', in Lionel Robbins, *Il federalismo e l'ordine economico internazionale*, Bologna: Il Mulino, pp. 9–20.
Morris-Suzuki, T. (1989), *A History of Japanese Economic Thought*, London, UK and New York, USA: Routledge.
Mussolini, Benito (1933), 'Discorso all'Assemblea del Consiglio Nazionale delle Corporazioni, Roma, 14 novembre 1933-xii', reprinted (1934) in Amerigo Montemaggiori (ed.). *Dizionario della dottrina fascista*, Torino: Paravia, p. 264.
Nakayama, Ichiro (1933a), 'Economic theory and economic sociology', in I. Nakayama (ed.), *A Study of Economics: in the Memory of Dr Fukuda*, Tokyo: Moriyama Shoten, pp. 79–100.
Nakayama, Ichiro (1933b), *Pure Economics*, Tokyo: Iwanami Shoten Publishers.

Nakayama, Ichiro (1957), 'An introduction: Robbins' economics', Preface to the Japanese translation of Robbins' *Essay*, pp. i–v.

Nakayama, Ichiro (1979), *My Way to Economics: An Autobiography*, Tokyo: Kodansha.

Negishi, Takashi (2001), 'Alfred Marshall in Hitotsubashi', in T. Negishi, R.V. Tamachandran and K. Mino (eds), *Economic Theory, Dynamics, and Markets*, Boston, MA: Kluwer Academic Publishers, pp. 357–67.

Negishi, Takashi (2002), 'The general equilibrium theory in 20th century Japan', *International Journal of Applied Economics and Econometrics*, **10** (3), 480–89.

Nomura, Kanetaro (1939), 'Theory and practice: recent British controversies on the methodology of economics', *Mita Journal of Economics*, **33** (8), 1–33.

Nomura, Kanetaro (1949), *A History of Japanese Economic Theory*, Tokyo: Keiso Shobo.

Noto, Sergio (2007), 'Le recezione di Hayek in Italia: gli anni '30 e '40' [The reception of Hayek in Italy: the 1930s and 1940s], *Quaderni di Teoria – Centro Studi e Documentazione Toqueville-Acton*, **5**, 160–69.

Ohkuma, Nobuyuki (1929), *A Tale of Robinson Crusoe in Marx*, Tokyo: Dobunkan.

Oka, Akiko (1958), 'A review of Robbins's new book *Robert Torrens and the Evolution of Classical Economics*', *Gakuto* (Maruzen), **55** (5), 51–4.

Palomba, Giuseppe (1933), 'Le economie non euclidee e l'economia corporativa', *L'economia italiana*, **18** (10), 456–8.

Palomba, Giuseppe (1934), 'Le forze extraeconomiche nella determinazione dell'equilibrio economico', *Rivista di Politica Economica*, **9–10**, 1010–15.

Pantaleoni, Maffeo (1925), *Erotemi di economia*, Bari: Laterza.

Papi, Giuseppe Ugo (1944), *Preliminari ai piani per il dopoguerra*, Roma: Istituto Internazionale di Agricoltura.

Parisi, D.F. (1981), 'Emmanuel Mounier e il dibattito sui rapporti tra scienza economica e giudizi di valore', *Il pensiero economico moderno*, **1** (marzo), 89–100.

Pyle, K.B. (1974), 'Advantages of followership: German economics and Japanese bureaucrats, 1890–1925', *Journal of Japanese Studies*, **1** (1), 127–64.

Resta, Manlio (1935), 'Cenni di teoria economica corporativa', *Rivista di Politica Economica*, **6**, 679–91.

Robbins, L.C. (1930), 'On a certain ambiguity in the conception of stationary equilibrium', *Economic Journal*, **40**, 194–214.

Robbins, Lionel C. (1932), *An Essay on the Nature and Significance of Economic Science*, London: Macmillan.

Robbins, L. (1934), *The Great Depression*, London: Macmillan.

Robbins, Lionel C. (1935a), *An Essay on the Nature and Significance of Economic Science*, 2nd edn, London: Macmillan.

Robbins, L. (1935b), *Di chi la colpa della grande crisi? E la via d'uscita*, Italian translation of (1934) *The Great Depression*, Torino: Einaudi.

Robbins, Lionel C. (1937a), *Economic Planning and International Order*, London: Macmillan.

Robbins, Lionel C. (1937b), 'The economics of territorial sovereignty', in Charles Antony Woodward Manning (ed), *Peaceful Change*, London: Macmillan, pp. 41–60.

Robbins, Lionel C. (1939a), *The Economic Basis of Class Conflicts*, London: Macmillan.

Robbins, Lionel C. (1939b), *The Economic Causes of War*, London: Jonathan Cape.

Robbins, Lionel C. (1940), 'Economic aspects of federation', in Melville Channing-Pearce (ed), *Federal Union: A Symposium*, London: Jonathan Cape, pp. 167–86.
Robbins, Lionel C. (1959), 'The present position of economics', *Rivista di Politica Economica*, **49** (8–9), 1347–63.
Robbins, Lionel C. (1981), 'Economics and political economy', *American Economic Review. Papers and Proceedings of the Ninety-Third Annual Meeting of the American Economic Association*, **71** (2), 1–10.
Robinson, Joan (1972), 'The second crisis of economic theory', *American Economic Review*, **62** (1–2), 1–10.
Robbins, L.C. (1933), 'Introduction', in P.H. Wicksteed (ed.), *The Common Sense of Political Economy and Selected Papers and Reviews on Economic Theory*, Vol. 1, London: Routledge, pp. v–xxiii.
Salin, Edgar (1934), 'List teorico del nazionalismo economico', *La Riforma Sociale*, **45**, 424–7.
Shibata, Kei (1933), 'Marx's analysis of capitalism and the general equilibrium theory of the Lausanne School', *Kyoto University Economic Review*, **8** (1), 107–36.
Shinohara, Miyohei (ed.) (1958), *Stability and Progress in Economies: In Celebration of 60th Birthday of Professor Dr Ichiro Nakayama*, Tokyo: Toyo Keizai.
Shionoya, Yuichi (ed.) (2001), *The German Historical School: The Historical and Ethical Approach to Economics*, London, UK and New York, USA: Routledge.
Skene Smith, N. (1929), *Economic Control: Australian Experiments in 'Rationalisation' and 'Safeguarding'*, London: P.S. King & Son.
Skene Smith, N. (1934), 'British economic theory during the last four years', *Journal of Economics*, The Society of Economics, University of Tokyo, **4** (3), 74–99.
Spengler, Joseph J. (1970), 'Notes on the international transmission of economic ideas', *History of Political Economy*, **2**, 131–51.
Spinelli, Altiero (1984), *Come ho tentato di diventare saggio. I. Io, Ulisse*, Bologna: Il Mulino.
Spinelli, Altiero (1993), *Machiavelli nel XX secolo. Scritti del confino e della clandestinità 1941–1944*, Piero Graglia (ed.), Bologna: Il Mulino.
Spinelli, Altiero and Ernesto Rossi (1941), *Il Manifesto di Ventotene* [The Ventotene Manifesto], new edition 1982, Napoli: Guida.
Suenaga, Takasuke (1950), 'The Great Depression and non-Marxian economics: with a central focus on Robbins' arguments', *Keizaigaku Zashi*, or *Journal of Economics*, Osaka University of Commerce, Nihon Hyoron Inc., **23** (4), 1–37.
Suenaga, Takasuke (1953), 'Modern economics', in Deguchi (ed.), *A History of Economic Thought*, Kyoto: Minerva Publishing Co., pp. 382–431.
Sugihara, S. and T. Tanaka (eds) (1998), *Economic Thought and Modernization in Japan*, Cheltenham, UK and Lyme, NH, USA: Edward Elgar.
Sugimoto, Eiichi (1953), *A History of Modern Economics*, Tokyo: Iwanami Shoten Publishers.
Sugimoto, Eiichi (1960 [1950]), *Explications of Modern Economics*, volumes 1 & 2, Tokyo: Rironsha.
Sugimura, Kouzo (1938), *A History of Economic Methodology*, Tokyo: Risosha.
Sugiyama, Chuhei (1994), *Origins of Economic Thought in Modern Japan*, London, UK and New York, USA: Routledge.
Takata, Yasuma (1949), *The Methodology of Economics*, Tokyo: Koishikawa Shobo.

Talamona, Mario (1960), 'Sull'evoluzione metodologica di Lionel Robbins', *L'industria*, **1**, 74–89.
Tomita, Shigeo (1950), 'Differences in thought patterns between materialism and scarcity definitions of economics', *Mita Journal of Economics*, **43** (3), 23–50.
Tsuji, Rokubei (1958), 'A methodological basis of economic science: a comment on Robbins's *Essay*', in M. Shinohara (ed.), *Stability and Progress in Economics: In Celebration of 60th Birthday of Professor Ichico Nakayama*, Tokyo: Toyo Keizai, pp. 133–66.
Vito, Francesco (1932a), Review article, 'Lionel Robbins, *An Essay on the Nature and Significance of Economic Science*, 1932', *Rivista Internazionale di Scienze Sociali*, 564–6.
Vito, Francesco (1932b), 'Depressione mondiale e crisi della teoria economica', *Rivista Internazionale di Scienze Sociali*, 637–46.
Vito, Francesco (1934), *La concezione biologica dell'economia. Considerazioni sul sistema del Marshall*, Milano: Vita e Pensiero.
Vito, Francesco (1935), Review article, 'Lionel Robbins, *Di chi la colpa della grande crisi? – La grande depression*', *Rivista Internazionale di Scienze Sociali*, **6** (6), 782–3.
Vito, Francesco (1936), Review article, 'Lionel Robbins, *An Essay on the Nature and Significance of Economic Science*, II edition', *Rivista Internazionale di Scienze Sociali*, **7** (6), 532–3.
Vito, Francesco (1937), 'Morale et économie', *Revue d'économie politique*, **51** (1), 43–9.
Vito, Francesco (1938), 'L'oggetto della scienza economica', *Giornale degli Economisti*, feb., 89–103.
Yamada, Yuzo (1938), 'Economic planning and price theory', *Hitotsubashi Review*, **1** (3), 37–56.
Yamada, Yuzo (1942), *Economic Theory of Planning*, Tokyo: Iwanami Shoten Publishers.
Yasui, Takuma (1933), Review Article, 'Lionel Robbins, *An Essay on the Nature and Significance of Economic Science*. 1932. pp. ix 141. Macmillan, London', *Journal of Economics*, The Society of Economics, University of Tokyo, **3** (6), 124–31.
Yasui, Takuma (ed.) (1980), *Modern Economics and Myself: Conversations with Four Specialists*, Tokyo: Bokutaku-sha.
Yasui, Takuma (1981), 'In the memory of Professor Nakayama', in T. Nakayama (ed.), *Ichio, his Eighty-Year Life*, Tokyo: Chuo Koron Business Publishers, pp. 261–7.
Uzawa, Hirofumi (1970), 'Problems of bewilderment in modern economics', *Nikkei*, 4 January.
Zagari, Eugenio (1982), 'Introduzione', in O. Mancini, F.D. Perillo and E. Zagari (eds), *Lateoria economica del corporativismo*, Napoli: ESI, pp. 1–12.
Zagari, Eugenio (2004), 'Il corporativismo come presunta sintesi fra liberismo e socialismo', in Piero Bini and Claudio Mazziotta (eds), *Sviluppo economico e istituzioni: la prospettiva storica e l'attualità. Scritti in memoria di Massimo Finoia*, Milano: Angeli, pp. 52–72.

10. The *Kyoto University Economic Review* (1926–44) as importer and exporter of economic ideas: bringing Lausanne, Cambridge, Vienna and Marx to Japan

Robert W. Dimand and Masazumi Wakatabe[1]

10.1 INTRODUCTION

The *Kyoto University Economic Review* (KUER) provided an outlet for English (and occasionally German) translations of articles by members of the Economics Department of Kyoto Imperial University, one of the two interwar Japanese imperial universities that had independent economics departments. Published twice a year from 1926 and then quarterly from 1939 until publication was suspended in 1944 (resumed 1950), it was based on translations of articles from a monthly scholarly journal in Japanese, *Keizai Ronso* (founded in 1915, superceding earlier, short-lived Kyoto academic journals), which gave considerable attention to the Western economic tradition, publishing substantial supplements to mark the 150th anniversary of the birth of Thomas Robert Malthus in 1916 and the bicentenary of Adam Smith's birth in 1923.[2] The *Review* was the first, and except for short-lived journals published by the Osaka College of Commerce from 1933 to 1937 and by the Kobe College of Commerce from 1938 to 1942, the only foreign-language economics journal in interwar Japan. It was also the first English-language economics journal founded, written and published by people whose native language was not English, followed a year later by the *Chinese Economic Journal* (founded in 1927: see Trescott, 2007). The *Indian Journal of Economics* began publication in 1916, but its founding editors, both at the University of Allahabad, were British: H. Stanley Jevons (son of William Stanley Jevons) and C.D. Thomson.

Beginning with its 73rd volume in 2004, the *Kyoto University Economic Review* changed its name to the *Kyoto Economic Review* and, instead of publishing translations of the research of Kyoto faculty members, became an open refereed journal inviting submissions.[3]

In the interwar *Kyoto University Economic Review*, Kei Shibata brought together general equilibrium analysis and Marxian economics; Yasuma Takata developed his power theory of economics (to which his student Michio Morishima drew attention in the 1990s); Hideo Aoyama analysed the monetary economics of D.H. Robertson and the Stockholm School; Shibata and Takata responded to J.M. Keynes's *General Theory*; and Shibata and Koji Matsuoka discussed Cassel's version of the quantity theory of money. As late as April 1943, during the Second World War (when writing in English about a British author was politically incorrect and perhaps dangerous for a Japanese scholar), Aoyama wrote about Hicks's general equilibrium analysis, specifically his theory of a group of commodities. Shibata's general equilibrium approach to Marx was noted by Maurice Dobb and Oskar Lange, but otherwise these ventures received little notice in the West at the time, despite efforts to attract attention by distributing many complimentary copies of the journal.

The *Review* not only provided exposition and critique of Western economics, but also published articles by Yasuzo Horie and especially by Eijiro Honjo on Japanese economic history and the history of Japanese economic thought and by Kinji Tajima and Fumio Hozumi on the history of Chinese economic thought, making the history of East Asian economic thought accessible to readers of English. Honjo's book *Social and Economic History of Japan* (Kyoto 1935, reprinted in New York, 1965), first published as a series of articles in the *Kyoto University Economic Review*, attracted the attention of specialists in Japanese history such as E. Herbert Norman (in a 1940 monograph reprinted in 1975, 120, 126, 130, 166, 167, 169, 170, 176) and G.C. Allen (1981, first edn 1946, 176, 178). Norman also cited KUER articles by Honjo and Yasuzo Horie and two books in Japanese by Horie (Horie 1935, 1938; Norman, 1975, 123, 152, 158, 166, 177, 185, 206), and Allen (1981 [1946], 290–92) listed KUER articles by I. Otsuka, Y. Yagi, and K. Taniguchi in his bibliography. Honjo's subsequent book on *Economic Thought and History of Japan in the Tokugawa Period* (Kyoto 1943, reprinted 1965), also originally a series of articles in the *Kyoto University Economic Review*, initially attracted less notice because of its wartime publication.

The *Review*, together with *Keizai Ronso*, provides insight into the reception of Western economic theory in interwar Japan (including the interplay between Marxian and non-Marxian economics), and also into the attempts made to display Japanese economic scholarship to the outside world in the generation preceding Michio Morishima, Takashi Negishi, Hakukane Nikaido, Nobuo Okishio and Hirofumi Uzawa, whose work succeeded in attracting the close attention of European and North American economic theorists.

From the 1890s to the First World War (plus a final contribution in 1923, 30 years after his first paper), Juichi Soyeda, who had attended Marshall's lectures in Cambridge and addressed the Cambridge Moral Sciences Club on national traditions in economics before becoming an undersecretary in the Finance Ministry and President of the Japan Industrial Bank, wrote a series of letters from Japan for the *Economic Journal* covering Japanese economic events as well as Japanese economic scholarship (see Soyeda, 1893 and 16 subsequent *Economic Journal* contributions by him; and Sugiyama and Mizuta, 1994),[4] but the *Kyoto University Economic Review* went beyond such a one-person venture to attempt systematically to make the scholarly output of a leading Japanese economics department available to readers of English. However, language of publication proved not to be the only barrier to international communication. To a much greater extent than the present, interwar economists published in their own national journals and did not read widely outside the national traditions in which they were trained (even in the post-war era, the Australian growth theorist Trevor Swan published only in the *Economic Record*, limiting international attention to his work).

In the literature, the *Kyoto University Economic Review* and contributions to the *Review* have not received due attention: Tessa Morris-Suzuki's *History of Japanese Economic Thought* (1989) and Koichi Hamada's 'The Impact of the *General Theory* in Japan' (1986) (and, following Hamada, Hadley, 1989) naturally focused on what Japanese economists wrote in Japanese, failing to mention that there were interwar publications by Japanese economists in English, attempting for instance to take part in the international debate over Keynes's *General Theory* (1936) (for which see Ikeo, 1993, 1997). Nor did Morris-Suzuki mention Soyeda's earlier writings. Shiro Sugihara's history of Japanese economic journals (Sugihara, 1987b) is published only in Japanese, and those articles in English that focus on the KUER and on interwar economics at Kyoto Imperial University (Negishi, 2004; Sakurada, 2004; Yagi, 2004) all appeared in the KUER and so did not reach Anglophone readers not already acquainted with the journal. Translations of some of Takata's books on his power theory of economics (Takata, 1995; Morishima, 1998) did not mention that, although Takata's theory had not previously been available in book form in Western languages, he had presented his power theory in the KUER in English in Takata (1929) and in German in Takata (1932).

By focusing on these attempts at international communication, this chapter will reconsider the meaning and boundary of dissemination of economic ideas and intellectual community. The fact that the *Kyoto*

University Economic Review did not receive much attention from Western economists despite the flourishing intellectual activities at Kyoto (which included an economic history journal, *Keizai Shi Kenkyu*, as well as the monthly *Keizai Ronso*), and despite vigorous attempts to reach out to a broader intellectual community, showed the extent of separation between intellectual communities in interwar economics.

10.2 ECONOMICS AT KYOTO IMPERIAL UNIVERSITY

Kyoto Imperial University (now Kyoto University) was founded in 1897, the second imperial university in Japan, preceded only by Tokyo Imperial University (now the University of Tokyo). Economics was taught in the School of Law (founded in 1899 with four economics professorships) until a separate Economics Department was created in 1919 with eight professorships (increased to ten in 1922). The first Kyoto economics professors, Kinji Tajima, Kaichi Toda[5] and Masao Kambe, were Tokyo Imperial University graduates who had studied in Germany under the influence of the German Historical School and joined the Association for the Study of Social Policy, the Japanese replica of the Verein für Sozialpolitik, as did their colleagues (and fellow Tokyo alumni) Hajime Kawakami and Shiro Kawada, who had not studied in Germany (Yagi, 2004).[6] Although Tajima never endorsed socialism and eventually became a conservative critic of Marxism, Yagi (2004, 14) reports that Tajima's 'brief summary of Marx's socialism in 1897 was probably one of the first publications to introduce the concept of Marxism to the Japanese public'.

The first issue of the *Kyoto University Economic Review* included articles by eight of the university's ten economics professors and by two associate professors. According to the second issue, 200 of the 1000 copies of the inaugural issue were placed on sale at the Maruzen Book Store and '800 copies were presented to universities, libraries, institutions and professors of various nations . . . 200 for England, 200 for America, 100 for Germany, 100 for France, 100 for Japan, and 100 for other countries', followed by a letter to the recipients asking them to confirm their subscriptions and suggest other recipients. Most of the articles in KUER were translated from *Keizai Ronso* by journalists who had worked on English-language newspapers in Japan, such as The *Japan Times* and The *Japan Chronicle*, with foreign professors in the Faculty of Letters supervising the translators (Sakurada, 2004, 3).

In the inaugural issue of KUER in July 1926, Hajime Kawakami's essay 'On Marx's "forms of social consciousness"' was balanced by

Kinji Tajima's (1926) 'New theory of surplus and the harmony of the various classes of society', which argued against the idea of class conflict. Masao Kambe, the Professor of Public Finance, offered a 'Proposal for a Personal Tax on Luxury Consumption', and continued to publish in each of the first 22 issues of the KUER up to December 1936, writing on taxation from the standpoint of the German Historical School, advocating progressive income and inheritance taxes. Although like all the other full professors of economics he left Kyoto University by 1946 (in his case, by retirement), Kambe reappeared in the KUER with articles on local public finance in April 1954 and April 1955. Eijiro Honjo, Professor of Economic History, contributed 'On peculiarities of the economic development of Japan' (Honjo, 1926) to the inaugural issue, and from July 1926 to July 1942 published in 27 of the first 40 issues of the KUER (including the articles collected as his books, Honjo, 1935, 1943). After the Second World War, while teaching at Osaka Prefectural University,[7] Honjo returned to the KUER with articles on 'Post-war national life in Japan' in October 1957 (Honjo, 1957b) and 'The development of the study on the history of Japanese economic thought' (Honjo, 1959) in October 1959. Together with Shibata (1956), these invited articles by Kambe and Honjo in the late 1950s marked the reconciliation between the Economics Department[8] of Kyoto University and its dismissed or otherwise departed former professors.

Saburo Shiomi, assistant professor and later Professor of Statistics, published in 26 issues of the KUER up to October 1942, discussing the index numbers of the Bank of Japan in the first issue and seasonal fluctuations in Japanese public finance in the second issue, but mostly writing about Japanese national income estimates and statistics of taxation. Seiji Takarabe, a full professor, contributed to three issues of the KUER, on surprising topics: 'Suicide statistics in Japan according to sex' in July 1926 (Takorabe, 1926a), 'A bird's-eye view of Japanese pickles' in December 1926 (Takorabe, 1926b), and 'On the fish-diet of the Japanese' in December 1932.

Political trends interfered with the development of economics at Kyoto Imperial University as at other Japanese universities. Hajime Kawakami, who had published on Marx's 'forms of social consciousness' in the inaugural issue of the KUER (Kawakami, 1926), was one of five Marxist professors dismissed from the imperial universities in 1928 (Bernstein, 1976; Mitchell, 1976; Marshall, 1992; Sugihara, 1996). Subsequently, such repression of 'dangerous thought' was extended beyond Marxists to social democrats, liberals, pacifists and internationalists, notably in 1933 when the Minister of Education dismissed Kyoto Imperial University law professor Yukitoki Takigawa despite the protests of the university's president, faculty and students, with Takigawa unable to publish until after the war (Hane, 1986; Tsurumi, 1986; Marshall, 1992). According to Mikiso Hane (1986, 285–6):

> In July, 1936, and then again the following February, there were mass arrests of Marxists as well as of socialist professors, who were engaged in academic disputations about the nature of the Meiji Restoration and where Japan stood in its stage of historical development . . . In the early 1930s, any work containing anti-war sentiments was rooted out and banned. Studies in economics were hit the hardest; not only Marxist writings but the works of classical economists were also prohibited. Any work with the word 'capitalism' in the title was immediately rejected. The only acceptable theories in this field, as one economist later remarked, were the kind to be found in the *Kojiki* [a mythological 'history' of Japan compiled in the 670s] or *The Analects of Confucius*.

Nonetheless, although Honjo, Hozumi, and Tajima wrote in the KUER on the long history of Japanese and Chinese economic thought, the KUER published studies of the theories of Keynes, Robertson and Hicks by Aoyama (1941a, 1941b, 1943), Shibata (1937, 1939b) and Takata (1937), and included the word 'capitalism' in the titles of Shibata (1933a) and Y. Horie (1936).[9] However, Kyoto economists were not immune to the wartime nationalism that swept up Japanese writers and scholars of diverse pre-war opinions (see Keene, 1964 [1981]; Crowley, 1971; Shillony, 1982), and the KUER published Taniguchi (1942) on the trade policy of the East Asia Wider Territory, Sakuda (1938) on 'Der Absolute Staat', and Nakagawa (1943) on 'The Nazis' human image as a historical realization'. Taniguchi was a member of Showa Kenkyukai, described by Yagi (2004, 17) as the 'policy think tank for Duke Fumimaro Konoe'. Konoe was Prime Minister until shortly before Pearl Harbor (after the surrender he committed suicide knowing that he would have been prosecuted as a Class A war criminal by war crimes courts).

According to Yagi (2004, 18):

> During wartime, philosophers of the Kyoto University were notorious for their legitimization of the war by a speculative 'philosophy of the world history' . . . During the post-war period, the GHQ of the Allied Forces suspected that Kyoto had been the cradle of 'militarism and ultra-nationalism' and purged nine professors by directly issuing a memorandum. Two of these were philosophers, one was a historian, and the remaining six were economists. Taniguchi, Shibata, and Ishikawa were on the list . . . Although Takata was not on the list [having retired from Kyoto Imperial University in 1944], he was judged 'unfit' for the teaching position by the examination committee that was organized by the faculty. He demanded a revision of this judgment from the Minister of Education and finally acquired it in 1949.

This enabled him to become a professor at Osaka University two years later.[10] Criticism by junior members of the Economics Department of the wartime conduct of their senior colleagues, notably through the well-funded Institute for East Asian Economy established in 1940 to promote the East Asia Wider Territory and the Greater East Asia Co-Prosperity Sphere (see Lebra, 1975), erupted at Kawakami's funeral in January 1946, and led to the resignation and departure of all the full professors, to be replaced in part by hiring new faculty and in part by promotion of the younger Kyoto scholars Hideo Aoyama, Yuzo Deguchi and Yasuzo Horie. This was not the last time that political upheavals affected economics at Kyoto University: publication of the KUER and *Keizai Ronso* became irregular during the 1970s: 'due to the outbreak and recurrence of the student unrest that annoyed the faculty for a decade starting from 1969' (Sakurada, 2004, 5).

10.3 HONJO, HOZUMI AND JAPANESE AND CHINESE ECONOMICS

The Institute for Research in Economic History of Japan was founded at Kyoto Imperial University in 1933 by Eijiro Honjo and Iwao Kokusho, with its own journal of economic history in Japanese (see Borton, 1961). Honjo published regularly in the KUER, but Kokusho, a full professor of agricultural history since 1926, never contributed to the KUER, presumably because his appointment was in the Department of Agriculture, rather than in the Department of Economics. Kokusho published the first Japanese translation of Max Weber's *General Economic History* in 1927, and the following year published a book on peasant riots in the Tokugawa period (Kokusho, 1928), concluding that these were not yet revolutionary class struggles, and that agrarian relations remained feudal (see also Borton, 1937 [1968]). After Kokusho's death, the Kyoto economist Hideo Aoyama published a revised second edition in 1954–55 with Aoyama and Kokusho listed as joint translators (Yagi, 2004, 16–17). After studying the formal economic theorizing of Robertson and Hicks (Aoyama, 1941a, 1941b, 1943), Aoyama (1944, 1950) turned to Weber's historical and sociological approach.

Eijiro Honjo wrote extensively in the KUER on Japanese economic and social history and on the history of Japanese economic thought, the latter a subject otherwise largely neglected (but see Neil Skene Smith, 1935, 1937). Honjo made exceptional efforts to communicate his research to an international audience, not only publishing dozens of articles in the KUER but also collecting these articles in English-language books published by his institute in Kyoto (Honjo, 1935, 1943, both reprinted in New York in

1965). He also published a note in the *Economic History Review* in Britain (Honjo, 1934) announcing the institute's economic history journal, and contributed to the International Statistical Institute's *Bulletin* an article on population problems in the Tokugawa period (Honjo, 1931), based on an article in the KUER (Honjo, 1927). While he did not find a wide readership outside Japan, his work on Japanese social and economic history (but not his work on the history of Japanese economic thought) attracted the notice of a few specialists, such as G.C. Allen (1981, first edn 1946) and especially the Canadian scholar of Japan, E. Herbert Norman, whose 1940 Harvard doctoral dissertation and Institute for Public Relations monograph cited Honjo more often than any other scholarly authority (Norman, 1975).

It is noteworthy that Honjo (1943 [1965]) chose to publish his second collection of KUER articles in English during wartime. However, Honjo (1942a, 1942b) wrote about the concept of a distinctive 'Japanese political economy' suited to Japan's 'national polity' and embodying economic principles different from those that might prevail in other societies, a politically-loaded approach that went far beyond drawing attention to the neglected history of Japanese economic thought prior to the opening to the West. Writing about the history of ancient Chinese economic thought, as Honjo's colleagues Kinji Tajima (1927) and Fumio Hozumi (1940, 1942, 1943) did in KUER, was also politically acceptable in the anti-Western atmosphere of wartime, but did not have the same inconvenient post-war taint of association with militant Japanese nationalism, so that Hozumi (1954, 1964) continued to publish his research on ancient Chinese economic thought in the KUER.[11] Thanks to Honjo and Hozumi, the KUER was the leading Western-language source for the history of Japanese and Chinese economic thought, although Western historians of economic thought failed to take advantage of that resource – not even Joseph Schumpeter, who had visited Japan in 1931, whose wife wrote on Japanese industrialization, and who consulted some Western books on ancient Chinese thought (Schumpeter, 1954, 53). After the war, teaching at Osaka Prefectural University (formerly Osaka College of Commerce, to which Honjo followed his Kyoto colleague Kawada in 1942), Honjo (1957a, 1962) published in the journal of his new university on the introduction of Western economics in Japan, but also returned once to the KUER to recall the beginnings of the study of the history of Japanese economic thought (Honjo, 1959).

After the war, Yasuzo Horie dominated economic history at Kyoto University as Professor of Economic History from 1945 to 1967. As a prewar fellow of Kokusho's and Honjo's institute, Horie had written on the formation of Japanese capitalism (Horie, 1936, 1938) and on the system of monopolies in Japan (Horie, 1935), daringly radical topics for the late 1930s. These works attracted the notice of Herbert Norman. Later, however, 'entrepreneurship' rather than 'capitalism' was the keynote of Horie's work (1965, 1966), as the young radical mellowed with age. The debate in the 1930s over the nature of Japanese capitalism, to which Horie (1936, 1938) contributed, was dominated by the dispute between the Koza school (proponents of the orthodox Stalinist or Comintern line that Japanese agrarian relations were still feudal, so that a bourgeois democratic revolution had to precede a proletarian revolution) and the Rono school (labelled Trotskyist by their opponents), who held that Japanese agrarian relations of production were no longer feudal in the orthodox Marxist sense of the term, so that Japan was ready for a proletarian revolution (see Borton, 1961; Tsuru, 1964; Yasuba, 1975; Hoston, 1986).

John Dower, in his monograph-length introduction to Norman (Norman, 1975, 35–8), denied that Norman's 1940 thesis *Japan's Emergence as a Modern State* reflected the rather mechanical formulas of the Koza–Rono debate, and pointed out that Norman never mentioned most of the leading Koza and Rono writings (with a few exceptions, such as the Rono scholar Takao Tsuchiya, 1937 [1977]). Quite so, but perhaps one should go beyond the list of Japanese scholars who did not influence Norman's view of the development of Japanese capitalism to consider those who did: the Kyoto economic historians Eijiro Honjo (1935 [1965], plus KUER articles later collected in Honjo, 1943 [1965]), cited by Norman (1975, 120, 126, 130, 166, 167, 169, 170, 176), Yasuzo Horie (1935, 1936, 1938), cited by Norman (1975, 123, 152, 158, 166, 177, 185, 206), and Iwao Kokusho (1928), cited by Norman (1975, 149, where Norman also cited a mimeographed 1935 study of peasant revolts by Kokusho's student Hidenosuke Numazaki).

10.4 MARX AND GENERAL EQUILIBRIUM: KAWAKAMI AND SHIBATA

Described by Takashi Negishi (2004, 2) as 'in a sense the first great economist in Japan', Hajime Kawakami (1879–1946) taught economics at Kyoto Imperial University from 1908 until his politically motivated forced resignation in 1928, and was imprisoned from 1932 to 1937 (see Bernstein, 1976; Sugihara, 1996; Inoue and Yagi, 1998; and his collected works, Kawakami 1982–86, 36 volumes). Initially, in addition to being influenced by the German Historical School, Kawakami 'was attracted by E.R.A. Seligman's economic interpretaion of history as well as by the marginalist economic theories of F.A. Fetter, J.B. Clark and I. Fisher' (Inoue and Yagi, 1998, 61). He became a Marxist-Leninist after the

Russian Revolution in 1917, although he did not formally join the (illegal) Japanese Communist Party until 1932, at the age of 53. Some of his Marxist studies of the historical development of capitalism, notably the 1928 Chinese translation of Kawakami (1923), were influential in Chinese translations in the 1920s and 1930s (Mita, 2003, cited by Yagi, 2004, 14). Kawakami began publishing his Japanese translation of Marx's *Capital* in serial form in 1927, but it was left incomplete upon his arrest in 1932.

Although he contributed extensively to *Keizai Ronso*, Kawakami (1926) only published once in English in the KUER before his dismissal from the university. Kawakami's teaching of principles of economics at Kyoto Imperial University then passed in 1930 to Yasuma Takata (1883–1971; Professor of Economics at Kyushu Imperial University 1925–30, and at Kyoto Imperial University 1930–44). Kei Shibata attended Kawakami's seminar on Marx's *Capital* and subsequently learned general equilibrium theory from Takata. The Kyoto economic historian Eijiro Honjo also studied with Kawakami. Through his former students, Kawakami had an influence on economics at Kyoto Imperial University, and on the growth of Marxian economics in Japan, much greater than might be suggested by his single article in the KUER.[12]

Influenced by his teachers Kawakami and Takata, Kei Shibata (1902–86) took up the project of combining Marx's schemes of simple and expanded reproduction with a simplified Walrasian general equilibrium system to advance Marxian economics in KUER articles (Shibata, 1933a, 1933b, 1934, 1937, 1939a) and in a two-volume treatise of more than 1000 pages on theoretical economics (Shibata, 1935–36). The author of 22 books and 122 articles, Shibata became a lecturer in economics at Kyoto Imperial University in 1929, associate professor in 1931, and full professor in 1939. Shibata was forced to resign in 1946 because of his wartime involvement in the New Order Movement, through which he advocated a non-communist planned economy (see Shibata, 1943; Yagi, 1997). He later taught at Yamaguchi University from 1952 and then from 1960 at Aoyama Gakuin University (see Sugihara, 1987a and Sugihara et al. 1991 on Shibata's life and writings).

Shibata (1933a) on 'Marx's general equilibrium analysis and the general equilibrium theory of the Lausanne School' attracted the notice of Oskar Lange ('Marxian economics and modern economic theory', 1935), Shibata (1934) was cited in a footnote by Maurice Dobb[13] (1937, 112n), and Shibata (1934, 1939b) were cited in a footnote by Paul Sweezy (1956 [1942], 105n). These mentions, together with the praise of Shibata (1937, 1939a) and Takata (1937) on Keynes by Dudley Dillard (1948, 57–8), were the high-points of contemporary Western attention to KUER articles on economic theory, but Shibata's main influence on Marxian economics outside Japan was delayed and indirect: Nobuo Okishio's well-known demonstration that the profit rate need not fall when technological improvements increase the organic composition of capital (Okishio, 1961) generalized and extended results that Shibata (1934, 1939b) had found for a very simplified case (Negishi, 1995, 1998, 2004, who uses the term 'Shibata–Okishio Theorem' for what is known oustide Japan as the Okishio Theorem; see also Rieu, 2009 on the 'Shibata–Okishio connection').

Shibata spent a year at Harvard studying with Joseph Schumpeter in 1936 (with a side-trip to New York City to meet Oskar Lange), and then went to England where, thanks to a letter of invitation from the Japanese ambassador, he lunched at Keynes's house in April 1937, although without achieving any serious discussion of economics with Keynes (Shibata, 1987, 60–63; Hamada, 1986, 464; Ikeo, 1997, 64–65). Shibata (1939b) reported that before that lunch, Shibata had sent Keynes a list of questions about Keynes's *General Theory* (1936) and received a reply, but Shibata (1987) recorded that both his letter and Keynes's reply were later lost. In October 1939, Shibata was invited to the Cowles Commission's 1940 summer conference, but had to decline because the Japanese government refused to pay his travel expenses (Ikeo, 1996, 126). Despite his junior academic rank until 1939, Shibata was better known among Western economic theorists in the 1930s, and his KUER articles were more often cited by them (even if only brief mentions in footnotes), than by any other Kyoto economist.

10.5 POWER, CAPITAL AND INTEREST THEORY

Japanese economists before the Second World War were quite well versed in a wide and diverse literature in economics. There had been a vigorous interest in the interactions between the economy and the society among economists such as Eugen von Böhm-Bawerk, Max Weber, Vilfredo Pareto and Joseph Schumpeter, which constituted the context. Yasuma Takata, whose research programme was influenced by, and shared with, those economists, took a serious interest in sociology: indeed he is considered now as one of the first sociologists in Japan.[14] Takata wrote a series of books on the topics. Although his works had not been translated in book form until Morishima, a student of Takata's, helped to make translations of various works of Takata on the 'power theory of economics' accessible to a wider audience (Takata, 1995; Morishima, 1998), it should be noted that the gist of Takata's arguments had been already available in German and English through the KUER (Takata, 1929, 1932, 1934, 1935).

The power theory of economics was the centrepiece of Takata's economics (Hayasaka, 1981, 133; Yagi, 1999, Chapter 6). Takata began with the examination of Böhm-Bawerk's famous article (Böhm-Bawerk, 1914) in which he claimed that extra-economic, social powers did not play a role in determining prices such as the wage rate. Takata countered that: 'the factor of social powers, or, to be more specific, of social powers as extra-economic powers, must not be neglected in any explanation of economic phenomena' (Takata, 1934, 95). However, as commentators noted, Takata changed his position towards the precise role of social powers in the economy several times, due to several criticisms (Hayasaka, 1981, 138; Negishi, 1998, 101). Takata considered the distinguishing feature of his power theory to be its general equilibrium theory framework against which the role of social powers was examined. He first maintained the impossibility of pure economic theory without the theory of extra-economic powers: the determination of price, factor prices in particular, would necessarily entail extra-economic powers.

He dealt first with wage determination: wages were determined by social powers rather than simply by the working of supply and demand. Of course he would deny the supply–demand analysis as such, admitting also that there were both upper and lower limits to wages. However, the supply price of labour, the 'requisite means of livelihood for them are what labourers have been *customarily* obtaining as wages or what their employers have been *customarily* paying them and estimating in their profit and loss accounts' (Takata, 1929, 20, emphasis added). The supply and demand curves derived were necessarily based on habit and customs. Culture would affect the quality of intellectual labour, and explain the disparity of wages between men and women, and between different nations (Takata, 1929, 32). In another article, turning to the simultaneous determination of wage and interest rates, Takata examined the validity of 'natural interest rate or interest in equilibrium' (1934). Examining also Wicksell's algebraic formulation (Wicksell, 1893), he claimed that equilibrium would be indeterminate without the quantity of labour being given exogenously, which he took as evidence that powers were necessary.

Then he shifted to the position which allowed the role of pure general economic equilibrium theory independent from extra-economic powers as a first approximation to the real economy, while it required the power theory as a second approximation. He once claimed that 'so long as the economy is pure in my sense and there is no action of powers, there can be no equilibrium interest', but now he conceded that Böhm-Bawerk's 'interest in equilibrium must be the real equilibrium interest and that accordingly the economic intervention of power is by no means an indispensable condition of the determination of an equilibrium interest' (Takata, 1935, 20).

Shibata sided with Takata on this topic, concentrating on Böhm-Bawerk's claim that: 'the attempt to raise wages over and above where they are, as determined by free competition, invariably causes the reduction of the total income of the working class' (Shibata, 1935, p. 113). The purpose of Shibata's 1935 paper was to reveal a concealed 'momentous assumption which has . . . not hitherto been pointed out by anybody – an assumption which has a necessary connection with his negation of "Macht-theorie"' (Shibata, 1935, 107). After elucidating Böhm-Bawerk's numerical examples, he demonstrated that the total amount of wages could increase when the wage rate increased. Shibata detected Böhm-Bawerk's 'error' in his 'assumption regarding the technical composition of capital of products of various kinds and on a peculiar assumption in regard to the annual product of the labourer' (Shibata, 1935, 122). Shibata further remarked that: 'labourers (or the State) can exert their influence on capitalists and can influence counter-measures which capitalists may decide to adopt against the labourers' demand for higher wages'.

However, both Böhm-Bawerk and Shibata assumed the value of the total wage fund, or K, to be given exogenously outside the system. Negishi pointed out that K should be an endogenous variable even in their model, in which it should be derived from the saving function in the stationary economy; he showed that the total amount of wages could increase when the wage rate increased (Negishi, 1995, 1998, 2004). In the end, Shibata's criticism was correct, but not on his ground.

As Negishi and others pointed out, it is fair to say that their venture, especially Takata's, however ambitious it might be, did not succeed as they planned. But their emphasis on and interest in the influence of social powers in the economy could not be dismissed easily. Martin Bronfenbrenner noted similarities between Takata's power theory and the bargaining theory of the Institutionalists of the Wisconsin School (Bronfenbrenner, 1981, p. 476). Kiichiro Yagi thought that Takata's research programme was still worth a re-examination in the light of the recent revival of economic sociology (Yagi, 1999, 148). Takata considered the 'irrational' factors such as emulation among labour unions as the driving force of the wage settlement. In this regard, one might also be able to point out the recent rediscovery of the 'irrational' in mainstream economics due to the development of behavioral economics as a further confirmation of their foresights.

10.6 THE QUANTITY THEORY OF MONEY: MATSUOKA, SHIBATA AND TANIGUCHI ON CASSEL, THE GREAT DEPRESSION AND THE GOLD STANDARD

The Kyoto economists contributed to monetary economics as well. Shibata started his academic career in economics by studying works of monetary economics such as those by the German and Austrian writers Karl Helfferich, Friedrich Bendixen, Karl Elster, G.F. Knapp, Ludwig von Mises and Joseph Schumpeter (Shibata, 1987, 17–18).[15] Although Shibata's teacher Hajime Kawakami was one of the first Japanese economists to introduce Irving Fisher's work to Japan, there was no sign that Shibata learned Fisher from Kawakami, mainly because Kawakami had become a Marxist when Shibata took Kawakami's seminar course at Kyoto Imperial University. Shibata ventured into other areas of economics, but monetary economics remained close to his heart. When the Great Depression hit the world's economies, Shibata thought that the 'Great Depression must have something to do with money' (Shibata, 1987, 24), and began investigating the works of Gustav Cassel (1927, 1930). The result was Shibata's 1932 paper.[16]

Cassel was then widely known as one of the authorities on money and exchange rates. His *Theoretische Sozialökonomie* (Theory of social economy) was translated into Japanese in 1926, three years after the English translation appeared in 1923.[17] Cassel's theory of long-run price movements was based on the quantity theory of money, but what received special attention was his empirical confirmation of the theory, which was later adopted as a basis for the First Interim Report of the Gold Delegation of the Financial Committee of the League of Nations, which appeared in September 1930. Cassel assumed that a certain rate of economic growth ('economic progress') required a certain rate of money growth; so, the argument went, what explained the long-run movement was not just the amount of gold stock, but the amount of gold stock relative to gold demand, which he called 'relative gold stock'. From this perspective, he distinguished between actual gold stock and normal gold stock, calculating the latter assuming a 3 per cent growth rate, and then he related the movement of the general price level to the relative gold stock, showing the positive correlation between the two series.[18]

Cassel (1926) wrote a short study of the Japanese currency for a Swedish ball-bearing company, which gave a copy of the study to the Japanese government, which gave copies to scholars at the Imperial University of Tokyo, after which it was published in Japanese translation and also summarized in *Toyo Keizai Shimpo* by the journalist (and post-war Finance Minister) Tanzan Ishibashi, who received a copy from from the Tokyo University mathematician Rikitaro Fujisawa (Ikeo, 1997, 54–5, 69). Cassel recommended that Japan return to the gold standard at the current exchange rate, rather than at the old parity.

After carefully surveying the relevant literature such as Kitchen (1930) and Woytinsky (1931), Shibata examined Cassel's theory in three steps: first he clarified what characteristics of data one should collect; second, he examined the available data; and third, he investigated whether the quantity theory of money could explain the variations of the price level since the First World War. Although he found Cassel's data and computing method quite wanting, he subscribed to the monetary explanation of the long-run price movements. Furthermore, Shibata extended the data set beyond Cassel's.[19] In this sense, Shibata went beyond what Cassel did, since Cassel's empirical investigation covered only up to 1910. The puzzle for Shibata was a wide gap between the general price level and the relative gold stock since the First World War (Shibata, 1932, 70). This failure was due to the large variations in the velocity of money due to the aftermath of the suspension of the gold standard during the war years:

> it was only because the currencies of almost all nations were ultimately connected with the stock of monetary gold that the variations of the stock of monetary gold had close connections with that of the general level of prices in gold; but with the Great War, the currencies of most nations of the world became emancipated from this yoke. (Shibata, 1932, 70)

He saw the deflation as the result of the contraction of the velocity of money *V* following the reconstruction of the gold standard system:

> V which was greatly expanded as the result of the emancipation of money from the yoke of gold was suddenly contracted to almost the normal size as soon as the United States took the decisive step in the direction of the gold standard system and all nations had to prepare themselves for a return to that system. (Shibata, 1932, 75)

However he also conceived the subsequent reversal of *V*, since the gold stock did not decrease, while the output stagnated, predicting even that 'the downward trend of prices is bound to come to a full stop' (Shibata, 1932, 77). Furthermore, he advocated the 're-suspension of the gold standard by some of the principal nations of [*sic*] and the devaluation of their currencies' (1932, 77) since that would raise the relative stock of gold and in turn the general price level.

In its emphasis on the deflationary role of the gold standard, what he termed the 'yoke of gold', in the interwar price movement and the role of its suspension in ending the Great Depression, Shibata's argument resembled the current international view of the Great Depression, or at least a part of the monetary interpretation of the Great Depression (Eichengreen, 1992). In the end, however, Shibata pointed out the fear of a 'general disturbance of its economic intercourse' caused by a prolonged suspension of the gold standard, and did not propose its abolition. Therefore, one cannot argue that Shibata was free from the gold standard mentality, but this was justifiable since he based his predictions on the post-First World War experience. A noted Japanese empirical business cycle economist, Miyohei Shinohara (1991, 60), remarked that one should appreciate Shibata not only as an economic theorist but also as a superb empirical economist, praising him as the first Kuznetsian and Friedmanian in Japan.

Koji Matsuoka, then an assistant professor, also examined Cassel and the League of Nations Interim Report of the Gold Delegation in a manner more critical than Shibata. First he pointed out that: 'The ideas and opinions of the Gold Delegation Report should in fact be described as a quantity theory of gold' (Matsuoka, 1934, 76–7). After casting doubts on the calculation method of Cassel's estimate,[20] he criticized Cassel's theory in two respects. First, he thought that Cassel already assumed the validity of his quantity theory before he examined it empirically. It required a separate analysis of economic growth: 'a dynamic examination of the general economic development or the increase of general economic transactions should take into consideration other causes, such as increase of population, technical progress, etc' (Matsuoka, 1934, 91). Second, concurring with Albert Aftalion's criticism of Cassel,[21] he pointed out that Cassel ignored the velocity of money component (Matsuoka, 1934, 92). Thus Matsuoka concluded his essay in an altogether negative tone about Cassel and the quantity theory:

> the quantity theory is not necessarily a key to the solution of the problem of the relationship between the gold supply and the general level of prices in the world today. The theory has no real importance in the world, being supported by the Gold Delegation merely to serve the purpose of certain financial capitalists. (Matsuoka, 1934, 93).[22]

Another assistant professor, Kichihiko Taniguchi (1932b), took issue with the inflation policy by the Hoover administration, which had so far failed. Although he diagnosed the cause of the ongoing depression as the 'lack of the people's purchasing power' (Taniguchi, 1932b, 53), endorsing the general purpose of raising the general price level, he found the policy seriously ineffective, since the current policy was to inject money to the top, 'finance capitalists'. Thus he conceived the 'Supplying Purchasing Power' Plan whose purpose was to inject funds directly to the people of the lower classes.[23]

At the same time in Western academia, the theory and empirics of Cassel and the 1930 League of Nations Report were under scrutiny. J.T. Phinney of Harvard University examined Cassel's estimates, casting doubt on his underlying assumptions concerning the methodology of computing 'normal gold growth rate' (Phinney, 1933); and Allan Fisher of the University of Otago, New Zealand, questioned Cassel's assumption of the proportionate relationship between gold demand and gold supply (Fisher, 1935), to which Cassel responded.[24] Cassel did not seem to have known Shibata's or Matsuoka's KUER papers, but George F. Warren and Frank A. Pearson, both farm economists at Cornell University and proponents of the 'gold purchase plan' to reflate the American economy, listed Shibata (1932) in their bibliography (Warren and Pearson, 1933, 126). There was a vigorous discussion about possible ways to reflate the world economy during the Great Depression: the KUER papers of Shibata and Taniguchi were offered as contributions to this international discussion. The monetary works in the KUER showed that Japanese economists were well versed in the literature and willing to contribute to the discussion.

10.7 CAMBRIDGE MACROECONOMICS REACHES JAPAN: SHIBATA, TAKATA AND AOYAMA ON KEYNES AND ROBERTSON

John Maynard Keynes and his economics received a great deal of attention in Japan. Hayashida's *Fifty Year History of the Studies of Keynes' General Theory* (1986, in Japanese) has a 17-page index of authors listing 970 Japanese names and a 55-page bibliography, mostly of Japanese titles (Ikeo, 1997, 39). Korekiyo Takahashi has sometimes been referred to as Japan's Keynes because he followed a policy of deficit finance and easy money as Finance Minister during the Depression from December 1931 until his assassination in 1936.[25] In November 1929 he also put forward an incomplete multiplier analysis, stressing secondary rounds of spending and employment, but without discussing the leakages that cause the spending multiplier to have a finite value (Nanto and Takagi, 1985; Cha, 2003; Smethurst, 2007). Such an incomplete mutliplier analysis had been advanced a few months earlier in 1929 by Keynes and Hubert Henderson in their pamphlet *Can Lloyd George Do It?* (Keynes, 1971–89, Vol. 9, 86–125). Keynes's writings were translated into Japanese soon after publication. In 1915, just two years after the publication of Keynes's *Indian Currency and Finance* (Keynes, 1971–89, Vol. 1), Saichiro Takashima translated the first three chapters from it as an appendix on the gold exchange standard to his textbook on money and prices, Kanji Okabe and Sanao Uchiyama translated *A Tract on Monetary Reform* (Keynes, 1971–89, Vol. 3) in 1924, the year after it appeared in English, and Nisaburo Kito translated Keynes's *Treatise on Money* (Keynes, 1971–89, Vols 4–5) in five volumes from 1932 to 1934, not long after the original publication in 1930 (Ikeo, 1997, 46, 50, 63). The Kyoto economists were thus very far from alone among Japanese scholars and policy-makers in giving close attention to Keynes (see Hayasaka, 1993 for interviews with leading Japanese who studied Keynes), but among Japanese economists only Shibata (1937, 1939b) and Takata (1937) in English, sought to take part in the international conversation about Keynes – a fact overlooked by Morris-Suzuki (1989), Hamada (1986) and Hadley (1989), although noted by Dillard (1948, 157–58).

In 'Unemployment and wages: a critical review of Mr Keynes' theory of unemployment', Takata (1937) agreed with Keynes about the possibility of involuntary unemployment. However, while he read Chapter 2 of Keynes's *General Theory* as being about downward rigidity of money wages, Takata argued that there is also downward rigidity of real wages. While Keynes rejected what he termed 'the second classical postulate' that the utility of the wage equals the marginal disutility of capital (the economy is on the labour supply curve) but accepted the 'first classical postulate' that the real wages equals the marginal product of labour (the economy is on the labour demand curve), Takata insisted that logical consistency should have led Keynes to reject both classical postulates. This would leave Keynes with no theory of wages, so Takata offered his own power theory to fill the lacuna.

Shibata (1939b, 60) complained that: 'Mr. Keynes entirely or almost entirely overlooks the relevance of such factors as wage, working day, intensity of labour, productivity, social unrest, and monopoly profit' (that section of Shibata's paper was titled 'Evils of monopoly capitalism'). Keynes's claim to be assuming a given money wage as a matter of convenience seemed to Shibata to evade much that belonged in a full analysis of capitalism. Shibata (1937, 90) insisted that: 'new investment may not necessarily increase the volume of employment but may possibly decrease it'. Increased investment might result from a diversion of resources from consumption to investment, rather than having a multiplier effect on consumption. Shibata did not find Keynes's paradox of saving at all persuasive.

Hideo Aoyama, a former student of Takata at Kyoto who became a lecturer there in 1936 (assistant professor 1940, full professor from 1946), expounded and critically examined D.H. Robertson's method of period analysis, J.R. Hicks's concept of a commodity group, and Hicks's temporary-equilibrium method (Aoyama, 1941a, 1941b, 1943). His teaching of Hicks and general equilibrium strongly influenced Michio Morishima. Although he was a full professor at Kyoto University until his retirement in 1973, Aoyama only published once in the post-war KUER (Aoyama and Nishikawa, 1958). Aoyama (1941b, 81) concluded that: 'the structure of liquidity preference is essentially incompatible with the postulates of period analysis and consequently it is impossible to analyse adequately by this method the effects of the interest rate on the price formation of illiquid assets accordingly of the commodities generally'. His articles are remarkable for their serious, insightful treatment of Robertson and Hicks that gave no hint of any political difficulties (or even, in 1943, full-scale war) between Britain and Japan. Aoyama's articles stand out from those of Takata and Shibata.

Takata (1937) and Shibata (1937, 1939b) were written by accomplished theorists (Dillard, 1948 praised Shibata's articles as 'excellent') and are interesting for their idiosyncratic reactions to Keynes, Takata proposing to supplement Keynes's theory with Takata's own power theory, as he would propose to supplement any theory. One would not, however, turn to their articles to learn what Keynes's economics was about, whereas Aoyama's articles are useful not just for Aoyama's reactions to Robertson and Hicks but also for understanding what Robertson and Hicks had to say.

In 'Fatal errors newly in Keynesian theory', Shibata (1956) returned to the KUER to argue that Keynes's economics had too many equations for the number of unknowns, that Keynes misrepresented classical economics and that, contrary to Keynes's paradox of saving, saving was the foundation of capital accumulation and wealth creation, views he further expounded in *Beyond Keynesian Economics* (1977). He also continued to participate in the post-war international conversation of economic theory in English with a 94-page monograph, *Critical Study of Mr Hicks' Cycle Theory* (Shibata, 1952). Takata also continued to wrestle with the Keynesian challenge, publishing a collection of his *Critical Essays on Keynes* (Takata, 1955), but in Japanese.

10.8 CONCLUSION: TOWARDS THE NEXT GENERATION

The *Kyoto University Economic Review* was a landmark effort in international communication in interwar economics. The Kyoto economists not only took part in importing many varities of Western economics into Japan, as with the translations of Marx's *Capital* by Kawakami, Weber's *General Economic History* by Kokusho and Aoyama, and of Aftalion's *Monnaie, Prix et Change* by Matsuoka. They also attempted, by publishing their own journal in English (with a few articles in German), to engage directly in discussion and debate with Western economists, despite the handicap of slow shipment of journals by sea. And also that of disruptions that mirrored the more general political history of Japan, from the dismissal of Kawakami in 1928 and his imprisonment in 1932–37, to the purge of Ishikawa, Shibata and Taniguchi by the Occupation authorities in 1945.

While Aoyama, Matsuoka, Shibata, Takata and Taniguchi engaged in critique and extension of the monetary, cycle, and interest theories of Böhm-Bawerk, Wicksell, Cassel, Aftalion, Keynes, Robertson and Hicks, Honjo and Hozumi made the history of Japanese and Chinese economic thought accessible to Western economists if they (apart from Neil Skene Smith) had cared to pursue the subject (Morris-Suzuki, 1989 cites Honjo, 1943, although by the date of the 1965 New York reprint, but otherwise makes no use of material from the KUER – or of Smith 1935). The KUER showcased the work of an extremely active department that published a monthly journal in Japanese; Takata alone published more than a 100 books and 500 articles (Shibata published 22 books and 122 articles; Aoyama 10 books and more than 200 articles). Other interwar Japanese economists undertook strategies to draw their research to the attention of foreign scholars, as when S. Ogata (1934 [1936]) published his paper about Japanese export control both in English in Japan in the newly founded journal of his university (Osaka College of Commerce, later Osaka Prefectural University), and in German in *Weltwirtschaftsliches Archiv*.

While their efforts at international communication by the Kyoto economists were prodigous, their success in attracting international attention was limited. Dudley Dillard (1948, 57–58) briefly noted Shibata and Takata on Keynes, and stated that 'Shibata's articles are excellent', but Keynes did not respond in print to Shibata or Takata, although he answered some of Shibata's questions (he also gave Shibata lunch, but without serious discussion). Warren and Pearson (1933) included Shibata's critique of Cassel in their bibliography, but Cassel took no notice of Shibata or Matsuoka. Lange (1935) cited Shibata's effort to apply the methods of general equilibrium theory to Marxian economics, but the subsequent literature chose to regard Lange (1935) as the originator of that project. Maurice Dobb (1937) and, through the influence of Shigeto Tsuru and following Shibata's visit to Harvard, Paul Sweezy (1956 [1942]), know Shibata's KUER articles on technical change and the falling rate of profit, but what Negishi calls the 'Shibata–Okishio Theorem' is known among Marxian economists outside Japan as the 'Okishio Theorem', so that Shibata (1933a, 1934, 1939a) exerted an international influence primarily indirectly, through the influence in of Shibata's writings in Japan on Okishio (1961).

When Takata's power theory was made available in book form in English (Takata, 1995; Morishima, 1998), it had been forgotten that Takata had made his theory available in German and English in the KUER (Takata, 1929, 1934, 1935). Contemporary Western specialists in

Japanese economic and social history, notably G.C. Allen and E. Herbert Norman, relied closely on the researches of the Kyoto economic historians Honjo, Kokusho and Y. Horie (although much less on Honjo's studies of the history of Japanese economic thought than on his writings on Japanese economic history). This influence has been overlooked in John Dower's study of Norman as an historian of Japan (in Norman, 1975).

Perhaps the strongest immediate impact of the KUER was through its long series of articles by Kawada and then by Y. Yagi (notably Y. Yagi, 1936) on land tenure in Japan, the leading source of such material available in English to guide the sweeping land reform imposed by the Supreme Command of the Allied Powers (SCAP) during the MacArthur shogunate.

Within Japan, scholarship on the Kyoto economists who published in the KUER includes substantial memorial volumes on the three major economic historians among them – Aoyama, Shibata and Takata – written mostly in Japanese but with a few contributions such as Bronfenbrenner (1981) in Western languages (Aoyama Hideo Chosakushu Kankokai 1999; Sugihara et al., 1991; Takata Yasuma Hakishi Tuisoroku Kankokai, 1981), as well as Sugihara (1987b) on Japanese economic journals. Three articles in English about the KUER – Negishi (2004), Sakurada (2004) and K. Yagi (2004) – appeared in the KUER's successor, the *Kyoto Economic Review*.

But there is a missing dimension in much of the English-language literature on the history of Japanese economics because of neglect of the KUER, just as the interwar Kyoto economists had only limited success to reaching a Western audience. By looking only at publications in Japanese about Keynes and Keynesian economics, Hamada (1986), Hadley (1989) and Morris-Suzuki (1989) present that story solely as one of importation of foreign ideas and their adaptation to Japanese conditions, overlooking the attempt to respond in Western languages and to engage Western economists in intellectual exchange (but compare Ikeo, 1997). The Kyoto economists were engaged in importing, critiquing and reformulating Western economic ideas, but also in making Japanese economic scholarship accessible to Western readers, engaging in the international development of economic theory (especially monetary and employment theory), and providing an account in English of Japanese economic history and the history of Japanese and Chinese economic thought.

The pre-1944 KUER had a considerable degree of continuity of tone due to long series of articles by the same handful of Kyoto professors, even though Honjo's topics, for example, were very different from those of Kambe or Shibata. After the KUER resumed publication in 1950 (without editorial comment on the six-year hiatus), the size and diversity of the post-war economics faculty worked against any such characteristic tone. It is difficult to identify the intended audience for the April 1971 issue, which consisted of three articles, on 'Modernization of the function of the assemblers in each local producing area in Japan' (Takemodo, 1971). 'On the Nash solution' (Sechiyams; 1971), and 'Rosa Luxemburg's arguments on the socialist movements' (Takemodo, 1971). In terms of international developments in post-war economics, perhaps three articles by Charles Yuji Horioka (1984, 1985, 1987) analysing saving in Japan are most notable. With the post-war internationalization of economics (Ikeo, 1996, 2006) and proliferation of journals, the postwar KUER was not as remarkable a pheomenon as the interwar KUER. While Aoyama, Shibata and Takata struggled to find an international audience in interwar and wartime economic theory, the post-war generation of Japanese economic theorists included such internationally renowned figures as Morishima, Negishi, Nikaido and Uzawa. Morishima was influenced by Takata (Takata, 1995; Morishima, 1998) and was introduced to the work of Hicks by Aoyama; Negishi (1995, 1998, 2004) has written repeatedly about Shibata and Takata; and, among Marxian economists, the very influential work of Okishio (1961) was influenced by Shibata. The interwar Kyoto economists had incomplete success with their extraordinary effort in international communication of economic ideas, but the post-war generation of Japanese economic theorists included several world-recognized scholars, some of whom were influenced and shaped by inter-war Kyoto economics and the KUER.

NOTES

1. We appreciate helpful comments from Hidetomi Tanaka and anonymous referees. Wakatabe would like to thank the Japan Society for the Promotion of Science (Grant No. 18530150), and Waseda University Grant for Special Research Projects (2006K-010) for indispensable financial assistance.
2. These supplements were early landmarks in the continuing Japanese tradition of scholarship on these British classical economists: see Kishimoto (1950) on Malthus's economics, the lead article in the first issue of the KUER after publication resumed, and Adamu Sumisu no Kai (1955 [1970]) for a bibliography of Japanese studies of Smith. See Sugiyama and Mizuta (1988) for later Japanese scholarship on the subject. Even in the early days, Kyoto economists engaged with the latest developments in Western economics, not just the classics: in 1913–14, Masao Kambe of Kytoto Imperial University engaged in a controversy with Kakujiro Yamazaki of Tokyo Imperial University and Senjiro Takagi of Keio University about Irving Fisher's compensated dollar plan (Ikeo, 1997, 43).
3. All papers of all volumes of the KUER are now available on the Kyoto University's Economic Review Database: http://www.econ.kyoto-u.ac.jp/review/.
4. Soyeda was not quite alone in interpreting Japanese economic development to European audiences at the turn of the century. For readers of German, Tokuzo Fukuda's Munich doctoral dissertation supervised by Lujo Brentano (published in

Stuttgart as Fukuda, 1900) discussed Japanese social and economic development (see Inoue and Yagi, 1998). The American Economic Association published Yeijiri Ono's monograph on 'The industrial transition in Japan' (Ono, 1890), and the Meiji era statesman Shigenobu Okuma (1900) wrote about 'The industrial revolution in Japan' in the *North American Review* (see Lebra, 1973 on Okuma, who was Prime Minister in 1898 and later founded Waseda University).

5. Kaichi Toda, prominent among the first cohort of economics professors at Kyoto Imperial University, died in 1924, two years before the start of the KUER.
6. See Pyle (1974) on the influence of the German Historical School of economics in Japan.
7. Honjo moved to the Osaka College of Commerce (later Osaka Prefectural University) in 1942, after his Kyoto colleague Shiro Kawada became president of that college. Kawada published on agricultural tenant systems in Japan, Korea and Taiwan in five of the first six issues of the KUER, up to December 1928. Subsequently, Yoshinosuke Yagi published on such agricultural topics in 16 issues of the KUER between December 1930 and January 1943. Kiichiro Yagi (2004, 16) reports that: 'It is said that American experts who drafted the post-1945 agricultural policy benefited from [Yoshinosuke Yagi's] articles printed in the KUER' (see Y. Yagi, 1936; Ikeo, 1993; Ikeo, 1994, 47–8).
8. Referred to as the Faculty of Economics in the KUER after it resumed publication in 1950, although its Japanese name (Keizai Gakubu) remained the same as when it was known as the Department of Economics.
9. As this example shows, Hane exaggerated the censorship of academic writings during the 1930s, although it is no doubt that the censorship existed. Neither were works on classical economics prohibited, nor was any work with 'capitalism' in the title was immediately rejected. We thank one anonymous referee for raising this point. According to NDL-OPAC, an online catalogue of the National Diet Library of Japan, there were 77 titles with the words 'capitalism' or 'capitalistic' published from 1937 to 1944. They include not only the Japanese translations of the works of Werner Sombart and Max Weber, but also the *History of World Economic Crises* by the Soviet Academy of Sciences.
10. Before being purged by the Allied Forces, Koji Ishikawa, full Professor of the History of Economics and Economic Philosophy at Kyoto since 1930 and a proponent of a 'Japanese political economy' suited to Japan's national polity (*kokutai*), had already lost his chair on a charge of 'disguised communism' for criticizing the aggressive policy of the Japanese militarists (Yagi, 2004, 18). Takata's rehabilitation was completed in 1965 with his designation as a Person of Cultural Merit (*Bunka Korosha*).
11. Political upheaval affected the reception of Kyoto economic history in other ways as well: the Canadian diplomat E. Herbert Norman, Honjo's most attentive Western reader, was driven to suicide by McCarthyite persecution for such youthful transgressions as taking part in a Marxist study group at Harvard with Paul Sweezy and Shigeto Tsuru (and the Canadian Keynesians Robert Bryce and Lorie Tarshis) that met five times in 1937 (see Bowen, 1986).
12. Kawakami was not forgotten at Kyoto University: the post-war KUER published articles about Kawakami by Yuzo Deguchi in October 1962 and by Eiji Ohno in October 1985.
13. After the KUER resumed publication in 1950, Dobb (1955) published in the KUER a reply to a critique by Hideichi Horie (1953) of Dobb's analysis of the historical development of capitalism.
14. A Japanese publishing company, Minerva Shobo, issued a three-volume selection of Takata's sociological writings in 2004. When a new research institute – now the Institute of Social and Economic Research – was established at Osaka University after the Second World War in 1954, Takata, the founder and first director, insisted on including the adjective 'social'. See Tominaga (1975) on Takata as a sociologist.
15. See Ellis (1934) for an overview of a rich German monetary tradition from which Shibata learned.

16. Shibata (1932) was incorporated in his *magnum opus* (Shibata, 1935–36, Vol. II, 819–38, 932–38) as parts of lengthy footnotes (see also Shibata, 1971).
17. The translation was based on the German third edition. Yasuma Takata used it as the textbook for his first 'Economic Principles' course at Kyoto Imperial University in 1929, which course Shibata attended, although he was already appointed as a tenured lecturer.
18. For discussion of Cassel's theory of long-run price movements, see Jonung (1979).
19. Shibata later recalled that he had to spend a considerable part of his inherited fortune to collect data (Shibata, 1987, 26).
20. Matsuoka was silent about Shibata's relevant works, perhaps because of his different and more critical attitude toward the quantity theory of money. Also Matsuoka had a Marxian bent, while Shibata was more critical towards Marxian economics (notwithstanding his contributions to integrating Marxian economics with general equilibrium theory and to the Shibata–Okishio Theorem about the falling rate of profit).
21. Matsuoka translated Aftalion's *Monnaie, Prix et Change* (Aftalion, 1927) into Japanese in 1937.
22. Matsuoka's KUER paper was incorporated into his 1933 book (Matsuoka, 1933) which began with a chapter on the gold exchange standard. He later wrote a paper on the history of the gold exchange standard system in Japan (1935) and another book on the topic (1937).
23. On this plan, he had already published a 300-page book in August of 1932 (Taniguchi, 1932a). However, his first contribution to the *Kyoto University Economic Review* concerned the correlation between spot and forward rice prices (Tanigachi, 1931).
24. Cassel thought that these criticisms were misunderstandings, and continued to uphold his main arguments (Cassel, 1935, 110–15, 118).
25. He was also Minister of Finance 1913–14, 1918–22 and 1927; Prime Minister 1921–22; and Governor of the Bank of Japan. Korekiyo Takahashi's translation of Alfred Marshall and Mary Paley Marshall's *The Economics of Industry* (1879 [1994]) was published by the Ministry of Education in 1886, so his attention to Cambridge economics was of long standing (Smethurst, 2007).

REFERENCES

Adamu Sumisu no Kai [Adam Smith Society] (1955), *Honpo Adamu Sumisu Bunken* [Works relating to Adam Smith in Japan], Tokyo: Kobundo; enlarged 2nd edition (1970), Tokyo: Tokyo Daihgaku Shuppan-kai.

Aftalion, Albert (1927), *Monnaie, Prix et Change: Expériences Récentes et Théorie*, Paris: Recueil Sirey; Japanese trans. (1937) by Koji Matsuoka, Kahei Bukka Kawaseron, Tokyo: Yuhikaku.

Allen, G.C. (1981 [1946]), *A Short Economic History of Modern Japan*, 4th edn, London: Macmillan.

Aoyama, Hideo (1941a), 'A critical note on D.H. Robertson's theory of savings and investment (I)', *Kyoto University Economic Review*, **16** (1), 49–73.

Aoyama, Hideo (1941b), 'A critical note on D.H. Robertson's theory of savings and investment (II)', *Kyoto University Economic Review*, **16** (2), 64–81.

Aoyama, Hideo (1943), 'On the extension of the concept of a commodity: a note on Hicks' theory of the "Group of Commodities"', *Kyoto University Economic Review*, **18** (2), 48–68.

Aoyama, Hideo (1944), 'Die rechnungsmassige Rationalitat als grundlegendes Merkmal der modernen Volkswirtschaft (I)', *Kyoto University Economic Review*, **19** (1), 44–60.

Aoyama, Hideo (1950), *Max Weber no Shakai Riron* [Sociological theory of Max Weber], Tokyo: Iwanami.
Aoyama, Hideo and Toru Nishikawa (1958), 'Business fluctuations in Japanese economy during the inter-war period', *Kyoto University Economic Review*, **28** (1), 14–39.
Aoyama Hideo Chosakushu Kankokai [Society for the Publication of the Works of Aoyama Hideo] (ed.) (1999), *Aoyama Hideo Sensei no Gakumon to Kyouiku* [The study and the education of Aoyama Hideo), Tokyo: Sobunsha.
Bernstein, Gail L. (1976), *Japanese Marxist: A Portrait of Kawakami Hajime, 1879–1946*, Cambridge, MA: Harvard University Press.
Böhm-Bawerk, Eugen von (1914), 'Macht oder ökonomisches Gesetz?', *Zeitschrift für Volkswirtschaft, Sozialpolitik und Verwaltung*, **23**, 201–71, translated (1962) as 'Control or Economic Law' in *Shorter Classics of Eugen von Böhm-Bawerk*, Vol. I, South Holland, IL: Libertarian Press.
Borton, Hugh (1937) 'Peasant uprisings in Japan of the Tokugawa period', *Transactions of the Asiatic Society of Japan*, Series 2, **14**, reprinted (1968), New York: Paragon Book Reprint Organization.
Borton, Hugh (1961), 'Modern Japanese economic historians', in W.G. Beasley and E.G. Pulleyblank (eds), *Historians in China and Japan*, Oxford: Oxford University Press, pp. 288–306.
Bowen, Roger W. (1986), *Innocence Is Not Enough: The Life and Death of Herbert Norman*, Armonk, NY: M.E. Sharpe.
Bronfenbrenner, Martin (1981), 'Professor Takata Yasuma, a foreigner's recollections', in Takata Yasuma Hakushi Tuisoroku Kanokai [Society for the Memorial Publication of Dr. Takata Yasuma] (ed.), *Takata Yasuma Sensei no Shougai to Gakusetsu* [The life and theory of Takata Yasuma], Tokyo: Sobunsha, 471–84.
Cassel, Gustav (1926), 'The Japanese currency', study on behalf of A.-B. Svenska Kullagerfabriken SKF, Japanese translation in *Ginko Tsushinroku*, **81** (483), 492–8.
Cassel, Gustav (1927), *Theoretische Sozialökonomie*, 4, Aufl. Leipzig: A. Deichertsche Verlagsbuchhandlung Dr. Werner Scholl.
Cassel, Gustav (1930), 'The supply of gold', *First Interim Report of the Gold Delegation*, Geneva: League of Nations.
Cassel, Gustav (1935), *On Quantitative Thinking in Economics*, Oxford: Clarendon Press.
Cha, Myung Soo (2003), 'Did Takahashi Korekiyo rescue Japan from the Great Depression?' *Journal of Economic History*, **63** (1), 127–44.
Crowley, James B. (1971), 'Intellectuals as visionaries of the new Asian order', in James Morley (ed.), *Dilemmas of Growth in Prewar Japan*, Princeton, NJ: Princeton University Press, 319–73.
Deguchi, Yuzo (1962), 'Two kinds of truth conceived by Hajime Kawakami – an analysis of *A Story of Poverty*', *Kyoto University Economic Review*, **32** (2), 39–53.
Dillard, Dudley (1948), *The Economics of John Maynard Keynes*, Englewood Cliffs, NJ: Prentice-Hall.
Dobb, Maurice Herbert (1937), *Political Economy and Capitalism*, London: Routledge & Kegan Paul.
Dobb, Maurice Herbert (1955), 'Capital accumulation – a note in reply to Professor Horie', *Kyoto University Economic Review*, **25** (1), 42–8.

Eichengreen, Barry (1992), *Golden Fetters: The Gold Standard and the Great Depression, 1919–1939*, New York: Oxford University Press.

Ellis, Howard S. (1934), *German Monetary Theory, 1905–1933*, Cambridge, MA: Harvard University Press.

Fisher, Allan G.B. (1935), 'Does an increase in volume of production call for a corresponding increase in volume of money?' *American Economic Review*, **25** (2), 197–211.

Fukuda, Tokuzo (1900), *Die gesellschaftliche und wirtschaftliche Entwicklung in Japan*, Stuttgart: Cotta.

Hadley, Eleanor M. (1989), 'The diffusion of Keynesian ideas in Japan', in Peter A. Hall (ed.), *The Political Power of Economic Ideas: Keynesianism Across Nations*, Princeton, NJ: Princeton University Press, pp. 291–309.

Hamada, Koichi (1986), 'The impact of the *General Theory* in Japan', *Eastern Economic Journal*, **12** (4), 451–66.

Hane, Mikiso (1986), *Modern Japan: A Historical Survey*, Boulder, CO: Westview Press.

Hayasaka, Tadashi (1981), 'Nihon Keizaigakushi ni okeru Takata Yasuma Hakushi' [The place of Dr Yasuma Takata in the history of Japanese economic thought]', in Takata Yasuma Hakushi Tuisoorku Kaknkokai [Society for the Memorial Publication of Dr Takata Yasuma] (ed.), op.cit., 112–55.

Hayasaka, Tadashi (ed.) (1993), *Keynes tono Deai* [The encounter with Keynes], Tokyo: Nihonkeizai-hyoronsha.

Hayashida, M. (1986), *Keynes Ippan Riron Kenkyu 50 nenshi* [A fifty-year history of the studies of Keynes's *General Theory*], Tokyo: Taga Shuppan.

Honjo, Eijiro (1926), 'On peculiarities of the economic development of Japan', *Kyoto University Economic Review*, **1** (1), 74–81.

Honjo, Eijiro (1927), 'Population problems in the Tokugawa era', *Kyoto University Economic Review*, **2** (2), 42–63.

Honjo, Eijiro (1931), 'The population and its problems in the Tokugawa era', *Bulletin de l'Institut International de Statistique*, **25** (2), 60–82.

Honjo, Eijiro (1934), 'The economic-history year-book of Japan', *Economic History Review*, **4** (4), 461–3.

Honjo, Eijiro (1935), *Social and Economic History of Japan*, Kyoto: Institute for Research in Economic History of Japan, reprinted (1965) New York: Russell & Russell.

Honjo, Eijiro (1942a), 'The formation of "Japanese Political Economy"', *Kyoto University Economic Review*, **17** (2), 1–19.

Honjo, Eijiro (1942b), 'The original current of "Japanese Political Economy"', *Kyoto University Economic Review*, **17** (3), 1–19.

Honjo, Eijiro (1943), *Economic Thought and History of Japan in the Tokugawa Period*, Kyoto: Institute for Research in Economic History of Japan, reprinted (1965) New York: Russell & Russell.

Honjo, Eijiro (1957a), 'The development of economics in Japan', *Bulletin of University of Osaka Prefecture*, Series D, **1**, 1–14.

Honjo, Eijiro (1957b), 'The post-war national life of Japan', *Kyoto University Economic Review*, **27** (2), 1–18.

Honjo, Eijiro (1959), 'The development of the study on the history of Japanese economic thought', *Kyoto University Economic Review*, **29** (2), pp. 1–16.

Honjo, Eijiro (1962), 'Introduction of Western economics into Japan', *Bulletin of University of Osaka Prefecture*, Series D, **6**, 1–19.

Horie, Hideichi (1953), 'Dobb's theories of economic history', *Kyoto University Economic Review*, **23** (1), 30–45.
Horie, Yasuzo (1935), *Waga Kuni Kinsei no Sembai Sendo* [The monopoly system in our country in present times], Tokyo.
Horie, Yasuzo (1936), 'An outline of the rise of modern capitalism in Japan', *Kyoto University Economic Review*, **11** (1), 99–115.
Horie, Yasuzo (1938), *Nihon Shihonshugi no Seiritsu* [The formation of Japanese capitalism], Tokyo.
Horie, Yasuzo (1965), 'Entrepreneurship in Meiji Japan', in W.W. Lockwood (ed.), *The State and Enterprise in Japan*, Princeton, NJ: Princeton University Press, pp. 183–208.
Horie, Yasuzo (1966), 'The role of the Ie (house) in the economic modernization of Japan', *Kyoto University Economic Review*, **36** (1), 1–16.
Horioka, Charles Yuji (1984), 'The applicability of the life-cycle hypothesis of saving to Japan', *Kyoto University Economic Review*, **54** (2), 31–56.
Horioka, Charles Yuji (1985), 'The importance of saving for education in Japan', *Kyoto University Economic Review*, **55** (1), 41–78.
Horioka, Charles Yuji (1987), 'The cost of marriages and marriage-related saving in Japan', *Kyoto University Economic Review*, **57** (1), 47–58.
Hoston, Germaine A. (1986), *Marxism and the Crisis of Development in Prewar Japan*, Princeton, NJ: Princeton University Press.
Hozumi, Fumio (1940), 'Ssu-ma Chen's economic outlook', *Kyoto University Economic Review*, **15** (1), 16–29.
Hozumi, Fumio (1942), 'On the monetary ideas as seen in the records of economics and finance in the Sung history', *Kyoto University Economic Review*, **17** (3), 36–59.
Hozumi, Fumio (1943), 'The Chinese ideas of money', *Kyoto University Economic Review*, **18** (1), 34–57.
Hozumi, Fumio (1954), 'The characteristics of the history of Chinese money', *Kyoto University Economic Review*, **24** (2), 18–38.
Hozumi, Fumio (1964), 'Paper currency theory of Wang Lin', *Kyoto University Economic Review*, **34** (2), 1–34.
Ikeo, Aiko (1993), 'Japanese modern economics, 1930–1945', in R.F. Hebert (ed.), *Perspectives on the History of Economic Thought*, Vol. 9, Aldershot, UK and Brookfield, VT, USA: Edward Elgar, pp. 192–202.
Ikeo, Aiko (1994), *20 Seiki no Keizaigakusha Nettowaaku* [The network of economists in the twentieth century: the development of economics as viewed from Japan], Tokyo: Yuhikaku.
Ikeo, Aiko (1996), 'The internationalization of economics in Japan', in A.W. Coats (ed.), *The Post-1945 Internationalization of Economics*, Durham, NC: Duke University Press, Annual Supplement to *History of Political Economy*, **28**, 123–41.
Ikeo, Aiko (1997), 'Keynes and Keynesian economics in Pre-WWII Japan', *Transactions of the Institute for Japanese Culture and Classics*, **80**, 37–74.
Ikeo, Aiko (2006), *Nihon no Keizei-Gaku: 20 Seiki ni Okeru Kokusaika no Rekisi* [Economics in Japan: the internationalization of economics in the twentieth century], Nagoya: Nagoya Daigaku Syppan-kai.
Inoue, Takutoshi and Kiichiro Yagi (1998), 'Two inquirers on the divide: Tokuzo Fukuda and Hajime Kawakami', in Shiro Sugihara, and Toshiriro Tanaka (eds), *Economic Thought and Modernization in Japan*, Cheltenham, UK and Lyme, NH, USA: Edward Elgar, pp. 60–77.

Jonung, Lars (1979), 'Knut Wicksell and Gustav Cassel on secular movements in prices', *Journal of Money, Credit and Banking*, **11** (2), 165–81.

Kawakami, Hajime (1923), *Shihonshugi Keizaigaku no Shiteki Hatten* [The historical development of the political economy of capitalism], Kyoto: Kabundo.

Kawakami, Hajime (1926), 'On Marx's "forms of social consciousness"', *Kyoto University Economic Review*, **1** (1), 27–37.

Kawakami, Hajime (1982–86), *Zenshu* [Collected works], 36 vol, Tokyo: Iwanami Shoten.

Keene, Donald (1964), 'Japanese writers and the Great East Asia War', *Journal of Asian Studies*, **23** (2), 209–5, reprinted (1981) in Donald Keene, *Appreciations of Japanese Culture*, New York, Tokyo and San Francisco: Kodansha International, pp. 300–321.

Keynes, John Maynard (1936), *The General Theory of Employment, Interest and Money*, London: Macmillan.

Keynes, John Maynard (1971–89), *The Collected Writings of John Maynard Keynes*, 30 vol, general eds D.E. Moggridge and E.A.G. Robinson, volume eds Elizabeth S. Johnson and D.E. Moggridge, London: Macmillan and New York: Cambridge University Press for the Royal Economic Society.

Kishimoto, Seijiro (1950), 'Malthus's theories in classical economics', *Kyoto University Economic Review*, **20** (1), 1–37.

Kitchen, Joseph (1930), 'The supply of gold compared with the prices of commodities', *First Interim Report of the Gold Delegation*, Annex 11, Geneva: League of Nations.

Kokusho, Iwao (1928), *Hyakusho Ikki no Kenkyu* [A study of peasant revolts], Tokyo: Iwanami Shoten.

Lange, Oskar (1935), 'Marxian economics and modern economic theory', *Review of Economic Studies*, **2** (3), 189–201.

Lebra, Joyce C. (1973), *Okuma Shigenobu: Statesman of Meiji Japan*, Canberra: Australian National University Press.

Lebra, Joyce C. (ed.) (1975), *Japan's Greater East Asia Co-Prosperity Sphere in World War II: Selected Readings and Documents*, Oxford: Oxford University Press.

Marshall, Alfred and Mary Paley Marshall (1879), *The Economics of Industry*, London: Macmillan; reprinted (1994) with introduction by Dennis O'Brien, Bristol: Thoemmes Press.

Marshall, Byron K. (1992), *Academic Freedom and the Japanese Imperial Universities, 1868–1939*, Berkeley, CA: University of California Press.

Matsuoka, Koji (1933), *Kin Mondai Kenkyu* [Studies in the gold issues], Kyoto: Yuhikaku.

Matsuoka, Koji (1934), 'On the quantity theory of gold – with special reference to Prof. Cassel's theory', *Kyoto University Economic Review*, **9** (1), 76–94.

Matsuoka, Koji (1935), 'An early history of the gold-exchange standard in Japan', *Kyoto University Economic Review*, **10** (2), 88–110.

Matsuoka, Koji (1937), *Kin Kawase Honni Sei no Kenkyu* [Studies in the gold exchange standard], Tokyo: Nihon Hyoron Sya.

Mita, T. (2003), *Yomigaeru Kawakami Hajime: Kindai Chugoku no Chi Gensen* [Reviving Kawakami Hajime: an intellectual origin of modern China], Tokyo: Fujiwara Shoten.

Mitchell, Richard H. (1976), *Thought Control in Prewar Japan*, Ithaca, NY: Cornell University Press.

Morishima, Michio (ed.) (1998), *Joseph A. Schumpeter and Yasuma Takata: Power or Pure Economics?* London: Macmillan.
Morris-Suzuki, Tessa (1989), *A History of Japanese Economic Thought*, London, UK and New York, USA: Routledge.
Nakagawa, Yonosuke (1943), 'The Nazis' human image as a historical realization', *Kyoto University Economic Review*, **18** (3), 46–61.
Nanto, Dick K. and Shinki Takagi (1985), 'Korekiyo Takahashi and Japan's recovery from the Great Depression', *American Economic Review*, **75** (2), 369–74.
Negishi, Takashi (1995), 'Böhm-Bawerk and Shibata on power or market', *Journal of Economics (Zeitschrift für Nationalökonomie)*, **61**, 281–99.
Negishi, Takashi (1998), 'General equilibrium theory and beyond: Yasuma Takata and Kei Shibata', in Shiro Sugihara and Toshiriro Tanaka (eds), *Economic Thought and Modernization in Japan*, Cheltenham, UK and Lyme, NH, USA: Edward Elgar, pp. 97–116.
Negishi, Takashi (2004), 'Kyoto school of modern economic theory', *Kyoto Economic Review*, **73**, 1–10.
Norman, E. Herbert (1940 [1975]), *Japan's Emergence as a Modern State*, New York: Institute of Pacific Relations, as reprinted in Norman (1975).
Norman, E. Herbert (1975), *Origins of the Modern Japanese State: Selected Writings of E.H. Norman*, John W. Dower (ed.), New York: Pantheon.
Numazaki, Hidenosuke (1935), 'Hyakusho Ikki Chosa Hokokusho' [Reports and investigations of peasant revolts], Kyoto, mimeo.
Ogata, S. (1934), 'The control of the export trade in Japan', *Journal of the Osaka University of Commerce*, **1** (2), 105–33; also (1936) in German as 'Probleme der Exportkontrolle in Japan', *Weltwirtschaftsliches Archiv*, May 472–507.
Okishio, Nobuo (1961), 'Technical change and the rate of profit', *Kobe University Economic Review*, **7**, 85–99.
Okno, Eiji (1985), 'Theory of economic policy by Young Kawakami – in relation to the controversy over taxation of imported rice', *Kyoto University Economic Review*, **55** (2), 1–31.
Okuma, Shigenobu (1900), 'The industrial revolution in Japan', *North American Review*, **171** (5), 677–91.
Ono, Yeijiro (1890), 'The industrial transition in Japan', *Publications of the American Economic Association*, First Series, **5** (1), 1–122.
Phinney, J.T. (1933), 'Gold production and the price level: the Cassel three percent estimate', *Quarterly Journal of Economics*, **47** (4), 647–79.
Pyle, Kenneth B. (1974), 'Advantages of fellowship: German economics and Japanese bureaucrats, 1890–1925', *Journal of Japanese Studies*, **1** (1), 127–64.
Rieu, Dong-Min (2009), 'The Shibata–Okishio connection: labor theory of value and rate of profit', *Journal of the History of Economic Thought*, **31** (3), 325–39.
Sakuda, Shoichi (1938), 'Der Absolute Staat', *Kyoto University Economic Review*, **13** (2), 1–20.
Sakurada, Tadae (2004), '*Kyoto University Economic Review*, 1926–2003', *Kyoto University Economic Review*, Supplement, 1–5.
Schumpeter, Joseph A. (1954), *History of Economic Analysis*, Elizabeth Boody Schumpeter, (ed.), New York: Oxford University Press.
Sechiyama, Satoshi (1971), 'On the Nash solution', *Kyoto University Economic Review*, **41** (1), 29–48.

Shibata, Kei (1931), 'The subjective theory of value and theories of the value of money', *Kyoto University Economic Review*, **6** (1), 71–93.

Shibata, Kei (1932), 'An examination of Professor Cassel's quantity theory of money', *Kyoto University Economic Review*, **7** (1), 52–84.

Shibata, Kei (1933a), 'Marx's analysis of capitalism and the general equilibrium theory of the Lausanne School', *Kyoto University Economic Review*, **8** (1), 107–36.

Shibata, Kei (1933b), 'The meaning of the theory of value in theoretical economics', *Kyoto University Economic Review*, **8** (2), 49–68.

Shibata, Kei (1934), 'On the law of decline in the rate of profit', *Kyoto University Economic Review*, **9** (1), 61–75.

Shibata, Kei (1935), 'On Böhm-Bawerk's theory of interest rate', *Kyoto University Economic Review*, **10** (1), 107–27.

Shibata, Kei (1935–36), *Riron Keizaigaku* [Theoretical economics], 2 vol, Tokyo: Kabundo.

Shibata, Kei (1937), 'Some questions on Mr. Keynes' general theory of employment, interest and money', *Kyoto University Economic Review*, **12** (1), 83–96.

Shibata, Kei (1939a), 'On the general profit rate', *Kyoto University Economic Review*, **14** (1), 40–66.

Shibata, Kei (1939b), 'Further comments on Mr Keynes' general theory', *Kyoto University Economic Review*, **14** (3), 45–72.

Shibata, Kei (1943), 'Economic theory of planning', *Kyoto University Economic Review*, **18** (4), 19–41.

Shibata, Kei (1952), *Critical Study of Mr Hicks's Cycle Theory*, Tokyo: Kobundo.

Shibata, Kei (1956), 'Fatal error newly uncovered in Keynesian theory', *Kyoto University Economic Review*, **26** (1), 13–42.

Shibata, Kei (1977), *Beyond Keynesian Economics*, Kyoto: Minerva Press.

Shibata, Kei (1987), *Keizai no Hosoku wo Motomete* [In search of economic laws], revised edn, Tokyo: Nihon Keizai Hyoron Sha.

Shillony, Ben-Ami (1982), *Politics and Culture in Wartime Japan*, Oxford: Oxford University Press.

Shinohara, Miyohei (1991), 'Shibata Keizeigaku to Choikihado' [Shibata economics and long-run cycles], in S. Sugihara, S. Kumon and M. Nitta (eds), op.cit., pp. 23–61.

Smethurst, Richard J. (2007), *From Foot Soldier to Finance Minister: Takahashi Korekiyo, Japan's Keynes*, Cambridge, MA: Harvard University Press.

Smith, Neil Skene (1935), *An Introduction to Some Japanese Economic Writings of the Eighteenth Century*, London: P.S. King & Son.

Smith, Neil Skene (ed.) (1937), 'Materials on Japanese social and economic history: Tokugawa Japan', *Transactions of the Asiatic Society of Japan*, Series 2, **14** (June), 1–176.

Soyeda, Juichi (1893), 'The study of political economy in Japan', *Economic Journal*, **3**, 334–9.

Sugihara, Shiro (1987a), 'Shibata, Kei', *The New Palgrave: A Dictionary of Economics*, Vol. 4, John Eatwell, Murray Milgate, and Peter Newman (eds), London: Macmillan, p. 325.

Sugihara, Shiro (1987b), *Nihon no Keizai Zasshi* [Economic journals in Japan], Tokyo: Nihon Keizai Hyoron-sha.

Sugihara, Shiro (1996), *Tabibito Kawakami Hajime* [The intellectual journey of Hajime Kawakami], Tokyo: Iwanami Shoten.

Sugihara, Shiro, S. Kumon and M. Nitta (eds) (1991), *Shibata Keizaigaku to Gendai* [The Shibata economics and today], Tokyo: Nihon Keizai Hyoron Sha.

Sugiyama, Chuhei and Hiroshi Mizuta (eds) (1988), *Enlightenment and Beyond: Political Economy Comes to Japan*, Tokyo: University of Tokyo Press.

Sugiyama, Chuhei and Hiroshi Mizuta (1994), *The Origins of Economic Thought in Modern Japan*, London, UK and New York, USA: Routledge.

Sweezy, Paul M. (1956 [1942]), *The Theory of Capitalist Development*, New York: Monthly Review Press.

Tajima, Kinji (1926), 'New theory of surplus value and the harmony of the various classes of society', *Kyoto University Economic Review*, **1** (1), 1–14.

Tajima, Kinji (1927), 'Economic ideas revealed in the Chung Yung (The Doctrine of the Mean', *Kyoto University Economic Review*, **2** (2), 1–27.

Takarabe, Seiji (1926a), 'Suicide statistics in Japan classified according to sex', *Kyoto University Economic Review*, **1** (1), 173–87.

Takarabe, Seiji (1926b), 'A bird's-eye view of Japanese pickles', *Kyoto University Economic Review*, **1** (2), 192–200.

Takarabe, Seiji (1932), 'On the fish-diet of the Japanese', *Kyoto University Economic Review*, **7** (2), 76–88.

Takata, Yasuma (1929), 'A power theory of wages', *Kyoto University Economic Review*, **4** (2), 14–51.

Takata, Yasuma (1932), 'Macht und Wirtschaft', *Kyoto University Economic Review*, **7** (1), 136–57.

Takata, Yasuma (1934), 'A critical analysis of Boehm–Bawerk's theory of capital', *Kyoto University Economic Review*, **9** (1), 95–145.

Takata, Yasuma (1935), 'Introductory discourse on the theory of interest', *Kyoto University Economic Review*, **10** (1), 18–34.

Takata, Yasuma (1937), 'Unemployment and wages: A critical review of Mr Keynes' theory of unemployment', *Kyoto University Economic Review*, **12** (2), 1–18.

Takata, Yasuma (1955), *Keynes Ronnan* [Critical essays on Keynes], Kyoto: Yuhikaku.

Takata, Yasuma (1995), *Power Theory of Economics*, Douglas W. Anthony (trans.), London: Macmillan.

Takata Yasuma Hakushi Tuisoroku Kankokai [Society for the Memorial Publication of Dr Takata Yasuma] (ed.) (1981), *Takata Yasuma Sensei no Shougai to Gakusetsu* [The life and theory of Takata Yasuma], Tokyo: Sobunsha.

Takemoto, Nobuhiro (1971), 'Rosa Luxemburg's arguments on the socialist movements', *Kyoto University Economic Review*, **41** (1), 49–77.

Taniguchi, Kichihiko (1931), 'Correlations between spot quotations and forward quotations of Japanese Rice', *Kyoto University Economic Review*, **6** (2), 68–85.

Taniguchi, Kichihiko (1932a), *Kobairyoku Hokyuan: Neo Infureishion* [The Supply Purchasing Power Plan: the case for neo-inflation], Tokyo: Chikua Shobo.

Taniguchi, Kichihiko (1932b), 'The "Supplying Purchasing Power" plan – an urgent proposal for breaking down of the world crisis by supplying people's purchasing power', *Kyoto University Economic Review*, **7** (2), pp. 50–60.

Taniguchi, Kichihiko (1942), 'The trade policy of East Asia wider territory economy', *Kyoto University Economic Review*, **17** (2), 20–43.

Tasugi, Kisou (1971), 'Modernization of the functions of the assemblers in each local producing area in Japan', *Kyoto University Economic Review*, **41** (1), 1–28.

Tominaga, Ken'ichi (1975), 'Yasuma Takata: an unknown giant of sociology', *Sociological Inquiry*, **45** (1), 31–41.

Trescott, Paul B. (2007), *Jingji Xue: The History of the Introduction of Western Economic Ideas into China, 1850–1950*, Hong Kong: Chinese University Press.

Tsuchiya, Takao (1937), 'An economic history of Japan', *Transactions of the Asiatic Society of Japan*, Second Series, **15** (December), reprinted (1977) Philadelphia, PA: Porcupine Press.

Tsuru, Shigeto (1964), 'Survey of economic research in postwar Japan', *American Economic Review*, **54** (4), Part 2 (Supplement), 79–101.

Tsurumi, Shunsuke (1986), *An Intellectual History of Wartime Japan, 1931–1945*, Tokyo: KPI.

Warren, George F. and Frank A. Pearson (1933), *Prices: Collapse of the Price System Real Cause of the Depression*, New York: John Wiley & Son.

Wicksell, Knut (1893), *Über Wert, Kapital und Rente*, Jena: G. Fischer.

Woytinsky, W. (1931), 'Das Rätsel der langen Welle', *Schmollers Jahrbuch*, **55** (4), 577–612.

Yagi, Kiichiro (1997), 'Economic reform plans in the Japanese Wartime Economy – the case of Shintaro Ryu and Kei Shibata', in Aiko Ieko (ed.), *Economic Development in Twentieth Century East Asia*, London, UK and New York, USA: Rotuledge, pp. 100–115.

Yagi, Kiichiro (1999), *Kindai Nihon no Syakai Keizeigaku* [The social economics of modern Japan], Tokyo: Chikuma Shobo.

Yagi, Kiichiro (2004), 'History-oriented economics in Kyoto', *Kyoto Economic Review*, **73**, 11–22.

Yagi, Yoshinosuke (1936), 'The current land problem and the establishment of peasant proprietorship', *Kyoto University Economic Review*, **11** (2), 60–84.

Yasuba, Yasukichi (1975), 'Anatomy of the debate on Japanese capitalism', *Journal of Japanese Studies*, **2** (1), 63–82.

11. The background of K. Akamatsu's *Gankou Keitai Ron* and its development: early empirical analysis at Nagoya

Tadashi Ohtsuki

11.1 INTRODUCTION

During his time at Nagoya from 1921 to 1939, Kaname Akamatsu (1896–1974) developed a theory of economic growth which was called *Gankou Keitai Ron*, a reference to a skein of geese, which image was more formally translated by M. Shinohara (1919–) as the 'Wild-Geese-Flying' (WGF) pattern theory or 'flying-geese' pattern theory, the name under which Akamatsu's work become known to non-Japanese economists (Ikeo, 2008, 199).[1]

Akamatsu's theory was also examined in relation to the 'product cycle' theory by Vernon (1966), and has been quoted or further developed internationally by many scholars such as Zimmerman (1964, 96–7), Suehiro (2000, 42–4, 48) and Ozawa (2005).[2] Kiyoshi Kojima (1920–), who is Akamatsu's pupil, should also be mentioned for his presentation of a more detailed theory elaborated on the basis of Akamatsu's original version.[3] In addition to these studies, the recent publication of Ikeo (2008) is the first biography of Akamatsu. However, Ikeo does not fully examine the development of WGF pattern theory or the theory of differentiation and uniformization of international economic structure from the viewpoint of wars and long wave theory. The context of WGF pattern theory has not been sufficiently studied; its background is described in Akamatsu's autobiography: 'through the empirical analysis of the spinning and woollen industries I grasped the Wild-Geese-Flying pattern of industrial development' (Akamatsu, 1975, 37).

The development of economics beyond the imperial universities, including some higher commercial schools such as Tokyo Higher Commercial School (HCS) (now Hitotsubashi University) or Kobe HCS (Kobe University) has not been sufficiently examined.[4] Very little work has been done on the empirical analysis carried out by Akamatsu. Describing the beginning of empirical analysis in Japan, for example Tamanoi (1971) writes: 'Empirical studies developed in the United States of America in 1920s to 1930s were not introduced into Japan before WWII. Large research institutes such as The Mitsubishi Economic Research Institute did not start such empirical analysis before the war' (Tamanoi, 1971, 223–4). But as we shall see, this view discounts work done at Nagoya HCS.

11.2 THE INTRODUCTION FROM HARVARD BUSINESS SCHOOL OF EMPIRICAL ANALYSIS INTO JAPAN

Akamatsu was appointed lecturer at Nagoya HCS in April 1921 following graduation from Kobe HCS in 1919, and then from Tokyo HCS in 1921.[5] In 1922 he became full professor at Nagoya HCS, and from 1924 to 1926 he was given an opportunity to study commerce and economics in Great Britain, Germany and the USA (Akamatsu, 1975, 24).[6]

At first Akamatsu informally attended the lectures[7] by Sombart (1863–1941) given at the University of Berlin (ibid., 25–6). According to Koide (1975, 275–7), Akamatsu did not attend the classes of a specific professor, but studied mostly on his own for about a year. Dissatisfied with Berlin, in 1925 he moved to Heidelberg and studied philosophy,[8] attending the seminars of Rickert (1863–1936) and Glockner (1896–1979).[9] Akamatsu intended to 'consolidate the foundation of economic policy as a matter of philosophy of economics' (Akamatsu, 1975, 25).

Although he spent most of his time abroad in Germany, his two-month visit to Harvard University was very beneficial to Akamatsu. He was especially interested in the case method education system at the Harvard Business School, business administration in general, and empirical studies conducted by the Harvard University Committee on Economic Research (ibid., 34, 84–5).

Regarding the case method education system, Ryusei Watanabe,[10] president of Nagoya HCS at that time, had instructed Akamatsu to attend the classes using this system. He attended M.T. Copeland's classes, and was 'somewhat surprised at the animated atmosphere of the discussion' (ibid., 33). According to Akamatsu, however: 'I could not become so interested in this, because another professor, Kiyozou Miyata[11] of Nagoya HCS, had already examined this system before me' (ibid.). After Akamatsu's return to Japan this teaching method was introduced at Nagoya HCS, for the first time in Japan. But it was soon discontinued because of the difficulty in collecting actual cases for this system at that time in Japan[12] (ibid.).

Akamatsu was however more interested in business administration, and the work of the Committee on Economic Research. Business administration in particular gave him the idea of WGF pattern theory. He was especially interested in the study of variation of management costs depending on the size of retailers, and the optimal number of retailers in each industry (ibid.). After studying business administration, he was aware that: 'I would be able to draw some regularities or laws from the research into the degree of activity of industries in manufacturing industry, just as statistical investigation of the economics of consumption by Ernst Engel had led to Engel's coefficient' (ibid., 35). This work began soon after Akamatsu's return to Nagoya.

He was also interested in the empirical analysis of business conditions. At the time, the Harvard University Committee on Economic Research was constructing its business barometer, together with three time-series curves denoting financial conditions, the security market and the commodity market (ibid., 34). Indices of general business conditions[13] had been constructed since 1919 under the direction of W.M. Persons of the University of Colorado at Boulder. The results were presented in the *Review of Economic Statistics* and *Weekly Letters* published by Harvard Economic Society. This analysis would also later be tried at Nagoya HCS.

Examining this work at Harvard, Akamatsu was also inspired by the philosophy of Hegel and Kant. He wrote as follows:

> In case of Kant, form of cognition and category are given a priori, thus frames of conception are constructed without any experiences. On the other hand, in Hegel's phenomenology, higher cognitions are generated step by step from the simplest intuition based on cognitions. Economics as an empirical science to which we are now going should start not from transcendental conception, but from intuitive events based on experiences. The aim of research bureaus is to understand intuitive events from experience, and furthermore to construct scientific concepts. Learning should not newly develop only by reading books as completed conceptions. Through such inspiration, Hegel and empirical studies at Harvard are connected in my mind. (Akamatsu, 1975, 34)

With these ideas in mind and following the investigation at Harvard, he left the USA for Nagoya in June 1926.

11.3 THE BEGINNING OF EMPIRICAL ANALYSIS AT NAGOYA HIGHER COMMERCIAL SCHOOL

Akamatsu, on his return to Japan, thought that: 'I have got a good idea as a souvenir – that I would like to introduce a research bureau like the one in

Harvard into Japan' (Akamatsu, 1975, 34). On his return to Nagoya in July 1926 Akamatsu suggested to Watanabe that a bureau of business research should be established (ibid.). That same year Sangyou Cyousashitsu (the Bureau of Business Research, NCC)[14] attached to Nagoya HCS was established. According to Akamatsu: 'our bureau intended to make indexes depending on empirical analyses and furthermore to draw or find some rules or regularities in these indexes' (ibid., 38). At that time no such attempt had been made in Japan (ibid., 37).

The main members of the bureau at first included Akamatsu and Saichiro Takashima (1884–1959, Finance),[15] who served as a senior adviser. Other professors such as Kikunosuke Koori, K. Miyata and Syouzaburou Sakai also participated. In addition to Japanese academics some foreign lecturers[16] such as Ernest Penrose (1895–1984)[17] contributed to work in Nagoya.

In the beginning, besides some chairs and desks, the bureau was equipped with only one electrically operated calculating machine, one Western-language typewriter and one Japanese typewriter. While today this seems extremely basic, for the time it was very advanced (Akamatsu, 1975, 34; Penrose, 1975, 324).

Immediately after the establishment of the bureau in 1926 several research projects were started. They included: the first study, an investigation into business administration in the Japanese spinning industry (Koide, 1975, 297); quantitative indexes of products made in Japan, which later became known as *Meikosho Shisuu* (the Index of Nagoya Higher Commercial School);[18] and creating a business barometer mainly for the textile industry.[19] It was the first of these that 'enabled me to develop WGF pattern theory' (Akamatsu, 1975, 37).

Akamatsu first analysed the variation of management cost depending on the size of retailer, and the optimal size of retailers in the Japanese spinning industry, applying methods learned in Harvard (ibid., 35). According to Akamatsu, it was very difficult to collect accurate data on management from each company. To deal with these difficulties he collected business reports from more than 60 industries and created a standard type of balance sheet[20] and profit and loss statement with the assistance of Professor Yutaka Kunimatsu (1880–1964) (Akamatsu, 1975, 35). Depending on the results, Akamatsu then made ratio analyses[21] which were aimed at grasping the relations between management scale and capital structure (Koide, 1975, 285). 'In those days management analyses . . . were in embryo in Japan, of course, and even in the world, thus its impact on the academia or the financial world in Japan was very large' (Akamatsu, 1975, 35).

According to Koide: 'management analysis in the private sector such as

The Mitsubishi Economic Research Institute began much later than the analysis at Nagoya H.C.S.'[22] (Koide, 1975, 285). But the Nagoya work ended with 'too much pain, too little reward'[23] (Akamatsu, 1975, 35). The detail and importance of this analysis was not sufficiently appreciated because the analysis of management was only in its early stages in Japan. In his later years, Akamatsu looked back on the beginning of empirical analysis: 'Since the bureau was very small, we could introduce only some parts of the Harvard system' (ibid.).

But at that time, even in imperial universities, Tokyo University of Commerce or Kobe HCS,[24] empirical analysis had not yet begun. Thus the empirical analysis at Nagoya HCS can be regarded as the first in Japan,[25] beginning only seven years after the case study method had been adopted at Harvard.

11.4 THE RESEARCH ON THE WOOLLEN INDUSTRY IN JAPAN: ITS MEANINGS TO AKAMATSU

Akamatsu's conception of the WGF pattern theory was prompted by his work on the woollen industry in the Bisai area of the Aichi Prefecture. This was the centre of the Japanese woollen industry in the 1920s, and was near Nagoya HCS. But this industry was not solely chosen because of its importance to the area.

The early industrialization of Britain was largely based upon woollen and cotton textiles, and this was noted as a model for development (Japan Textile Council, 1958a, 21). Textiles were also important in Japanese development, growing rapidly from 1886 (Okazaki, 1997, 31).

As is clear from Table 11.1, the percentage of textile industry grew from 29.12 per cent in 1885 to 44.51 per cent in 1893. Thereafter the proportion of textiles decreased to 32.53 per cent because of the development of heavy chemical industries. In fact, the percentage of the output of the heavy chemical industry in all the industries increased from 14.83 per cent in 1893 to 24.94 per cent in 1914, while the percentage of light industries decreased from 85.17 per cent in 1893 to 75.06 per cent in 1914 (Okazaki, 1997, 30; Shinohara, 1972, 140–43).

The textile industry was therefore important to early Japanese industrialization, and was divided between cotton, wool, silk, hemp and other artificial textiles (Sakai and Akamatsu, 1935, 3). Cotton and wool were the most significant from the point of view of economic development (ibid., 3–5). But there were important differences between cotton and wool. Cotton was already cultivated in Japan, and cotton spinning had

Table 11.1 Structure of production in manufacturing industry: nominal (%)

	1885	1893	1914
Food	42.45	30.72	31.94
Textiles	29.12	44.51	32.53
Timber and wood products	3.74	2.36	2.78
Stone, clay and glass products	1.29	1.90	2.40
Printing	0.40	0.31	1.14
Iron and steel	0.16	0.23	3.05
Non-ferrous metals	0.94	1.00	1.97
Machinery	1.39	1.45	7.69
Chemicals	14.20	12.15	12.23
Other	6.30	5.30	4.28
Total	100	100	100

Source: Okazaki (1997, 30), Shinohara (1972, 140–43).

developed before the Meiji Restoration (Akamatsu, 1935, 130). When Japan opened up to foreign trade, new technologies such as spinning machines were imported from European countries like France into Japan, further stimulating the development of the cotton industry.[26]

Wool by contrast was not so widespread, and the woollen textile industry had not really developed prior to Meiji era. The woollen industry was therefore a new venture for Meiji Japan, presenting Akamatsu with the opportunity of studying a new industry: 'Through the examinations of the woollen trade more than through the investigations of the cotton trade, we can investigate in purer form how an entirely new industry develops' (ibid.)

The Meiji period saw a rapid shift in fashion from traditional Japanese clothing to a more Western style. This trend was especially marked for military and women's clothing. Faced with such increasing demand, the Meiji government built the national weaving factory[27] in Senjyu, Tokyo in 1879 under a government policy aimed at promoting industry (Japan Textile Council, 1958b, 270–72). In the same year a private woollen factory was also established by Jyosaku Goto (1858–129) in Hongou, Tokyo[28] (ibid., 272–3). The woollen yarn spinning factory in Osaka followed in 1888 (ibid., 272). From around this period the industry expanded rapidly, centred especially on Tokyo, Osaka and Hyogo prefectures, which were (and remain) important commercial and industrial areas in Japan. Akamatsu explains this process as follows:[29] (1) the change in preference from traditional Japanese to Western dress; (2) technological development of the production process; (3) changes in customs tariffs; and (4) the outbreak of the First World War and the collapse of stock exchanges (Akamatsu, 1935, 157–8).

In fact, taking the actual data on this point, the export of woollen yarn and woollen textiles only averaged 137000 yen during the period of 1903–07, this being shortly after the inauguration of the Japanese woollen industry. This sum was 0.038 per cent of all goods exported (357293 yen). By 1934 the proportion of woollen exports had risen to 2 per cent of all exports, representing a fiftyfold increase over 1903–07 (Akamatsu, 1935, 139). Around 10 per cent of all woollen textiles originated in Aichi Prefecture in 1916 (Tamaki, 1957, 256–7), rising to around 50 per cent in 1930 and 67 per cent in 1937.

In the Aichi Prefecture the centre of the woollen industry was the Bisai area in the northwest Noubi plains, including Ichinomiya city, Nakashima county, Ama county and Haguri county (Koide, 1938, 149). This industrial area developed more than 25 years later than that in Tokyo, but quickly established a strong base. This was partly because cotton, silk and hemp manufacturing had long been established in the Bisai area[30] (Sakai and Akamatsu, 1934a, 2). These industries were seriously damaged by the Noubi earthquake in October 1891; but in the aftermath many gradually changed over from cotton to woollen textiles (Japan Textile Council, 1958b, 713). Even though new technological skills such as dyeing and weaving were required for the newly introduced woollen industry, the experience and ability of the workforce made this possible (Japan Textile Council, 1958b, 813; Koide, 1938, 150). Coincidentally with this was the fear that the change towards Western dress would undermine the sales of cotton products (Japan Textile Council, 1958b, 813).

In addition to this the humidity of the Bisai area was also ideal for weaving wool, and a major river, the Kiso River, ran through the area (Sakai and Akamatsu, 1934a, 2). Social conditions were also important. The small and medium-size scale of the established production units made it easier for them to respond to changes in demand (Japan Textile Council, 1958b, 813). Bisai was also the centre of both land and water traffic, with the significant industrial and commercial city of Nagoya close by. The Great Kanto Earthquake in September 1923 also disrupted manufacturing in the Tokyo area, enabling the Bisai area to expand production (Japan Textile Council, 1958b, 282).

While the data are not complete, it can be said that in 1907 the percentage by value of woollen textile production in the Bisai area was very small, merely 0.86 per cent of total Japanese production in woollen textiles. This grew rapidly up to 1916, reaching between 1 and 6 per cent. By 1917 it was 10.84 per cent, and 21.04 per cent in 1923. Comparing the data of 1922

Table 11.2 National structure of the woollen textile industry

	Amount of production		Number of factories		Number of machines		Number of workers	
	Yen (000)	%	Number	%	Number	%	Number	%
Aichi Prefecture	84260	50.45	944	87.35	13536	50.98	16081	38.65
(Bisai area, Aichi)	(60694)	(36.34)	(766)	(67.31)	(9476)	(35.69)	(9991)	(24.01)
Hyogo	29966	17.94	10	0.88	3476	13.09	9152	22.00
Tokyo	16165	9.68	14	1.23	3093	11.658	5903	14.19
Osaka	11317	6.78	77	6.77	1697	6.39	4187	10.06
Gifu	9360	5.60	9	0.79	1343	5.06	1926	4.63
Shizuoka	6110	3.66	4	0.35	986	3.71	753	1.81
Mie	4424	2.65	10	0.88	646	2.43	636	1.53
Gunma	1672	1.00	4	0.35	382	1.44	831	2.00
Tochigi	1196	0.72	1	0.09	82	0.31	388	0.93
Total	167010	100	1138	100	26554	100	41606	100

Source: Sakai and Akamatsu (1934a, 4).

with that of 1932, the percentage of total output doubled from 18.09 per cent to 36.34 per cent (Sakai and Akamatsu, 1934a, 6; 1935, 13). Table 11.2 shows this expansion on a nationwide scale, taking the data in 1932 as an example. This table clearly shows the weight of the woollen textile industry in Bisai area.

If we use Table 11.2 as a base, the industrial characteristics of the Bisai area become more apparent, as shown in Table 11.3. In output per factory, the Bisai area had the smallest average unit size of all prefectures in Japan. This is also true for the number of machines and workers per factory.

11.5 THE DEVELOPMENT OF WILD-GEESE-FLYING PATTERN THEORY

At first, when Akamatsu and other researchers visited small or medium-sized factories, they had difficult experiences. For example, a factory manager would ask, 'Why are you asking such useless things?' or, 'Are you researchers from the customs house?' Nonetheless, five reports from this research were published. First was the report on management research of the woollen industries in Bisai Area in 1934 (Sakai and Akamatsu, 1934a). In the same year a report on the historical development of the woollen industries in Britain appeared (Sakai and Akamatsu, 1934b). Akamatsu

Table 11.3 Production in the woollen textile industry by unit of production

	Amount of production per factory (yen, 000s)	Number of machines per factory	Number of workers per factory
Aichi Prefecture	89	14	27
(Bisai area, Aichi)	79	12	13
Hyogo	2997	348	915
Tokyo	1155	279	422
Osaka	147	22	54
Gifu	1040	149	214
Shizuoka	1528	247	188
Mie	442	65	64
Gunma	418	96	208
Tochigi	1196	82	388

Source: Sakai and Akamatsu (1934a, 5).

here sought to forecast the future development of the woollen industry in Japan, which he thought would move into first place in the world woollen market in the near future (Sakai and Akamatsu, 1934b, 1–2). Third was the report on the condition of the Japanese woollen industry in Japan in 1935 (Sakai and Akamatsu, 1935). This includes an historical overview of the woollen trade and production problems in the Japanese industry. The fourth report (Sakai and Akamatsu, 1936) examined large-scale establishments. Finally in 1937 a report on the Japanese foreign woollen trade (Akamatsu and Sakai, 1937) was published.[31] Akamatsu also presented a paper on the trend in Japanese woollen products (Akamatsu, 1935).

Historical analyses gave Akamatsu the idea of WGF pattern theory. He first used the expression *Gankou Keitai*, which refers to a skein of wild geese, in 1935. He summarized the development of one industry in one country as follows. In the first stage, finished goods are introduced and then imported to a country; this period lasts some considerable time (Akamatsu, 1935, 130). In the second stage, semi-finished goods are imported and then finished in the country. In the third stage, raw materials are imported, and the process for making the finished goods is developed. In addition, finished goods are then exported from the country (ibid., 130–31). The stages of development from import to export in one industry in a country are the essence of WGF pattern theory. Akamatsu presented the table given as Table 11.4 here, showing the composition of imports for the Japanese woollen industry.

Table 11.4 The composition of the imports of the woollen industry in Japan

	Raw wool		Woollen yarn		Woollen goods/ textiles*		Total of woollen industry: (A)	Total	Total amount of all imports: (B)	(A) / (B)
Five-year average	Yen (000s)	%	Yen (000s)	%	Yen (000s)	%	Yen (000s)	%	Yen (000s)	%
1883–87	110	3.1	66	1.9	3328	95.0	3504	100	32 789	10.7
1888–92	296	4.7	302	4.8	5728	90.5	6326	100	69 508	9.1
1893–97	842	7.5	896	8.0	9504	84.5	11 242	100	145 195	7.7
1898–1902	3295	21.5	993	6.5	11 053	72.0	15 341	100	262 543	7.2
1903–07	9358	35.1	3340	12.5	13 974	52.4	26 672	100	418 057	6.4
1908–12	11 469	41.3	5786	20.9	10 492	37.8	27 747	100	485 498	5.7
1913–17	29 502	72.9	3420	8.5	7539	18.6	40 461	100	729 971	5.5
1918–22	66 774	61.5	14 535	13.4	27 219	25.1	108 528	100	1 936 448	5.6
1923–27	95 647	48.9	53 966	27.6	45 923	23.5	195 536	100	2 312 986	8.6
1928–32	92 617	73.7	16 529	13.1	16 614	13.2	125 760	100	1 725 148	7.3
1933	165 817	94.2	3 020	1.7	7213	4.1	176 050	100	1 917 220	9.2
1934	187 668	96.4	1708	0.9	5199	2.7	194 575	100	2 282 531	8.5

Note: * Includes muslin, woollen cloth, serge, blanket and others.

Source: Akamatsu (1935, 132).

As already noted, the woollen industry was barely developed at the beginning of the Meiji era. During this first stage, the percentage of the woollen goods and textiles, which are finished goods, shows that the woollen industry began through the import of especially finished products into Japan (ibid., 133). Until 1892 finished goods formed more than 90 per cent of all imported woollen textiles. In the second stage this fell to around 50 per cent by 1903–07. Over the same period the percentage of woollen yarn imported rose to more than 20 per cent. This period did not last as long as the first stage. At the same time the import of raw wool was rapidly increasing. In the period 1883–87 this had been only 3.1 per cent of imports; but by 1913–17 this had increased to over 70 per cent, and by 1933 was more than 94.2 per cent (ibid., 135). After 1933 almost all Japan's woollen textiles were domestically produced. Furthermore, an export trade developed, by 1936 being more than three hundred times the level of 1903–07 by value (Akamatsu, 1935, 139; Akamatsu and Sakai, 1937, 8–9).

Akamatsu went on to investigate the developmental stages of the woollen industry, dividing it into various kinds of woollen textiles: rough woollen textiles, muslin, woollen cloth, serge, woollen yarn and raw wool. During the first stage, mainly rough woollen textiles were imported: during the period from 1868 to 1872 this formed 67 per cent of total woollen imports (Akamatsu, 1935, 154–5). This percentage gradually decreased, while the percentage of the amount of the imported muslin in the total imported woollen textiles was increasing (ibid. 155). This rose to 34.4 per cent in the period of 1873–77, reaching 53.4 per cent in 1878–82. While there was a decrease after this period, it remained at more than 35 per cent until 1902 (ibid.).

In the same period flannel and Italian cloth was also imported. Flannel cloth in 1888–97 peaked at around 12 per cent of total woollen imports; while Italian cloth peaked at around 20 per cent in the period 1883–92. Both items quickly declined to a negligible volume (ibid., 155–6).

In the period 1903–07 the import of woollen cloth and serge began to increase, from 57.3 per cent to 90.4 per cent in the period 1923–27 (ibid., 156–7). Akamatsu argued that the subsequent period would see an increase in the import of semi-finished products (woollen yarn), and then raw materials (raw wool) would increase (ibid., 157). Rough woollen textiles, muslin, woollen cloth, serge, woollen yarn and raw wool came to be imported into Japan in this order.

Akamatsu also turned to the exports of these items from Japan, using the table given here as Table 11.5.

The limitation of the data for the period of 1903–07 makes it difficult to assess the export of woollen textiles. But the amount of rough woollen

Table 11.5 Exports of woollen yarn and textiles, 1903–34

	Woollen yarn		Woollen textiles										Total	
			Muslin		Woollen cloth, serge		Blankets		Others		Total			
Five-year average	Thousand yen	(%)	Thousand yen	(%)	Thousand yen	(%)	Thousand yen	(%)	Thousand yen	(%)	Thousand yen	(%)	Thousand yen	(%)
1903–07			64[1]	46.7					73[1]	63.6	137	100.0	137	100
1908–12	131[1]	14.2	181	19.7	286[2]	31.1	153[2]	16.6	170	18.5	790	85.8	821	100
1913–17	1033	12.4	1338	16.0	5343	64.0	322	3.9	312	3.7	7315	87.6	8348	100
1918–22	1422	17.2	2618	31.6	2528	30.5	991	12.0	721	8.7	6858	82.8	8280	100
1923–27	611	18.0	1761	51.8	547	16.1	221	6.5	262	7.7	2791	82.0	3402	100
1928–32	963	22.1	524	12.0	2202	50.7	160	3.7	498	11.5	3384	77.9	4347	100
1933	5293	29.3	1200	6.6	8020	44.4	392	2.2	3157	17.5	12769	70.7	18062	100
1934	12185	28.6	2185	5.1	19099	44.8	572	1.3	8565	20.2	30421	71.4	42606	100

Notes:

1. three years average
2. 1912 only.

Source: Akamatsu (1935, 139).

textiles, including muslin, dominated during this period (ibid., 194). The outbreak of the First World War altered matters, shifting the emphasis to the export of woollen cloth and serge, reaching 64 per cent of the total. With the end of the war the situation changed again, exported muslin resuming first place throughout the period of 1918–27. During 1928–32 this proportion decreased rapidly, being replaced once more by woollen cloth and serge until the woollen yarn industry fully developed. This period should therefore be treated as the period of the export of woollen cloth and serge (ibid.). As Akamatsu forecast: 'the woollen yarn industry is the most recent; the export of this product will expand considerably after this industry has become completely established' (ibid.). It can also be also pointed out that rough woollen textiles, muslin, woollen cloth, serge, woollen yarn and raw wool would in the future be exported from Japan in this order.

The product which was imported first also came to be produced and then exported first. In respect of rough woollen textiles, muslin, woollen cloth, serge and woollen yarn, these were imported, produced and then exported in this order. In the conclusion to Akamatsu (1935) he used for the first time the expression *Gankou Keitaiteki Hatten* (meaning the pattern of development whose curves look like skeins of flying geese), as in Figure 11.1, which shows the amount of the import, production and export respectively of muslin, woollen cloth, serge and woollen yarn.

He summarized his idea as follows:

> In most cases, the rise of a new industry in a country was stimulated by an increase in the import of the product concerned. Capitals then flows to the industry producing those finished or half-finished goods that are predominantly imported, and this industry develops fully when conditions permit. Soon after the rapid increase in imports, domestic production of this good develops and displaces this inflow. When this industry has fully developed domestically, it will convert to an export industry . . . In this way we can formulate the Wild-Geese-Flying pattern development of import, production and export in one industry.' (ibid., 210)

He later realized that: 'the same pattern could be found in the trend of import, production and export of almost all products imported into the modern Japanese economy' (Akamatsu, 1975, 39). The origin of the name 'Wild-Geese-Flying pattern' (originally in Japanese *Gankou Keitaiteki*) is described by Akamatsu as follows: 'I have an image of flocks of geese flying in the autumn night making shapes like mountains' (Akamatsu, 1974, 174).

As we can see from Figure 11.1, he compared each shape of the 'flying geese' to the import, production and export curves. Akamatsu recalled the research at Nagoya HCS as follows:

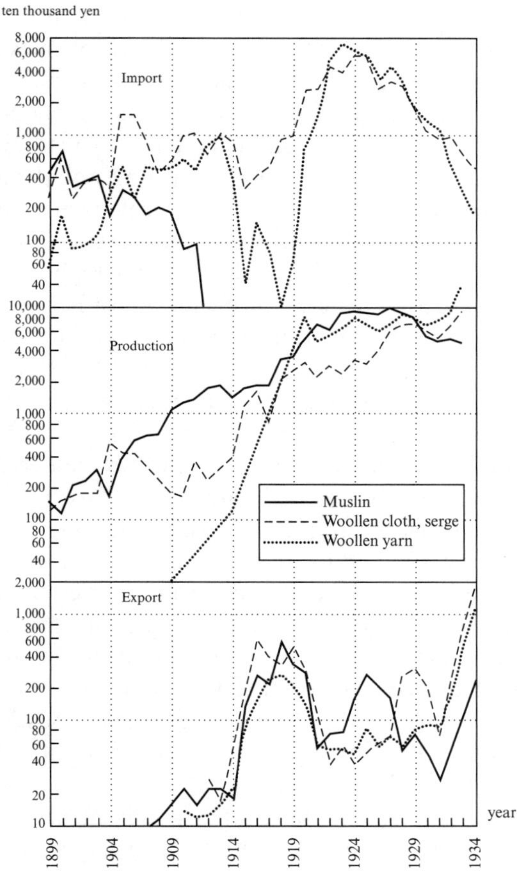

Source: Akamatsu (1935, 209).

Figure 11.1 The first graph of Gankou Keitai

> through the empirical analysis of the spinning and woollen industries I grasped the Wild-Geese-Flying pattern of industrial development and the theory of differentiation and uniformization of international economic structure. (Akamatsu, 1975, 37)

While his paper on WGF pattern theory was published in 1935, his first paper on the theory of differentiation and uniformization of the international economic structure had already been published in 1932. He argued that the process of differentiation and uniformization of international economic structure could be divided into approximately seven stages (Akamatsu, 1962, 4).

The first stage is the period when native Asian industry develops as a result of the exchange of native Asian products for Western European industrial products (ibid., 3). The second stage is the period when native handicraft industry crumbles, manufactured consumer goods flowing into Asia after the Industrial Revolution in Western Europe (ibid.).

The third stage is when Western European capital and technology penetrate the Asian area aimed at the large-scale production of primary goods, such as raw materials and provisions necessary for the Western European economy, constructing railroads and highways. During this period the exchange of Western European consumer goods for native primary products is established (ibid.). In these first three stages there is a clear structural differentiation between Asian and Western Europe industries. During the subsequent stage this begins to change.

In the fourth stage Western European capital flows in to develop modern industries, including the industries processing raw materials (ibid.). The fifth stage is when domestic capital enters the industries processing raw materials. This creates a conflict between consumer goods imported from advanced countries and those of the domestic processing industries. Capital goods are imported from advanced countries for the consumer-goods industries in the developing countries and, in consequence, there is a marked change from consumer to capital goods in the import structure (ibid., 3–4). Next the volume of imports of finished products decreases, being displaced by the import first of semi-finished goods, then raw materials. There is a structural change towards a uniformity of industries in developing and advanced economies.

The sixth stage is when manufactured goods in general begin to be produced by domestic industries, whether the raw materials are domestically available or not. The capital goods required by these industries are financed by the introduction of foreign capital and the export of primary products (ibid., 4).

The seventh stage is the period when the industrialization of the developing countries becomes so advanced that the export of manufactured consumer goods is possible, and when the domestic production of some capital goods increases (ibid.). In the last two stages industries in developing areas become fully advanced; the exports of finished products from these areas increases, followed by structural changes in the industry of developing countries.

As is clear from the above, the Wild-Geese-Flying pattern of economic development is part of the process of differentiation and uniformization in the world economy.

He further developed his thinking in Akamatsu (1937a, 1939), using the framework of long wave theory. He placed especial emphasis on the role of wars. During the 1920s and 1930s studies of long waves or cycles were popular in Western countries.[32] These found an echo in Japan, especially after Kondratiev's work was published in German (1926b), the original Russian version of which having been published in 1925. Once this appeared in *Archiv für Sozialwissenschaft und Sozialpolitik*, economists in Japan took up the study of long waves or cycles,[33] and especially the work of N.D. Kondratiev (1892–1938).[34]

Among these economists one of the first was Yasuma Takata (1883–1972), then a member of Kyoto Imperial University. Takata directed criticism to two main points. First, he criticized Kondratiev's idea of investment. According to Kondratiev, large-scale investment is made only when the accumulation of capital reaches a certain point. However, Takata argued that: 'This idea can not be applied once limited liability, debenture loans and banks have developed' (Takata, 1931, 36–7). Secondly, 'Kondratiev provides no evidence that durable but obsolescent capital goods are replaced about every fifty years' (ibid., 37). The same arguments and criticisms were also made by Kei Shibata (1902–86). Quoting Takata, Shibata argued that long waves cannot be explained endogenously[35] (Shibata, 1932, 107–8).

Although economists[36] went no further than introducing and criticizing Kondratiev's theory, Akamatsu advanced a theory which originally adopted the framework of long waves. Akamatsu emphasized the influence of war, while Kondratiev had argued that major cycles are caused by the replacement of durable and obsolescent capital goods.[37]

At first Akamatsu pointed out three long waves, using the British price index. The first wave declined from the end of the Napoleonic Wars to 1850, followed by a rising period from around 1850 to 1870 and the Franco-Prussian War. The second saw a decline in reaction to this war up to around 1895, with an upward movement from around 1895 to 1920. The third involved a decline from 1920 to 1932, and recovery after 1932 (Akamatsu, 1937a, 65). He added that: 'immediately after the great wars there occurred the peaks of long waves' (ibid., 67).

As regards the relationship between changes in prices and the outbreak of wars, he continued:

> The beginning of a long wave decline just after the war means that wars and its consequences have an important impact on the economic structure, and that this change promotes the structural conflicts inherent to capitalism. (ibid.)

Then he explained the process of the structural conflicts brought by wars:

> Through a war and the expansion of armaments, huge amounts of capital and labour are invested in munitions factories, especially in heavy industry. The products of light and consumer-goods industries become scarce, leading

> to rising prices during the war and just after its end. As soon as the war ends the demand for heavy industry ceases, making it very difficult for capital and labour to switch into peacetime industry. This change also take a great deal of time. What is worse, these peacetime industries have already developed in countries during the war who had not been involved in the fighting, preventing industrial change in belligerent countries, and further adding to long-term structural contradiction. (ibid.)

He went on to examine the impact of war: 'when a tendency for oversupply of capital and labour recede, and social unrest and disturbance are apt to occur. When this oversupply is externalised such conflicts are subdued inside the country, and business conditions recover' (ibid., 69). When the conflict of oversupply of capital and labour do not exist, this secures social stability. When such conflicts exist, social life becomes unstable, and the country or the people seek to expand outward. According to Akamatsu, this expansion explains the drive for colonies, occurring inevitably because of a natural increase of population and the structural conflicts of industry (ibid.). These processes promote the expansion of armaments production and an increase of expenditure (ibid.).

In short, colonial wars turn depression into prosperity, overcoming structural conflicts. And larger scale wars and the expansion of the armaments in powerful countries accelerate the expansion of major heavy industries (ibid., 70). Following the war, however, structural conflicts re-emerge, prolonging the depression. Akamatsu argued that: 'wars should be endogenous to long waves' (ibid.).

Akamatsu's theory was further developed in his work of 1939. He first dealt with the conditions under which the oversupply of capital and labour recede or are projected outside the country. He states that this 'depends on the level of economic development and the percentage of the increase of population in a country' (Akamatsu, 1939, 26). Oversupply recedes when economic development ceases or the increase of population stops. In the opposite case, this oversupply is projected outside the country.

The second point concerns the relationship between small-scale and large-scale wars. Admitting that large-scale wars break out during a rising wave, he also argued that there was a connection between large- and small-scale war in the trough of a declining wave (ibid., 21). A small-scale war between a strong and a weak country usually occurs at the bottom of the declining period. In this process, the falling wave changes into the next rising one. He treated warfare as endogenous to long waves.[38]

Akamatsu also briefly criticized the account of technological innovation put forward in J.A. Schumpeter's *Theorie der wirtschaftlichen Entwicklung* in 1912.[39] (ibid., 29) According to Akamatsu, long waves cannot be understood in the absence of the unbalanced investment of capital during wartime periods, the decline of munitions industries after wars and the tendency to oversupply non-military products during peacetime (ibid.).

11.6 CONCLUSION

WGF pattern theory has its roots in the historical analysis of the woollen industry in Japan. This analysis also played a part in the development of local industry, especially in the Bisai area of Aichi Prefecture. The theory of differentiation and uniformization of international economic structure, or Wild-Geese-Flying pattern development, can be regarded as a stages theory of economic development, and so relates to the theory of economic development espoused by the German historical school, Kondratiev,[40] A. Gerschenkron (1904–78) and W.W. Rostow (1916–2003).

Akamatsu was conscious of the way in which his empirical work at Nagoya HCS had implications for his later work, writing in 1944 that: '[My studies and researches at Nagoya HCS] have the most important role in my investigations of the international economy' (Akamatsu, 1944, 2).

NOTES

1. Editors' Note: The image of flying geese evoked here draws mainly on the way that skeins of flying geese look from the ground – whether in loose V-shaped formations, or in straggling echelons – as in Figure 11.1 below; but the image also relates to the way in which the birds land successively from these formations.
2. For further information, see Ikeo (2008, 209–18).
3. Recent publications are Kojima (2003–06).
4. Tamanoi (1971) and Yagi (1999, Chapter 1) could be taken as examples.
5. As to his personal history, see Akamatsu (1958, 1975). And regarding his bibliography, see Ikeo (2008, 227–36).
6. Regarding his studies abroad, see Akamatsu (1975, 24–37) and Koide (1975, 275–80).
7. According to Akamatsu (1975, 26), the lectures by Sombart were what was later published in 1934 as *Deutscher Sozialismus*.
8. Regarding Akamatsu's visit to Germany, see Akamatsu (1975, 24–32). Many students in Japan at that time, including Akamatsu, were influenced by the introduction of Kantianism into economics by Kiichiro Souda (1881–1927). Akamatsu also read the works of Souda, and studied philosophy (Akamatsu, 1975, 16–17). With this academic background Akamatsu developed his theories on the foundation of synthetic dialectics.
9. Glockner had a high opinion of Akamatsu's paper entitled 'Wie ist das vernünftige Sollen und die Wissenschaft des Sollens bei Hegel möglich? Zur Kritik der Rickert'schen Abhandlung "Über idealistische Politik als Wissenschaft?"', published in *Archiv für Geschichte der Philosophie und Soziologie*, Bd.XXXVIII. 1 und 2 Heft 1927, 1–17.
10. He was the first president of Otaru Higher Commercial School from 1911 before he became President of Nagoya HCS. For further information see Hotta (2005, 23–30).
11. K. Miyata (1896–1977) and Akamatsu, who were in the same class at Tokyo HCS, attended the same seminar of Tokuzou Fukuda (1874–1930).

12. The case method of teaching at Nagoya HCS is described in Akamatsu (1975, 40–41).
13. On this index see Koori (1934).
14. This English translation is quoted from Koide (1975, 283). Another translation, 'The Industrial Research Bureau of NCC', also can be seen on the back cover of Akamatsu and Sakai (1937). This bureau is now known as the Economic Research Centre, School of Economics Nagoya University.
15. Takashima is known as one of the first scholars who introduced the works of J.M. Keynes into Japan. For details see Kamikubo (2003, 119–123).
16. Many lecturers came from overseas to Nagoya HCS to teach foreign languages and economics. Before Penrose, G.C. Allen (1900–1982) taught at Nagoya HCS from 1922 to 1925. As to his activity and memories of Japan, see Allen (1983).
17. With a recommendation from A.C. Pigou, and on the advice of D.H. Robertson and A. Robinson (Penrose, 1987, 6), Penrose came to teach at Nagoya HCS in 1925 after his graduation from Cambridge University, and stayed for about five years. In 1944 he married a widow whom he had met at Johns Hopkins, Edith Denhardt (née Tilton), who therefore became Edith Penrose.
18. The indexes were made through the efforts of especially Koide and Penrose. At first Penrose created the quantitative indexes of agricultural products, mineral and animal foodstuffs during his five years' stay at Nagoya. After he left for the Food Research Institute of Stanford University in 1930, this work was taken up by Koide. He completed the quantitative index of all products in Japan from 1894 to 1931, thought to be the first quantitative index in Japan (Koide, 1975, 287–8). Afterwards Penrose introduced this analysis into his English works, and especially through the publication of Penrose (1940) the work at Nagoya HCS came to be widely known. This index was later called *Meikosho Shisuu* or the 'Koide Index' (Koide, 1975, 289–90).
19. According to Akamatsu (1975, 37): 'I can not forget the business barometer of Harvard, thus tried applying this method to the research of the textile industry in Japan . . . But we did not obtain good results through this research'.
20. The actual balance sheet is printed in Akamatsu (1928, 4–5).
21. This study is printed in Akamatsu (1928).
22. The Mitsubishi Economic Research Institute was established in 1932.
23. According to Akamatsu (1975, 35), this expression was originated by Professor Youjirou Masuchi (1896–1945).
24. These universities or higher commercial schools had a research bureau. But their research style was that of German bureaus, which aimed mainly at gathering articles from newspapers. Such bureaus were not therefore what Akamatsu had planned (Akamatsu, 1975, 37).
25. Hence Tamanoi's previous description is inappropriate here.
26. For more detailed information see Iijima (1949) and Japan Textile Society (1958a, Chapter 1).
27. The name of this factory in Japanese is Senjyu Seijyu-Sho; its first director was Syouzou Inoue (1845–86). For further information, see Japan Textile Council (1958b, 270–72).
28. On this point, see Japan Textile Council (1958b, 272–73).
29. The details of these points will be discussed in a later paper.
    For further information, see Akamatsu (1935, 158–70), Japan Textile Council (1958a, 664–752, 733–5; 1958b, 273–4, 277–8, 803).
30. For a historical overview of the cotton industry in this area, see Tamaki (1957, 31–82).
31. Even though this report was published in 1937 by Akamatsu and Sakai, it is almost identical to Akamatsu (1935) written by Akamatsu alone.
32. For an overview of these studies see Goldstein (1988, Chapters 2 and 3).
33. Attention should be paid to the difference between 'wave' and 'cycle'. In particular, Kondratiev distinguished them in his Russian works. As Barnett (1998, 107) points out, for Kondratiev a 'wave' was half a 'cycle'. But in the title of Kondratiev (1926b) the German word *Wellen* was used, so that in Japan the expression 'Kondratiev wave' has often been used.

34. Another writer to whom some Japanese economists paid attention was De Wolff (1924). But his work was at first not examined directly.
35. In his later works, analysing the existence of long waves from the viewpoint of the production of gold, Shibata argued that long waves were 'only an accident' (Shibata, 1936, 930).
36. Kinnosuke Ohtsuka (1892–1977) and Seiichi Tanaka also criticized Kondratiev's theory. For an overview of these studies, see Ichihara (2001, 183–94).
37. Kondratiev did not explain this point in Kondratiev (1926b). Regarding his theory of major cycles, see Barnett (1998, Chapter 5) and Ohtsuki (2007, 37–40). Indeed, Akamatsu did not examine Kondratiev (1926a), probably because of the language barrier, or the difficulty of obtaining his work.
38. We could point here to the similarity between the theory of Akamatsu and that of J.H. Åkerman (1896–1982). On this point see Ohtsuki (2008, 96).
39. After the Second World War, however, Akamatsu further developed his theory of technological innovation in Akamatsu (1965).
40. See Barnett (1998, 169–87).

REFERENCES

(Titles in [ ] are abridged English translations of the Japanese title by the author)

Works by K. Akamatsu

(1928), *Cyousa Houkoku 4th*, Nagoya: The Bureau of Business Research of Nagoya Higher Commercial School (B. of N.). [*Management Research of the Spinning Industries in Japan. Researches of the Ratio of Capital*].

(1932), 'Sekai-keizai no Ishitsuka to Doushituka' [Differentiation and uniformization of the world economy] *Syougyou Keizai Ronsou* (*Journal of Nagoya Higher Commercial School*), **10** (1), 237–77.

(1935) 'Wagakuni Youmou Kougyouhin no Boueki Suusei' [Trend of the trade of woollen products of Japan], *Syougyou Keizai Ronsou*, **13** (1), 129–212.

(1937a), *Sangyoutousei Ron*, [Theory of industrial control] Tokyo: Chikura Syobou.

(1937b), 'Wagakuni Keizai-Hatten no Sougou-Bensyouhou' [Economic development of Japan by synthetic dialectics], *Syougyou Keizai Ronsou*, **15** (2), 179–210.

(1939), 'Cyouki Hadou nitsuite' [On long waves], in Sakanishi Yoshizou Hakushi Kanreki Syukuga Ronsyu Kankou-kai (ed.), *Keizaigaku Keizaishi no Syomondai*, Tokyo: Iwanami Syoten, pp. 1–29.

(1944), *Keizai Shin-Chitsujyo no Keisei Genri*, [Principle of the formation of the new economic order] Tokyo: Risou Sya.

(1958), 'Jisaku Nenpu', [Akamatsu's career] in Akamatsu Kaname Hakushi Kanreki Kinen Ronsyu Kankou Kai, (ed.), *Keizai Seisaku to Kokusai Boueki*, Tokyo: Syunjyu-sya, pp. 497–512.

(1961) 'A theory of unbalanced growth in the world economy', *Weltwirtschaftliches Archiv* **86** (2), 196–217.

(1962), 'A historical pattern of economic growth in developing countries', *The Developing Economies*, Institute of Asian Economic Affairs, **1** (Mar.–Aug.), 3–25.

(1965), *Sekai Keizai Ron* [Theory of world economy], Tokyo: Kunimoto Syobou.
(1974), *Kin-Haika to Kokusai-Keizai*, [Demonetizing of gold and international economy] Tokyo: Toyo Keizai Shinpou-sya.
(1975), 'Gakumon Henro' [Autobiography], in Kojima (ed.), op. cit., pp. 9–68.

Works by K. Akamatsu with other authors

Akamatsu, K. and S. Sakai (1937), *Cyousa Houkoku 20th*, (B. of N.) [Our Foreign Trade in Woollen Industry: Researches of Woollen Industries in Japan.].
Sakai, S. and K. Akamatsu (1934a), *Cyousa Houkoku 15th*, (B. of N.) [Researches of Woollen Industries in Japan 1: Management Research of Woollen Industries in Bisai Area of Aichi Prefecture].
Sakai, S. and K. Akamatsu (1934b), *Cyousa Houkoku 16th*, (B. of N.) [Researches of Woollen Industries in Japan 2: The History of the Development of Woollen Industries in Britain].
Sakai, S. and K. Akamatsu (1935), *Cyousa Houkoku 17th*, (B. of N.) [Researches of Woollen Industries in Japan 3: The Present Status of Woollen Industry in Japan].
Sakai, S. and K. Akamatsu (1936), *Cyousa Houkoku 18th*, (B. of N.) [Researches of Woollen Industries in Japan 4: Business Analysis of Large Scale Establishments in Our Woollen Industry].

Works by Others

Allen, G.C. (1983), *Appointment in Japan*, London: Athlone Press.
Barnett, V. (1998), *Kondratiev and the dynamics of economic development*, London: Macmillan.
Bureau of Business Research, Nagoya HCS (1933), *Cyousa Houkoku 14th*, (B. of N.) [Quantitative index of all products in Japan: 1894–1931].
de Wolff, S. (1924), 'Prosperitäts-und Depressionsperioden', in O. Jensen (ed.), *Der lebendige Marxismus*, Jena: Thüringer Verlagsanstalt und Druckerei, pp. 13–43.
Goldstein, J. (1988), *Long Cycles*, New Haven, CT, WA and London, UK: Yale University Press.
Hotta, S. (2005), *Nagoya Koutou Syogyo Gattukou* [History of Nagoya Higher Commercial School], Nagoya: Nagoya Daigaku Daigaku Bunsyo Shiryou-shitu.
Ichihara, K. (2001), *Shihon-syugi no Hatten to Houkai*, Tokyo: Chuo Daigaku Syuttupan-bu. [Development and Collapse of Capitalism].
Iijima, M. (1949), *Nihon Bouseki-Shi* [History of spinning in Japan], Osaka: Sougen-Sya.
Ikeo, A. (2008), *Akamatsu Kaname* [Biography of Akamatsu], Tokyo: Nihon Keizai Hyouron Sya.
Japan Textile Council (ed.) (1958a), *Nihon Seni Sangyou-shi: Souron Hen* [History of textile industry in Japan: general remarks], Tokyo: Seni Nenkan Kankoukai.
Japan Textile Council (ed.) (1958b), *Nihon Seni Sangyou-shi: Kakuron Hen* [History of textile industry in Japan: details], Tokyo: Seni Nenkan Kankoukai.
Kamikubo, S. (2003), *Nihon no Keizaigaku wo Kizuita Gojyu-nin* [50 Japanese economists who contributed to the development of economics in Japan], Tokyo: Nihon Hyouron-Sya.

Koide, Y. (1938), 'Aichi Ken Keorimono-Kougyou no Cyousa Kenkyu' [Investigation on the woollen textile industry in Aichi Prefecture], *Nihon Toukei Gattukai Nenpou 7th Year*, 149–61.
Koide, Y. (1975), 'Akamatsu-sensei no Gakumon to Nagoya Jidai' [Akamatsu at Nagoya], in Kojima (ed.), op. cit., pp. 265–313.
Kojima, K. (ed.) (1975), *Gakumon Henro*. Sekai keizai Kenkyukai. [*Akamatsu: His Life and Works*].
Kojima, K. (2003–06), *Gankou-gata Keizai Hatten-ron. 1–3* [Theory of Flying-Geese Pattern development. 1–3.], Tokyo: Bunshin-Dou.
Kondratiev, N.D. (1993 [1925]), 'Большие циклы конъюнктуры', in *Избранные сочинения*, М.: ЭКОНОМИКА: 24–83.
Kondratiev, N.D. (2002 [1926a]), 'Большие циклы экономической конъюнктуры', in *Большие циклы конъюнктуры и теория предвидения*, М.: ЭКОНОМИКА: 341–99.
Kondratiev, N.D. (1926b), 'Die langen Wellen der Konjunktur', *Archiv für Sozialwissenschaft und Sozialpolitik*, **56**, 573–609.
Koori, K. (1934), 'Persons no Ruisuiteki Keiki Yosokuhou nituite' [Analogical business forecasting by Persons], *Syougyou Keizai Ronsou*, **11** (3), 1–15.
Ohtsuki, T. (2007), 'N.D. Kondratiev to S. de Wolff no Daijyunkan Kenkyu' [Major cycles in the theories of N.D. Kondratiev and S. de Wolff: an important difference in the 1920s], *History of Economic Thought*, **49** (2), 35–51.
Ohtsuki, T. (2008), 'Akamatsu Kaname no Sekai Keizai Kouzou no Hendou Riron wo Megutte' [Akamatsu Kaname's theory of changes of international economic structure: advanced at Nagoya Higher Commercial School], *Language, Area and Culture Studies*, Tokyo University of Foreign Studies, **14**, 81–101.
Okazaki, T. (1997), *Kougyouka no Kiseki* [Track of industrialization of Japan], Tokyo: Yomiuri Shinbun-sya.
Ozawa, T. (2005), *Institutions, Industrial Upgrading, and Economic Performance in Japan*, Cheltenham, UK and Northampton, MA, USA: Edward Elgar.
Penrose, E.F. (1940), 'Japan, 1920–1936', in E.B. Schumpeter (ed.), *The Industrialization of Japan and Manchukuo 1930–1940*, New York: Macmillan, pp. 80–270.
Penrose, E.F. (1975), 'My Nagoya era and professor Akamatsu', in Kojima (ed.), pp. 323–7.
Penrose, E.F. (1987), 'Memoirs of Japan, 1925–1930', in R. Dore and R. Sinha (eds), *Japan and World Depression: Then and Now: Essays in Memory of E.F. Penrose*, London: Macmillan, pp. 6–13.
Shibata, K. (1932), 'Cyouki-Hadou to Sekai-Kyoukou' [Long waves and world-wide crisis], *Keizai Ronso*, **34** (3), 102–21.
Shibata, K. (1936), *Riron Keizaigaku 2* [Theoretical Economics 2], Tokyo: Koubundou Syobou.
Shinohara, M. (1972), 'Kou-Kougyou' [Estimates of long-term economic statistics of Japan since 1868: mining and manufacturing].
Suehiro, A. (2000), *Catch-up gata Kougyouka-Ron* [The catch-up pattern of industrialization], Nagoya: University of Nagoya Press.
Takata, Y. (1931), 'Cyouki-Hadou nitsuite' [On long waves], *Keizai Ronso*, **33** (3), 19–39.
Tamaki, H. (1957), *Aichi-Ken Keorimono Shi* [History of woollen textiles in Aichi Prefecture], Toyohashi: Aichi Daigaku Chyu-Bu Chihou Sangyou Kenkyu-Sho.

Tamanoi, Y. (1971), *Nihon no Keizaigaku* [Economics in Japan], Tokyo: Cyuou kouron-sya.
Vernon, R. (1966), 'International investment and international trade in the product cycles', *Quarterly Journal of Economics*, **80** (2), 190–207.
Yagi, K. (1999), *Kindai Nihon no Syakai Keizai-gaku* [Social economics in Modern Japan], Tokyo: Chikuma Syobou.
Zimmerman, L.J. (1964), *Arme en Rijke Landen*, Den Haag: Albani.

12. Was *Sozialforschung* an Aesopian term? Marxism as a link between Japan and the West

Kiichiro Yagi

12.1 FELIX WEIL'S FRANKFURT LECTURE, MAY 1973

On 14 May 1973, Felix Weil, the founder of the Frankfurter Institut für Sozialforschung, delivered a lecture at Frankfurt University which I was fortunate enough to attend. It had been originally announced as a colloquium, but because the institute's seminar room could not accommodate the large audience, the lecture was held in a classroom on the university's main campus.

Weil, old and gray-haired, spoke about a series of fascinating episodes regarding the foundation of the institute and his involvement in it, from its conception right up to his departure from Frankfurt in 1929. He revealed that the original aim of the institute was to provide an institutional guarantee for continuing research in Marxism and that its members had been not alien to politics. According to Weil, the institute was primarily aimed at advancing Marxism on an academic level. Although Weil himself was not a Communist Party member, several members of the institute were Communist activists, and Weil closely collaborated with them in research and publication. It was in the basement of the Institute that a photocopy of Marx's manuscript in the possession of the Social Democratic Party was made for the editorial work of the *Collected Works of Marx and Engels* (MEGA) which was published in Moscow in 1927–35. Thus the pre-war institute was different in nature from that of its post-war successor, which distanced itself from orthodox Marxism and actual leftist politics.

What particularly caught my attention was that Weil twice mentioned 'ein Japaner' in his speech. The first occasion was when the young Weil was closely associated with Karl Korsch. In Jena, Korsch gave private lessons on Marxism to a Japanese scholar and used the fee, which he received in foreign currency, to support his family. The second instance referrred to a time when Weil and his friends were searching for an appropriate name for the planned institute which would conceal the original intention of a Marxism institute. They then hit on *Sozialforschung* because they had heard that a similar term was already used in Japan. Weil stressed in his lecture that at that time *Sozialforschung* was an Aesopian word denoting Marxism. All this took place at a study meeting on Marxism that was held in Ilmenau, Thüringen, in which a Japanese scholar also participated. To my regret, I was not able to determine whether Weil credited this Japanese person with any positive role in the creation of the word, or its adoption in the title of the planned institute. This Japanese person might have been a sponsor of the institute, or he might simply have indicated that an institute of such a name already existed in Japan.

At the end of Weil's lecture, I raised my hand and asked him the name of the Japanese man. Weil answered that the man's name was Fukumoto, and explained that Korsch had accompanied him to a study meeting on Marxism held in Ilmenau. I assumed that he was referring to Fukumoto Kazuo (1894–1983), who had lived in Germany as a researcher for the Ministry of Education of Japan and had guided the rebirth of the Communist Party of Japan after his return. From Weil's smile, I felt that he was encouraging me, a young Japanese man who came to study in Germany, just as Fukumoto had done half a century ago. This was the experience which prompted all my inquiries over a period of three decades.

12.2 INQUIRY IN JAPAN

Upon returning to Japan, I had two tasks to accomplish. First, I had to confirm whether the Fukumoto in Weil's speech was indeed Fukumoto Kazuo, the legendary theoretician of the Communist Party of Japan in 1926.[1] Second, I needed to determine whether the Ohara Institute for Social Research (Ohara Shakai Mondai Kenkyusho), founded in Osaka in 1919, might have exerted any influence in the nomenclature of the Frankfurt Institute, because of either Fukumoto's discussion with Weil, or for another reason.

The significance of the Ilmenau meeting (*Erste Marxistische Arbeitswoche*, EMA) on the intellectual history of Western Marxism was first made public through Martin Jay's *Dialectical Imagination* (Jay, 1973), which was apparently based on his interview with Weil. Jay's book, published in the same year as Weil delivered his lecture at Frankfurt, did not mention Fukumoto's name among the list of participants in the Ilmenau meeting. However, in an article on Karl Korsch (Buckmiller, 1973), which was also published in 1973, I found a biographical table that contained the name of Fukumoto at the end of the list of participants in the meeting. Korsch's biographer M. Buckmiller seemed to have based the list on the memory of Korsch's widow, Hedda Korsch, who had also attended the meeting. However, the date of the meeting was still questionable. While according to Jay (1973) and Buckmiller (1973) the meeting took place in the summer of 1922 and May 1922, respectively, Migdal (1981) claimed that it took place in early 1922.[2]

I also found that the journal *Archiv für Sozialismus und Arbeiterbewegung*, edited by Carl Grünberg, the first director of the Frankfurt Institute, contained some articles related to Kazuo Fukumoto. In Vol. 14 (1929), Yoshitaro Hirano wrote a review of Fukumoto's book, *The Methodology of the Criticism of Political Economy (Keizaigaku Hihan no Hohoron)* (1926b).

I made contact with Kazuo Fukumoto, who lived in Fujisawa, and with the Ohara Institute, which was affiliated with Hosei University, Tokyo. First, I was able to conduct an extensive interview with Fukumoto on 18 September 1974. One of my teachers had advised me that careful preparation would be required in order to interview such a difficult person. Accordingly, I prepared for the interview by reading Fukumoto's recollections (Fukumoto, 1952) in which he wrote about his life in Germany and Paris, although there was no mention of either Korsch or his participation in the Ilmenau meeting. Fukumoto may have had reasons for not revealing this information, because the affinity of his theory to those of Korsch and Lukács had been one of the reasons he had received criticisms among communists since the 1920s.

Fukumoto, who at 80 years old retained his vigour, received me warmly, allaying my anxiety. He seemed to have prepared for the interview and often talked with a memorandum in his hand. The following is a summary (abridged reconstruction[3]) of the interview, from Fukumoto's perspective.

1. Association with Korsch

After I [Fukumoto] arrived in Germany at the end of May or June 1922, I looked for books on the materialistic view of history and found Korsch's pamphlet *Kernpunkte der materialistischen Geschichtsauffassung* [1922]. It was not excellent, but it did motivate me to talk with him. I carried some money every time I visited him. It was a trivial amount for me, but it might have been valuable for him under such difficult circumstances. At that time, he lived in the upper floor of a newspaper publisher in Jena. He contributed significantly to papers and journals, but I did not know about his activities in detail. Since I travelled quite often, I did not stay continuously in Jena. Nevertheless, I remember meeting him on Christmas in 1922. After my move to Paris, I had no correspondence with him, and I was not aware of his purge from the Communist Party in 1926. I was unsatisfied with his works, which were much too inclined to juristic discussions rather than true socio-economic research.

2. Participation in the Ilmenau meeting
I attended it on Korsch's suggestion. Since I took a photo of Marx's grave in the Highgate Cemetery in London on 22 May 1922, it was unlikely that the meeting took place in May that year. The meeting took place in a small town with [a clear view of] an open field. The participants I remember were Lukács, Korsch and his wife, Weil, and Wittvogel, among whom Lukács was outstanding. Due to difficulties in language, I was unable to join the discussions actively. Still, it was amusing that I was introduced as a professor from Japan. Because I started travelling again soon after this meeting, I was not aware of the results of this meeting.[4]

3. Talk with Weil and social research
I have never visited Frankfurt; I met Mr Weil only at the Ilmenau meeting. I think it was his suggestion that I visit the *Rote Fahne* (Organ of the Communist Party of Germany; KPD) editorial office when I visited Berlin. He talked about his plan to establish an Institute, and I talked about my idea of 'research of society' (*shakai no kenkyu*). I would like to explain why I talked about the 'research of society'. As you can see immediately from the title of my book, *The Process of Construction and Transformation of the Society (Shakai no Kosei narabini Henkaku no Katei)* [1926a], the object of my research was society itself, not the state. In those days, everyone was a supporter of statism; for instance, Professor Shinkichi Uesugi's theory of the divine power of the emperor (*Tenno Shinken-setsu*), the courses of state science at the Law Faculty of the Imperial University of Tokyo, and its journal, *Kokka Gakkai Zasshi* [Journal of state science]. The faculty of letters had a chair of sociology, which was just trivial. Hajime Kawakami's journal, *Research of Social Problems* (*Shakai Mondai Kenkyu*) reflected the old style of its editor/author, 'contemplating in a quiet room with a clear desk under the moonlight from the window'. I felt the need for a complete investigation of society that subsumes the state, rather than a partial research into labour or social problems. I believed that I had searched for the materialistic view of history. However, when talking about 'society', it might have also influenced me that as a student in the Law Department, I had read G.D.H. Cole's book, *Social Theory* [1920].

4. Relations with leftist movement
I had no direct contact with the political movement in Europe. My association with Korsch was not a political one. When I visited *Rote Fahne* in Berlin, I declined its request to write about the political situation in Japan. Indeed, I read the so-called Lenin's Testament in Paris,[5] but I did not receive it by any particular political route.

Regarding the origin of the term *Sozialforschung*, Fukumoto talked a great deal about the formation of his own viewpoint. In the term *shakai no kenkyu* (research or study of society), he apparently recognized the possibility of a theory that can critically subsume the state under a more general entity of society as a whole. He believed that this was precisely Marxism's materialistic view of the society. It was clear that Fukumoto's interpretation of the word coincided with that of Weil.

However, I could not discount the possibility that this word was derived from the name of the Ohara Institute or Kawakami Hajime's journal, *Shakai Mondai Kenkyu* [research of social problems]. Therefore, after my first interview, I wrote to Fukumoto to ask whether he might have used this word in such a context. In his letter dated 22 January 1975, he responded by emphasizing the distinction between *shakai mondai kenkyu* (study or research of social problems)[6] and *shakai kenkyu* (*Sozialforschung*; study or research of society as a whole) and declared that he had never experienced any confusion when distinguishing one from the other.

I also inquired with the Ohara Institute about whether it had used the term *Sozialforschung* before the Frankfurt Institute had and whether any of Ohara's researchers who were sent to Germany during that period had contacts with the circle around Weil and the Frankfurter Institute.[7] During the course of this investigation, I discovered that one of the ex-researchers of Ohara, Professor Samezo Kuruma (1893–1982) wrote the name of the Ohara Institute in German as 'Ohara Institut für Sozialforshung' in the *Marx Lexikon*, which he published around 1970. I received the provisional answer from the Ohara Institute[8] with three items of photocopied pages.

The first was Samezo Kuruma's research report on consumers' unions in Japan (Kuruma, 1923), which was published in the *Schriften des Vereins für Sozialpolitik*. In this German publication, Kuruma's affiliation was written not in German but in English: 'Research Member of the Ohara Institute of Social Research.'

The second was the English back cover of the Institute's official journal, *Ohara Shakaimondai Kenkyusho Zassi*, **7** (3) (December 1930). Here, the English name of the institute also read as 'The Ohara Institute for Social Research'.

The third was the cover of a catalogue of the literature collection on anarchism that the Ohara Institute purchased in the 1920s. The term *Soziale Forschung* appeared as 'Verzeichnis der Eltzbacher-Bibliothek des Anarchismus im Ohara Institut für Soziale Forschung' in the second part, which was printed in December 1930.

From these materials I concluded that hitherto, no evidence had been found that the Ohara Institute used the word *Sozialforschung* or *Soziale Forschung* before the Frankfurt Institute was founded. Since the Ohara Institute used the English term 'social research' as early as 1923, it is possible that researchers of Ohara unofficially translated the term into German as *Sozialforschung* or *Soziale Forschung*. However, no contact between the Ohara and Weil's circle in Frankfurt has been confirmed before the latter was founded.

Fukumoto had asked me to convey his greeting to Weil, which I did, stating that I had confirmed his talk in Frankfurt by directly interviewing

BOX 12.1

25 Nov. 74

Sehr geehrter Herr Yagi:
Haben Sie besten Dank für Ihren Brief vom 11. Oktober, der mich über das Institut in Frankfurt fort hier erreicht.
Ich freue mich, zu hören, daß es Fukumoto noch gibt. Bitte richten Sie ihm meine besten Grüße aus.
Ihre Mitteilung kam noch gerade rechtzeitig, um in meiner Autobiografie verwendet zu werden.
Mit freundlichsten Grüßen
Ihr Felix Weil

Dear Mr Yagi,
Thank you for your letter of 11 October, which was forwarded to me from the Frankfurt Institute.
I am pleased to learn that Fukumoto is still alive. Please give him my warmest greetings.
Your news came just in time for me to use it in my autobiography.
Best wishes,
Felix Weil

Fukumoto.[9] Given above is the transcription of Weil's response to me in German, with an English translation.

This was how far I had got in 1974–75; and I assumed that the details of the story would become common knowledge with the publication of Weil's autobiography. Accordingly I wrote a provisional report, together with my brief thoughts on the implications thereof on the intellectual history of the 1920s, for an annual bulletin of a local association of researchers in Nagoya (Yagi, 1976).

In the meantime, my correspondence with Fukumoto and Weil was printed in a private circular of Fukumoto's group. Further, a group of researchers in the history of social thought knew of my discovery. Researchers interested in the Frankfurt School as well as those with an interest in Lukács and Korsch showed interest in this personal relationship. Buckmiller corresponded with Fukumoto and sent him a group photo (Figure 12.1) of the participants of the Ilmenau meeting, in which Fukumoto was sitting in the front row. It was originally in the possession of Hedda Korsch, a copy of which Fukumoto had given me.

When Fukumoto Kazuo died on 16 November 1983, I was asked to contribute to a special commemorative issue of the *Undoshi Kenkyu* [Studies in the history of social movement]. I revised my 1976 article, and I published it in 1984 with the photo in issue 13 of the *Undoshi Kenkyu*.

Figure 12.1 *Group photograph of EMA participants (in the author's possession)*

This article is now included in an anthology on Fukumoto (Kojima, 2005).

12.3 WEIL'S AUTOBIOGRAPHY

In 1984 I had to admit that my research remained incomplete until Weil's autobiography became available, particularly since I was uncertain of my comprehension of Weil's German lecture in 1973. Weil had died on 18 September 1975, leaving an almost complete manuscript on his desk. His widow Anne Weil devoted herself to working on it day and night, and she died six days after sending the manuscript to a publisher in Germany. However, the publisher felt it required considerable revision, and then abandoned its publication after a year. I acquired this information through an inquiry to Felix Weil's heir, Frank G. Weil. In his first letter dated 29 September 1977, he promised me that he would send me a copy of the book when it was published. In his second letter, dated 14 February 1979, after the publisher's final decision, he promised he would look for the passage in which his father mentioned Fukumoto.

In the mid-1980s, when I received no further correspondences from

Frank G. Weil, I inquired with the then director of the Frankfurt Institute, Professor Gerhard Brandt, regarding the whereabouts of Weil's autobiography. He kindly informed me that Frank Weil had also died and that the manuscript was being transferred to the City Library of Frankfurt. It was, at least temporarily, not accessible, even to academic researchers. Eventually, Professor Brandt also died, and I heard that the Frankfurt Institute was going to be drastically modernized, at which point I lost all connection with it.

It has been fashionable in recent years to conduct historical reflections on the social sciences of modern Japan.[10] Previously, most of such histories were written with a partisan slant toward some political group or academic schools. Such partisanship seems to have disappeared now. Further, the project of the *Collected Works of Fukumoto* (Fukumoto, 2008–2011) is ongoing. This reminded me of my task to establish the facts regarding the origin of *Sozialforschung*.

When I checked the Frankfurt Institute's website, I was surprised to find another group photo of the Ilmenau participants, from which Fukumoto was missing. Both photos were apparently taken in the same place and at the same time. Neither Korsch nor Lukács, let alone Fukumoto, were mentioned in the text of the official history of the institute. Although the photo of the Ilmenau meeting is shown on the first page, the meeting itself has been neglected.[11] It seems to me that the institute had intentionally overlooked its origins in radical left intellectualism. I had a similar impression from the latest history of the Frankfurt School by Wiggershaus, although it did mention the Ilmenau meeting. Because Wiggershaus acknowledged that he could not use the material from the City Library of Frankfurt, I decided to resume the effort to as far as possible approach Weil's autobiography.

The City Library of Frankfurt was reorganized, and its historical materials were shifted to a special historical archive. From the electronic catalogue of this archive, *Institut für Stadtgeschichte Frankfurt am Main*, I discovered the manuscript I had sought for over three decades, and fortunately, I was able to obtain a CD copy[12] in the summer of 2008. The manuscript was not well ordered. Although it had a contents page, the order had been changed, and materials were intermingled with the text. While there was a cover page for the second version, most of the text remained as written in the first version. It had two paginations, one typed and the other handwritten. Apparently, someone had tried to reorder the manuscript and left it half done.

In this manuscript, I found stories similar to those that I had heard from the author in 1973. I have extracted and presented below some texts related to the Ilmenau meeting. I will cite these in my English translation, (the typed pagination of the MS is shown in roman, the handwritten in italic):

> I hit upon the idea to provide Marxist research with an academic home in the early year of 1922 at the Erste Marxistische Arbeitswoche (First Marxist Working Week) in Ilmenau, Thüringen. Karl Korsch and I invited the participants, and I paid the charges. (MS80: *200*)
>
> In early 1922, Karl Korsch and I invited a number of interested theoreticians – some of them were sympathizers of the Communist Party, and others were party members – to an Erste Marxistische Arbeitswoche (First Marxist Work Week), which was held at an inn in Ilmenau, Thüringen. They were all my guests – it was the first time that I spent a large amount of money from my inheritance toward the cause. Twenty-five participants attended the EMA. They included Kurt Albert Gerlach, Richard Sorge, Julian Gumperz, Kurt Alexander, Georg Lukács, Karl Korsch, Friedrich Pollock, Fritz Sternberg, Felix Weil, Gyury Fogarasy, Karl August Wittfogel, Konstantin Zetkin, Karl Schmückle, Boris Roniger, and their wives Käthe Gumperz, Rose Wittfogel, Christiane Sorge, Hedda Korsch, and Käthe Weil. (MS84: *277*)
>
> I do not remember the content of the programme except that Lukács talked on History and Class Consciousness, out of which his famous book that appeared in 1923 from Malik-Verlag emerged. The great discussion between Lukács and Korsch was the central focus of the meeting. I remember that Wittfogel reported on the Science of Bourgeois Society, which also appeared in 1922 from Malik-Verlag. He talked further on his theory of Chinese society. In addition, I know that Fritz Sternberg first reported his theory of imperialism in this meeting, which he continued then at the Institute. (MS85: *278*)

Fukumoto's name was missing in this manuscript. He appeared only as 'ein Japaner' at the end of the introduction of the participants of the Ilmenau meeting.

> From the group photo printed on page XX [*sic*], which does not show all of the EMA participants, I can see there were several more men, women and students who accompanied Karl Korsch. I cannot recall their names, but among them, there was a Japanese man, to whom Karl Korsch gave private lectures on Marxism, from whose tuition fee paid in dollars Korsch's entire family could live – this was during the truly wild inflation. (MS85: *278*)

Regrettably, my correspondence with Weil was not used for the revision of the manuscript. However, on the other hand, the question emerges as to why in May 1973 Weil mentioned Fukumoto in his response to me. He may have had additional information, or a better recollection after writing this manuscript.

The origin of the word *Sozialforschung* was explained as follows:

> It was during the occasion of the EMA that the idea of establishing a university institute for the study of Marxism came to my mind. I talked over this idea with

> Gerlach and Pollock. We were soon in accord that for the sake of independence the institute should not be placed under the essentially still reactionary Faculty of Economics and Social Sciences. It must be an institute affiliated to the university, but not an institute of the university. Further, it was also clear that the title of 'Institute for Marxist Research' should create considerable resistance. As with my dissertation, the title of the institute must have an Aesopian disguise. At that time, Pollock reminded that a few years ago an institute of social research, Institut für Sozialforschung, was founded in Japan, and the concept of 'Sozialforschung' could indeed mean something related to his own view. Thus we decided to adopt it to achieve our purpose, and that I should write a memorandum on the necessity for the founding of the Institut für Sozialforschung. (MS87–8: *286–7*)

Here, the English name of the Ohara Institute provided Weil and Pollock with the inspiration for *Sozialforschung*, by which they meant Marxism. The manuscript offered no information as to the source from which Pollock learned of the foundation of the Ohara Institute.

It is clear that the dating of the Ilmenau meeting in 1922 was mostly based on Weil's testimony. In the meantime, however, an invitation letter to a meeting that seems to refer to the EMA was discovered in the papers of Gertrud Alexander.[13] It was written by Richard Sorge (1895–1944) and sent on 9 May 1923 to Gertrud's husband, Eduard Ludwig Alexander (1884–1945), a theoretician of the Communist Party. From this document it is reasonable to assume that the EMA (Erste Marxistische Arbeitswoche) was held over eight days,[14] beginning 20 May 1923, at the Bahnhofshotel Geraberg, Thüringen.[15] It is not clear why Weil mentioned Ilmenau as the meeting place. But since Geraberg is close to Ilmenau, and the participants got there by local trains bound for Ilmenau, it is logical to refer to the place of the meeting by the name of the better-known town in Thüringen, Ilmenau.[16] From this document, we can see that the agenda of the meeting had three themes:

I. On dealing with the current problem of crisis (guided by Ludwig [i.e. E. Alexander]).
II. On questions of method (guided by Lukács and Korsch)
III. Organizational questions for the Study of Marxism (guided by Fogarasi)[17]

The highlight of the meeting was probably the discussion led by Lukács and Korsch. With respect to the third theme, however, there may have been the possibility that Weil's plan for the new institute was openly discussed. Fukumoto may well have joined the discussion and revealed his conviction about the total view of society. Since the first proposal for the Institute, *Denkschrift über die Begründung eines Instituts für Sozialforschung*, written by Weil and Aachen economist Kurt Albert Gerlach in the autumn of 1922, had already used the word *Sozialforschung*, it was not at the Geraberg meeting that Weil (and Pollock) chose this Aesopian word to signify their aim.

12.4 THE FOUNDATION OF THE FRANKFURT INSTITUTE

According to Weil's original plan, one of his senior friends, Kurt Albert Gerlach, would have been the director of the new institute. However, in October 1922, Gerlach suddenly died of diabetes, which forced Weil to look for another scholar who could occupy the position of professor. Korsch was very deeply involved in politics. Therefore Weil first approached Professor Gustav Mayer, the biographer of Friedrich Engels, but Mayer and Weil did not get along. Eventually, Weil found an appropriate candidate in Carl Grünberg, a Viennese economic historian who edited the journal *Archiv für Geschichte des Sozialismus und der Arbeiterbewegung*.

> As soon as he read the memorandum with Gerlach's signature and I explained its aim using Aesopian terms, he declared that he was in principle willing to follow. 'Comrade Felix,' said he, 'you can trust me, if the task is to make Marxism 'look respectable'[18] in the University.' He showed his understanding of our need to formulate the memorandum and other official documents in Aesopian terms. (MS95–6: *288–9*)

> Without any great difficulty, Grünberg gained the approval of the economics faculty of Frankfurt University for a new chair that accompanied the directorship of the institute. On 22 June 1924, he delivered his inaugural lecture and declared the aim of the institute to be to function as a research centre for labour movements and social studies. Grünberg gave Weil and his close friend F. Pollock a free rein in the area of theoretical research. According to Weil's self-evaluation, 'the Institute fulfilled what had been promised. The promise of the Institute to become the home for a non-dogmatic – at present we can say a pluralistic – Marxism was maintained.' (MS98: *299*)

One of the Frankfurt Institute's most significant contributions during the 1920s was the acquisition and preparation for publication of the original manuscripts of Marx and Engels. Weil made the most of the advantages that academic institutions have by making photocopies of materials in the possession of the SPD (Social Democratic Party of Germany):

> The photocopy of the Marx-Engels Nachlass was also made in the studio of the institute with the consent and collaboration of the executives of the SPD. Rjazanov, the Director of the Marx–Engels Institute in Moscow, planned to publish a *Collected Works of Marx–Engels* (MEGA) in Germany, and our institute collaborated with him toward this aim. The Nachlass was ca. 150 000

> pages. Twice a week, I organized a despatch with an old Menschewik, Boris Nikolajewski, who brought a load of manuscripts by train from the central office of the SPD to the Frankfurt Institute, where the camera was set up in the cellar to make negative – black and white – copies. Rjazanov wanted everything copied without making a distinction of whether it was being published or not. Nikolajewski was assisted by six people in two shifts. On his next visit, the courier brought new manuscripts again and gave the Soviet Embassy in Berlin the copies, which were sent as diplomatic post to the Marx–Engels Institute in Moscow. The entire Nachlass was copied in this way. Then in the Marx–Engels Institute the volumes were prepared for publication. It was published under my direction from Marx–Engels Archivverlag, located at first in Frankfurt. In 1924, initially under the direction of Pollock and myself, the Society of Sozialforschung and the Marx–Engels Institute in Moscow jointly founded the publisher, a limited company. (MS110: *296*)

The foundation of the Marx–Engels Archivverlag created tension between Weil and the university. The university, which strictly separated academic research from politics or business, exerted pressure on the institute. Partly because of this conflict, Weil abandoned his hopes of earning his *Habilitation* in Frankfurt.

The cooperation between these two institutes was recently investigated using materials from the Moscow Institute (Hecker, 2000), emphasizing the tense relation between the leaders of the SPD and Moscow. According to Weil, however, the real reason for terminating the arrangement was Moscow's ideological concerns.

> The collaboration for the MEGA between our institute and the Moscow Institute came to an abrupt end in 1927. The personnel who worked in the photo studio of our institute consisted mostly of students, of whom at that time, at least from the view of Russians, six belonged to the so-called ultra-radical supporters around Karl Korsch. Consequently, collaboration with the Frankfurt Institute was forbidden in Moscow because of their fear of Trotskyism. (MS117: *300*).

When Grünberg's retirement approached, the continuing conflict with the economics faculty led Weil to entertain moving the directorship of the institute from economics to philosophy:

> Soon after this, I submitted a new idea to the Ministry that was accepted more easily: after Grünberg's retirement, the professor chair should move from the Faculty of Economic and Social Sciences to the Faculty of Philosophy with the transformation to a chair of social philosophy. My friend, a private lecturer (since 1925) Dr Max Horkheimer – who belonged to the group at the institute from the beginning – should be invited to take up that chair. (Before this, there was no such thing as 'Social Philosophy' – *Sozialphilosophie*. Since the Faculty of Philosophy would not call the chair 'Philosophy and Sociology', the concept

was founded by us.) The Philosophy Faculty approved my idea, and it happened then, on 24 January 1931, that Horkheimer made his inaugural lecture.' (MS119: *301*)

Horkheimer was not an expert in the field of political economy; he made no distinction between *Sozialphilosophie* and *Sozialforschung*. In the Preface of the newly founded journal of the Institute, *Zeitschrift für Sozialforschung*, he redefined the term *Sozialforschung*:

> The word 'Sozialforschung' is not intended to demarcate a new borderline in the map of learning, which is at present so problematic. The investigations intended here in various fields as well as on various levels of abstraction are integrated with the aim of contributing to the theory of present society as a whole. It is this principle of integration, according to which each investigation is performed under unrestricted empirical rigour while at the same time aiming to address a central theoretical problem, that distinguishes the social research (*Sozialforschung*), to which this journal (*Zeitschrift für Sozialforschung*) will contribute from mere descriptions of facts or empirically irrelevant constructions. It seeks to reveal the process of society as a whole, and so presupposes that beneath the surface of chaotic phenomena the structure of the causal forces can be detected.[19]

When Hitler became the Chancellor of Germany the Frankfurt Institute in exile minted the term 'Critical Theory', a Marxian epistemology, as Horkheimer understood it. Critical theory recognized the social reality of thinking subjects, in contrast to 'traditional theory', which ordered empirical data according to the criterion of abstract rationality:

> The subject of critical theory is the individual that forms real relations with other individuals and groups, confronts particular classes, thus through such intermediation is involved with the contradictions within the society as a whole, and with nature. The subject of critical thinking is not the Ego of bourgeois philosophy. The description of the content of this individual is nothing other than the construction of the historical present.[20]

Critical theory was different from the idea of *Sozialforschung* in two respects. First, individuals, not classes or class-consciousness, were the subjects of research or theory. Second, critical theory could not identify itself with Marxism or Leninism as the living form of *Sozialforschung*.

12.5 DEVELOPMENT OF THE OHARA INSTITUTE

The origin of the Ohara Institute was similar to that of its Frankfurt counterpart – a donation from a successful entrepreneur. Magosaburo

Ohara (1880–1943), born in Kurashiki, Okayama Prefecture, took over his father's business and made his fortune as a result of the growth of the Kurashiki Spinning Company (Kurashiki Boseki). He became a philanthropist under the influence of an enthusiastic Christian, Ishii Juji, who founded an orphanage in Okayama. Ohara established clinics and schools through his spinning company and supported various sorts of social and cultural works. After Ishii's death in 1914, Ohara expanded Ishii's office in Osaka into a social work foundation and established a research office for social work.

At the end of 1918, when the so-called Rice Riot awoke Japanese concerns regarding social problems, Ohara moved to establish an institute for research into social problems, with the belief that it was necessary to conduct systematic research into the origin of social problems and their possible remedy. He invited professors of Kyoto University, including Hajime Kawakami, to be members. The Ohara Shakai Mondai Kenkyusho had its inaugural meeting on 9 February 1919, with Professor Iwasaburo Takano (1871–1949) of the University of Tokyo as its director.[21] After merging the twin institutes for remedial works in July, the Ohara Institute issued its foundational declaration on 21 September 1919, as follows:

> Since the World War, the solution of social problems has become urgent in our nation. Solutions to these problems require an approach from a fair and purely fundamental viewpoint, not from the partial viewpoints of interest-bearing participants. For this sake, we must look for the roots of the problem, consider the real situation in our country, compare real examples in other countries, and make a thorough investigation. Our institute is founded on this aim, and its activities are according to the following stipulations.[22]

Following this mission statement, the following tasks of the institute were outlined:

1. Inquiry and research into labour problems, social work, and other social problems;
2. Entrusting specialists with inquiry and research into particular areas of social problems;
3. Publication of the inquiries of researchers in Japan in the field of social problems;
4. Translation and publication of foreign literature on social problems;
5. Call for the submission of essays articles for a prize, their evaluation, and announcement of the decision;
6. Supporting inquiry and research into social problems;
7. Organizing academic lectures on social problems and maintaining educational classes;
8. Collecting domestic and foreign literature and materials on social problems and making them publicly available to researchers;

Over the next year, the Ohara Institute started publication by issuing the first numbers of *Nihon Rodo Nenkan* [Annual Labor Register of Japan], *Nihon Shakaijigyo Nenkan* [Annual Social Work Register of Japan], and *Nihon Shakai Eisei Nenkan* [Annual Register for Social Hygiene of Japan]. The first of these, which collected objective data on the condition of workers and farmers and their social movements, continues to the present day, despite a break of several years during and after the Second World War. The second publication was absorbed into the first in 1928, and the third was transferred to another research institute in ergonomics, which was separated from the institute in 1922. The journal *Ohara Shakai Mondai Kenkyusho Zasshi*, which started in 1923, soon became one of the most influential economics journals in Japan. The educational class for workers gave rise to many labour movement leaders. It published many research monographs and translations related to social movements and social work, and it sent its researchers to study abroad and to form collections for the institute. In 1920, it sent Samezo Kuruma (1893–1982) and Tamizo Kushida (1885–1934) to Europe, followed by Tatsuo Morito (1888–1984) and Hyoe Ouchi (1888–1980) in 1921, to study and to collect literature.

Takano had majored in social statistics and social policy. As a loyal disciple to his mentor in Germany, Lujo Brentano, Takano always supported socially progressive workers' movements. He was furthermore very indebted to his elder brother, Fusataro Takano, who had devoted himself to the early Japanese labour movement and had died while Takano was studying abroad. Takano organized a thorough investigation of the living conditions in the workers' residential area of Tokyo and established the tradition of social research in Japan. Many of his students who were involved in the first student movement in Japan ended up entering social movements. Shortly after Takano assumed the directorate of the Institute, he resigned from the university, accepting his nomination as workers' representative of the Japanese delegate to the International Labour Office assembly. The government believed that Takano would be acceptable to all of the workers' unions in Japan. In fact, union leaders, many of whom were Takano's ex-students, were not necessarily opposed to the person nominated, but they were against the idea of the government nominating workers' representatives. This induced Takano to devote himself to the management of the institute.

Takano's position was social-liberal, in the sense that he was more favourable to the autonomous movement of workers and consumers than to authoritarian social policies or patrimonial measures within firms. On the political scene he could be classified as a social democrat. He was often nominated as a symbolic leader of the working class party (*Musan Seito*) in the 1930s, and after 1945, he was one of the senior trio that called for the formation of the Socialist Party of Japan (Nihon Shakaito).

However, it is difficult to determine his attitude toward Marxism. While he kept his distance from the sectarian activities of Communists in leftist politics, he had a high regard for Marxism and Marxian economics, and encouraged research in these subjects in his institute. Of the eight researchers that the institute sent to Europe in the 1920s, four – Samezo Kuruma, Tamizo Kushida, Hyoe Ouchi and Karoku Hosokawa – were Marxists.[23] Takano's institute in the 1920s and 1930s was undoubtedly one of the principal cradles, and probably the safest, of Marxian studies in Japan.[24]

Takano himself showed his closeness to Marxism when he was involved in the planning of the Japanese version of the *Collected Works of Marx and Engels* (*Marx Engels Zenshu*) in 1928. In the previous year, Takano had made his third tour to Europe and attended the party congresses of both the Communists and the Social Democrats in Germany, although he seems to have been more impressed by the Communists. He also met David B. Rjazanov at the Soviet Embassy in Berlin and visited the Marx–Engels Institute in Moscow. The aim of his visit was to learn about the organization and activity of the institute itself, and its statistical information regarding the populations and living conditions of workers. He also viewed the photocopies of Marx's manuscript that had been prepared under Weil's collaboration in the Frankfurt Institute.[25]

It was natural that after his return Takano became the key man for the amalgamated publishers' version of the Japanese *Collected Works of Marx and Engels* (*Renmei-ban Marx Engels Zenshu*). However, a single publisher, Kaizosha-ban Zenshu, also vigorously pursued the same publication plan, and eventually won out over the joint project. Takano was probably very pleased with the quality of the translation of the amalgamated publishers' version, on which researchers from his institute had worked. In the final stages of the collapse of this version Takano vainly sought its rescue by assuming the entire editorial responsibility for the *Zenshu* as an official task of the Institute.[26]

In 1930, in an explanatory article on the Ohara Institute, Takano wrote the following:

> In short, as this Institute is no more than a small private Institute, we cannot expect its performance to be as great in the future as it has been in the past. However, given that, except for the Marx–Engels–Lenin Institute in Moscow and the Institute for Social Research in Frankfurt, very few institutions in the world are equipped for such specialized research into social problems, the existence of this Institute in Japan surely encourages those who are concerned with social problems. The obligation of this Institute, to provide the emerging

> working class movement in Japan with a theoretical base and to register its perpetual struggles without delay, is not a private matter for the members of the Institute but a public matter that corresponds to the reasons for its foundation.'[27]

It is not difficult to detect Marxism and empirical social research among the common features of the three institutes mentioned in parallel. If the amalgamated publishers' version of *Zenshu* had continued, the Marxian linkage of the three institutes would have been more apparant.

12.6 THE TRANSFORMATION OF *SOZIALFORSCHUNG*

The sharing of a holistic approach to society first became apparent in the Marxian spirit of the participants in the Ilmenau (Geraberg) meeting. This was the first link between young intellectuals in the West and their counterparts in the East. Lukács's presentation privileged the consciousness of the working class in seeking a total view of the society. Korsch proposed grasping the Marxian critique of the political economy as the substantial philosophy of the working class. Fukumoto sketched the formation of social structure and its transformation process, with an emphasis on consciousness. His interpretation of Marxism dominated the thinking of young Communists seeking theoretical foundations for the reformation of the Japanese Communist Party, causing a dispute with the older leaders around the time of Hitoshi Yamakawa (1880–1958).

In 1924, Lukács was criticized by the Comintern orthodoxy for subjectivist deviation and, in 1926, Korsch was excluded from the Communist Party of Germany (KPD) for leftist deviation. In 1927, the dispute among Japanese Communists was decided not in Japan, but in Moscow. Fukumoto was displaced from the leadership of the Communist Party of Japan (JCP) on charges of an orientation to idealistic sectarianism. From that point on, 'Fukumotoism' was regarded as a sin that the JCP had committed in its juvenile phase.[28] Weil was neither an ideologue nor a party member. However, without ever stating this explicitly, he was also a leftist radical who sought a total critical view of society combined with revolutionary activities.

The next discovery was of the two parallel institutes: Frankfurt and Ohara. My guess about the origin of the name *Sozialforschung*, based on the foundation of the Ohara Institute, is that it was a creative translation of the English term 'social research'. In the late 1920s, the two institutes converged in terms of research guided by Marxism. This could develop into a visible linkage through the *Collected Works of Marx and Engels* (MEGA) whose motor was the third institute in Moscow.

Now, to finish this story, two questions must be answered. First, how should we understand the relationship of the above two linkages? Did Fukumoto not make a clear distinction between 'research into social problems' and 'social research' in the spirit of *Sozialforschung* commonly shared by the participants in the EMA?

It is true that the Ohara Institute originated from the idea of a philanthropic capitalist. The original aim of its research was social problems and their remedies, rather than a total view of society. However, the director and most researchers were well aware that social problems could not be fully grasped without a systematic study of the society by which they were caused. The term 'social problem' sounds like the partial view of philanthropists or *Kathedersozialisten* (professional socialists) that presupposed the immunity of their privileged position, or state power. However, in Japan around 1920, many scholars sought an 'ultimate solution to social problems'. In 1919, Hajime Kawakami (1879–1946), who could not offer a definite solution to modern social problems in his widely read *Bimbo Monogatari* [Tales of poverty] (1917), launched his own journal, *Shakai Mondai Kenkyu* [Study of social problems], to look for the 'ultimate solution to social problems'.[29] To many Japanese, the solution was either social revolution towards socialism, or moral revolution against private egoism.

Marxism suffused both institutes. Thus Marxism can be viewed as the core of the linkage both between the young intellectuals at the Ilmenau meeting and between the two institutes. However, the fresh radicalism of Fukumoto and Korsch or Lukács could not be contained within in the frame of the institutionalized study of Marxism. This was, I suppose, an intellectual version of Leninism that stressed the active elements of social criticism. Compared to them, both Grünberg and Takano were scholars who retained the traits of empiricism, since they were scholars in the camp of the social policy school.

The second question is with respect to how we should understand the relationship between Ilmenau's Marxism and Critical Theory from the Frankfurt perspective. On the Japanese side, the question is whether a similar outcome to Critical Theory can be found in the heritage of the Ohara Institute. At the end of section 4, I suggested that Horkheimer's Critical Theory abandoned the supposition of the class as the subject of recognition and rejected its identification with Leninism. In this respect, the attitude of social scientists in the Ohara Institute was ambiguous, and they handed the heritage of Marxian scholarship to the post-1945 generation. However, I see no changes in their outlooks in the areas of social philosophy. Seemingly, in the area of political thought, they simply retained the positions that they had adopted in the 1920s. I wonder whether they sensed the twin chimeras of Nazism and Stalinism as strongly as their European counterparts did.

NOTES

1. The Communist Party of Japan (JCP) was originally founded in July 1922 by a group of socialist activists. When Fukumoto returned to Japan, the JCP was dissolved under the influence of the old party leader, Yamakawa Hitoshi, who sought for a legal, unified mass party. Fukumoto was received by young Communists who were discontent with Yamakawa's direction. When the JCP was re-established in the end of 1926, Fukumoto was its leading theoretician.
2. I suppose that all these dates were in accordance with their interviews or correspondence with Weil. See Weil's recollections, cited in section 12.3 of this chapter.
3. I sent the record of the interview to Fukumoto, to which he answered in a letter dated 23 January 1975. This summary is based on the interview and his letter.
4. Later, in my talk with Fukumoto, he assumed that the date of the meeting was the spring of 1923, before he moved to Paris.
5. After one year's stay in Germany, Fukumoto moved to Paris, where he concentrated on writing his notes on the materialistic view of history, methodology of political economy, and the organizational problems of the revolutionary movement, which were later published in Japan and referred to as 'Fukumoto's trilogy' (Fukumoto, 1926a, 1926b, 1926c).
6. A this time, *shakai mondai* refers to problems such as urban pauperism, health and sanitary conditions of the masses, and labour disputes, which social policies broadly dealt with.
7. Author to the Ohara Institute, 5 February 1975.
8. Ohara Institute to author, 1 March 1975.
9. Author to Felix Weil, 11 October 1974.
10. See Kato (2006, 2008) and Yagi (2007, 2008). Barshay (2004) and Hein (2004) were translated into Japanese and welcomed by the public.
11. Friedeburg (2009) on the home page of the Institut für Sozialforschung, http://www.ifs.uni-frankfurt.de/index.html, accessed 20 January 2009.
12. Felix Weil, 'Erinnerungen' (fragment), [CHRONIKEN S5/421] housed in the Institut für Stadtgeschichte der Stadt Frankfurt am Main (Weil, 1973–75). The Institute admitted that the use of the text was free because no heir of the author was known after Frank Weil's death.
13. See Alexander (1985), Buckmiller (1988) and Hecker (2000).
14. It was during the Whitsun holidays in 1923. This date fits Fukumoto's recollection that he received Lukács's book, which was published in May 1923. Further, Fukumoto moved to Paris in June 1923.
15. Alexander (1985), S. 53. According to Mader (1985, S.12–13) the newborn KPD occupied the majority in the council of Gera, a village of ca. 1400 residents, and the manager was a loyal party member.
16. Mader (1985) maintained that another meeting was held in 1922 in Ilmenau, which was the EMA concerned. However, the basis of the existence of this first meeting was scarce and weak, while the second meeting in Geraberg was well documented. Buckmiller (1988, S.154–55) too was sceptical on the first meeting in 1922. My guess is that participants of the 1923 meeting used the name of a more renowned neighbouring town for some reason, such as to hide the exact place of the meeting.
17. Alexander (1985), S.53.
18. Orig. *Hoffähig*.
19. Horkheimer (1932, S.1).

20. Horkheimer (1937, S.265).
21. The differences in their views on social problems and the role of the institute for their research are explored in Wada (1997).
22. 'Ohara Shakai Mondai Kenkyusho Setsuritsu Shuisho' [Grounds of the Foundation of Ohara Institute of Social Research], in Ohara Shakai Mondai Kenkyusho (1971, 14).
23. In addition, Uno Kozo (1897–1977), whose theory founded a new school of Marxian Economics in post-1945 Japan, was an affiliated researcher of the institute, although his study in Germany (1921–23) was not financed by it.
24. From 1928, when the first nationwide repression of Marxist studies occurred, the maintenance of the institute became a matter for discussion between Takano and Ohara. Despite his company's difficult situation, Ohara did not reduce his financial support until 1936. After Ohara's support ceased, the institute moved to Tokyo in 1937.
25. Takano (1961) contains essays and extracts of his diary that are related to this tour.
26. Takano's correspondence with Rjazanov was found in Moscow and printed in Rolf Hecker (1997). See also Omura (2005).
27. 'Ohara Shakai Mondai Kenkyusho', in *Shakai Kagaku Daijiten* [Great dictionary of social science], 1930, in Takano (1961, 169f.).
28. Fukumoto was arrested in 1928 and imprisoned for 14 years. After his release, he began his folklore and historical studies. Although he returned to the JCP in 1949 and ran for election, he was critical of the leadership and maintained an independent journal. Until he was in his eighties, he continued his research on Japanese cultural history, particularly of the Edo Period, in which he believed a 'Renaissance of Japan' existed (Iwami, 1993).
29. In Kawakami's case, the 'ultimate solution' had a moralistic connotation that condemned private egoism. Kushida and Fukumoto rejected this moralism. See Yagi (2007).

REFERENCES

Alexander, Susanne (1985), 'Marxistische Arbeitswoche', *Beiträge zur Geschichte der Arbeiterbewegung*, **27** (1), 53–54.

Barshay, Andrew E. (2004), *The Social Sciences in Modern Japan: The Marxian and Modernist Traditions*, Berkeley, CA: University of California Press.

Buckmiller, Michael (1973), 'Marxismus als Realität. Zur Rekonstruktion der theoretischen und politischen Entwicklung Karl Korschs', in C. von Pozzoli (ed.), *Jahrbuch der Arbeiterbewegung, Bd.1, Über Karl Korsch*, Frankfuer a. M.: Fischer, pp. 411–13.

Buckmiller, Michael (1988), 'Die Marxistische Arbeitswoche 1923 und die Gründung des Instituts für Sozialforschung', in Willem van Reijen and G. Schmid Noerr (eds), *Grand Hotel Abgrund: Eine Photobiographie der Frankfurter Schule*, Hamburg: Unius Verlag, pp. 141–82.

Cole, G.D.H. (1920), *Social Theory*, Methven.

Friedeburg, Ludwig v. (2009), 'Geschichte des Instituts für Sozialforschung', http://www.uni-frankfurt.de/ accessed January 2009.

Fukumoto, Kazuo (1926a), *Shakai no Kosei narabini Henkaku no Katei* [Process of the construction and transformation of society], Tokyo: Hakuyosha.

Fukumoto, Kazuo (1926b), *Keizaigaku Hihan no Hohoron* [Methodology of the criticism of political economy], Tokyo: Hakuyosha.

Fukumoto, Kazuo (pseudonym Hojo Kazuo) (1926c), *Musan Kaikyu no Hoko Tenkan* [Change in direction of the proletarian movement], Tokyo: Kibokaku.

Fukumoto, Kazuo (1952), *Kakumei wa Tanoshi karazuya: Kaikoroku Mutki-hen* [How enjoyable was the revolution: Recollections Part 1, Foghorns], Tokyo: Kyoiku Shorin.

Fukumoto, Kazuo (2008–2011), *Fukumoto Kazuo Chosakushu*, 10 vols, Tokyo: Kobushi Shobo.

Hecker, Rolf (1997), 'Zu den Beziehungen zwischen dem Moskauer Marx-Engels-Institut und dem Ohara-Institut für Sozialforschung in Osaka', *Beiträge zur Marx-Engels-Forschung Neue Folge Sonderband 1, David Boriscovic Rjazanov und die erste MEGA*, Berlin and Hamburg: Argument, pp. 85–107.

Hecker, Rolf (2000), 'Erfolgreiche Kooperation: Das Frankfurte Institut für Sozialforschung und das Moskauer Marx-Engels-Institut (1924–1928)', *Beiträge zur Marx-Engels-Forschung Neue Folge Sonderband 2, Erfolgreiche Kooperation: Das Frankfurter Institut für Sozialforschung und das Moskauer Marx-Engels-Institut (1924–1928)*, Berlin and Hamburg: Argument Verlag, pp. 9–120.

Hein, Laura Elizabeth (2004), *Reasonable Men, Powerful Words: Political Culture and Expertise in Twentieth Century Japan*, Berkeley: University of California Press.

Hirano, Y. (1929), 'K. Fukumoto, *Zur Methodologie der 'Kritik der Politischen Ökonomie*, Tokio 1926, 439S', *Archiv für die Geschichte des Sozialismus und der Arbeiterbewegung*, **14**, 157–9.

Horkheimer, Max (1932), 'Vorwort', *Zeitschrift für Sozialforschung*, **1**, i–iv.

Horkheimer, Max (1937), 'Traditionelle und Kritische Theorie, Philosophie und Kritische Theorie', in *Zeitschrift für Sozialforschung*, **6**, 245–94.

Iwami, Takashi (1993), *Fukumoto Kazuo: Nihon Renaissance-ron wo meguru Shiso to Ningen*, Tokyo: Ronso-sha.

Jay, Martin (1973), *Dialectical Imagination: A History of the Frankfurt School and the Institute for Social Research 1923–1950*, Boston/Toronto, MA, USA and Toronto, Canada: University of California Press.

Kato, Tetsuro (2006), 'Personal contacts in Japanese–German cultural relations during the 1920s and early 1930s', in Christian W. Spang and Rolf-Harald Wippich (eds), *Japanese-German Relations, 1895–1945: War, Diplomacy and Public Opinion*, London, Abingdon, and New York: Routledge, pp. 119–38.

Kato, Tetsuro (2008), *Weimar-ki Berlin no Nihonjin: Yoko-Chishikijin no Hantei-Network* [Japanese in Berlin of the Weimar Republic: anti-imperialism network of overseas Japanese intellectuals], Tokyo: Iwanami Shoten.

Kawakami, Hajime (1917), *Bimbo Monogatari* [Tale of poverty], Kobundo.

Kojima, Ryo (ed.) (2005), *Fukumoto Kazuo no Shiso* [Ideas of Fukumoto Kazuo], Tokyo: Kobushi Shobo.

Korsch, Karl (1922), *Kernpunkte der materialistischen Geschichtsauffassung – Eine quellenmässige Darstellung*, Berlin: VIVA.

Kuruma, Samezo (1923), 'Das Konsumgenossenschaftswesen in Japan', in G.J.W.F. Goedhart, Samezo Kuruma, Siegmund Kaff and Karl Pettermand (eds), *Die Konsumsvereine in Holland, Japan, Österreich und der Schweiz* München and Leipzig: Schriften des Vereins für Sozialpolitik, vol. 150.

Lukács, George (1923), *Geschichte und Klassenbewusstsein*, Berlin: Malik-Verlag.

Mader, Julius (1985), *Dr. Richard Sorge in Ilmenau, Geraberg und Suhl. Festschrift zum 90. Geburtstag des Helden der Sowietunion*, Ortsparteileitung der SED in Geraberg [Geraberg Local Social Unity Party Executive].

Migdal, Ulrike (1981), *Die Frühgeschichte des Frankfurter Instituts für Sozialforschung*, Frankfurt. a. Main: Campus Verlag.

Ohara Shakai Mondai Kenkyusho (Hosei Daigaku) (ed.) (1971), *Ohara Shakai Mondai Kenkyusho Gojyunenshi* [Half century history of Ohara Institute for Social Research], Tokyo: Hosei Daigaku Shuppankyoku.

Omura, Izumi (2005), 'Takano Iwasaburo to D. Rjazanov tono Ofukushokan (1928nen–1930nen)' [Correspondence of D. Rjazanov and Takano Iwasaburo 1928–1930], *Ohara Shakaimondai Kenkyusho Zasshi*, **559**, 16–35.

Shakai, Shiso-sha (ed.) (1930), *Shakai Kagaku Daijiten* [Great dictionary of social science], Kaizo-sha.

Takano, Iwasaburo (1961), *Kappa no He* [Farts of Kappa], Suzuki Koichiro (ed.), Tokyo: Iwanami Shoten.

Wada, Tsuyoshi (1997), 'Ohara Magosaburo – Takano Iwasaburo – Kawakami Hajime: Ohara Shakaimondai Kenkyusho wo meguru Shiso ni kansuru Shoron' [An essay on the ideas around the Ohara Institute of Social Research], *Keizai to Keizaigaku* (Tokyo Toritsu Daigaku), **82**, 31–48.

Weil, Felix (1973–75), 'Erinnerungen', manuscript kept in the Institut für Stadtgeschichte Frankfurt a. M. [CHRONIKEn S5/421].

Yagi, Kiichiro (1976), 'Shakai Kenkyu (Sozialforschung) to Marukusu-shugi', [Sozialforschung and Marxism], *Nagoya Jinbun Kagaku Kenkyukai Nenpou*, **2**, 62–77.

Yagi, Kiichiro (1984), 'Fukumoto Kazuo to Frankfurt Shakai Kenkyusho' [Fukumoto Kazuo and Frankfurt Institute for Social Research]', *Undoshi Kenkyu*, no. 13, Tokyo: Sanichi Shobo, pp. 157–66, reprinted in Ryo Kojima (ed.), *Fukumoto Kazuo no Shiso*: *Kenkyu Ronbun Shusei* [Ideas of Fukumoto Kazuo: collection of research], Tokyo: Kobushi Shobo.

Yagi, Kiichiro (2007), 'Emergence of Marxian scholarship in Japan: Kawakami Hajime and his two critics', *Rekishi to Keizai*, **194**, 34–45.

Yagi, Kiichiro (2008), 'Japanische Wirtschaftswissenschaftler in der Deutschland der Weimarer Periode', Vortrag gehalten am Sitzung des Dogmenhistorischen Ausschusses des Verein für Sozialpolitik, Berlin, May.

13. The contributions of two eminent Japanese scholars to the development of economic theory: Michio Morishima and Takashi Negishi

Heinz D. Kurz

13.1 INTRODUCTION

This chapter scrutinizes and compares the contributions of two eminent and internationally renowned Japanese scholars to the history of economic thought: the late Michio Morishima and Takashi Negishi. Both are leading theorists who, however, saw their own analytical work as firmly embedded in the flow of economic ideas of the past three centuries, since the inception of systematic economic thought. They learned from past authors, benefitted from combining some of their ideas in order to create something new, and rejected the view that the history of economic thought is a grave containing the dead ideas of dead people. They rather saw it as a treasure trove, rich with ideas and concepts that still have to be explored, developed and brought to fruition by cross-breeding them with other ideas and concepts.[1] The two also referred to each other's works and commented on the ideas contained therein. They even involved each other in debate and controversy on a number of issues.

Michio Morishima is especially known for his innovative work on the multisectoral theory of economic growth and income distribution, generalizing John von Neumann's model (1945) in order to cover a number of phenomena not dealt with in its original formulation. These include, *inter alia*, a discussion of different savings propensities out of wages and profits, different forms of technical progress, the turnpike problem, and the role of money, credit and interest in the growth process (see Morishima, 1964, 1969, 1992). Morishima is concerned with developing 'a new formulation of general equilibrium', hence the subtitle of one of his books (Morishima, 1992), or, more precisely, an alternative formulation to the general equilibrium theory in the tradition of Arrow and Debreu. The new formulation is supposed to offer 'a more satisfactory model of general equilibrium' (1992, 2) that is not tied to Say's law and therefore may incorporate important ideas of Marx, Walras, Keynes and Schumpeter, in particular the problem of unemployment. Takashi Negishi is especially known for his innovative contributions to general equilibrium theory in the tradition of Arrow and Debreu. Among other things, he provided an alternative proof of the existence of a competitive general equilibrium by searching for a Pareto-optimal allocation of resources at which the budget constraints of all the consumers are satisfied at efficiency prices. The proof was first published in *Metroeconomica* (Negishi, 1960), a journal I have had the privilege of editing together with Neri Salvadori for the past few years. The method of proof has since then been used especially in numerical computations of general equilibria.

In this chapter special attention will be paid to the two authors' studies of the works of some of the most important economists ever, in particular Adam Smith, David Ricardo, Karl Marx, Léon Walras, Eugen von Böhm-Bawerk, Knut Wicksell and John Maynard Keynes. While Morishima's contributions are mostly in the form of books devoted to the works of major authors (see especially Morishima, 1973, 1977, 1989), Negishi's are mostly in the form of short articles that are conveniently collected in three volumes (Negishi, 1993d, 1994, 2000; but see also Negishi, 1989). How did the two scholars interpret the works of leading economists? Which of their ideas did they find convincing and which not?

13.2 THE CLASSICAL ECONOMISTS

Both Morishima and Negishi carefully studied the classical authors. Morishima's main interest appears to have been David Ricardo's magnum opus, the *Principles*, and the contributions of those who developed Ricardo's ideas, especially Piero Sraffa, Nicholas Kaldor (1955–56) and Luigi Pasinetti (1960). In addition to Ricardo, Negishi focused on Adam Smith and especially his 'magnificent dynamics', that is, Smith's view of the process of capital accumulation, population growth and the growth of labour productivity entailed by a widening and deepening of the division of labour. Here we deal first and foremost with the two authors' disquisitions on Ricardo.

In the preface to his book *Ricardo's Economics: A General Equilibrium Theory of Distribution and Growth*, Morishima states that 'this volume is not primarily a book on history of economic analysis but a reappraisal of past great economists from the viewpoint of contemporary economic theory' (1989, vii). Together with *Marx's Economics* (1973) and *Walras's Economics* (1977), on which more below, it forms a trilogy. In terms of the conventional (but problematic) distinction between historical and rational reconstructions, all three works mentioned belong predominantly to the second class.

13.2.1 Value and Distribution

The characteristic feature of Morishima's respective works is that he looks upon past authors through the lens of an extended version of John von Neumann's paper 'A model of general economic equilibrium' (1945). It is this perspective that makes him maintain that the analyses of the three authors are much more similar than is generally held. He actually contends that they are characterized by a *unité de doctrine* (1989, 4).

One may wonder whether this contention can be sustained. One difference between the classical authors and Marx on the one hand, and Walras and the marginalist authors on the other, is too obvious to be overlooked. The former treated wages and property incomes (profits and rents) asymmetrically, and explained the latter in terms of the surplus product or residual that remains after all means of production that have been used up and the means of subsistence in the support of workers have been subtracted from gross outputs levels. On the contrary, the latter treated all kinds of incomes alike, that is, symmetrically, with reference to the 'forces of demand and supply' interacting in the respective factor markets, and thus in terms of the relative scarcities of the different factors, or their marginal productivities. In the former, real or commodity wages are taken to be part and parcel of the inputs needed in production and are thus essentially reckoned as an element of the capital advanced at the beginning of the production period, whereas in the latter they are treated as a part of the product that emerges as the result of the cooperation of the different productive forces.[2]

Before I proceed, it is interesting to note that the von Neumann model, which forms the basis from which Morishima develops his argument, shares a similar outlook on economic phenomena as the classical economists (see Kurz and Salvadori, 1993). Von Neumann takes the real wage rate as given and paid *ante factum*. Technically, he explicitly subsumes the means of subsistence of workers under the coefficients of the input matrix **A** of his model, that is, employs what he called the 'augmented matrix' (Morishima, 1964, 1969). At given levels of the operation of the different processes of production, profits (or interest, as von Neumann prefers to call them) consist physically of the net product, or social surplus. As Ricardo stressed: 'Profits come out of the surplus product' (Ricardo,

Works, II, 130–31; similarly I, 95). When it comes to the determination of the rate of return on capital and relative prices, real wages are thus treated as a given magnitude both in the classical authors and in von Neumann. Also Marx adopted this approach from the classical authors, and especially Ricardo, and attempted to ascertain the general rate of profit as the ratio of the labour value of the surplus product, or surplus value, and the labour value of the social capital, consisting of a constant (means of production) and a variable (wage goods) capital. While Ricardo and Marx were able to expound and develop in some detail the classical surplus-based approach to the theory of value and distribution, they did not succeed in providing a logically coherent version of it. This was only achieved by John von Neumann, apparently without being aware of the classical features of his approach, because it can safely be assumed that he was not familiar with the writings of the classical authors;[3] and then, in a more general analytical framework and with a thorough understanding of the classical authors, by Piero Sraffa (1960).

Morishima deals not only with Ricardo's theory of value and distribution, but also with other aspects of his analysis, including rent theory, durable instruments of production, the problem of the standard of value, the natural wage doctrine, the theory of comparative advantage and Say's law in connection with the problem of machinery. For a critical assessment of his respective discussions, see Kurz and Salvadori (1992). Here I comment only on the last three issues mentioned.

13.2.2 Natural Wages

Ricardo distinguished, not only with regard to commodities but also with regard to labour, a 'natural' and a 'market' price. In some places, apparently focusing attention on a self-replacing state of the economic system, he defined the 'natural wage' as that wage that is just sufficient to allow for the reproduction of the labour force, without any increase or diminution. However, with the rate of profit falling as capital accumulates and population grows due to extensive and intensive diminishing returns in agriculture, and setting aside technical progress, Ricardo's doctrine has widely been interpreted as revolving around the concept of a given and constant long-run subsistence wage. While in an 'improving society' natural wages are typically higher than in a stagnant one because via the wage rate the growth of population is adjusted to the requirements of accumulation, in a stationary state they are down to the subsistence level. Yet this is too narrow a view of Ricardo's doctrine. While several of Morishima's statements on the issue I find problematic, I think he is right in pointing out that the concept of the natural wage in Ricardo is a much more complex concept than is usually understood, and that it is often defined in conjunction with the rate of capital accumulation. The two are attuned to one another in such a way that the natural level of the real wage rate, via the growth in the working population, sustains the accumulation rate, and the accumulation rate, via its impact on the demand for labour, sustains the real wage. Hence Ricardo's position in this regard is not all that different from Adam Smith's.[4]

There is a point of contact here between Morishima's analysis and an argument put forward by Negishi in a paper on Adam Smith's theory of growth (Negishi, 1993c). As regards the population mechanism Smith sees at work, it anticipates an important element of Thomas Robert Malthus's analysis in that it also contemplates a positive relationship between the real wage rate and the growth rate of polulation.[5] We may express the idea in simple terms as involving a relationship of the following kind:

$$w = (1 + g)w^*$$

where g is the rate of growth of the work force, w^* is the real wage rate in a stationary system and w is the wage rate that attunes g to the requirements of capital accumulation. One might incorporate a ratchet effect in this, reflecting Ricardo's conviction that with a higher level of the real wage rate workers will adjust to the new situation and develop needs and wants that render necessaries what previously were comforts or even luxuries.

The above ideas coexist in Ricardo's writings and reflect the complexity of his thoughts and variability of the conditions contemplated. It should therefore come as no surprise that different interpreters, focusing attention on differents parts of his analysis, would come to different conclusions concerning his doctrine. The fact is that these elements are all there. What should be clear, though, is that the natural wage must not be mistaken for a purely physiological minimum of subsistence (Ricardo, *Works*, I, 96–7). Ricardo, like other classical authors with their emphasis on the social and historical factors shaping economic behaviour, even anticipated what was to become a most important empirical fact, namely, that economic development and the emergence of new institutions endogenously eroded the Malthusian population mechanism. Thus Ricardo contemplated the possibility that 'population may be so little stimulated by ample wages as to increase at the slowest rate – or it may even go in a retrograde direction' (Ricardo, *Works*, VIII, 169).

Ricardo also discussed the case of workers participating in the sharing out of the surplus product.[6] In this case he felt the need to replace the concept of a given real (that is, commodity) wage rate by a share concept, or 'proportional wages' (Sraffa, 1951, p. lii), that is, 'the proportion of the annual labour of the country . . . devoted to the support of the labourers'

(*Works*, I, 49). It was on the basis of the new wage concept (and on the premise that the social capital consisted only of, or could entirely be reduced to, wages) that Ricardo then asserted what was called his 'fundamental proposition on distribution': that the rate of profits depends on proportional wages, and on nothing else.

13.2.3 Foreign Trade

I do not think that the criticism Morishima levels at Ricardo's trade theory, contained in Chapter VII, 'On foreign trade', of the *Principles*, can be sustained. According to Morishima the chapter 'begins on the wrong foot and results in confusion and incomprehensibility' (1989, 128). Ricardo is said to have been particularly wrong in rejecting Smith's view that the opening of trade increases the rate of profit. However, there appears to be a misunderstanding on Morishima's part here. On the assumption of a given real (or commodity) wage rate, the opening of trade, by rendering some wage goods less expensive, implies a reduction in the nominal wage rate. Ricardo concluded that profitability will increase for a given and constant real wage rate, if trade entails a lowering of the price of (some) wage goods, whereas a lowering of the price of luxuries would have no such effect. This is an important insight which carries a distinction encountered in Ricardo's discussion of different forms of technical progress over to the realm of international trade. In Ricardo's view trade and specialization typically involve larger rates of profits of the countries involved and thus corroborate his conviction that foreign trade and improved machinery may have similar effects: 'If . . . by the extension of foreign trade, or by improvements in machinery, the food and necessaries of the labourer can be brought to the market at a reduced price, [the rate of] profits will rise' (Ricardo, *Works*, I, 132).

This view is neatly corrobrated by Negishi in his paper 'The labor theory of value in the Ricardian theory of international trade' (1982c) which focuses attention on Ricardo's famous numerical example of comparative costs.[7] He takes issue with the received marginalist (or neoclassical) interpretation of the example which contends that the latter is based on the assumption that there is only a single factor of production, labour. Negishi rightly insists that this is not so, because Ricardo's argument is naturally developed against the background of an economic system that involves the use of land, produced means of production (and means of subsistence, or capital) and labour. Interestingly, Negishi also rejects the view that Ricardo cannot determine the terms of trade without having recourse to considerations concerning the demand for commodities, as a long tradition of interpreting Ricardo taking off from John Stuart Mill contends. In this regard he elaborates on an argument put forward by K. Kojima. Negishi stresses that Ricardo was aware of the fact that the opening of trade increases the domestic rate of profits for a given real wage rate (provided wage goods and not only luxuries are involved).[8]

Let us immediately turn to the gist of Negishi's argument. He assumes that the real wage per unit of labour employed is the same in both countries, Portugal (P) and England (E), and is given in terms of a fixed bundle of wage goods, consisting of c_1 units of cloth and c_2 units of wine. Both products are produced with constant returns to scale production processes that employ only wage capital. Hence in autarky the price equations in the two countries are given by:

$$p_{1j} = (1 + r_j)\, l_{1j}\, (c_1 p_{1j} + c_2 p_{2j})$$

$$p_{2j} = (1 + r_j)\, l_{2j}\, (c_1 p_{1j} + c_2 p_{2j})$$

where $j = P, E$. From the two equations and Ricardo's numerical example $[(l_{1P} = 90;\ l_{2P} = 80), (l_{1E} = 100;\ l_{2E} = 120)]$, it can immediately be seen that:

1. in autarky the price ratio of the two commodities, p_{1j}/p_{2j}, equals the ratio of direct national labour inputs, l_{1j}/l_{2j}: cloth is relatively less expensive in England and wine is relatively less expensive in Portugal.
2. The rate of profits in autarky is the higher the higher is labour productivity (the lower is the direct labour coefficient) in each domestic sector, given the real wage rate.
3. In autarky the rate of profits is higer in Portugal than in England, because Portugal exhibits a higher productivity of labour than England in both industries.

After trade begins, the prices of cloth and wine are taken to become the same in the two countries, because transportation costs and the like are set aside. This means, as Negishi points out (1982c, 206), that with a given and uniform real wage rate money wages are equalized between the two countries. According to the principle of comparative advantage, Portugal will specialize in the production of wine and England in the production of cloth. Negishi shows that in the trade situation the three distributive variables r_P, r_E and the (common) real wages rate (c_1, c_2) are related in the following way:

$$R_P R_E - 100c_1 R_P - 80c_2 R_E = 0, \qquad (*)$$

where $R_P = 1/(1 + r_P)$ and $R_E = 1/(1 + r_E)$.

Obviously, the case in which $r_P = r_E$ (and thus $R_P = R_E$) is a very special constellation implying riskless and costless capital investment in both countries. Yet if that constellation prevails it is clear that relative prices are fully determined, because in this case Portugal and England have been replaced by a larger economy that produces the two commodities in two industries only instead of in four, where industry 1 uses the English method of production and industry 2 the Portuguese one.

Yet as Negishi rightly points out, this is not the most interesting case that Ricardo contemplated in his chapter on trade. The reason is that capital movements may face difficulties and insecurities. Ricardo in fact stressed:

> Experience . . . shews, that the fancied or real insecurity of capital, when not under the immediate control of its owner, together with the natural disinclination which every man has to quit the country of his birth and connexions, and intrust himself with all his habits fixed, to a strange government and new laws, check the emigration of capital. These feelings, which I should be sorry to see weakened, induce most men of property to be satisfied with a low rate of profits in their own country, rather than seek a more advantageous employment for their wealth in foreign nations. (Ricardo, *Works* I, 136–7)

In such cases capital mobility will be hampered and together with it from a certain point onwards a tendency towards a uniform rate of return on capital worldwide. In Ricardo's example, a higher rate of profits in Portugal can, in principle, be expected to attract English capital. Yet if English importers and exporters are satisified with a decent rate of profits at home rather than seek a higher rate abroad, there will be no full equalization of profitability. Negishi (1982c, 207) formulates the basic idea by defining a 'rate of conversion a (< 1)' by which English capitalists 'discount' r_P in case it is higher than r_E:

$$\mathrm{R}_P = a\mathrm{R}_E.$$

Then equation (*) becomes

$$R_E = 100c_1 + (80/a)c_2.$$

Clearly, a larger a involves a smaller R_E and thus a larger r_E: English capitalists benefit from their discounting profitability elsewhere. For a given conversion rate a, r_E is determined and together with it r_p and the price ratio of the two commodities in the 'world market' (consisting of Portugal and England). Negishi conludes: 'Ricardian theory can determine the terms of trade on the basis of cost–price relations without having recourse to reciprocal demands' (1982c, 208). And in another paper he insists:

> Neoclassical theory of international trade cannot determine the terms of trade, without taking the reciprocal demand into consideration. Those who consider Ricardo's theory as a special case of the neoclassical one naturally regard the former as merely a partial theory of international trade, which by itself cannot determine the terms of trade, having no consideration of the reciprocal demand. This interpretation of Ricardo is, however, clearly a misunderstanding of neoclassical economists. (Negishi, 1996a, 234)

He adds:

> The lesson from [this] reinterpretation of Ricardo's magic numbers of comparative advantage is that the study of the classical theory from the point of view of modern theory should not be a cutting or stretching of the former theory in a Procrustean bed of the latter. It should be a mirror in which modern theory finds the importance of what it forgot to learn from the classical theory, in this case, the role of exporters and importers in international trade and investment. (Negishi, 1996a, 235)

Negishi's is an interesting reconstruction of a central element of Ricardo's theory of trade that for simplicity sets aside the problem of scarce land(s).

Seen from a higher standpoint, Negishi's reconstruction may be said to be covered by the so-called 'Non-Substitution Theorem'.[9] The theorem applied to the present case states that relative prices and the rate of profits in the two countries are independent of the pattern of final demand provided: (1) there are constant returns to scale throughout both economies; (2) there is no joint production (and thus no fixed capital); (3) there is only a single original factor of production (homogeneous labour); and (4) the real wage rate and the ratio of the two domestic profit rates are given (from within a feasible range).[10] These conditions are met by Negishi's reconstruction of Ricardo's argument.[11]

13.2.4 Machinery and Say's Law

As is well known, in the third edition of the *Principles* Ricardo recanted his previously held view that improved machinery cannot be injurious to the interests of the class of labourers. He had convinced himself that the mechanization of production – the substitution of machine power for labour power – involves a destruction of the circulating capital and thus of necessity leads to a 'diminution in the demand for labour, population will become redundant, and the situation of the labouring classes will be that of distress and poverty' (*Works*, I, 390).

Morishima (1989, 11) contends that Ricardo's argument is fundamentally flawed and that Say's law does not admit of unemployment. Morishima therefore feels entitled to modify the famous numerical example that Ricardo had elaborated in order to illustrate the case of technologically induced unemployment.

I see especially two problems with Morishima's argument. First, he interprets Say's law in the modern (marginalist) sense as involving the clearing of all markets, including a 'labour market'.[12] Yet, this is not the sense in which Ricardo or his contemporaries used it: they confined Say's law to markets, in which commodities are exchanged that have been produced in the hope and expectation of making profits, that is, capitalistically. Labour (or, in Marx's terminology, labour power) does not belong to them: it is not capitalistically produced. Hence the law does not apply to it, and indeed we do not find in Ricardo a discussion of the 'labour market'. Ricardo rather stressed that 'M. Say . . . has most satisfactorily shewn, that there is no amount of capital which may not be employed in a country, because demand is only limited by production.' And, 'there is no limit to demand – no limit to the employment of capital while it yields any profit' (*Works*, I, 290, 296). Ricardo's finding that the introduction of improved machinery may displace workers therefore does not contradict the then prevalent version of the 'law of markets'.

Secondly, Morishima's reworking of Ricardo's numerical example empties Ricardo's reasoning of its very content. As Negishi (2000, 103) stressed: 'Apparently, Morishima's problem is different from Ricardo's machinery problem.' Ricardo is interested in the problem of whether the production of a new machine, and then its productive use, changes the overall composition of the capital stock of the miniature system under consideration, away from criculating capital, which is (for the main part) used to employ workers, and towards fixed capital, which is not used to do so. Ricardo identifies this shift as the source of the trouble. Contrary to his claim, Morishima's alternative construction contains no discussion of the replacement of human labour by machinery, which was Ricardo's main concern. Interestingly, Negishi (1998a) in a critical comment, rejected Morishima's argument on the ground that it did not contain a faithful interpretation of Ricardo's reasoning and therefore could not disprove the latter's opinion on the matter.

We may conclude by saying that while Morishima's interpretation of Ricardo contains some interesting observations on how to develop the argument and formalize certain parts of it, in important respects the interpretation is difficult to sustain. The view that Ricardo, Marx and Walras shared a similar approach to the problems they investigated is particularly dubious, as the following discussion will show.

13.3 KARL MARX AND THE MARXISTS

Karl Marx's contribution to political economy is dealt with in numerous works of Morishima and Negishi. Their attention focuses first and foremost on the theory of value and distribution and the theory of capital accumulation and economic dynamics, including Marx's explanation of a long-run tendency of the rate of profit to fall. Morishima's main works in this regard are two books: his *Marx's Economics: A Dual Theory of Value and Growth* (1973) and, together with George Catephores, *Value, Exploitation and Growth* (1978). Both books met with considerable interest and in the aftermath of the controversies in the theory of capital contributed to a sometimes heated debate about the merits and demerits of Marx's economic analysis.[13]

Negishi published a number of papers on Marx and compared Marx's analysis especially with Eugen von Böhm-Bawerk's (see Negishi, 1980a). He is basically in agreement with Morishima in that also in his view the 'essence of the labor theory of value lies . . . not so much in the proportionality of relative values and quantities of labor embodied as in the explanation of the profit created not in the process of circulation but in the process of production' (1982c, 199). This comes close to what Morishima dubbed the 'Fundamental Marxian Theorem'.

13.3.1 Value and Distribution

It does not come as a surprise that Morishima also approaches Marx from a von Neumann perspective. In his view the labour theory of value was used by Marx essentially as a device to aggregate microeconomic magnitudes and arrive at macroeconomic ones which are supposed to allow him to establish the 'laws of motion' of the economy as a whole (see, for example, 1973, 3). I think this is a valid observation in the light of the fact that Marx appears to have been convinced that this method provided him with a correct expression of the general rate of profit – the key variable of a capitalist economy. Once this rate was known, prices of production could be ascertained in a second step by appropriately marking up costs of production.

However, Marx's two-step procedure, or what Ladislaus von Bortkiewicz called Marx's 'successivism', cannot generally be sustained. As von Neumann and then Sraffa showed, the general rate of profit and relative prices can be determined without any recourse to labour values. Yet this aspect will concern us here only incidentally. We rather focus attention on Morishima and Catephores's reconsideration of the labour theory of value in their 1978 book, because it is here that they themselves see a chief innovation in the discussion of Marx's economics. Whereas labour values are conventionally (and also in Morishima, 1973) determined in terms of systems of simultaneous equations of the sort:

$$\mathbf{Bv} = \mathbf{Av} + \mathbf{l},$$

where **B** is the (square) output coefficient matrix, **A** the (square) matrix of input coefficients of means of production, **l** the vector of direct labour input coefficients and **v** the vector of labour values.[14] Provided the inverse of matrix (**B** – **A**) exists, one gets:

$$\mathbf{v} = (\mathbf{B} - \mathbf{A})^{-1}\mathbf{l}$$

This approach the two authors reject and replace it with an approach that ascertains labour values in terms of a von Neumann linear programming approach. The 'true value' of a commodity *i* is said to be obtained as a solution:

$$v_i^* = \mathbf{q}^*\mathbf{l}$$

to the following problem:

$$\text{Minimize } \mathbf{ql}$$

$$\text{subject to } \mathbf{qB} \geq \mathbf{qA} + \mathbf{e}_i, \ \mathbf{q} \geq \mathbf{0},$$

where **q** is the vector of the operation of processes and $\mathbf{e}_i$ is the *i*-th unit vector (whose element *i* is unity, all the other elements being zero). Hence Morishima and Catephores's 'true values' are those that minimize the amounts of labour needed directly and indirectly in the net production of one unit of the respective commodity.

What has motivated this reconsideration? In his 1960 book, Sraffa had pointed out that:

> in the case of joint-products there is no obvious criterion for apportioning the labour among individual products, and indeed it seems doubtful whether it makes any sense to speak of a separate quantity of labour as having gone to produce one of a number of jointly produced commodities. (p. 56)

He went on to argue that with joint production it cannot be excluded that a *ceteris paribus* increase in the net output of one commodity might request a change in the proportions in which the different processes of production are activated such that a reduction in the total amount of (direct) labour employed results. Hence, one would have to conclude that the commodity under consideration 'is in fact being produced by a *negative* quantity of labour' (1960, 60). Taking up Sraffa's finding, Steedman (1975) then showed that there are cases in which positive profits may go together with a negative surplus value. This, however, flew in the face of Morishima's 1973 'Fundamental Marxian Theorem' (1973, 53–4) that positive surplus value is a necessary and sufficient condition for positive profits. In order to save the theorem, or some version of it, the concept of labour values had to be reconsidered with special regard to joint production: 'negative' labour values had to be avoided.

On the basis of their new definition Morishima and Catephores proved the following two propositions:

1. The surplus to necessary labour ratio, which the authors consider as the full measure of 'exploitation', is generally greater than the rate of surplus value, because of the non-additiveness of 'true values'.
2. The capitalist system is profitable and capable of expansion if and only if workers are exploited. This finding the authors now dub the 'Generalized Fundamental Marxian Theorem' (1978, 45–53).

While the new concept of 'true value' manages to accomplish the predefined task, there are a number of features of this approach that are disquieting. First, some of the processes selected by the above labour-minimization problem need not be chosen by cost-minimizing producers at the given real wage rate, as analysed by John von Neumann (1945) and Sraffa (1960). Hence the solution that Catephores and Morishima propose in order to get rid of negative labour values may relate to an economic system that differs substantially from the one actually in use (according to the solution of the choice of technique problem). It may be asked: what is the relevance of methods of production that are not employed for the actual economy and its characterization? Secondly, and closely related to what has just been said, Marx insisted that in the case where differently 'productive' methods are used side by side, what matters is not the most productive one, but an average of those actually employed. Hence, Marx insisted that what matters are the actually employed methods and not some other methods. Finally, in their treatment of the 'transformation problem' of labour values in prices of production (1978, Chapter 6) the authors surprisingly do not start from 'true values' but from those conventional labour values that result from solving a system of simultaneous equations (see above). It thus remains somewhat unclear what labour values do mean and for what purpose they are needed.

13.3.2 Falling Tendency of the General Rate of Profit

In two papers Negishi (1998b, 1999b) takes issue with the conventional interpretation of Marx's law of the falling tendency of the rate of profit and its criticism in terms of the Shibata–Okishio Theorem. The theorem states that a new (single product) method of production, which reduces the unit cost of a (basic) product,[15] will be introduced by cost-minimizing producers and, for a given real wage rate, of necessity raises the general (or competitive) rate of profit. This may well go along with an increase in the organic composition of capital. Hence, Marx's respective argument in Volume III of *Capital* is seen to be flawed.

Negishi disagrees with this assessment. The formalization, he insists, does not faithfully represent Marx's argument: 'the model of an economy used to prove the Shibata–Okishio theorem may be too restrictive for Marx' (1998b, 253). The world that Marx had in mind, Negishi surmises, exhibits two crucial features not taken into account in the respective literature: (1) diminishing unit costs due to economies of scale; and (2) firms facing downward-sloping demand curves. It is competition among capitalists vis-à-vis these two facts, which, in Negishi's interpretation, is responsible for Marx's law of a falling rate of profit. Marx's basic idea, Negishi maintains, can be rendered clear in terms of Cournot's model of oligopoly or Chamberlin's model of monopolistic competition.[16] These models, Negishi surmises, are appropriate for discussing the falling tendency of the rate of profit along Marx's lines, whereas the 'Walrasian assumptions of constant returns to scale and perfect competition' (1998b, 258) are not.[17]

It suffices to limit this discussion to Negishi's adaptation of Cournot's model. Negishi assumes that each of n identical firms has a linear cost function:

$$K_i = C + Dx_i,\ i = 1, \ldots, n$$

where K is the total cost of a firm, C and D are positive constants and x_i is the output of the firm. D gives real wages per unit of output, where the real wage rate per unit of labour is assumed to be constant throughout the exercise. The demand function for the industry as a whole is given by:

$$p = A - B(x_1 + x_2 + \ldots + x_n)$$

where p is the price of the product and A and B are positive constants. Firms are taken to maximize profits, $P_i = px_i - K_i$. Negishi then calculates the Cournot–Nash solution of this simple model.

Next he assumes that a new method of production is available which exhibits higher fixed costs *C*, which Negishi identifies with Marx's 'constant capital' (or rather fixed capital), and lower variable costs (wages), which are said to largely correspond to Marx's 'variable capital'. The new method will be introduced by an innovating firm, provided it is profitable to do so, which is the case if a certain condition is met. The innovating firm will reap extra profits by exploiting the increasing returns, which, however, requires to increase the firm's output and, *a fortiori*, thus aggregate output. Other firms will follow in adopting the new method, which leads to a general expansion of output. This, however, reduces the price of the product along the given and unchanging demand function and depresses the profits of each single firm. Under well-specified conditions the rate of profits on fixed capital is bound to fall.

Is this reconstruction convincing? Interestingly, Negishi himself has drawn the attention to a fact that raises doubts. He writes: 'we have to admit that our analysis . . . is limited to that of the partial equilibrium, while the Shibata–Okishio theorem is obtained in the general equilibrium analysis of the perfect competition' (1998b, 262). This is indeed the case. Put differently, while the technique used by the economic system under consideration changes, and economies could make themselves felt at an ever larger scale, they are prevented from doing so by a market demand function that stays put indefinitely. Hence, we get the peculiar result that despite technical advancement the real wage per unit of labour is constant and the general rate of profit falls. We might also say that the model tries to cross-breed a long-period (technical change) and a short period (given demand) perspective. I have doubts that it can successfully challenge the Shibata–Okishio Theorem.[18]

13.3.3 Unequal Exchange and Exploitation

In a number of papers Negishi (1991, 1993a, 1999a) enters into a discussion of the problem of unequal exchange and exploitation of workers as it was put forward in the 1970s. It is interesting to recall the motivation of these papers: Negishi stresses that the theory of the classical economists and Marx is fundamentally different from the neoclassical one and that it is therefore of interest to see what an alternative research programme has to offer. His attention focuses on the works of A. Emmanuel and then S. Amin and J.C. Saigal who argued *inter alia* that a country with a given low wage level is exploited by a country with a given higher wage level when the two trade with one another and capital is imported by the former. 'Being alerted by this Marxian attack on the neo-classical orthodoxy, Samuelson stood up quickly and tried to show the illogicality of neo-Marxian doctrine of unequal exchange.' Negishi adds:

'Samuelson seems, unfortunately, [to] misunderstand the main point of Emmanuel's argument' (1991, 37). Samuelson's demonstration within a neoclassical framework of the gains from trade is said to be beside the point, because Emmanuel's focus of attention is the possible deterioration of the terms of trade of the country with lower wages in comparison with the situation in which there are no wage differentials. It is an exogenously given level of real wages for each country which constitutes the distinguishing feature of Emmanuel's approach. In his second paper on the theme Negishi stresses that: 'even neoclassical economists may not be uninterested in classical and Marxist theories of international trade that are based on wage theories quite different than the neoclassical ones' (1993a, 353).

To begin with, it is interesting to emphasize that in Negishi's view the theory of income distribution constitutes the main difference between classical and marginalist (neoclassical) theory. I believe this is a valid observation. While the neoclassical theory tries to ascertain the distributive variables, especially the rate of profit (or interest) and the wage rate, in a symmetrical way in terms of the marginal contributions of 'capital' and labour to the product, the classical theory takes the real wage rate as given (and determined in another part of the theory) and ascertains the rate of profit residually, that is, asymmetrically. Therefore, Negishi insists, it is not possible to assess Emmanuel's analysis strictly from a neoclassical perspective, as was done by Samuelson. Such a perspective of necessity involves putting the theory of unequal exchange into a Procrustean bed.

This does not mean that Negishi subscribes to the analyses of Emmanuel and his followers. He points out that specialization of countries is driven by comparative costs and thus relative prices which generally differ from relative labour values.[19] This is due to the well-known fact that relative prices depend not only on the technical conditions of production actually in use, but also on the division of the product between workers and capitalists. The impact of distribution on relative prices may be such that the pattern of specialization, as one would expect it on the basis of labour values (which result in the special case in which the rate of profit is nil), is turned upside down: in terms of Ricardo's famous numerical example, one could construct cases of the time profile of labour employed in the production of the different commodities in which at the prevailing rate of profit Portugal would specialize in cloth, and England in wine. Negishi admits, however, that a model with an equalized rate of profit worldwide and differential, country-specific wage rates 'does fit present-day reality much more than the orthodox neo-classical model, that is, the so-called Heckscher–Ohlin model with international factor price equalisation'

(1991, p. 38). Yet, properly formalized, such a model does not lend support to some of the views proposed by Emmanuel, Saigal and so on. Negishi is therefore on the lookout for a condition that would save the argument and, interestingly enough, discerns it in Ricardo's assumption, discussed in the above, that the rate of profit need not be equalized even though capital can, in principle, move freely between countries. Negishi concludes: 'It is quite ironical that unequal exchange in the sense of Saigal is impossible . . . in a free capitalist world, while it may be possible in a socialists' world when an advanced country imposed a wrong pattern of specialisation to other countries' (1991, 47).

13.4 THE MARGINALIST ECONOMISTS

In their various papers and books Morishima and Negishi deal with all major early marginalist authors, especially William Stanley Jevons, Léon Walras, Eugen von Böhm-Bawerk, Alfred Marshall and Knut Wicksell. Due to space constraints, I focus attention on some of their comments on, and interpretations of, Walras, Böhm-Bawerk and Wicksell.

13.4.1 Léon Walras

The third book of Morishima's trilogy is devoted to *Walras's Economics: A Pure Theory of Capital and Money* (1977). According to a widespread view, Walras's concern was first and foremost the theory of exchange and allocation. This view is rejected by Morishima who insists that the theory of exchange and allocation was: 'but an overture to his general equilibrium theory of capital formation and circulation' (pp. vii–viii). The amount of work devoted to rendering the ouverture mathematically rigorous Morishima considers excessive and culminating in a 'complete sterilization' of Walras's theory. This criticism is explicitly levelled at models developed by Hicks (1967), Arrow and Debreu (1954) and Arrow and Hahn (1971) (see, for example, p. 207).

I think that some of Morishima's criticisms of received interpretations of Walras are sound, whereas others cannot be sustained. He is right that Walras was not merely concerned with static problems of allocation, but with a system in motion, in which capital accumulates, the population grows and technical knowledge increases over time. In the system contemplated money and credit play an important role. These dynamic aspects have typically been set aside in some interpretations, which therefore have distorted Walras's analysis. He is also right in stressing that as to the problems tackled there are several parallels between the analyses of

Ricardo, Marx, Walras and Keynes: the ultimate aim of all four authors was to investigate 'how the capitalist system works' (Morishima, 1977, 4). Walras even arrived at somewhat similar results as Ricardo with respect to the long-term development of important variables of the economic system, such as wages, rents and the rate of profit, in the case in which diminishing returns due to the scarcity of land are not fully counteracted by the effects of technical progress (see Walras, 1954, 390–91). However, this does not mean, as Morishima is inclined to think, that the analyses of the authors under consideration are essentially cast from a single mould. He is led to this opinion because he reinterprets both Ricardo, Marx and Walras in terms of the von Neumann model, or rather the 'Walras–von Neumann model' (1977, 199). It is this uniform garb that he puts on all three of them that makes them look alike, although under the garb they differ in important respects from one another.

Fundamental objections can be raised against the view that there is a direct lineage and basic *unité de doctrine* leading from Ricardo and Marx to Walras and then Keynes (Morishima, 1977, 5–7). First, Walras himself saw the relationship between his work and that of Ricardo not as one of continuity, but rather as one of discontinuity and incompatibility. It suffices to recall the title of Part 7 of the *Elements of Pure Economics*, 'Exposition and refutation of the English theory'. In it Ricardo is accused of having committed 'fundamental errors' and of having failed to develop 'a unified general theory to determine the prices of all productive services in the same way' (Walras, 1954, 416). Secondly, such a unified general theory, Walras contended, has been elaborated by himself by generalizing the principle of 'scarcity', which the classical economists had limited to natural resources, to all goods and factors of production alike. A careful investigation of the classical and the Walrasian analyses shows indeed the main differences between the two, in particular, the surplus-based approach to the explanation of profits and rents of the former as opposed to the scarcity-based approach to all shares of income of the latter. Scrutinising Part 7 of the *Elements* is also interesting because it demonstrates vividly that Walras could not but try to understand the contributions of Ricardo and the classical economists from the point of view of his own intellectual style, that is, demand-and-supply analysis. He was therefore bound to misinterpret their main message and accuse them of errors, logical and other, which are not there and simply reflect Walras's misapprehension of their doctrines; for a detailed exposition, see Kurz and Salvadori (2002). It is interesting to note that misinterpretations of Walras's kind, based as they are on taking some type of approach or intellectual style as an absolute measure to assess all other approaches or intellectual styles, abound in the history of economic thought.[20]

13.4.2 Eugen von Böhm-Bawerk and Knut Wicksell

Triggered by a paper by Bo Sandelin (1980), there has been a debate about Knut Wicksell's Austrian theory of value and distribution that is known as 'Wicksell's missing equation'. The emphasis is on Wicksell's treatment of the economy's endowment of capital at a given point in time in order to ascertain the rate of interest as a (relative) scarcity index of capital, reflecting marginal productivity of this factor of production. The issue under consideration is whether or not Wicksell had put forward a theory of capital and interest that is closed in the sense that the data, or independent variables, from which he started suffice to determine the unknowns, or dependent variables, especially the 'natural' rates of wages, rents and interest. The claim was put forward that there is one equation 'missing' in Wicksell's theory and that therefore his formal system of equations is underdetermined. The question then is how to close the system in a way that is faithful to Wicksell. The authors that contributed to the debate differ in terms of the closures they suggest.

It is interesting to note that the view was widespread that there was indeed an equation missing in Wicksell's construction. The authors that advocated this view also agreed that a consistent closure necessitated taking the overall 'quantity' and composition of social capital as endogenously determined. This in turn implied that the system had to be assumed to be in a stationary state in which there was neither accumulation nor decumulation of capital, because in such a state the capital stock is fully adjusted to the other data of the Wicksellian (or, more generally, marginalist) system, that is: (1) the preferences of agents; (2) the technical alternatives from which cost-minimizing producers can choose; and (3) the given amounts of the other factors of production, labour and land. In a stationary state all independent variables (including factor endowments) do not change any longer, nor do the dependent variables. With a zero rate of accumulation, incentives to invest and incentives to disinvest must obviously just balance each other. This means that the (overall) rate of interest equals the (overall) rate of time preference.

In a comment on Sandelin's paper, Negishi (1982a, 310) confirms Sandelin's claim as to the missing equation. In a related paper dealing with Eugen von Böhm-Bawerk's famous 'Three Grounds' of interest he rightly stresses that closing the system via a given amount of capital in value terms, which is Wicksell's closure, deprives the analysis of much of its explanatory power (1982b, p. 164). He makes essentially the same point in Chapter 9 of his *Economic Theories in a Non-Walrasian Tradition* (Negishi, 1985).

While Negishi sides with Sandelin, he is very clear that Wicksell actually closed the system by considering the available 'amount of *capital*' (Wicksell, 1934 [1901], 204) at the beginning of the production period as given in value terms, representing a certain quantity of the numeraire. In equilibrium that sum of value (the 'supply of capital') must then be equal to the value of capital employed (the 'demand for capital'), which consists of 'labour power capital' and 'land power capital'. The different quantities of the latter, employed in different periods of time, have to be appropriately discounted forward. There is clear evidence that Wicksell did not like this closure and therefore vacillated a good deal in his analysis. To be forced to take the capital endowment in value terms destroyed the sought analogy between the different factors of production, with labour and land all given in terms of their natural physical measures, whereas heterogeneous capital goods had to be given in terms of an abstract standard in an attempt to determine the competitive rate of return on social capital. There can be no doubt that Wicksell thought that there was no equation missing. He actually insisted with reference to the equation just described: 'we shall then obtain the *necessary* [additional] relation, and the problem will at last be completely determinate' (Wicksell, 1934 [1901], 204–5).

As Negishi appears to imply in his contributions, Wicksell's failure puts in sharp relief the fact that marginalist long-period analysis cannot generally be sustained. In the stationary state the forces that it contemplates have seized to exert their influence, and the stationary state is at any rate rather uninteresting because no real economy, as Wicksell stressed, can ever be taken to come close to it or even be in it.[21] Negishi does not attempt to save long-period marginalist analysis; he rather points out that the closures mentioned in the literature do not exhaust the set of alternatives, and suggests two further variants. In one he introduces explicitly the saving behaviour of the capitalist, which derives from intertemporal utility maximization. This involves, he stresses, considering 'the value of capital as an endogenous variable' (1982a, 310). In his other contribution (Negishi, 1982b) he develops an overlapping generations model with a stationary population, where each agent lives for two periods; the first being the working period, the second the retirement period. In the former the income of the agent exceeds their consumption, that is, they save, whereas in the latter things are the other way round, that is, they dissave all the capital previously built up. Negishi demonstrates that even assuming away time preference, the rate of interest may be positive due to the individual agent's concern with better provision for wants in the second than in the first period, and the superiority of more roundabout processes of production. Hence, Wicksell is said to have been right in his criticism of Böhm-Bawerk that time preference was not all that important in the theory of interest.

13.5 JOHN MAYNARD KEYNES[22]

Keynes, as is well known, singled out a few economists, including Thomas Robert Malthus, as anticipating, in one form or another, the 'principle of effective demand'. This principle states that there is no reason to presume that investment demand can be expected to gravitate around levels that equal savings at full employment-cum-full capacity income. Keynes chastised as 'classical economics' those views that were based on Say's law, where he interpreted this law in the neoclassical sense as involving also the clearing of the labour market, that is, full employment.

Keynes's view of Malthus and the classical economists is difficult to sustain. Negishi is right in arguing that Malthus was not a precursor of Keynes, but despite appearances to the contrary, 'a supply-side economist who emphasized the motives to produce as a function of the rate of profit' (1993c, 116; see, in greater detail, Negishi, 1989, 139, 143–7). By assuming that every act of saving will swiftly be followed by an act of investment of the same magnitude, Malthus deprived himself of the possibility of arguing that there can be a general glut of commodities. In his criticism Ricardo mercilessly uncovered the logical inconstistencies of Malthus's argument (see on this Kalmbach and Kurz, 2008).

While Walrasian general equilibrium theory is said to be 'a paradigm of modern economics, Keynesian economics may perhaps be called another paradigm of modern economics' (Negishi, 1993b, 53). However, Negishi maintains, the so-called 'Keynesian revolution . . . was not a thorough-going revolution, since it could not penetrate micro-economics' (ibid.). Neoclassical economists responded to the challenge of Keynesianism in terms of developing models based on theories of expectations, uncertainty, adjustment cost and disequilibrium, which were able to explain unemployment due to rigidities etc. In Negishi's view, these models have not pre-empted the need for some alternative theory: 'we still need Keynesian economics to explain persistent large-scale depression and unemployment' (ibid., 54). This assessment Negishi put forward in 1993, after he had himself, in the 1970s, developed some non-Walrasian general disequilibrium models based on sticky or rigid prices; see especially his book *Microeconomic Foundation of Keynesian Macroeconomics* (Negishi, 1979). Yet these models, whatever their merits, were not fully satisfactory to him. Firstly, they did not faithfully represent Keynes's argument, which was not based on sticky prices, but rather contended that with flexible prices the situation might get worse due to the destabilising effects of deflationary tendencies; and secondly, they left in the dark why prices were what they are and under what circumstances they would change. In short, Keynes's analysis could not be reduced to the economic effects of rigidities.

In Negishi's view, as I interpret it, the Keynesian revolution is still to be accomplished. As regards explaining persistent unemployment, Negishi singles out Azariadis's theory of implicit contracts between firms and workers and the difference between the two parties as to risk aversion as one of the most promising alternatives; see, especially, Negishi (1979, 227–35).

Morishima originally had the plan to write also a book on Keynes's economics, but then changed his mind. One of the reasons for this was that he was convinced that the problem of unemployment emerged once Walras's theory was properly formalized. As he was keen to show in Chapter 7, 'Towards Keynes', of his *Walras's Economics*, the Walrasian equilibrium is overdetermined, which he interpreted as implying that we must consider a Keynesian unemployment equilibrium.

Morishima's argument was not well received in the literature. William Jaffé accused him of confusing his own problems with those of Walras, while Negishi (1980b) questioned the correctness of the derivation of Morishima's surprising result. In terms of simplified versions of Morishima's model, he established the fact that there was no overdeterminacy. He did this, first, with respect to a model in which Say's law holds; more specifically, in which savers are also investors.[23] He then turned to an economic system with four classes: workers, landowners, capitalists and entrepreneurs. According to Morishima this is the socio-economic stratification that Walras had in mind, with savings coming (almost) exclusively from capitalists and with investments decided (almost) exclusively by entrepreneurs. In this perspective Walras is much closer to Keynes than is generally assumed, because the behaviour of entrepreneurs is different from and independent of the behaviour of capitalists and necessitates the introduction of an investment function in addition to a savings function.

For the sake of the argument, Negishi follows Morishima's proposition and adds an investment function to the system. However, with the additional equation there comes an additional variable, the rate of interest. The result is that 'the introduction of the Keynesian investment function into the Walrasian system does not lead to the over-determinacy of the Walrasian system . . . Thus the problem of over-determinacy cannot be a proper starting point for the journey from the Walrasian towards the Keynesian system' (Negishi, 2000, 260).

13.6 CONCLUDING REMARKS

Some conlusions can now be drawn from the above analysis, focusing on a comparison of the two authors under consideration. The first point is that both Morishima and Negishi are authors with a thorough interest in and knowledge of some of the most important traditions in the history of economic thought. They are very well read and erudite and have studied with great care and circumspection the contributions of many of the great economists from Adam Smith (and before) to our times. Secondly, both are interested in the history of economic thought because they consider the works of the old masters as a fertile source of valuable ideas, only some of which have been absorbed into contemporary economic theory. A study of these works thus has nothing to do with morbid antiquarianism. It rather expresses the conviction that even nowadays we can still learn from Adam Smith, David Ricardo, Karl Marx, Léon Walras, Knut Wicksell, John Maynard Keynes and so on. Thirdly, according to the views of these two authors, such learning often requires that old ideas are incorporated into modern analytical frameworks – an elaborated version of the von Neumann model in the case of Morishima, or a partial or general equilibrium model in the case of Negishi. It is the combination of reconfigured existing ideas, old and new, that embodies the potential of analytical progress and can be expected to improve our understanding of economic facts and processes. However, as especially Negishi admits, there are cases in which certain old ideas run counter to, and therefore are incompatible with, modern analytical frameworks. In such cases the respective ideas cannot be made to speak to us by integrating them into some existing theory or model. It is, rather, necessary to develop a framework that is conducive to them.

Fourthly, in at least one important respect the two authors approach the history of economic thought from rather different perspectives. While Morishima appears to be convinced that such diverse authors as, in particular, Ricardo, Marx, Walras and Keynes can all be brought together and their ideas synthesized and integrated into a coherent whole, Negishi variously expresses the view that there are differences between different authors that cannot (easily) be overcome. These different perspectives are reflected in the very different characters of the two authors' works. Morishima attempted to elaborate a sort of metatheory that incorporates various old masters' analyses. His trilogy in particular expresses his concern with building an overarching system of economic analysis. Negishi is much more cautious in this regard and refrains from engaging in such a demanding enterprise. His contribution consists mostly of short papers, each of which is dedicated to a particular problem at hand which is then typically, but not always, dealt with in terms of a formalization.

These different perspectives, and this is my fifth and final observation, imply somewhat different attitudes towards the historical material. Morishima emphasizes time and again that his main concern is not with a comprehensive, let alone complete, historical reconstruction of the works under consideration, but with identifying those elements that point beyond the respective author's own work and contribute to the genealogy of modern theory. Hence, Morishima sees past authors first and foremost from the perspective of what they contributed to modern theory, as conceived by Morishima. He attempts to localize their works as processing elements in this development. Compared with him, Negishi places a good deal more attention on historical reconstructions that are faithful to the authors under consideration. He insists on the variety and complexity of ideas and is less prepared to try to integrate them into an allegedly coherent whole.

But whatever may be the differences between their approaches to the history of economic theories, both deserve praise for having broadened and deepened our understanding of past authors, alternative approaches to economic problems and contemporary economic theory. They belong to a small group of truly remarkable economists who combined an interest in economic theories with an interest in their emergence and development, and in the yet unexploited potential of elaborating on and judiciously combining received and new ideas. As one of the two scholars succinctly put it: 'Economics is a science which cannot dispense with its history' (Negishi, 1993b, 55).

NOTES

1. The combinatoric metaphor as an abstract description of the process of how new knowledge is generated by reconfiguring and recombining old pieces of knowledge can be traced far back in the history of natural philosophy. It was used by, amongst others, Adam Smith and Joseph Alois Schumpeter; see, for example, Kurz (2006, 2008).
2. For a counterposition of the analytical structures of the approaches to the theory of value and distribution of especially Ricardo and Walras, see Kurz and Salvadori (1995, Chapter 1; and 2002). (As will become clear below, Negishi also appears to see the main difference between the two different schools of thought as consisting in different theories of income distribution.) As regards the classical authors' treatment of workers' participation in the sharing out of the surplus product, see below.
3. On a possible link between Ladislaus von Bortkiewicz, who was well read in the classical authors and Marx and had formalized some of their ideas, on the one hand, and von Neumann via Robert Remak, on the other, one of his mathematical colleagues, see Kurz and Salvadori (1993).
4. For a different view, see Negishi (1988; 1994, xiii), who exclusively credits Smith with considering the natural wage rate as interdependent with the growth rate.
5. Since Malthus also contemplates the case of unemployment, what matters for the rate of population growth is the real income of families, which depends not only on hourly wages paid, but also on the levels of employment of the different members of a family. This aspect need not concern us here.
6. According to Morishima: 'Ricardo considered both capitalists and landowners as savers'. In fact he even also contemplated the possibility of workers saving. Ricardo

may thus be said to have anticipated the basic idea underlying what became known as the Post-Keynesian theory of growth and distribution; see especially Kaldor (1955–56) and Pasinetti (1962).

7. Negishi (1996a, 1996b) are closely related papers. In each of them Negishi takes the contributions of K. Kojima to Ricardo's trade theory as one of his starting points; see below.
8. In Negishi's model we discuss below there are only two commodities both of which enter the real wage rate and are thus what the classical economists called 'necessaries' as opposed to luxuries. For a discussion of the latter, see Negishi (1989, 136–8).
9. See Kurz and Salvadori (1995, 26–8; on the application of the Non-Substitution Theorem to Ricardo's trade argument, see p. 152).
10. The possible range of a satisfying Ricardo's numerical example is $80/120 \leq a \leq 90/100$; see Negishi (1982c, 208).
11. It goes without saying that with non-constant returns to scale in one or both industries, the argument would have to be adopted. Diminishing returns are typically associated with agriculture where the scarcity of land may make itself felt in increasing unit costs as output increases, whereas increasing returns to scale may result from an increase in the extent of the market and the ensuing scope for a deeper social division of labour. These themes are, however, beyond the scope of Negishi's and also the present chapter.
12. Morishima says so explicitly: 'we define the law in the same way that Keynes did' (1989, p. 54; see also p. 164). Now Keynes, as is well known, defined the law in the received marginalist full employment sense (which he, erroneously, considered to be the 'classical' sense as well).
13. The capital controversies had been triggered by a paper by Joan Robinson (1953), but as time went by it gradually became clear that she had benefited from discussions with Piero Sraffa whose 1960 book rekindled and broadened the debate; see Robinson (1970).
14. For a discussion of the determination of labour values in the presence of joint production, see Kurz and Salvadori (1995, Chapter 8).
15. Using Sraffa's definition (in the case of single production): a basic product is a product that enters directly or indirectly into the production of every product, whereas non-basics do not.
16. Negishi (1999b, 235–8) extends the analysis somewhat and employs also a version of Krugman's model of monopolistic competition and economies of scale.
17. I set aside the problem of whether the discussion of the law in terms of linear models of production with free competition as they were used by Okishio, Morishima or Steedman are well characterized as 'Walrasian'.
18. It should be noted that Volumes II and III of *Das Kapital* were not yet ready for publication when Marx died in 1883. Frederick Engels prepared the two volumes out of Marx's unfinished notes, manuscripts and preliminary drafts and interpolated bits and pieces of material whenever he felt the need for it. The material was written at different times, and there is no reason to presume that Marx would have sustained all the views expressed in it. Therefore it is not at all clear what would have been Marx's opinion on the various matters had he been given the time to prepare the two volumes for print. See, on this, Gehrke and Kurz (2006) with respect to Sraffa's doubts as to the conventional interpretation of Marx's law of the falling rate of profit.
19. In systems with single production as assumed by Emmanuel and then Negishi, prices can be reduced to dated quantities of labour (Sraffa, 1960), which express this fact in a straightforward manner.
20. For example, recently Sraffa's reformulation and rectification of the classical approach to the problem of value and distribution has been discussed by some commentators as if it was a contribution to intertemproal general equilibrium theory (see Hahn, 1982).
21. Contrary to Wicksell, Robert Lucas (1988, p. 11) maintained that: 'for *any* initial capital $K(0) > 0$, the optimal-capital consumption path $(K(t), c(t))$ will converge to the balanced path asymptotically'. He added: 'That is, the balanced path will be a good

approximation to any actual path "most" of the time [and that] this is exactly the reason why the balanced part is interesting to us'. This is a bold statement that sounds rather strange, especially at the time of a deep economic crisis worldwide.

22. In this section I comment only on a few issues discussed by the two authors in regard of Keynes's contribution to economics. In particular, Morishima's huge project of incorporating the ideas of Keynes (and other non-orthodox economists) in a new formulation of general equilibrium theory, culminating in Morishima (1992), can only be mentioned in passing.
23. It goes without saying that this is a very special case of Say's law.

REFERENCES

Arrow, K.J. and G. Debreu (1954), 'Existence of an equilibrium for a competitive economy', *Econometrica*, **22**, 265–90.

Arrow, K.J. and F.H. Hahn (1971), *General Competitive Analysis*, San Francisco, CA: Holden-Day.

Gehrke, C. and H.D. Kurz (2006), 'Sraffa on von Bortkiewicz: reconstructing the Classical theory of value and distribution', *History of Political Economy*, **38** (1), 91–149.

Hahn, F. (1982), 'The Neo-Ricardians', *Cambridge Journal of Economic*, **6**, 353–74.

Hicks, J.R. (1967), *Critical Essays in Monetary Theory*, Oxford: Clarendon Press.

Kaldor, N. (1955–56), 'Alternative theories of distribution', *Review of Economic Studies*, **23**, 83–100.

Kalmbach, P. and H.D. Kurz (2008), 'Malthus: Vorgänger von Keynes?' in H. Hagemann, G. Horn and H.-J. Krupp (eds), *Aus gesamtwirtschaftlicher Sicht. Festschrift in honour of Jürgen Kromphardt*, Marburg: Metropolis, pp. 163–82.

Kurz, H.D. (2006), 'Whither the history of economic thought?', *European Journal of the History of Economic Thought*, **12** (3), 493–523.

Kurz, H.D. (2008), 'Innovations and profits: Schumpeter and the classical heritage', *Journal of Economic Behavior and Organization*, **67**, 263–78.

Kurz, H.D. and N. Salvadori (1992), 'Morishima on Ricardo: a review article', *Cambridge Journal of Economics*, **16**, 227–47.

Kurz, H.D. and N. Salvadori (1993), 'Von Neumann's growth model and the "Classical" tradition', *European Journal of the History of Economic Thought*, **1** (1), 129–60.

Kurz, H.D. and N. Salvadori (1995), *Theory of Production. A Long-Period Analysis*, Cambridge: Cambridge University Press.

Kurz, H.D. and N. Salvadori (2002), 'One theory or two? Walras's critique of Ricardo', *History of Political Economy*, **34**, 365–98.

Lucas, R.E. (1988), 'On the mechanics of economic development', *Journal of Monetary Economics*, **22**, 3–42.

Morishima, M. (1964), *Equilibrium, Stability and Growth: A Multi-sectoral Analysis*, Oxford: Clarendon Press.

Morishima, M. (1969), *Theory of Economic Growth*, Oxford: Clarendon Press.

Morishima, M. (1973), *Marx's Economics: A Dual Theory of Value and Growth*, Cambridge: Cambridge University Press.

Morishima, M. (1977), *Walras's Economics: A Pure Theory of Capital and Money*, Cambridge: Cambridge University Press.

Morishima, M. (1989), *Ricardo's Economics: A General Equilibrium Theory of Distribution and Growth*, Cambridge: Cambridge University Press.

Morishima, M. (1992), *Capital and Credit: A New Formulation of General Equilibrium Theory*, Cambridge: Cambridge University Press.

Morishima, M. and G. Catephores (1978), *Value, Exploitation and Growth*, Maidenhead: McGraw-Hill.

Negishi, T. (1960), 'Welfare economics and the existence of an equilibrium for a competitive economy', *Metroeconomica*, **12**: 92–7.

Negishi, T. (1979), *Microeconomic Foundation of Keynesian Macroeconomics*, Amsterdam: North-Holland.

Negishi, T. (1980a), 'Marx and Böhm-Bawerk in the theory of interest', *Économie et Sociétés*, **14**, 287–304.

Negishi, T. (1980b), 'A review of Michio Morishima, "Walras's Economics"', *Economic Review*, **31** (1), 89–91.

Negishi, T. (1982a), 'Wicksell's missing equation: a comment', *History of Political Economy*, **14**, 310–11.

Negishi, T. (1982b), 'Wicksell's missing equation and Böhm-Bawerk's three causes of interest in a stationary state', *Zeitschrift für Nationalökonomie*, **42**, 161–74.

Negishi, T. (1982c), 'The labor theory of value in the Ricardian theory of international trade', *History of Political Economy*, **14** (2), 199–209.

Negishi, T. (1985), *Economic Theories in a Non-Walrasian Tradition*, Cambridge: Cambridge University Press.

Negishi, T. (1988), 'The role of demand in Adam Smith's theory of natural price', *Seoul Journal of Economics*, **1** (4), 357–65.

Negishi, T. (1989), *History of Economic Theory*, Amsterdam: North-Holland.

Negishi, T. (1990), 'Ricardo and Morishima on machinery', *Journal of the History of Economic Thought*, **12** (2), 146–61.

Negishi, T. (1991), 'Samuelson, Saigal and Emmanuel's theory of international unequal exchange', in Shri Bhagwan Dahiya (ed.), *Theoretical Foundations of Development Planning*, **4**, 37–49.

Negishi, T. (1993a), 'International exploitation in Marxist and neo-Marxist economics', in H. Herberg and Ngo Van Long (eds), *Trade, Welfare, and Economic Policies: Essays in Honor of Murray C. Kemp*, Ann Arbor, MI: University of Michigan Press, pp. 353–64.

Negishi, T. (1993b), 'General equilibrium theory and the history of economics', in A. Heertje (ed.), *The Makers of Modern Economics*, Vol. I, Hemel Hempstead: Harvester Wheatsheaf, pp. 47–66.

Negishi, T. (1993c), 'A Smithian-growth model and Malthus's optimum propensity to save', *European Journal of the History of Economic Thought*, **1** (1), 115–27.

Negishi, T. (1993d), *The Collected Essays of Takashi Negishi*, Volume I, *General Equilibrium Theory*, Aldershot: Edward Elgar.

Negishi, T. (1994), *The Collected Essays of Takashi Negishi*, Volume II, *The History of Economics*, Aldershot: Edward Elgar.

Negishi, T. (1996a), 'Different interpretations of Ricardo's theory of foreign trade', *Surugadai Economic Studies*, **5** (2), 227–38.

Negishi, T. (1996b), 'Japanese studies of Ricardo's theory of foreign trade', *Japanese Economic Review*, **47** (4), 335–45.

Negishi, T. (1998a), 'Machinery', in H.D. Kurz and N. Salvadori (eds), *The Elgar Companion to Classical Economists*, Vol. II, Cheltenham, UK and Northampton, MA, USA: Edward Elgar, pp. 62–5.

Negishi, T. (1998b), 'Marx, economies of scale, and the falling rate of profit', *Japan and the World Economy*, **10**, 253–63.
Negishi, T. (1999a), 'Unequal exchange and exploitation', *Japanese Economic Review*, **50** (2), 113–21.
Negishi, T. (1999b), 'Technology and profit under global monopolistic competition', in R. Sato, R.V. Ramachandran and K. Mino (eds), *Global Competition and Integration*, Boston, MA, USA, Dordrecht, Netherlands and London, UK: Kluwer Academic Publishers, pp. 229–40.
Negishi, T. (2000), *The Collected Essays of Takashi Negishi, Volume III: Economic Thought from Smith to Keynes*, Cheltenham, UK and Northampton, MA, USA: Edward Elgar.
Neumann, J. von (1945), 'A model of general economic equilibrium', *Review of Economic Studies*, **13**, 1–9.
Pasinetti, L.L. (1960), 'A mathematical formulation of the Ricardian system', *Review of Economic Studies*, **27**, 78–98.
Pasinetti, L.L. (1962), 'Rate of profit and income distribution in relation to the rate of economic growth', *Review of Economic Studies*, **29**, 267–79.
Ricardo, D. (1951–73), *The Works and Correspondence of David Ricardo*, Piero Sraffa (ed.) with M.H. Dobb, 11 vols, Cambridge: Cambridge University Press.
Sandelin, B. (1980), 'Wicksell's missing equation, the production function, and the Wicksell effect', *History of Political Economy*, **12**, 29–40.
Sraffa, P. (1951), 'Introduction', in Ricardo, op. cit., Vol. I, pp. xiii–lxii.
Sraffa, P. (1960), *Production of Commodities by Means of Commodities*, Cambridge: Cambridge University Press.
Steedman, I. (1975), 'Positive profits with negative surplus value', *Economic Journal*, **85**, 114–23.
Walras, L. (1954), *Elements of Pure Economics*, London: Allen & Unwin.
Wicksell, K. (1934), *Lectures on Political Economy*, Vol. I, translation from the Swedish of the 3rd edn (1st edn 1901), London: George Routledge & Sons.

Index

Akamatsu, Kanamu 292
Akerlof, George 9
American Civil War 1, 108
American Economic Association 109f.
Arias, Gino 232f.
Azpilcueta, Martin de 23ff.

Balance of Power, European 43, 45
Bastiat, Frédéric 4, 108
Bielfeld, Baron 5, 68, 72–3
Blacque, Alexander 163
Böhm-Bawerk, Eugen von 114, 271–2, 355
Booth, Charles 136
Bosanquet, Helen 132f.

Caird, Edward 141
Cameralism 5, 13ff., 65ff., 79
Carey, Henry 171
Cassel, Gustav 273–4
Chapman, Sydney 147
Chevalier, Michel 169
Chinese Economic Journal 260
Clark, John Bates 110, 120, 121
Cole, G.D.H. 143
Commons, J.R. 117
Croce, Benedetto 226

Davenant, Charles 5, 41ff.
Dobrogeanu-Gherea, Constantin 172

Economics, Historical School of 6, 20, 108f., 119–20, 238f.
Economics, Marxist 3
Economics, Mercantilist 14, 49, 67
Economics, Scholastic 14
Economics, Walrasian 239f.
Einaudi, Luigi 230, 234
Ely, Richard T. 109–10, 117, 121
Empire, Holy Roman 20
Empire, Ottoman 20, 45, 161f.

European Society for the History of Economic Thought 1, 4, 8

Fawcett, Henry 3
First World War 116, 142

Garnier, Joseph 4
Grotius, Hugo 14
Grünberg, Carl 325, 326

Hansen, Alvin 195, 199f.
Harvard Business School 8, 293–4
Hayek, Friedrich 7, 193, 201ff., 224
Hermann, F.W.B. von 91
Hicks, John 277
Hill, Octavia 136
Hitotsubashi University 1, 8–9, 292
Horkheimer, Max 326–7
Horsfall, Thomas Coglan 135f.

Indian Journal of Economics 260
Institutionalism 117

Japanese Society for the History of Economic Thought 1, 4, 8, 9, 36
Justi, Johann Heinrich Gottlob von 67f.

Keynes, John Maynard 7, 9, 126, 194, 199, 210, 224, 240f., 276f., 357
King's College Cambridge Research Centre 4
Kingsley, Charles 136
Klock, Kaspar 4–5, 16ff., 29ff.
Knies, Carl 114
Knight, Frank 117
Kondratiev, N.D. 307
Korsch, Karl 315–18, 331
Kyoto University Economic Review 7, 260ff.
Kyoto University 8, 263

Lessius, Leonardus 27ff.
Lisbon Earthquake 73–4
List, Friedrich 6, 101, 165, 171
Lluch, Ernst 72
Loch, Charles Stewart 135
Louis XIV of France 43
Lukács, Georg 323, 331

MacGregor, D.H. 6, 149f.
Machiavelli, Nicolo 5, 41, 46–7, 52, 54, 56–7, 59, 62
Magnusson, Lars 67, 68
Malthus, T.R. 100
Mardin, Şerif 200–201
Marshall, Alfred 3, 7, 113, 115, 125ff.
Industry and Trade 139, 142
Principles of Economics 139, 241
Marx, Karl 4, 9, 26, 89, 100, 168, 178, 268, 330f., 339, 347ff.
Marxism 204f., 208, 239f., 241f., 263–4, 265, 323–4
Maurice, F.D. 136
Meiji Restoration 1, 2, 237f.
Meinecke, Friedrich 60–61
Menger, Carl 87
Methodenstreit 110, 115–16, 118, 120
Mill, James 88
Mill, John Stuart 3, 6, 87, 94, 103–4
Mitchell, Wesley Clair 121
Mizuta, Hiroshi 2
'Modernization' 3–4, 7
Money, theory of 24–5
Morishima, Michio 8
Mussolini, Benito 225

Negishi, Takashi 8
Neumann, John von 337, 339

Palomba, Giuseppe 229
Petty, William 42
Pigou, Arthur C. 3, 7, 143f.
Economics of Welfare 144–5
Pocock, J.G.A. 41–2, 48, 60
Polanyi, Karl 7, 194, 200ff., 213f.
Pollock, Friedrich 325
Police 5, 65ff., 69
Policy, fiscal 44, 49
Public finances 74, 78
Pufendorf, Samuel 14

Rau, Karl Heinrich 6, 87ff., 175
Ricardo, David 94, 169, 338, 340f., 353
Richelieu, Cardinal 5, 42, 46ff.
Rjazanov, David 8, 326, 330
Robbins, Lionel 7, 223ff.
Roover, Rayond de 13–14, 32f.
Roscher, Wilhelm 6, 87ff., 96f.
Rossi, Pellegrino 167
Ruskin, John 136

Salamanca, School of 13, 17, 20, 31
Say, Jean-Baptiste 88, 108, 346
Catéchisme d'économie politique 163, 166–7
Schmoller, Gustav 6
Schumpeter, Joseph 7, 9, 193, 202–3, 241f., 270, 308
Capitalism, Socialism and Democracy 197f.
Second World War 2
Seebohm Rowntree, Benjamin 146
Seligman, E.R.A. 112
Serra, Antonio 14–15
Shiller, Robert 9
Skinner, Quentin 59
Smith, Adam 2, 3, 13, 32, 42, 101, 129, 169
Sombart, Werner 293
Sonnenfels, Joseph von 67
Soutsos, Ioannes 166–7
Soyeda, Juichi 262
Spiethoff, Arthur 18–19
Sraffa, Piero 8, 340
Stere, Constantin 171–2

Taxation, systems of 21, 31, 75
Trikon, Charles 163
Tuck, Richard 59

Ülgener, Sabri 198f., 212
Usury 27ff.

Verein für Sozialpolitik 1, 263
Vecchio, Giorgio Del 229–30
Vito, Francesco 227

Wakefield, Andre 71
Walras, Léon 339, 353f.
Webb, Beatrice 136
Webb, Sidney 155
Weil, Felix 8, 315ff.
Westcott, Brooke Foss 137f.
Wicksell, Knut 355
Wieser, Friedrich von 114

Xenopol, Alexandru 171

Young, Allyn 117